FAIRFIELD P.N.E.U. SCHOOL
FAIRFIELD WAY
BACKWELL
Nr BRISTOL
BS19 3PD

CHERRYTREE BOOKS

THE LIVING PLANET

WEATHER

EDITED BY TOM MARINER

A Cherrytree Book

Adapted by A S Publishing from
El Tiempo © Parramon Ediciones S.A. 1996
Text: Miquel Àngel Gilbert
Illustrations: Miquel Ferrón, Txema Retama
Design: Beatriz Seoane

This edition first published in 1997
by Cherrytree Press Ltd
a subsidiary of
The Chivers Company Ltd
Windsor Bridge Road
Bath BA2 3AX

© Cherrytree Press Ltd 1997

British Library Cataloguing in Publication Data
Weather. – (The living planet)
 1. Weather – Juvenile literature
 I. Mariner, Tom
 551.6

 ISBN 0 7451 5318 6

Typeset by Dorchester Typesetting Group Ltd, Dorset
Printed in Spain

Lightning, the most dramatic of all weather effects, lights up the night sky.

CONTENTS

THE POWER OF THE SUN

THE CONDITION of the atmosphere – cold or warm, wet or dry, windy or calm – in a particular place at any particular time is what we call the weather. Although our weather may change from day to day, it does so according to a pattern that is repeated from season to season and from year to year. This pattern of weather in a particular region is known as its climate. Both weather and climate affect our lives in many ways.

Weather is the condition of the atmosphere at one place at one time. Climate is the pattern of weather over a long period in a particular region.

What causes weather? Why does it vary from region to region? Why does it vary from day to day within the same region? The answer to all these questions is the sun. The sun heats the earth. Its rays travel through the atmosphere – the air around us – and they heat the ground. The heated ground warms the air. Because the earth is spherical, the sun does not heat the earth evenly. The sun is almost directly overhead at the equator. Its rays hit the ground straight on and the heat is intense. Further away from the equator, the sun is lower in the sky. Its rays hit the earth at an angle and are spread over a greater area, making the heat less strong overall. This is why it is always cold at the poles and warm in the tropics, the regions north and south of the equator. In the tropics plants grow thick and fast; at the poles it is so icy that nothing will grow.

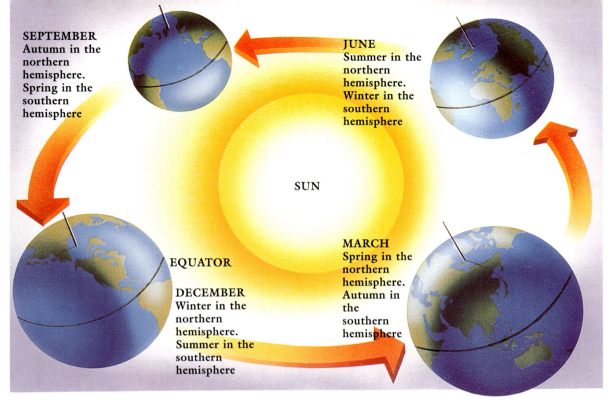

SEPTEMBER
Autumn in the northern hemisphere. Spring in the southern hemisphere

JUNE
Summer in the northern hemisphere. Winter in the southern hemisphere

SUN

EQUATOR

DECEMBER
Winter in the northern hemisphere. Summer in the southern hemisphere

MARCH
Spring in the northern hemisphere. Autumn in the southern hemisphere

The earth spins like a top in space. It makes one complete turn every twenty-four hours. Night follows day as it turns. As well as spinning on its own axis, the earth also travels round the sun, taking a year to make each circuit. But the earth does not spin upright; its axis is tilted at an angle of $23\frac{1}{2}°$. This tilt points first one side of the orbiting earth and then the other towards the sun. Although the heat and light given out by the sun is always the same, the parts of the earth leaning towards the sun receive more light and heat than the parts tilted away from it. These variations cause the seasons.

In regions leaning towards the sun it is summer. In regions tilted away from the sun it is winter. In between times it is either spring or autumn. The exceptions are at the poles and at the equator. In these regions the temperature is almost constant all the year round; very low at the poles and very high near the equator. At the poles themselves the sun stays below the horizon for half the year. During the other half it hangs low in the sky but never sets.

The regions in between have four distinct seasons. Their climate is temperate. It is good for growing crops. It is not too hot or too cold, nor too wet or too dry.

The rhythm of the seasons is caused by the tilt of the spinning earth from the vertical to its path round the sun.

SUMMER

WINTER

SPRING

AUTUMN

THE PROTECTING ATMOSPHERE

THE ATMOSPHERE is a layer of air surrounding the earth. Air is a mixture of transparent gases. Nitrogen accounts for 78 per cent and oxygen 21 per cent. The remaining 1 per cent consists of argon and carbon dioxide and minute traces of other gases. Water vapour is also present in the air in varying amounts. In desert regions it is less than 1 per cent of the air while in the tropics it may account for more than 4 per cent.

The atmosphere is vital to life. Without oxygen, we could not breathe and without carbon dioxide plants could not grow. As

The atmosphere shields the earth from harmful rays of the sun and helps keep it warm.

EXOSPHERE (500km-space)

THERMOSPHERE (80-500km)

MESOSPHERE (50-80km)

OZONE LAYER

STRATOSPHERE (10-50km)

TROPOSPHERE (up to 10-16km)
EARTH'S SURFACE

well as providing these essentials, the atmosphere protects us. It acts like a shield and a blanket. It prevents the earth from overheating during the day and from losing too much heat at night.

The atmosphere reaches as high as 500km above the earth and is composed of five layers. The lowest, the troposphere, is next to the earth. It is here

that the clouds, winds and other weather features are found. Above it is the stratosphere where supersonic aircraft fly. The ozone layer at the upper edge of the stratosphere stretches like a thin skin around it and merges into the mesosphere.

In all these layers the temperature decreases with height. In the mesosphere the temperature falls to minus 120°C. A dramatic change

occurs in the next layer, the thermosphere, for here the temperature rises with height and can exceed 2000°C. It is here that shooting stars and the polar auroras are found, and where the space shuttle flies. Beyond is the exosphere, even hotter than the thermosphere, where the earth's atmosphere gradually merges into space. Some satellites orbit the earth in this region.

The troposphere is the lowest layer of the atmosphere and the one that supports all human and animal life. It is only about 16km deep at most but it contains three-quarters of the gases of the atmosphere and almost all its humidity. Its temperature decreases by about 6°C for each 1000m of height. Its lowest level also contains dust particles and salt crystals. The dust in the atmosphere is what makes sunsets red.

The air in the troposphere acts as a thermostat, maintaining temperatures over the earth. It moderates the heat from the sun and prevents it from escaping too rapidly into space. Together the heat and water in the troposphere combine to give us our weather.

As well as infrared heat rays that warm us, the sun also emits ultraviolet rays. These tan and burn the skin and can cause cancer. The earth is shielded from over 95 per cent of these rays by a layer of ozone gas in the upper stratosphere. Ozone (O_3) is a form of oxygen (O_2) with three rather than two oxygen atoms. Chemicals called chlorofluorocarbons (CFCs), used in refrigerants and aerosol sprays, react with the ozone molecules and break them down into oxygen molecules. Without the ozone, too many damaging ultraviolet rays can reach earth.

The bottom layer of the atmosphere, the troposphere, is where the weather takes place.

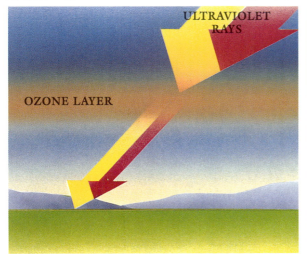

ULTRAVIOLET RAYS

OZONE LAYER

ULTRAVIOLET RAYS

OZONE LAYER DESTROYED

HOT AND COLD

THE HOTNESS or coldness of the air (air temperature), the amount of moisture in the air (air humidity) and the weight of the air (air pressure) are the elements in the atmosphere that create weather. The element we are most aware of is temperature.

Weather is a combination of three elements in the atmosphere: temperature, humidity and pressure.

Temperature varies according to the time of the day and the time of the year. It is cold in winter when the earth tilts us away from the sun and at night when our side of the earth faces away from the sun.

To measure temperature we use a thermometer. The most common type of thermometer consists of a glass tube that contains mercury or alcohol. When these liquids become warm their volume increases and they move up the tube. When the temperature decreases the liquid moves down the tube. A scale on the outside of the tube allows the change in temperature to be measured exactly.

The U-shaped maximum and minimum thermometer uses mercury and alcohol. The figures opposite the lower ends of the tiny metal markers in the two columns record the highest and lowest temperatures respectively.

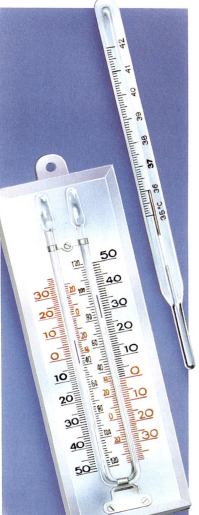

Temperature is measured in specific units, usually degrees Celsius (°C). These form a scale from 0°C, the temperature at which water freezes, to 100°C, the temperature at which it boils. This scale superseded the Fahrenheit scale on which water freezes at 32°F and boils at 212°F. Scientists use the Kelvin scale. On this water freezes at 273K and boils at 373K .

The average temperature of anywhere in the world depends on the amount of the sun's heat it receives. As the map of temperature zones shows, the closer an area is to the equator the hotter it is likely to be. The lowest temperatures are found at the poles.

 COLD AIR

 WARM AIR

	Cold all year
	Warm summer Cold winter
	Hot summer Cold winter
	Cool summer Mild winter
	Hot summer Mild winter
	Hot all year

Other factors complicate this simple picture. Sea water warms up and cools down more quickly than the land. On a sunny day the land warms rapidly. The air above gets lighter and rises, and a cool breeze from the sea moves in to replace it. At night the opposite happens. Cooler land air replaces warmer air over the sea. As a result, coastal areas tend to have even temperatures.

Height also affects temperature. The temperature of dry air falls by 1°C for every 100m of height. Mountainous areas are therefore normally cooler than lowland areas. A mountain, however, can have a cooling effect on land at its base. On a clear, calm night cool mountain air may sink downhill to replace the warmer air below, creating a cold downhill wind.

The normal temperature of a place depends not only on its nearness to the equator. It is also affected by altitude and by how close it is to the sea.

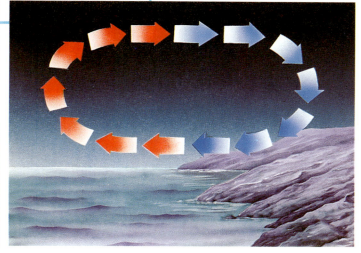

AIR PRESSURE

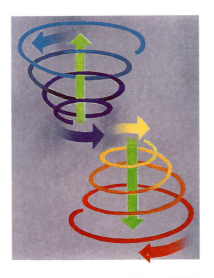

ALTHOUGH IT feels weightless, air has weight. We do not notice its weight because the pressure of the air in our bodies is the same as that of the air around us. Air, or atmospheric, pressure changes from place to place and from time to time. Heat makes air less dense, so warm air is lighter than cold air. Being lighter, warm air rises while heavier cold air sinks and flows to take its place.

If the earth were still and not spinning, the hot air at the equator would rise and go directly to the poles, while cold air from the poles would flow straight to the equator to replace it. But the spin deflects the flow of air to form spirals. In the northern hemisphere, these flow from left to right in areas of high pressure and from right to left in areas of low pressure. They flow in the opposite directions south of the equator.

Warm rising air causes low pressure, cold descending air causes high pressure. Winds, which are air on the move, naturally blow from high pressure to low pressure. Hot air at the equator rises and creates areas of low pressure. The rising air cools and spreads out to the north and south, where it sinks and becomes warmer, causing areas of high pressure. The warm air flows towards the equator, and the whole cycle begins again.

Weather maps show air pressure by means of isobars. Isobars are lines linking places where the pressure is the same, just as contour lines on ordinary maps join places of the same height. Air pressure is measured in millibars. Average pressure at sea level is 1013 millibars. Circles at the centre of isobar systems indicate areas of high and low pressure.

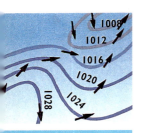

On weather maps air pressure is shown by isobars. The higher the figure in millibars the higher the pressure.

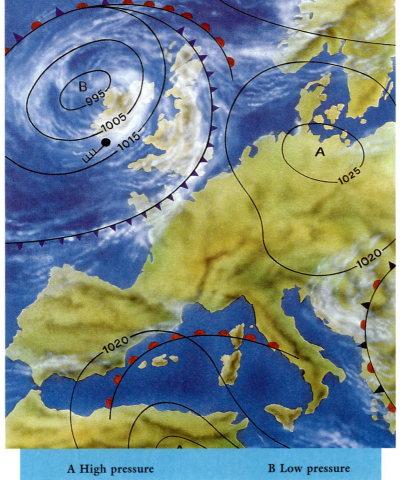

A High pressure   B Low pressure

Air pressure is measured with a barometer. This simple instrument was discovered by chance in 1643 by the Italian scientist Torricelli while he was trying to produce a vacuum. Torricelli filled a fine tube with mercury, turned it upside down and plunged it into a bowl of mercury. As soon as the tube was in position the column of mercury sank down the tube until it remained steady at a height of about 76cm. Inside the empty tube, above the mercury, was the vacuum that Torricelli had been looking for. It soon became obvious that the mercury level changed with the weather and that it rose or fell according to height above sea level. This led to the discovery of air pressure and that it is higher at sea level than in the mountains.

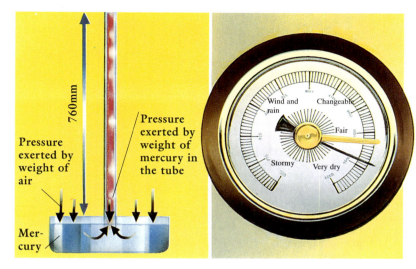

760mm

Pressure exerted by weight of air

Pressure exerted by weight of mercury in the tube

Mercury

Mercury barometers have largely been replaced by aneroid barometers. These instruments are based on a flexible metal box containing a partial vacuum. Changes in air pressure squeeze or relax the box which is linked to a pointer. The pointer moves round a dial graduated in millibars and marked with the weather conditions to be expected.

The words on the dial of a barometer – stormy, wind and rain, changeable, fair and very dry – give an idea of the weather to be expected.

WHAT A WIND!

1. Prevailing westerlies
2. Northeast trade winds
3. Equatorial doldrums
4. Hurricanes
5. Southeast trade winds
6. Prevailing westerlies
7. Southern polar winds
8. Typhoons
9. Cyclones

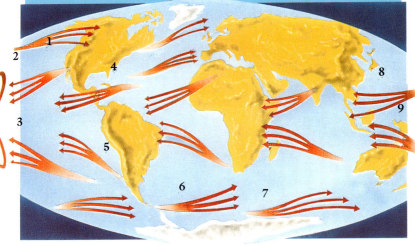

IN SPITE OF many local variations there is a general pattern of air circulation around the world. It takes the form of broad bands circling the earth parallel to the equator. Apart from the almost windless zone on the equator, each of these bands is dominated by a prevailing wind. Such winds are not constant but they blow more often than any other wind in the same area.

Winds are caused by differences in temperature and air pressure. Their direction is affected by the earth's rotation and by local conditions.

Rising air at the equator causes calm conditions known as the doldrums. Immediately to the north is a zone where steady northeast winds blow. These are the trade winds, so called because merchant ships in the days of sail took regular advantage of them. Farther north still is a band of prevailing westerlies. Beyond it are bitter polar winds blowing from the east. This wind pattern is true of the northern hemisphere. The pattern in the south is the same. Some violent winds blow only for a short time, but bring dreadful devastation with them. Areas both north and south of the equator experience particularly violent winds at certain times of the year. Called typhoons or cyclones in the Pacific, and hurricanes in the Caribbean, they are whirlpools of air up to 600km across blowing at very high speeds. They form over warm sea but die away over land.

Some local winds blow so regularly that they are given names. The sirocco is a southeast wind that carries desert dust from the Sahara to parts of Europe. The same name is given to a warm damp wind that blows from the same direction but brings rain. The harmattan is a cool wind that blows southwards from northwest Africa. It is so dry that it withers vegetation and may cause people's skin to peel.

Wind speed is measured with a simple instrument called an anemometer. This consists of cups mounted on arms that rotate round a central spindle. The wind fills the cups and makes them turn. The stronger the wind the faster the cups rotate. The number of turns they make in a second is shown on a dial by a pointer coupled to the spindle. This tells us the wind speed in metres per second.

Wind direction is shown by a weather vane or a wind sock. A weathercock is the traditional kind of weather vane. The cock's beak points to where the wind is coming from. The wind sock is a more reliable device. It is a tube made of sturdy cloth, open at both ends. One end is tethered to a rigid ring. When the wind blows the sock rises and trails in the wind, showing at a glance the direction it is coming from and its strength.

Wind speeds are measured with an anemometer. Wind direction is indicated by means of weather vanes. For centuries corn was ground in wind mills. Today wind is harnessed to generate electricity.

In 1805 the British admiral Francis Beaufort devised a scale to estimate wind speeds. A variation on the scale is shown above: 1. Light air: smoke drifts with air. 2. Light breeze: smoke is blown and leaves rustle. 3. Gentle breeze: leaves and twigs move. 4. Moderate breeze: small branches in constant motion. 5. Fresh breeze: small trees sway and waves form on inland waters. 6. Strong breeze: large branches sway and electric cables whistle. 7. Near gale: trees bend and it is difficult to walk into the wind. 8. Gale: twigs break and it is very difficult to walk. 9. Strong gale: tiles ripped from roofs. 10. Storm; trees uprooted, buildings damaged. 11. Violent storm: widespread severe damage. 12. Hurricane: devastation. When it is dead calm the wind force is 0.

WATER IN THE AIR

WATER VAPOUR is a gas that you cannot see, feel or smell. Humidity is the amount of water vapour in the air. Air is saturated when it cannot hold any more water vapour. Warm air can hold more water vapour than cold air, so when warm, moist air cools down, the air eventually become saturated. As the air becomes saturated the water vapour it holds condenses to form tiny water droplets which appear as mist or fog. Fog (A) is defined as any condensation that reduces visibility to less than a kilometre. Mist (B) is a haze that reduces visibility only slightly.

You can make your own fog if you breathe on a window on a cold day. Your breath, which is saturated air, cools when it hits the cold glass and turns into water droplets.

A

B

Air contains water in the form of an invisible gas called water vapour. As air cools the water vapour turns into water droplets which become visible as fog or mist.

Relative humidity is the amount of water vapour in the air compared to the amount required for saturation at the same temperature. It can be measured with a hair hygrometer. This uses human hair which is at its shortest when dry and gradually lengthens as it gets wet. A bundle of hair is anchored at one end and attached to a lever at the other. As the hair length changes, the lever moves a pointer on a scale.

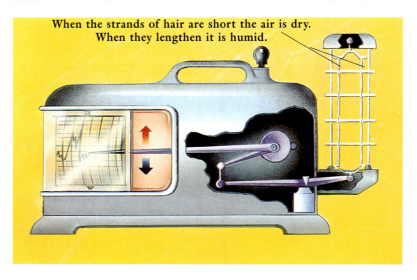

When the strands of hair are short the air is dry. When they lengthen it is humid.

CONDENSATION

PRECIPITATION

EVAPORATION

Water moves in an unending process like a turning wheel. As water vapour, it rises into the sky where it turns into water droplets and forms clouds. The water droplets join together to make larger drops which fall to earth as rain.

The sun's rays heat the surface of the oceans, seas and lakes. The heat makes the water evaporate and turn into water vapour. As the air is warmed by the sun's heat it becomes lighter and some sweeps towards the land. When the moisture-laden winds meet the land, they are forced to rise, often by high mountains. As the air rises it cools. The water vapour in the colder air condenses to form minute water droplets. The tiny droplets formed in rising air join together in larger drops which collect to become clouds.

The drops become too heavy to float in the air so they fall back to earth as rain, or if it is cold enough, snow or hail. Rain, snow and hail are grouped together under the term precipitation. Almost all of the water that evaporates from the oceans falls back into them. The rest mostly falls on the land, soaks into the soil and seeps into the rocks. This water finds its way back to a river and is carried to the sea.

Once the water has returned to the sea, the processes of evaporation, rising, cooling, condensation and rainfall are repeated and go on without ceasing. This never-ending process is called the water cycle.

CLOUDS

A CLOUD IS a great mass of billions of tiny water droplets or ice crystals. When air rises and is cooled enough to reach its saturation point, the water vapour in it condenses. A boiling kettle illustrates this process. The water vapour at the spout is cooled by the air it meets. It condenses and forms steam – a small cloud.

Clouds are formed by air cooling below its saturation point. When air passes over a warm land surface it heats up and rises. As it rises it cools and forms clouds. Air has to rise when it blows over mountains and this makes it form clouds. Lighter warm air rides upwards over heavier cold air.

Clouds change their shape all the time as they evaporate or condense. Some are white and fluffy, others dark and menacing. Their names describe their appearance. Cirrus clouds are wispy (cirro means curl), cumulus clouds are like heaps of cotton wool (cumulo means heap) and stratus clouds are sheets that often cover the whole sky (stratus means layer). Different clouds form at different heights in the sky. The main cloud names are used in various combinations to describe their appearance and height.

When warm air rises and cools down, the water vapour it holds condenses as water droplets to form clouds.

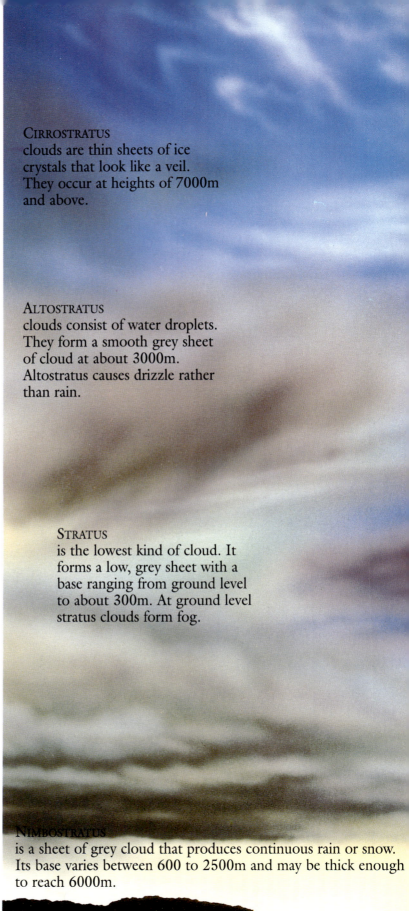

CIRROSTRATUS clouds are thin sheets of ice crystals that look like a veil. They occur at heights of 7000m and above.

ALTOSTRATUS clouds consist of water droplets. They form a smooth grey sheet of cloud at about 3000m. Altostratus causes drizzle rather than rain.

STRATUS is the lowest kind of cloud. It forms a low, grey sheet with a base ranging from ground level to about 300m. At ground level stratus clouds form fog.

NIMBOSTRATUS is a sheet of grey cloud that produces continuous rain or snow. Its base varies between 600 to 2500m and may be thick enough to reach 6000m.

CIRROCUMULUS
is caused by strong winds at very high altitudes. It usually appears in small patches that may look like fish scales. This kind of cirrocumulus is known as a mackerel sky.

CIRRUS
clouds look like wispy streaks of white hair, sometimes called mares' tails. They are composed of ice crystals and found as high as 10,000m.

CUMULONIMBUS
are towering anvil-shaped thunderclouds that pile up high in the sky and discharge rain, hail and lightning. They may be 10km across and 10km high.

ALTOCUMULUS
is found between 2500 and 6000m. Made of water droplets, it appears as layers of puffy white or grey clouds that signal a change in the weather.

CUMULUS
are white puffy clouds that often float in the sky on sunny days. Sometimes they join together and produce rain or cumulonimbus clouds.

Get to know the ever changing cloud types and you will always know what kind of weather to expect.

STRATOCUMULUS
clouds form in pale and dark layers, often extending over thousands of square kilometres. They create an overcast sky but rarely give rain.

RAIN, SNOW AND HAIL

THE WATER particles in a cloud are so tiny that it takes millions of them to form one rain drop. They grow bigger as they collide with each other or as more moisture condenses on them. Eventually they become heavy enough to fall as raindrops. Raindrops measure between 2 and 5mm in diameter. Larger drops splash as they hit the ground. The smallest land lightly as drizzle.

Rain is vital to life. In parts of the world where rain is scarce, there are few plants, animals or people.

Rain gauge

Rainfall is measured with a rain gauge. This instrument is a cylinder with a removable lid. Inside is a funnel leading to a tube. The mouth of the funnel is ten times the diameter of the tube, so if one centimetre of rain falls it will measure ten centimetres on the tube. This makes it possible to measure very small amounts of rain. The gauge should be placed on the ground in the open.

If air cools enough, some of the water vapour in it condenses. On a clear, cold night the ground loses heat quickly. If the air above it is cooled sufficiently, it becomes saturated and condenses as droplets of dew on plants and on the ground. The air temperature at which dew begins to form is called the dew point. When the temperature is below freezing ice crystals are deposited as frost.

When the temperature in a cloud falls to below −10°C, water vapour turns to ice crystals. The upper parts of many clouds consist of ice crystals. If these grow heavy enough they fall through the cloud, colliding with water droplets that freeze on to them. The crystals join together to form snowflakes. A typical snowflake may consist of 50 or more individual ice crystals. As the snow crystals pass through warmer air they may melt and fall as rain. But if it is cold enough they fall as snow. Sometimes snow and rain fall together as sleet.

If you look at a snow crystal under a magnifying glass, you will see that it has six sides or points. Look at another and you will see the same, but the pattern will be different. Every individual snowflake has its own beautiful shape. No two are ever exactly the same.

Snow takes up more space than rain composed of the same amount of water. As a rough guide 5cm of rain equals a 50cm fall of snow.

Water also falls as hail. Hailstones are made of layers of ice. They form in high cumulus clouds. Droplets of water are tossed up and down the freezing levels of the cloud by air currents. Water condenses on them as they fall and freezes as they rise. Eventually they fall to earth as hail. Some hailstones are as big as tennis balls. A large hailstone cut open will show the layers of ice it is made of.

AIR MASSES AND FRONTS

AIR MASSES are enormous bodies of air that form over areas of land or sea with a fairly constant temperature. They may be warm or cold; humid or dry. Air masses move at different speeds and do not readily mix. The boundary zones between them are called fronts. Most changes in the weather occur along fronts. There are two main types of front: cold and warm.

Air masses blow from one area to another. The boundaries between air masses of different temperature and humidity are known as fronts.

In a cold front, cold air catching up with warmer air burrows underneath it, causing it to rise rapidly and cool down. As it cools the water vapour in the warm air condenses and falls as heavy rain. As the front passes it brings colder weather.

A warm front is the result of warm air overtaking cooler air. The warm air rides up gradually over the colder air, causing the water vapour it holds to fall as gentle rain or drizzle. As the front passes it brings warmer weather.

Cold air moves faster than warm, so a cold front often catches up with a warm front to form an occluded front. An occluded front generally results in persistent cloud and rain.

On weather maps cold fronts are indicated on their leading edge by triangles, warm fronts by semicircles, and occluded fronts by alternating triangles and semicircles.

Cold front

Warm front

Occluded front

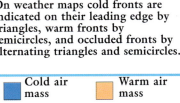
Cold air mass   Warm air mass

WARM FRONT   Cirrus   Altocumulus   Nimbostratus

Cirrus clouds are the first indication of the arrival of a warm front. Then the sky begins to cloud over. Altocumulus appear and the wind gets up. The clouds thicken to altostratus and soon turn to a low, dark blanket of nimbostratus. It starts to rain – or snow – steadily for hours at a time. A warm front advances slowly at about 8km/h. The clouds that are the first signs of its approach may be seen 1500km in advance of the front at ground level and 48hrs before the front's arrival.

Cold fronts often follow warm fronts. They move at some 30km/h, considerably faster than warm fronts. The front's arrival is signalled by strong gusts of wind, large clouds and bursts of heavy rain, hail or even thunderstorms. When the storm passes and the clouds clear, it is cooler. Some cumulus clouds may remain, causing further downpours.

Warm fronts and cold fronts both bring rain. Warm front rain tends to be persistent and moderate. Rain from cold fronts is usually violent but short-lived.

COLD FRONT   Wind   Rain or hail   Cumulus

STORMY WEATHER

Tornado

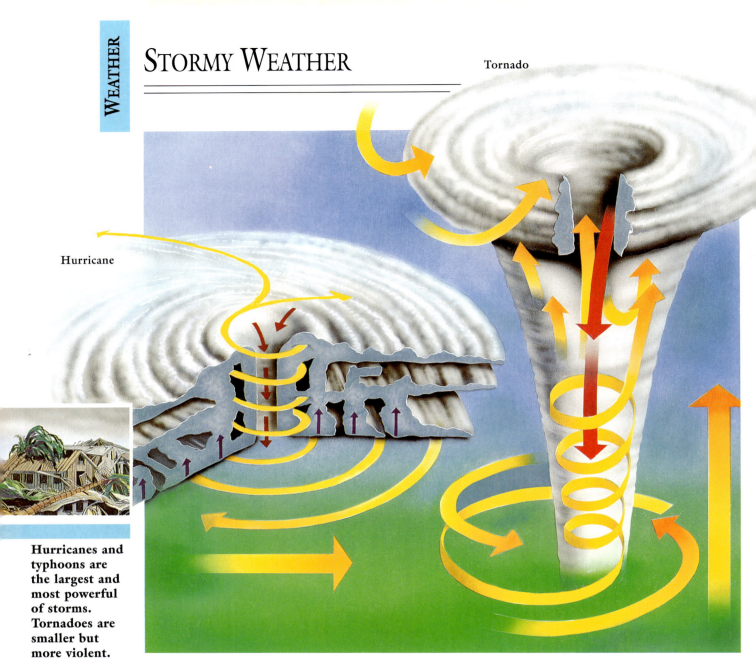

Hurricane

Hurricanes and typhoons are the largest and most powerful of storms. Tornadoes are smaller but more violent.

TROPICAL STORMS can be predicted but they still bring devastation and death. Known as hurricanes in the Atlantic and typhoons in the Pacific, cyclones are huge whirling storms born in hot, moist air masses over the oceans a little north or south of the equator. There, in late summer and early autumn, trade winds from the northern hemisphere meet trade winds from the south. The twisting effect of the earth's rotation sets them whirling around each other.

Cyclones feed on the energy they get from warm moist air as they move over the ocean. Their winds grow ever more violent, reaching speeds of 240km/h rising to 360km/h in sudden gusts. At the centre, or eye, of the cyclone is an area of calm about 11km across. Cyclones wreak enormous havoc in coastal areas but die down as they move inland.

Tornadoes are small cyclones. They occur on land in spring and summer in places where moist warm air and cold air masses meet. They consist of funnels of wind whirling at speeds of up to 450km/h or more round a centre where air pressure is so low that it sometimes causes buildings to explode. Tornadoes are short-lived and rarely measure more than 1500m across. The most violent occur in the United States.

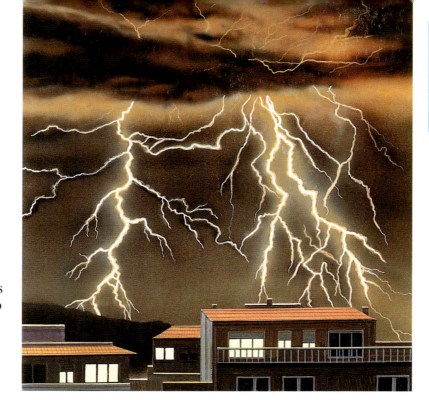

Thunderstorms occur when warm, moist air is forced upwards by air currents or by a mass of cold air burrowing under a mass of warm air. They are set going by updraughts of air, usually in large cumulonimbus clouds. These winds cause water drops and ice crystals in the cloud to rub together, building up gigantic charges of static electricity. Cloud particles become alternately positively and negatively charged. When enough electricity has been produced it is released as a lightning flash between two clouds or between a cloud and the ground. Thunder is the sound made by air in the path of the flash expanding violently as it is heated by the electricity in the flash. The most violent thunderstorms occur almost daily in equatorial regions. They occur least often in the polar regions which lack the heat that generates thunderstorms.

Because light travels much faster than sound, you always see lightning before you hear the thunder it causes.

Rainbows occur when sunlight is seen through raindrops. The raindrops break up the sun's white light and reflect it back to an observer as seven different colours – red, orange, yellow, green, blue, indigo and violet – the colours of the rainbow. You can only see a rainbow when you stand with your back to the sun. Large raindrops produce the best rainbows. Sometimes you may be lucky enough to see a double rainbow.

WEATHER FORECASTING

IN DAYS GONE by, people looked for clues in nature to help them predict the weather. Frogs croaking loudly was a sign of rain on the way. Closed pine cones meant wet weather; open meant fine. The rhyme 'Red sky at night, shepherd's delight. Red sky in the morning, shepherd's warning' is probably the best-known example of traditional weather wisdom. Watch the sky and see if it is true.

A weather forecaster explains tomorrow's weather using a meteorological chart prepared with the aid of the latest scientific developments.

Satellites and sophisticated modern computers have revolutionised weather forecasting. Satellites in stationary or variable orbits provide pictures of weather worldwide. Radar provides details of cloud-cover and rainfall. Further contributions come from weather ships, weather observatories and balloon-borne equipment. This diverse information is digested and processed by weather-forecasting computers capable of making billions of calculations per second. Meteorologists translate the computer results as weather forecasts for aircraft, ships and farmers; as reports for radio and television; as maps for newspapers and as temperature forecasts for the gas and electricity industries.

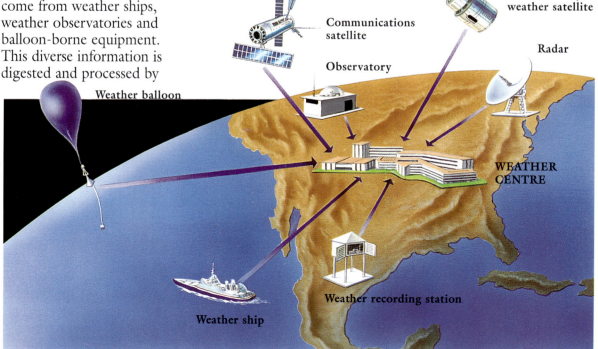

Communications satellite

Geostationary weather satellite

Observatory

Radar

Weather balloon

WEATHER CENTRE

Weather recording station

Weather ship

There are basically three types of climate: hot, temperate and cold. Temperatures go from hot at the equator to cold at the poles. But it is not just latitude that affects temperature. It is also altitude, ocean currents and distance from the sea. Rainfall also varies from place to place, depending on the prevailing winds and the rise and fall of the land.

TROPICAL CLIMATE

DESERT CLIMATE

MEDITERRANEAN CLIMATE

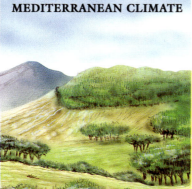

CONTINENTAL CLIMATE

Equatorial climates are hot and humid all year. Tropical climates have humid summers and dry winters. Rain forests thrive in these regions but the soil is poor and it is hard to grow crops. Oceanic regions mostly have mild summers and winters. The Mediterranean climate gives hot, dry summers and gentle, damp winters. The continental climate inland has hot summers and cold winters.

The frozen wilderness of the polar regions and the damp heat of equatorial forests represent the opposite extremes of world climates.

The frozen wastes of the Arctic and Antarctic are dry and know nothing but extreme cold. The same climate occurs in mountainous regions that have snow and ice all year. These areas are as hostile to life as hot deserts. Little grows in them and eking an existence in them is difficult. Because temperate regions are not too hot or too cold, too wet or too dry, they are good for growing crops and grazing animals.

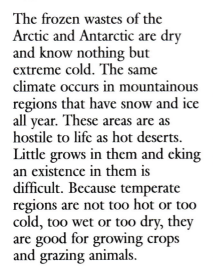

POLAR CLIMATE

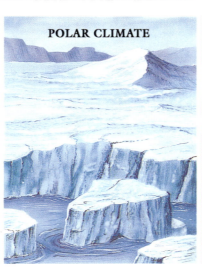

MOUNTAIN CLIMATE

25

FUTURE WEATHER

IN THE PAST, the earth's climate has changed many times. From 80,000 to 10,000 years ago much of northern Europe, Asia and North America was covered in ice, in places 2km thick. This ice age was only the most recent of many and we are still not sure what caused it or its predecessors. We are now living in a warmer phase but it seems that the global climate is set to change again.

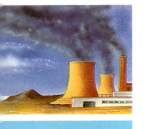

Pollution is changing the balance of gases in the atmosphere and causing global warming.

Whatever may have caused them, past climatic changes have arisen from natural causes. The change to a warmer global climate that many scientists now predict is due not to natural forces but to human activity. Attempts are being made to halt the change but they may be too late.

Carbon dioxide and other gases that occur naturally in the atmosphere help to keep the earth warm enough to sustain life. These gases let the sun's rays through to heat the earth but prevent too much heat from being radiated back into space. They are called 'greenhouse gases' because they act like the glass in a greenhouse. Heat passes through the glass into the greenhouse, the surfaces and plants inside get hot and heat the air. The heat does gradually pass out through the glass but only very slowly.

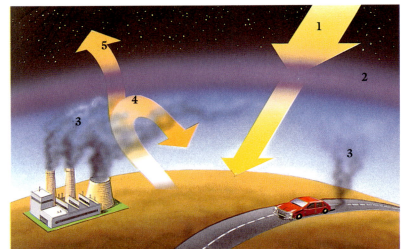

GREENHOUSE EFFECT

1. **Heat from the sun**

2. **Natural gases**

3. **Pollution gases**

4. **Radiation trapped**

5. **Heat escaping into space**

Too much carbon dioxide in the atmosphere, however, increases the greenhouse effect so that extra heat is trapped. During the last half century cars and factories have been pouring huge and increasing volumes of carbon dioxide and other pollutants into the atmosphere. It is impossible to predict accurately what will happen as a result. The polar ice-caps may well melt and rising seas may flood low-lying coastal areas.

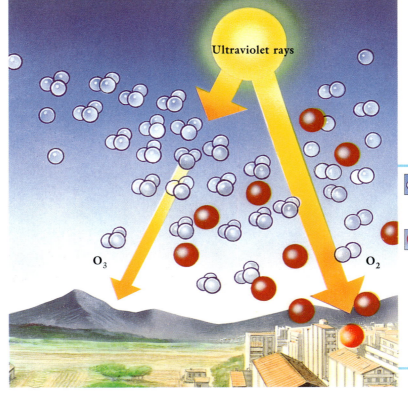

Ultraviolet rays

O_3 O_2

 Ozone decomposes into oxygen

CFCs destroy ozone molecules and allow more ultraviolet rays to reach the earth

When smoke from factories and car exhausts combines with natural fog, the lethal mixture known as smog is created. Smoke particles and sulphuric acid in smog may be fatal to anyone with breathing difficulties. In some big cities the combination of pollutants and hot sunshine produces a photochemical smog that blocks out the sun and causes a temperature inversion. What should be a warm, sunny day becomes cool and gloomy.

The ozone layer shields the earth from overexposure to ultraviolet radiation which can cause skin cancer and eye diseases. Widespread use of CFCs has caused large holes to open up in the ozone layer over the poles. The use of these chemicals has now been limited but not yet totally banned. Though ozone high in the atmosphere protects us, at ground level it is a pollutant, a component of photochemical smog.

The earth's forests are shrinking fast as they are cut down for their wood or cleared for cultivation or industrial developments. This too is changing the world's climate, for trees absorb carbon dioxide and give off water vapour. A square kilometre of tropical forest evaporates more moisture than the same area of ocean. More carbon dioxide increases global warming and less water vapour means less rain.

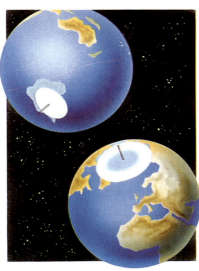

Trees are also damaged by acid rain. Emissions of sulphur and nitrogen compounds by factories, power stations and cars combine with water vapour to form acids. These acids fall to the ground by themselves or in rain. They collect in rivers and lakes, weakening and killing fish and other wildlife. Clouds blown from industrial areas may dump their lethal rain on forests far away, causing the trees to die.

Pollution shrouds cities in smog or subjects them to showers of acid rain.

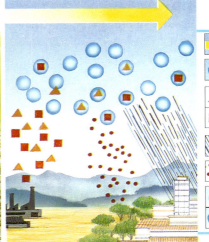

Wind

Water vapour

Oxides of sulphur and nitrogen

Rain

Dust

Acid droplets

WORKING WITH WEATHER

Meteorology is the science of weather. As well as watching the weather and forecasting future weather, meteorologists work out why the weather is the way it is and what causes it. Like other scientists, they test their theories. With the aid of simple, everyday things it is possible to prove for yourself some of the processes that cause weather.

WHICH HEATS FASTER?

Take two plastic glasses and fill one with dry soil from a shady place and the other with cool water. Put both out in hot sun and after an hour take their temperatures with a thermometer. Then move both into the shade for an hour and do the same. Which substance warms more quickly and which cools more quickly?

MAKE A RAIN GAUGE

Ask an adult to cut off the top of a plastic bottle. With sticky tape fix the top upside down in the bottom part. Stick a paper strip marked in half centimetres on the side of the bottle and fill the bottle to where your scale starts. Put your rain gauge in a flower pot and leave it out in the open. Now take daily readings of the rainfall.

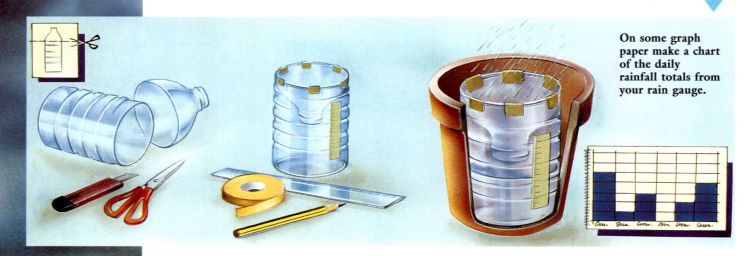

On some graph paper make a chart of the daily rainfall totals from your rain gauge.

Testing for acid rain

First make an indicator. Ask an adult to boil some chopped red cabbage in a little distilled water for a few minutes, then let it stand for an hour. Strain the cabbage and keep the cabbage water. Don't let it drain down the sink. Pour equal amounts of the purple cabbage water into a glass of distilled water and a glass of rainwater. If the rain water turns red you have acid rain in your area.

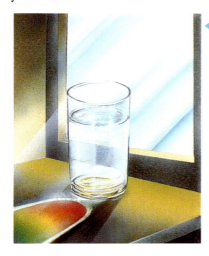

Make your own rainbow

You will need a clear glass of water and a sheet of white paper for this experiment. Lay the paper on a window ledge and place the glass on it in full sunlight. What can you see on the paper in the shade of the glass? If you do not see a rainbow, put a piece of card between the glass and the window with a narrow slit in it so that only a sliver of sunlight can get through.

Make a weather record

Draw up a weather chart like this one for each month. Watch the sky every day and record what you see. Every day look at your rain gauge and at a thermometer and enter the results on your weather chart.

Glossary

ACID RAIN Rain that contains high levels of acids derived from pollution.

AIR Mixture of gases, including nitrogen, oxygen and carbon dioxide, that make up the atmosphere.

AIR MASS Large body of air in which the temperature, humidity and pressure are much the same throughout.

AIR PRESSURE Weight of air. Also called atmospheric pressure.

ALTITUDE Another word for height.

ANEMOMETER Instrument that measures wind speed.

ANEROID BAROMETER See BAROMETER.

ATMOSPHERE Blanket of air surrounding and protecting the earth.

ATMOSPHERIC PRESSURE See AIR PRESSURE.

ATOM Tiny particle of matter, once thought to be indivisible.

AURORA Sheet of coloured light sometimes seen in the night sky at the poles.

BAROMETER Instrument for measuring air pressure.

BEAUFORT SCALE Scale of numbers used to indicate the strength of the wind.

CLOUD Mass of condensed water vapour floating in the air.

CONDENSATION Process in which a gas turns into a liquid, as when water vapour turns into rain.

CYCLONE Winds spiralling round a centre of low pressure. Hurricanes, typhoons and tornadoes are cyclones.

DEW Moisture deposited overnight by cool air condensing on plants and other cold surfaces.

DOLDRUMS Area of calm weather and low pressure near the equator where the northeast and southeast trade winds meet.

EQUATOR Imaginary line running east-west round the middle of the earth.

EVAPORATION Process in which a liquid turns into a gas. The opposite of condensation.

FOG Cloud at ground level that restricts visibility.

FRONT Boundary between two different air masses. A cold front is one where colder air is overtaking warmer air. A warm front is one where warmer air is catching up with colder air. An occluded front occurs when a cold front overtakes a warm front.

FROST Frozen dew.

GLOBAL WARMING Increase in temperatures worldwide that some scientists believe is occurring as a result of increased carbon dioxide emissions.

GREENHOUSE EFFECT Ability of atmospheric gases to hold a layer of warm air near the earth's surface. Too much carbon dioxide increases the effect, trapping extra heat.

HAIL Pellets of frozen rain formed from layers of ice.

HARMATTAN Dry local wind in West Africa.

HEMISPHERE Half of a sphere. The earth is divided into eastern and western hemispheres and northern and southern.

HUMIDITY The amount of water vapour in the air.

HURRICANE Violent cyclone that forms in the Caribbean or eastern Pacific.

ICE AGE Period of several thousand years in which large parts of the earth were covered in thick ice sheets.

INFRARED RADIATION Rays from the sun that heat the earth.

ISOBAR Line on a weather map that joins points of equal air pressure.

MERCURY Liquid metal used in thermometers and barometers.

METEOROLOGY Study of the atmosphere and particularly weather.

MILLIBAR Unit of air pressure, one-thousandth of a bar.

MIST Thin cloud at ground level.

MOLECULE Unit of matter composed of atoms.

OCCLUDED FRONT See FRONT.

OZONE Form of oxygen that forms a layer in the stratosphere and absorbs harmful ultraviolet radiation from the sun.

CHLOROFLUOROCARBONS (CFCs) Chemical compounds used in refrigerants, aerosols and other products that rise as gases into the atmosphere and damage the ozone layer.

POLES Points, north and south, that mark the ends of the earth's axis.

PRECIPITATION Rain, snow or hail that falls from a cloud.

PREVAILING WIND Wind that blows most often from one direction.

RADIATION Rays of light and heat, and other rays from the sun.

SATURATED Full of moisture. When the air is saturated, the water condenses to form dew.

SHOOTING STARS Bright, moving trail of light seen in the night sky as a meteor (matter from outer space) burns up in the atmosphere.

SIROCCO 1. Dry wind that reaches Europe from the Sahara. 2. Warm rainy wind that blows in southern Europe.

SMOG Mixture of smoke and fog.

TEMPERATE Moderate climate with four seasons.

TEMPERATURE Degree of heat.

THERMOMETER Instrument used to measure temperature.

TORNADO Violent whirlwind.

TRADE WIND Wind that blows steadily towards the equator. North of the equator trade winds come from the northeast while south of it they come from the southeast.

TYPHOON Name used for a hurricane that arises in the western Pacific.

ULTRAVIOLET Rays in sunlight that can tan and damage the skin.

WATER VAPOUR Water in the form of an invisible gas in the atmosphere.

WEATHER State of the atmosphere in a particular place at a particular time; it includes temperature, pressure, humidity, wind and cloudiness.

WEATHERCOCK Traditional instrument that indicates wind strength and direction.

WIND Moving air.

WIND SOCK Device that indicates wind strength and direction.

INDEX

The Library of
Nordic Literature

Dreams of Roses and Fire

Dreams
of Roses and Fire

EYVIND JOHNSON

Translated from the Swedish by
Erik J. Friis

Introduction by
Monica Setterwall

Hippocrene Books / New York

The Library of Nordic Literature
Erik J. Friis, *General Editor*

Volume 2
Dreams of Roses and Fire, by Eyvind Johnson

This book was originally published in Sweden under
the title *Drömmar om rosor och eld* © 1949
by Albert Bonniers Förlag.

This English translation copyright © 1984
by Erik J. Friis.

For information, address: Hippocrene Books, Inc.,
171 Madison Avenue, New York, N.Y. 10016.

Printed in the United States of America

Library of Congress Cataloging in Publication Data

Johnson, Eyvind, 1900–
Dreams of roses and fire.

I. Title.
PT9875.J6D713   1984   839.7'372   83-26690
ᵉʰ ISBN 0-88254-897-2

Contents

Introduction

THE TITLE OF Eyvind Johnson's novel *Dreams of Roses and Fire*, from the original *Drömmar om rosor och eld* (1949), deserves a moment of reflection. The "dreams" must refer to that nebulous area underneath wakened sensibilities and objective reality, where imagery is prompted by unspoken desires. Roses are associated with glowing colors, passion, and beauty, and so is fire. But fire is also destructive. Or rather, the purpose of fire is to destroy or to cleanse, but the nature of fire is simply to consume. To dream of roses and fire is to dream of passion, and perhaps of being consumed by passion. It is clear at least that with the title at hand, subliminal and symbolic aspects of roses and fire may be expected in the narrative.

Both roses and fire appear as highly concrete entities in the novel. The priest Grainier always carries a rose stuck in among the pages of his breviary. When the nuns in the Ursuline convent begin to have dreams troubled by demons, they wake up with thorns in their hands. The smoke of a big fire hangs heavy over the last part of the novel. Some welcome the cleansing power of this particular fire, others see only its tragic destructiveness. Roses are an emblem of beauty for the priest, but they only leave behind the sharpness of thorns in the hands of the nuns. Roses and fire are made symbolic of an ambiguous tendency in man, both life-promoting and life-destructive. In this manner, the title is indicative of Johnson's interest in the psychological motivations of his characters, as well as of his complex interweaving of realistic and symbolic detail, a trademark of his narrative art.

What the title does not suggest, however, is the historical background of the novel. Its setting is early seventeenth-century France with its political and religious clashes between Catholics and Huguenots, and with Cardinal Richelieu as the central power factor working for Catholic supremacy. The historical issue should be given some attention here for two reasons. First, it is Johnson's belief that man remains essentially the same at different points of time, only his outer circumstances change. To illuminate varying facets of the human condition, Johnson frequently places his novels within a specific historical framework. From Homer's time to our present day there are few centuries of European history that do not appear in the novels of this erudite writer. Secondly, a look at Johnson's treatment of historical facts gives a wider perspective to an understanding of his narrative technique.

In 1628 Cardinal Richelieu's troops conquered La Rochelle, the Huguenot stronghold. This put an effective stop to the political power of the Huguenots which had been established by the Edict of Nantes in 1598. The Huguenots still claimed religious freedom, however, and the struggle continued. In the small city of Loudun in the district of Poitou, a Jesuit priest by the name of Urbain Grandier—in Johnson's novel he appears as Urbain Grainier—was caught in the power machinations. Siding with the leading Huguenots in the city, he tried to save the city walls, which Richelieu had ordered to be torn down on the grounds that they protected the heretics. Grandier's part in defending the walls had been conspicuous, to say the least, earning him Richelieu's suspicion and distinct lack of appreciation. Richelieu's negative feelings were further intensified when Grandier was rumored to be the author of a widely circulated libelous pamphlet against him.

The controversial Grandier was an impassionate man, and he made enemies with numerous citizens in Loudun as well, because of his attraction to women, his arrogance, and his political intrigues. He was eventually accused of trafficking with demons, and of leading them to seduce the nuns at the local Ursuline convent. Following several exorcist sessions, he was finally sentenced to death for witchcraft in 1634 and burnt at the stake. During the trial and the torture, he repeatedly stated his innocence in the crimes for which he was sentenced. The event stirred up a vivid debate concerning demonic power in general and Grandier's guilt or innocence in particular, a debate which has reverberated in religious, judicial, medical, literary, and cinematic comments in later and more contemporary years.

By the late 1600s and the revocation of the Edict of Nantes, a certain Huguenot by the name of Nicolas Aubin fled to the Netherlands together with thousands of other Huguenots. Among his papers he had an account of a first-hand witness to the events in Loudun. The witness was his aunt, Maria Aubin, who was a young girl in 1634, and who had been a boarder at that time at the Ursuline convent. Nicolas Aubin wrote a book based on her account, *Histoire des diables de Loudun*, and had it published in Amsterdam, 1716.

Aubin's detailed presentation of the exorcist proceedings have supplied much of the content in Johnson's fictional version. Even Marie Aubin plays a small, peripheral part. At one point Nicolas Aubin reports a sudden exclamation from a man in the group of observers who had been invited to witness the Church's subjugation of demonic power. The man, identified as Daniel Drouin in the novel, is not impressed by the demon's faulty Latin, and he makes a caustic remark about it. With this remark we enter Johnson's fictional world, the opening paragraph of the novel, where the echo of Daniel Drouin's words about the devil provides the starting point for the narrative.

This echo of historical facts is the spark that ignites Johnson's novel. The echo has intrinsic significance in the narrative too. Part I, "Out of the Past," contains portrayals of two nuns and of the exorcist Barrot. They are the characters who experience the demons, the nuns by being subjected to the demons' advances, the exorcist by subjugating the demons. In these three chapters, the characters reflect on their childhood memories, and on the causes that led to a cloistered life and to the recognition and fighting of demons. Common to these childhood echoes is a violation against the individual. None of them has experienced love or human nearness. The absence of love is closely related to the presence of demons. What appears as an onslaught of demons from the outside may also be seen as a projection of an individual's imprisonment, be it inside cloister walls, or in the narrow cell of distorted vision.

Interspersed with these three chapters are excerpts of Daniel Drouin's diary. The echo principle is at work here as well. Like the main narrator, Drouin is interested in historical facts. He is the chronicler of the city and its inhabitants, and he provides the ongoing commentary on selected events. In this manner, he functions as an echo for the main content of the text: Urbain Grainier's involvement in the power intrigues of the city, his personal ambition and defense of the walls, eventually leading to his death. It is soon made evident by the ironic but sympathetic narrator, however, that Drouin as an echo is not altogether impartial or trustworthy. He is divided by his outward role as a loyal civil servant and his secret admiration for Grainier's magnetic personality. With characteristic Johnson humor, the secrets of Drouin's life are made very obvious, very human.

With this complex weaving of voices, the narrator makes several points from the outset. Historical facts can only be transmitted as echoes through the subjective eyes of the beholder or listener. Human interaction is also the result of echoes of a person's individual past, and some of those echoes one would rather not reveal to the outside world. Submerged, imprisoned echoes become strong driving forces leading to a conflict situation between inner being and outer role of interaction. According to the narrator, such a conflict is especially attractive to demons.

Part II is simply called "The Story," another hint by the narrator of the significance of the echo. For just as Drouin's criticism of the devil brings about the introduction to the novel, just as childhood memories of the nuns and the exorcist lead to their close relations with the demons, so Part I is necessary for the story itself to commence. The testimony in Part I produces the echoes or sound waves that lead to accusation, sentencing, and death in Part II.

There is an inner rhythm of echoes in Part II as well. As in Part I, Drouin's diary excerpts are interlaced with chapters on Grainier and the priest Minet, with Drouin's wandering in the city, and with Grainier's own reflections on his guilt and innocence. Woven into the conversation between Grainier and Minet is the voice of Philippe Tranchant, the young woman whom Grainier made pregnant and then rejected. Her sad fate is central to Minet's accusations against Grainier, and her voice transmits to the reader the echo of her unhappiness. The purpose of Drouin's wandering is to find another biting remark against the devil, one that will resound, make appreciative echoes in the city. The chapter on Grainier's reflections, finally, is called "Exercise in Silence." The immediate reference here is the silence he imposes on himself during the torture. But his silence in the presence of suffering has a certain message for posterity. The absence of screams or of his confession will reverberate as a statement of his innocence to later judges of historical facts.

Not only Grainier is concerned with the judgment of posterity. At one point or another, all the characters turn to posterity, sometimes to clarify their standpoint, generally to ask for help in finding the underlying causes to the chain of events that lead inexorably to Grainier's death. Drouin begins his diary as a self-confident chronicler of facts. By the end, both his tone and purpose have changed. He is no longer as willing to take notes, and he discovers that it was not the facts, after all, that he wanted to leave with posterity. It was the nuances, his breath, the small gestures of his friends. Similarly, the whole narrative can be seen as reverberations of echoes that invite the reader to take a stand and contribute to an understanding of why humans are vulnerable to demons.

A look at the different functions of the walls offers a related approach to this question. On a figurative level the city walls and the city inhabitants have certain characteristics in common. First of all, the walls have an esthetic value. They render architectural beauty to the city, and they delimit and define the city as a living body. The walls also have a protective function. They defend the inhabitants from outside intrusion. Similarly, the role that each individual assumes in societal coexistence constitute the walls that define and protect that individual. In this sense, literal and figurative walls have a positive function. But if the gates of the city walls are razed, protection becomes meaningless, and if the gates are bolted against the outside world, protection becomes imprisonment. Similarly, if the individual loses his societal definition, the meaning of coexistence is lost. If the individual out of fear of what he might find "bolts the gates" to his inner being, thereby excluding the outside world, protection becomes imprisonment, open vision becomes distorted. These walls, or individuals, who have lost a meaningful interaction with the world outside, are attractive to covetous demons and are liable to breed demons on the inside.

Why then does Grainier lose the struggle for the city walls? He certainly does not suppress unwanted desires. It may be said that his eloquence, good looks, and magnetic personality accentuate the shortcomings of those around him making him a welcome target in the religious and political conflict. This is part but not all of his dilemma. As he is confronted by the screaming women who accuse him of having seduced them, he knows that this is not true, that it has not happened. And yet, there is something inside him that responds to their screaming, that seems to remember this. The sounds from the women produce echoes inside him against all reason and common sense. No one goes free from demonic intrusion, Johnson seems to say, it is part of the human condition.

In this moment of bleakness it is good to remember Johnson's emphasis on the smile that disarms the most insufferable of situations. Truly, by the end of the novel it is too late to smile, but during one of the exorcist sessions the narrator makes a lengthy reflection on the possibilities of the smile. Drouin's wandering through the city in search of another biting remark also belongs to the smile-provoking passages.

This short survey on echoes and walls to illustrate the meeting place for historical and fictional reality, Johnson's view of human vulnerability to demons, and polyphony as an aspect of Johnson's narrative technique, offers an approach not only to *Dreams of Roses and Fire* but to Johnson's oeuvre as a whole.

Johnson's sensibility to the demonic is never far afield. This characteristic appears already among his early socio-critical novels. In *Kommentar till ett stjärnfall* (1929; "Commentary to A Falling Star") the diabolical machinations of Laura Stormdal leads to her husband's mental collapse. The vulnerability of the entire capitalist society is exposed by the demonic magnetism of Bobinack in the novel of the same name (1932). In the *Krilon* trilogy (1941–1943) the demonic is attributed to a real estate agent and his cohorts, who are Nazi representatives in disguise, or at least on an allegorical level. Together with *Strändernas svall* (1946; *Return to Ithaca*, 1952) *Dreams of Roses and Fire* mark the transition from socio-critical to mythical-historical themes, and the demonic element persists. It is very vividly a part of Johannes Lupigis' temptation to assassinate Charlemagne in *Hans nådes tid* (1960; *The Days of His Grace*, 1968). In Johnson's last novel, *Några steg mot tystnaden* (1973; "Some Steps Toward Silence") the demonic Mr. X appears with unnerving closeness. He is one facet of the narrator's persona, described as a manipulative parasite on life.

In the recurrent theme of demonism it is only the figure of Grainier—Bobinack shows a similar tendency but it is unconvincing—who represents the demonic as a human potential for both good and evil. The demonic power that surrounds him, and to which he has perhaps contributed, shares the characteristics of demonic presence in the other novels: distorted vision, sadistic manipulation, and above all, the misuse of power. The fascination with power is present from the very beginning in Johnson's writing, but his fascination is combined with his reluctance to use power. In the early novels this dilemma is expressed as the inability to take action in the face of wrongdoing. The Hamlet dilemma of passivity is the center of concern in *Avsked till Hamlet* (1930; "Farewell to Hamlet"), where the protagonist Mårten Torpare is able to free himself from the inability to act as he learns to accept his past.

With the same freedom of spirit Johnson undertakes his autobiographical tetralogy *Romanen om Olof* (1934–1937; "The Novel about Olof"). Most significant here is the fact that Olof's maturing process centers on the discovery of words. Johnson's emphasis is not on the injustices of a rigid class-structured society, or on the effects of poverty, but instead on Olof's realization that words are powerful, they have communicational force, and they open up vast fields of knowledge. The power of the word remains the last stronghold, as the pacifist dilemma of militant action in face of war recurs in the novels *Nattövning* (1938; "Night Maneuvers") and *Soldatens återkomst* (1940; "The Return of the Soldier"). With the Krilon trilogy, called Johnson's military service in words and one of his most important novels, the power of the word to spread knowledge, to illuminate suffering, to console, and to avert oppression, is the basic theme. Krilon appears as a guardian of western civilization, and of humanist concern.

Johnson's preoccupation with the power of the word is central also for the polyphony of his narrative. In his later novels the intricacies of story-telling is evident in the number of narrating voices, which at different times and from different vantage points illustrate the course of events, as in *Hans nådes tid*. In *Livsdagen lång* (1964; "Life's Long Day") the Narrator and the Historian define their respective roles as mediators of reality, but gradually their roles become exchanged. Similar to this dissolving of outlined mediation is the dissolving of biological time and life

xiv

spans. For the man and the woman of this legendary tale meet and separate in the course of centuries always recognizing each other, always drawn apart.

Johnson's themes may be socio-critical or mythical-historical, his narrative technique may develop into highly specialized narrative art, his represented reality becoming gradually more elusive in the process, but his experimentation with his medium and his deep-seated humanist concern remain in full force. Johnson's commitment was to protect the freedom of the spirit from violation, to disarm darkness with the power of the smile, to sharpen and refine his verbal medium by mingling saga and fantasy with everyday reality. In the best of Johnson's writing there are always roses and fire.

Eyvind Johnson was born in the village of Svartbjörn in Norrbotten on July 29, 1900. He was one of six children, his father was disabled by silicosis, and it was at times hard for the family to make ends meet. The young Eyvind was adopted by relatives, and he was not even in this teens when he started working for his living. He became politically active with the syndicalist movement for whom the Russian revolution of 1917 held the promise of a brighter future. Such hopes dwindled, however, and Johnson left his syndicalist affiliation in 1924. In 1919 Johnson moved south to Stockholm, decided on a career as a writer, appearing frequently in the socialist magazine *Brand*. But it was time to move on, and in 1921 Johnson arrived in Berlin. Except for two brief returns to Sweden, he spent the 1920s in Germany and France. He learned German and French, read much of German and French literature, absorbed the intellectual currents of the time, and barely managed to survive on articles sent to Sweden for publication. The experience of being a starving writer on the continent in the 1920s is well documented in two novels, *Romantisk berättelse* (1953; "Romantic Tale") and *Tidens gång* (1955; "The Passage of Time").

During World War II Johnson was the editor of the

underground magazine *Håndslag*, which was made small enough in size to be fitted into shoes and in this way smuggled across the border to Norway. After the war Johnson again lived abroad for long periods of time with his family. The young worker with a minimum of schooling from northern Sweden had made Europe his home and western civilization his area of learning. At his death, August 25, 1976, he had among other honorary achievements become an elected member of the Swedish Academy, 1957. In 1974, he shared the Nobel Prize with the poet and novelist Harry Martinson.

Johnson is not among the most widely read novelists in Sweden. Only a few of his approximately 40 works belong to the novels that are generally treasured by Swedish readers. Among them are the tetralogy *Romanen om Olof*, the Ulysses-version *Return to Ithaca, Dreams of Roses and Fire*, and *The Days of His Grace*.

However, those who place Johnson at the very top of Swedish novel writing are appreciative of the fact that Johnson is widely read abroad. He has been translated into all European languages, and some non-European as well. Together with the translation at hand, four novels have made it into English, namely those four that were mentioned above as the most popular ones in Sweden. It should be noted that only Part I of *Romanen om Olof* has been translated into English, *Nu var det 1914* (1934; *1914*, 1970).

It is no easy task to translate Johnson's prose into English. His sentence structure is characterized by subordination and a complexity of modal phrases. Unless drastic measures are taken, the English version becomes stilted, almost archaic. Mr. Friis must be commended for the painstaking care with which he has managed to divide lengthy sentences and arrive at a more paratactic sentence structure without losing either tone or flavor. It is to be hoped that this successful rendering will be followed by others.

MONICA SETTERWALL
The University of Chicago

PART I

Out of the Past

1

Portrait of a Minor Character Born in 1592

Daniel Drouin, who was an assessor and at times was styled councillor—*conseiller*—in the office of Monsieur de Cerisay, who was the *bailli*, or district bailiff, and the highest civilian official in the city, on one occasion uttered a few words which are far from being the most obtuse that have gone down in history. His words, which I shall revert to further on, implied a rather severe and audacious criticism of the way in which a dark power used the Latin language. People laughed heartily, and for good reason, at what Drouin had said at that time, on November 24, 1632; through various documents, the echo of his witty and bitter remark has even reached our own time.

Here is some information about the Drouin family.

Daniel Drouin's grandfather was a master joiner in the city of L. in the present-day department of Vienne in the northern part of what is known as Southwestern France. He lived on one of the narrow streets up on the hill between the Church of Saint-Pierre and the castle wall. Whether he was a Huguenot or a Catholic is not quite clear; it is my guess that he was a mixture of both, which at that time and in that city was not uncommon. He made windowsills and doors and later on plain furniture and still later on beautiful benches, chairs, beds, cabinets, and tables of oak and walnut for burghers and soldiers of different religious persuasions. The life of the old man was governed by the tall and square Nerra Tower, which had been built in the twelfth century. In the city at that time there were about twenty castle and fortress towers, but the square one was his favorite tower.

Daniel Drouin I was, like all of us, at the very center of the world, that is, in his own life. While the old man's furniture was carried into or broken to pieces or burned up in the houses, his son grew up with his glance ever fixed at the square tower and later at the royal court in Paris. Daniel Drouin II, whom we here may call Middle-Drouin, did not become a furniture-maker, but nevertheless stayed fairly close to his father's profession, in that he changed over to dealing in rugs. Was he a Huguenot or a Catholic? For some decades the inhabitants of the city consisted predominantly of Huguenots. Middle-Drouin said on many occasions, "I try to live in the best way possible."

At first he had a shop in the house up by the castle wall but moved after some years to a recently purchased house on the Square of Sainte-Croix, right across from the church of the same name. He kept the house by the castle wall even after his parents had died, but his actual work was carried on down in the city. The business was conducted in such a way that he with great care, and with the help of his wife, put costly rugs—woven or knotted here in France, in Turkey, and even more distant places in the East and the South—into heavy chests of oak or even finer and fragrant woods with ingenious locks. On each rug he sprinkled insect powder, consisting mainly of crushed wormwood, dried grass, and lavender. Another aspect of the business took place when he carefully and quite often, with the aid of his wife and, at certain times, his only son,

4

brought out the rugs—as well as other things kept in the chests—and showed his stock to selected, reliable customers. At times his servant, Mathieu Archer, a growling serf, was standing for security reasons in the yard with a big ax over his shoulder, a weapon shaped like an executioner's ax. The fellow stood there as if by chance, staring at a pile of wood.

Every Sunday as long as he could make it on foot (he was a big and fat man), Middle-Drouin visited the house up by the castle wall which he had rented out. He could have afforded a carriage or a sedan chair, but he felt ashamed of that kind of showing off, and besides he only very grudgingly paid out any money. He was quite well off, but nevertheless rented out the second floor of his house on the Square of Sainte-Croix. On the first floor there were three rooms and a kitchen for the use of the family. On the other side of the archway, facing Rue des Marchands—the Street of the Merchants—there was a stairway to the right for the tenant, and past that one would enter a small yard which was separated from the houses next door by tall gables or garden walls. An oak tree and a weeping willow were growing in the yard. In the wall facing the side street, which led up to the Church of Saint-Pierre and on to the castle, there was a gate with a knocker and a heavy barrier; if one knew the trick, the gate could also be opened from the outside.

In the above-mentioned archway between the Square of Sainte-Croix and the yard there was a side-door on the left, that is, right opposite the stairs. Through it one entered directly into what one could call the store, a single room with grated windows facing the Rue des Marchands and furnished with a large oak table, a few chairs, and a cabinet in the corner which contained eight glasses, silver beakers, and a wine jug; by the inner wall there were a couple of large chests with metal ornamentation and on the table lay a dark and well-worn ell-measure. Beyond was the bedroom with a wide but not too pretentious canopy bed, its head close to the wall; it stood near a corner of the room but one could pass between the wall and the bed. The bed of their only son, Daniel, would be placed at the other end of the room, below the grated window looking out on the yard, whenever he visited them; to the right and the left of it and wherever there was space around the room stood tall, securely locked chests filled with rugs. In the innermost room there were three more chests with the very finest rugs, a chest with linen, fine clothing and silverware, and a wide cabinet which contained the everyday dinner service, wine tankards, beakers of pewter, and glasses; bookkeeping and writing materials were also kept there. The room had a grated window facing the yard. From that room as well as from the bedroom was a door leading to the long, narrow kitchen. Beyond that was a tiny sleeping closet. Mathieu Archer lived in this little room, but the maid slept in the kitchen on a bed close to the fireplace. The servant and the maid were the parents of a daughter; her name was Séraphique, and she became an extra maid in the house. In the yard, there was a stable for a horse and a donkey, a wagon shed, a pigsty, a chicken coop, and a small garden plot.

Middle-Drouin's looking furtively toward the royal court and Paris was not done on his own account. The rug merchant was thinking of his son. He had him study Latin and other subjects. The first two years with Canon Poussaut who taught school in the house of a relative in Rue Pasquin. The canon spoke through his nose; he was a dirty fellow who drank in the open as well as on the sly, and he beat his pupils for no apparent reason. He did not beat learning into them, as do respectable, knowledgeable, and experienced pedagogues, but instead he beat a fear of learning into them, and in the case of many he quickly whipped out of them whatever learning they might have acquired before they came to him. Stammering increased a great deal in the city and its environs during his years as a teacher. After this beginning, Middle-Drouin sent his son to the Jesuit school in the cathedral city of Poitiers, and in two years there Daniel discovered that Latin also held poetry, that Greek and Hebrew were accessible languages, and that a person could learn Italian, Spanish, and English without any great difficulty, if he only wanted to.

It is doubtful that Middle-Drouin underwent any religious crises. If, in the midst of a religious war and in a city that for decades had been markedly Protestant, he sent his son for his further education to the Jesuit Fathers at Bordeaux, it had more to do with his sidelong glances at the court, his obvious, though fearful, ogling at Paris, than with taking sides. Young Daniel himself evinced decidedly Protestant traits—as will become apparent further on. Like his grandfather and his father, he was tall of stature, but he had a more slender build. Like his immediate ancestors, he loved good food, which he was accustomed to at home, and he hated the fare at the schools he was sent to. He was a voracious reader; perhaps he had ambitions for an intellectual career, but during his years of study he was always vacillating between the urge to obtain knowledge, especially in languages and law and to some extent medicine, and his loathing for the refectories at the boarding schools. He was, one might now say, a refined glutton with a great hunger for knowledge.

His piety, like that of his father, is rather dubious. The old man said, "I tolerate religion." Was Middle-Drouin a Catholic or a Protestant? He attended mass but approved of the Edict of Nantes, and what was thought to be free exercise of religion. What had he dreamed about his son and the Paris court? Now we cannot grasp it all in detail. After so many years, we merely glimpse a few distinct desires felt by these people, who are long since gone: to be able to eat one's fill, to have the ability to satisfy other physical and possibly spiritual needs.

Middle-Drouin wanted his son to be purveyor by appointment to the king of fine rugs, a Drouin who was the king of rugs of the provinces and at least the rug-baron of Paris, a *Drouin de Vienne* or *de Poitou* with his own palace near the Louvre;—a super-merchant in rugs who, besides practical knowledge of legal proceedings, would master several languages and reel off exact quotations in Latin which, the old man shrewdly calculated, would considerably raise the prices of his rugs. This was a dream. In reality, the young Drouin in time came to Bordeaux, the seat of the archbishops Sourdis, in order to study with the Jesuits. Daniel the Younger even then dreamed of becoming a government official. And he did become a government official. Very early he wrote off anything having to do with rugs.

Madame Drouin died in the spring of 1611 (she was a kind woman with markedly Protestant leanings—she was born a Thiboust). The son remained at home the entire summer and helped his father chase moths, sprinkle insect powder, negotiate with customers, and work a little in the vineyard at their country home near Ainsay.

"How are your Latin studies coming along?" Middle-Drouin would ask once in a while.

"Oh, fairly well."

"I hope that it won't be merely Miserere and Ave Maria," said the father, whose face was pale-gray from lack of sunshine and whose back was bent from all the bowing before his rugs; a contributory cause was his wife's death. "It's a good thing you don't want to become a priest," he said. "Here they're running around like black and gray and brown cats with their Latin and they don't get to be anything."

8

"Some of them get to be something," the son replied. "As, for example, a friend of mine in Bordeaux. He will go far, he will no doubt become a bishop, and perhaps a cardinal. His name is Grainier. He comes from Le Mans."

Middle-Drouin didn't care to listen. He was now fifty-four years old and felt that it was high time for his son to enter the rug business.

"You are nineteen now, Daniel. Why don't you go to Paris and look around for a year or two. I can get you the right connections, and I can guarantee that you get the right kind of rugs. Later on, when you are firmly established there, you might move the entire business up there, if you wish. I am not going to meddle, but I'll come up to Paris and watch you drive out in your splendid carriage. For you'll no doubt be the kind who likes the latest style in carriages. Right?"

He laughed, feeling very pleased, until he noticed the silence.

One evening the following summer, Drouin Junior was standing with the sixteen-year-old Séraphique Archer behind the oak tree in the middle of the yard. It was late, pitch dark, and hot.

Séraphique and Daniel were occasionally together out in the country. On hot evenings they would walk out to the country house and look at how the vines were growing.

"If you lie down on the ground, you can even *hear* them grow," Daniel Drouin said.

And they heard the vines grow.

In the spring of 1613, Middle Drouin fell seriously ill, and his son, who had stayed home the entire winter doing nothing but reading, listened attentively to his last words.

"Think of it carefully, Daniel," Middle-Drouin said. "Do you know how many government officials there are in this

9

city alone? Men who have become jurists merely because they have heard another jurist twist the laws, persons who have become civil servants only because they know five words of Latin and because their parents have purchased a position for them at the city hall, in the bailiff's or in the governor's office! They will never get that money back unless they learn to steal or at least commit some minor misfeasances. We have eighteen who call themselves 'pro-curators' and 'solicitors,' twenty 'royal advocates' and 'prosecutors,' eight 'notaries' and 'administrators,' and seventeen 'excutors' and 'distrainors,' and I do not know how many there are who call themselves 'assessors' and 'councillors'!"

Even though he was a dying man, Middle-Drouin pronounced all the quotation marks very distinctly.

"Well, do as you wish," he concluded. "My son, I do not leave behind me many relatives, but I still hope that you will make out well in life."

He did not receive extreme unction. It was too late, people said. With Mathieu Archer, the maid, and their daughter Séraphique, Daniel stood in front of the canopy bed, crying. Daniel was holding Séraphique's hand; no one thought but that it was right and proper.

Then Daniel became the only Drouin in town. He had a whole lot of Poitiers and Bordeaux Latin together with some jurisprudence in his head and his hands were literally full of costly rugs. He sold the rugs, and not for a song, but he did not buy any new ones. He used his money to good purpose. On account of his money, his good, indeed very good, Latin, his knowledge of the law, his amiable manners, and his sometimes smart repartees, which for the most part were well-chosen quotations, he was at first employed as a clerk and assistant administrator (settlements of estates, etc.) at the city hall and in time advanced to the position of assessor in the office of the bailiff, the town's highest official, M. de Cerisay. At times he would be addressed, as was customary, *conseiller*—councillor.

Daniel Drouin had certain ideas, one of them concerning the liberation of women. He also had very strong carnal inclinations. He liked to talk, as often as he had the opportunity, to a girl by the name of Corisande Dolet, whose parents were Huguenots. She married his only relative in the locality, his cousin Mathurin Thiboust, a coachbuilder. Daniel Drouin himself waited long before he entered into matrimony. Mathieu Archer died in 1619. The maid, who now was on in years, and her and Archer's daughter, Séraphique, did the housekeeping. The maid died in late autumn of that year; her daughter was left all alone. She was very capable, and besides, strong and wellbuilt. She became the mother of two children, who both died the same year they were born: a boy in 1620 and a girl in 1621. Their deaths made Daniel Drouin feel depressed for some time.

When Daniel Drouin married in 1624, Séraphique left his employ. She had disappeared when he returned from Saumur with his bride. People said that she had run away with a soldier.

His wife's name was Charlotte Coton; she was the daughter of a government official in Saumur. Like the religion of many people from Saumur, hers was rather vague: among her relatives were Huguenots as well as Catholics. She was a brunette, of a buxom, soft, and housewifely type. She knew a little Latin, and she did learn even more. It was said that the loving couple would coo and conjugate Latin verbs at the same time. She bore in the minimum time possible three boys and two girls; then another boy and two girls. All the children were baptized in the Church of Sainte-Croix on the other side of the square.

Daniel Drouin felt skeptical about certain things. He was

not a religious man. He did not openly deny the necessity of the marriage ceremony or of baptism, but deep inside his breast there was yet another assessor who scrutinized, weighed, and saw through things. His grandfather's and his father's yardstick reposed in his heart: he was a judge of quality and a just man even though at times he might deviate from the principle of absolute right.

Man ought to enjoy his time on earth too, he thought. A woman ought not to be burdened with more than seven, at the most eight, children, and she ought to bear them as quickly as nature and her body allow so as to get a few good years in her middle age. She ought to receive the help of her husband wherever he can be of help and where the maids can't manage, above all for moving furniture, polishing pewterware and silver, and to some extent for the cooking of superior foods and dishes.

Both Daniel Drouin and his wife loved country living, although only in moderation. During the summer, they stayed for several weeks at their little country place. Although she was the wife of an official, Charlotte helped him when he puttered in the garden. He, in turn, and although he was an assessor, would on certain occasions accompany her to the butcher and the marketplace and select fresh meat for her. He liked to do it. He knew most of the town's butchers, bakers, grocers, fishmongers, and wine and vinegar merchants and could discuss their wares with them like an expert. He knew the prices of grain and of food not only in his capacity as a government official but also because he was interested in all this. He knew that one ought to be able to get a good brisket of beef for three sols per pound, prime veal or mutton for at most four sols and six deniers—the same price as for cow's udders—and that one should not pay more than 26–28 sols for a dozen liver sausages or 6–8 sols for a pair of sheep's kidneys. The prices fluctuated a bit, at times very much, from year to year and were regulated by war, plague, harvest prospects and harvest results and political changes. The food prices were influenced by the various kinds of disputes in which the King, the Church, and (later on) Cardinal Richelieu were involved and by the restless greed for power of Maria de Medici and Gaston of Orléans; but Daniel Drouin had the price list more or less in his head and could offhand quote the price of such very special and much sought-after necessaries as partridges, woodcocks, pheasants, young boars, or peacocks and swans—the last-named about 40-50 sols apiece.

Due to his fondness for good food and his desire to derive something delectable from world literature, he procured in the course of years some of the cookbooks that might be needed by a skeptical, friendly and helpful, well-to-do man, someone who was happy in his work and his learning. At times as he sat reading in the dining room he would interrupt himself, walk into the kitchen and himself turn the meat on the spit, observe developments, inhale the aroma, wipe his fingers on a rag, and then return to the dining room table to read some more by low fire, as it were. A bit anxiously, his wife saw to it that the maid tended the fire on the hearth so that the flames were just the way they ought to be, and now and then Daniel Drouin would come back in and supervise both his wife and the maid. "Turn it gently, oh, very gently,—so that the juice doesn't drip out. Rub in just another hint of garlic, just a hint! May I taste it?" He cut off a small piece, put it on an iron stick or fork, smelled it, did not lick the piece but let it just touch the tip of his tongue, blew on it, put it in his mouth, closed his eyes, and readied himself for the experience. He chewed very slowly, swallowed, opened his eyes and turned his glance toward the ceiling and then toward Madame Charlotte, his smile spreading from his eyes to his mouth and all over his face, indeed throughout the entire very tall although not especially broad-shouldered figure. "A few minutes more, Charlotte, and you'll see, it will turn out to be perfect!"

He was proud of his gastronomic skills and expanded them constantly. He knew of many tricks used by Queen Anne's master chef, de Forger; he knew how the king's chef, Maître Georges, made fish dishes, and if he lived long enough and his strength held out, he would surely obtain detailed information about the methods used by the famous Maître Nicolas, who performed his life's work in the house of Bishop Monseigneur d'Estampes de Valençay, a glutton who demanded much from his chefs.

But Daniel Drouin was not ignorant of the fact that people were starving in France as well as in the world at large. A remark of his deserves to be quoted; it was made late one evening in his favorite tavern, "The Golden Hen": "I am not blind. I can think and I can add figures. With better organization and with the common sense we get from information and experience, there is still hope of eliminating hunger and war from this earth."

His books stood on a shelf and were not hidden in chests and cabinets. The cookbooks were by themselves, on top, and they were spotless but filled with notes in the margins. There were such works as *Agriculture, or the Home of the Farmer* by Charles Estienne and Jean Liebault, printed in 1564; *The Agricultural Scene and Farm Management* by Olivier de Serres, printed in the year 1600; and *The Image of Health* by Joseph de Chesne, which among other things contained useful recipes for baking cakes. He had several guides on vineyards and wine making, on distillation, and how to add flavor to beverages, and a few works on the practice of medicine, in which the application of chemical advances of course was represented by the famous

14

Théophraste Renaudot, who was born in the town but now devoted himself to organizing the poor relief of Paris.

Yes, Daniel Drouin read much and enjoyed different kinds of literature. Above all, his gift was that of the reader of good books, the one who can make prompt quotations. He had a sense for dates and for juridical, clerical, and historical relationships. Who knows, perhaps at heart he was a historian who had not yet started writing his city's or his country's history? The fact that he had written poems in Latin as well as in French goes without saying. He recited them at times before selected friends and colleagues who now and then visited his home and were treated to good food. By "friends" one meant in those days only those who defended the castle and the fortifications against the destructive forces, whose names one would rather not mention out loud, at least not while criticizing them.

As we have said, he read a lot. He could reach out and get hold of Messire François Rabelais, who once upon a time was born in the neighboring city of Chinon. He knew many verses by Malherbe; he was not at a loss if the conversation touched on Clement Marot or François Villon; he read Margaret of Navarre, Ronsard de Bellay, and Montaigne with as much interest as he kept up with the great number of pamphlets (not to be seen on his shelves, however) regarding Cardinal Richelieu. He could quote Chaucer in English and Dante in Italian. He ordered many books printed in Lyons, Paris, and Holland. And his favorite author was Cicero, whose thoughts about old age he quoted and thoroughly enjoyed already in his younger days.

It should come as no surprise if later in life (after all that happened!) and with a smile of melancholy skepticism,

15

bitterness, and irony, which also held linguistic satisfaction, he was to read out loud the concluding words, both in Latin and Italian, of the abjuration that Galileo Galilei was forced to sign on June 22, 1633:

Io Galileo Galilei sopradetto ho abiurato, giurato, promesso, e mi son obligato. . . .

Daniel Drouin sat several hours every day in a pleasant although not very large room in the city hall building together with another assessor, Charles Calvet, whose brother, Louis, was assistant public prosecutor. Assessor Drouin's chief occupation consisted in the settling of estates, investigations in lawsuits regarding inheritance claims, and language scrutiny in missives sent to the governor, Monsieur Jean d'Armagnac (who had his headquarters in the city but stayed most often at the royal court in Paris or at Saint-Germain), to the central government and the High Court in Paris, or to the ecclesiastical authorities at Poitiers and Bordeaux.

He liked to drink one or two glasses of wine, or a few small glasses of absinthe in the inn "The Golden Hen," located on the square known as Henhouse Square. There he generally met his only relative in town, his cousin Mathurin Thiboust, the coach-builder. He was married to Corisande Dolet, a woman whom Daniel Drouin had been very fond of at one time in his youth, a woman whom he still thought of with a feeling of strong desire.

He wrote a diary in the form of a continuing protocol. He was a rather happy man, but there were periods in his life when he felt worried and ill at ease.

2

Per Flores

Men die out—most of them through fire. No doubt many die through flowers but this is also through fire. The fire of slow or intense fragrance, and that of love, and of hate.

Some are consumed directly, on a pyre, the smoke envelopes their cries or exposes them. Others rot away while still alive.

Women not infrequently come to their end through fire. It used to be named the fire of blood and heart; now they have other names for it. Some are consumed by a slow, gentle flame over many years, some char quickly. The coal keeps its color or turns gray but the ashes always turn white, sooner or later, and time sweeps them away from our streets and squares so as not to hinder us in our activity: to be consumed by fire.

Men often come to their end through fire, and I mean not only war between men, or catastrophes, which are nature's war against mankind. Glands and acids in their bodies consume them. Certain individuals are led up on the pyre and concerning this one may say at the present time:

The man is obliterated. But all those who have brought him here, all those who have carried firewood and are standing in a circle around the fire, spectators at close

17

range, they are consumed at the same time. What we later see of them are merely the ashes not yet blown away.

Yes?

All those who take the lives of human beings are themselves killed by the blows they inflict on others. All those who burn people are themselves burned to death. Consciousness of this alone may save the humanity that crawls or bounces on the surface of the earth.

Yes?

All those who build prisons make themselves prisoners because they are a part of the mass of humanity, merged with it. All those who guard prisoners guard a part of themselves. All those who worship princes, worship the dreamt-of prince within themselves. All those who tear down prisons, try to free themselves by freeing others. All true crimes are crimes against humanity. There are no other crimes; there is hunger, there are games; there are diseases. We don't fully know, at this early stage, in this dawn which still clings tightly to the primeval darkness, what crime is.

Yes?

All those who gather women and men and children around them and say, "I will speak to you about the truth," are lying. With such a short span of human time behind us, we cannot know the truth. Instead they ought to say, "I will show you what I believe is one of the possibilities leading to truth." All those who speak lies are themselves consumed by them.

No?

Many die through flowers, *per flores*. Why do I, who have so little time, since my days will not suffice for more than the most essential, why do I use such a strange old word from a language which I know only superficially? A dead language?

My friend, my problematic friend, Daniel Drouin, who has been gone from the surface of the earth for nearly

18

three hundred years, yes perhaps three hundred and ten or three hundred and twelve years, often used it in moments of great stress: the inner moments, when in anguish he sought to express what could not be fully expressed with lips and tongue. I have not come any further. A dead language? It is not dead as long as many things and circumstances can best be expressed in it. No, there is no word that can simultaneously express the fragrance of life and the smell of death with such delicacy and validity. One sees lilies, they are the first to be seen when one closes one's eyes. The others are roses. Life and death are blended here like rose-lilies and lily-roses. Then there are other ways to live and die *per flores:* through violets and forget-me-nots and through sticky flowers whose names will not be mentioned. All those who die through flowers die through fire.

*

Leading Characters: Madeleine and Urbain

He reached out his hand to the women and they took it, at times quickly, at times with hesitation. They burned themselves. Or they reached both hands out to him and he took them in his. They burned their hands. Last came Madeleine, and she held on to his hands.

He could have said to her, "Madeleine, that is what I want." At the same moment he had the full inner right to say, "I do not want to any more. I will test your resistance to me a while longer. While you are groping blindly for me, now and during the years that lie behind us, behind that which is ours, I freely close my eyes creating for myself a darkness in which I grope for you, for that which is us, that which is ours. We will both be ruined, but *I know.*"

She never asked him about the girl with the boy's name, Philippe Tranchant, who now was married to one of the many Poussauts living here, Louis Poussaut. But she knew

19

of her, knew or had known her in an indestructible and spiteful second-cousin relationship. She resembled her, she thought. But she had been used up just like he had used others before and after her, and as he will use me.

She recalled his arrival here, in 1617; she was twenty-two years old then. He was crossing the Square of Sainte-Croix, carrying his breviary in his folded hands. It was in September. She recalled that he had a flower inserted among the pages of his prayer book, a red rose. Later he told her that she remembered wrong; still later he said that perhaps she was right. But wasn't it a white rose? "I learned to wait for you then," she said. "My maidenhood was waiting for you. You took it even though I was wedded to Christ. No, not wedded, but as good as promised to him. You are a priest of lies. Can't you let me remember that you had a red rose in your breviary fifteen years ago?"— He replied that he would let her remember that. "You are wedded to me," he said. "I was wedded to you, at night, in the Church of St. Pierre," she said. "No one saw it, there were no witnesses, I was wedded in darkness, and you have written your tract against priestly celibacy in order to save my soul and your soul and our conscience," she said. "To save you for me," he said. "No, Urbain," she said, "it was to save yourself for yourself."

She was the woman who followed him in the shadows, in darkness, through many years. She was the lady Madeleine de Brone, the wealthy, the lonely and independent one, who was now living in Assessor Daniel Drouin's house on the Square of Sainte-Croix, across from the church. From her windows she could see the women walk toward him, to him—to them he became the Church.

With him she lived her secret life. A relative of hers, Pierre Milouin, reached out his hands for her. He was an official of the king, an assistant public prosecutor here, a cousin who wanted to be the protector of the orphans, a future great man in this city. His heart was full of love for her. A year later it was brimful with hatred. "You didn't enter a convent, Madeleine," he said. "You waited until you could become the priest's whore." What she replied to these words, which were true, was that it was not the truth. "If you repeat that, Pierre Milouin," she said, "I'll take you to court for defamation of character." "What I said is the truth," he said. "If you repeat it in public, I will bring a suit against you, Pierre Milouin," she said. "You were the woman who could have married me, Madeleine," he said; "now you are the woman who lies down under a priest just because he can talk better than others. Just because people think, that they believe, that he can talk better than anyone else. But a day will come for him too. We all know it. He has been consecrated to death. Death is his true bride. You are only a concubine, Madeleine," he said. "And you are full of hatred, Pierre Milouin," she said. "Yes, hatred, my dear cousin, my dear Demoiselle," he replied.

*

"Urbain (she said at one time), I don't want you to be inside the walls of our city."

"Madeleine," he answered, "the walls are to be torn down, as you know."

"I don't want you to be a priest," she said. "Instead you ought to be a governor, a real governor, and not only an adviser in the shadow of Armagnac. You ought to be a bailiff like my cousin Cerisay or a police official or a civil servant like my cousin Calvet or like Daniel Drouin. No, not like Drouin, he is insufferable with his cooking and his Latin and his tippling. But you shouldn't be a priest."

"You might have said royal *procureur* and public advocate and prosecutor and commanding officer like your relative Louis Tranchant," he said. "But that you didn't do. You didn't think about the gossip about me and his daughter. That was very nice of you."

"I'm thinking of you," she replied. "And that you should not be a priest."

"Madeleine (he then said and it was long ago but the

21

words remained in her memory, constantly repeated), Madeleine, it is a calling. If I leave it, I will be a lost human being. I want to die as a priest."—She replied (then, long ago) that his life was a lie and he agreed to that; but in order to get out of it he had to enter another lie, which was another life.

"Madeleine, you know what they have done to me. For over ten years I have been fighting half the city. They have pushed all their guilt on me; I have been their old cart, their manure cart. They wanted me banished. It was because of the women and other things. They had me sentenced to be banished and their tool was Bishop Roche-Pozay of Poitiers. I sat for two months in his jail. Do you remember the autumn of 1629? I sat in a dark and dank cell in the tower and was ill and about to go to rack and ruin. I wrote to the bishop and said that I forgave all my enemies. That was that time. I believe that I meant it. But then they thought up so much to harm me—which I have not yet learned to forgive. Monsieur de la Roche-Pozay, incidentally, did not reply to my letters. It was Archbishop Escoubleau de Sourdis in Bordeaux who saved me. He also mentioned the word 'forgiveness.' But I have not learned to forgive yet. I try once in a while."

"One mustn't fight all the time," Madeleine said. "But you do."

"It only appears that way. I defend myself. And I have to win. If I don't win—time after time—then I am lost. There is no middle way, no compromise for me. Not any longer."

"Urbain, you could leave everything here," she said.

"I could become a soldier and kill with weapons. I could have joined a war and become a general killing Huguenots and others. I could have come with the Cardinal's troops to La Rochelle and played the Cardinal's game, or gone with Duke de Rohan along the course he has taken and gambled at his cards. But I stayed here and played my own game in order to save city walls and fortifications and myself, and it is already a lost game. I am not lost as long as I am playing my game—even though the game is lost. I am myself, I'm alive."

"I don't understand you, there is no wholeness in you," she said on one of those spring evenings at the beginning of the thirties when he had come to her and let his clerical garb drop to the floor. "You lie us both straight into hell."

"I know," he said, "but I choose a minor lie to get us a shorter time in purgatory."

"But what am I, Urbain? A harlot?"

"You are my woman, I am your man, we have been wed at night in my Church of Saint-Pierre and we live on this lie: I am your father confessor and you are my pupil in sacred things; in reality, you are one of my many daughters. I give you the sacrament of the body and you give me that of love."

"You are a Jesuit priest," she said.

"That is what saves me," he said, "I can think, I have been attacked from my first day here, because I was a stranger—and for no other reason. To be a stranger may mean that the women look at one differently from the way they glance at their male cousins or playmates. Gossip spread around me. Gossip provided the easiest way to mix with people. I could think, I could defend myself, my tongue became sharp."

"You were arrogant, too," she said.

"Yes, that too."

"Urbain," she said, "are you good or evil?"

"I *am*," he said. "No, I am *with you*. Don't talk any more about it. I am not happy when you talk about it."

"You are seldom happy," she said. "But I want you to be with me. Many women want you to be with them. God has given you a face and a body which perhaps do not go with your soul."

"What do we know about that?" he said.

"Women turn around and look at you in the street. They want you. And when I walk in the street, they think to themselves: There goes the priest's whore, one of the priest's tarts. They don't stone me, they say: Good day, dear madame, sweet Demoiselle de Brone, how are you? How is your sister in Chinon, we have heard that she is so weak after the last child? How is our dearly beloved Helène du Rothay and how is your youngest sister, the lovely little Madame Renée Bogier? And you who live alone all by yourself! Isn't it lonely to have a lonely apartment in times like these? Isn't it noisy down at Assessor Drouin's? Is it true that he drinks heavily at times and that he's running after women even though he has such a sweet wife, and that he makes all the meals himself even though he is an assessor?"

She heard him chuckle in the darkness.

"Do you know what they think when they see *me* in the street, Madeleine? Yes, they think: There goes the beautiful lady's father confessor. The one to be envied!"

"You don't have faith," she said.

"I don't know, Madeleine. But I am loyal to my mother."

"Do you mean the Church or your own mother?" she said.

"Both," he answered.

"We're sitting in a prison, Urbain. But it is possible to escape."

"There are only prisons," he said. "To escape—for me— is to change cells: to live the life of a runaway priest is also being in a prison. To live a soldier's life is a prison. In that of the Church there is most peace. Not complete peace but a whole lot. Unless one is—"

She waited:

"What, Urbain?"

"A mathematician, Madeleine. Like that man in Padua. Galilei."

"You don't want to stay there, in the Church," she said. "We could live in a foreign land. In the New World on the other side of the oceans."

"Be a savage?" he said. "Or one who kills savages? How

24

old am I now? Forty. And you are thirty-six. We are still young. Travel—"

And then he said, "In the Church I find the balance that I need."

"But you don't *want* to stay there, Urbain? Say that you don't want to. Tell me the truth."

"I don't know, Madeleine," he said.

*

She never asked him about the girl Philippe Tranchant, but she thought about her often: She looks like me. Or: She looked like me. She was used up, just as he has used many, as he perhaps will use me. No, not in the same way.

*

A few years earlier, on a spring day in 1626, she had been in the neighboring town of Chinon on the hill, visiting her sister Helène who was staying there. She got off by the Church of Saint-Mexme and sent the carriage away. As she crossed the small square, a priest came up directly behind her. She quickly turned around, and looked at him closely. He was middle-aged, short and thin, with a crooked back, and round-shouldered. She knew his name and what he was best known for. "The exorcist!" she thought with dismay. In the middle of the square he walked right beside her a few paces. His face was very sinewy, his skin was gray as if it had been powdered with ashes. The tightly shut mouth was so small that one immediately noticed it. His forehead was full of wrinkles and his watery eyes were soft brown. He looked down and mumbled, as if addressing the ground:

"Aren't you Madeleine de Brone?"

"Yes."

"You are a very beautiful woman," he murmured. "You are very, very beautiful."

"That is not a proper thing to say, Father Barrot."

"You are very, very beautiful, Madeleine de Brone," he

murmured without looking up again and then walked away from her, right across the square.

He has no right to say that! she thought. It is for Urbain I am beautiful. Not for that rat!

When she had returned from Chinon, she and Urbain G. sat together late at night in the room where she lived. There had been a little party down at Assessor Drouin's, but now everything was quiet: the assessor was out on the town.

"My sister was so melancholy," she said. "I think she is very fond of someone. Someone who is not her husband. She is grieving."

"She grieves with some composure, I hope," he said.

"We have always been very composed in our family."

"Not you," he said.

"No. Not I.—What have you been doing this week?"

"First of all, I have been longing for you," he said and touched her hand. "Second, I have been longing for you. Third, I have given the governor some good advice, since he asked me for it. Fourth, I have today baptized Daniel Drouin's son and rejoiced to see how insanely happy and proud Daniel D. is of his child. Fifth, I have noted that the gossip about me is continuing, and I have not expected anything else. Sixth, I have been longing for you. Seventh, I can tell you that it has been decided that some Ursuline nuns from Poitiers are to stay in Poussaut du Frène's old hovel in Rue Pasquin. There will be eight of them to start with. Perhaps some of them are good-looking."

"They will surely want you as their father confessor," she said. "Your reputation is spreading far and wide."

"It will probably be Frène's old cousin," he said. "So that it remains with the Poussaut family. I have been longing for you."

"You are an unworthy priest, Urbain."

"I am still a young man," he said. "You are my wife before God."

"Yes—," she said. "In Chinon—. Just as I stepped down from the carriage—."

"Yes?"

"It was nothing," she said.

*

The Beginning of Jeanne

The following year he told her that the Ursuline Sisters had a new prioress, a young woman with, it was said, changeable moods—Sister Jeanne.

"I have heard of her," Madeleine said. "Her name sounds so beautiful: Jeanne de Beaucil."

"I know the family," he said. "They come from Saintonge."

During the summer of 1631, after old Poussaut had died, the Ursuline Sisters asked him to become their father confessor. They didn't ask him directly but someone whispered in his ear that he ought to go see the prioress. He hadn't done so. In his stead had been appointed his colleague at the Church of Sainte-Croix, Minet, called the Lame One.

It so happened that old Poussaut began to haunt the place. For some months following his death, he walked through the corridors of the cramped Ursuline convent in Rue Pasquin and disturbed the nuns, the serving sisters, and the girls who boarded there. He used unbelievably foul language—it was rumored—especially to those who were reserved and bashful. He tossed off words that were so crude and vile that the walls started mouldering, said one of the sisters in the kitchen who had been subjected to his behavior. He had been inside several cells and in the dormitories and had tried to get close to some of them, but they were feeble attempts, said the girls. He was old and decrepit even as a ghost. In his prime he had been a tormentor of children, at the time he had been teaching La-

27

tin. The new father confessor, his nephew Jehan Minet, drove him back into Purgatory with a few words, and Uncle Poussaut never returned.

But he opened the way for others.

On a moonlit night in March 1632, three demons climbed into the Ursuline convent.

The first one, of middling height and very nimble, was called Ashtaroth; the second one, heavier in his movements and more thoughtful, was called Sabulon, and the third one's name was Asmodeus; he was exceptionally nimble and lively. They whispered together in Latin, not of the best sort, but what they said could not be comprehended.

Ashtaroth, Sabulon, and Asmodeus arrived on a wave of earth smell, scents of the fields, the scent of early flowers, and with stenches from the latrines. They wore black, tight-fitting clothes, and every muscle and limb were clearly silhouetted underneath the silky material. Ashtaroth's muscles were especially clearly seen; and around him there was a particularly rank smell of goats and a smell of bulls.

They climbed quickly up the grayish-yellow-white limestone wall leaving flickering shadows on the walls. Now and then they would stop, getting a hold like lizards in cracks and around joints, whispering eagerly. When they came to a small window, their clawlike fingers grasped the worn iron grating. They pressed together in front of the window and looked in: their heads made a cluster but their bodies were spread over the wall forming a six-fingered, pendulous fan. When they reached the edge of the roof— the house was three stories high—they sat down on the gutter and deliberated. Then Ashtaroth crawled and climbed on the slate roof up to the biggest chimney, the one in the middle, and looked around. He waved, and the others followed, Asmodeus making a series of quick jumps. They sat for a while on the edging around the chimney looking at the pale spring moon. They surveyed the city rising above the plain; the towers, the soon-to-be-razed fortifications, and the walls were bathed gently in the milky light of the moon. There was silence now by the gates, the Chinon Gate, the Bartray Gate, and the others soon to be gates without walls. Toward the northeast they saw the castle of Chinon, its heavy mass and pointed towers, and further north the towers of Saumur, where there was much heresy with great possibilities for work by demons. They could dimly make out the blue ribbon of the Loire and the glittering Vienne River. Tours was far to the northeast, and Orléans was still further away; far to the northwest and west was Angers with its heavy prison fortress and Nantes, the old town of the Namnetes, Portus Namnetum, a place known for struggle, faith, and doubt; and to the south was Poitiers with its bishop's castle and prison, churches, and judges, experienced, prepared.

The city below them seemed hunched-up for the night. The houses bent toward one another across the narrow streets, and the whole area was smaller than during the day, shrunken. Ashtaroth, Sabulon, and Asmodeus viewed the scene in contemplation. Their glances rested for a while on the Church of Sainte-Croix, very near them, and the Church of Saint-Pierre, further up on the castle heights. For a long while they looked, watchfully, at the tall, square North Tower as if they expected it to move, walk away wrapped in veils of moonlight, stumbling among the fortress and city walls which surrounded all but were even now condemned and largely razed.

"We should have had Isaacarum and Behemoth with us," Asmodeus said, after a while of watching and musing on the chimney.

"And Guelman, he is quite effective," Sabulon said, pensively. "And Gresil and Carmim."

"Well, let's get going." Asmodeus said.

"I want to look around and think a while yet," Ashtaroth

said. "I want to remember the city the way it is now, before the changes come. The plague will be here in a month. And in a year much more will have been razed and gone."

They continued looking for a while yet. The bell in Sainte-Croix struck one, the one up in Saint-Pierre responded. Bells that were not too damaged were pealing across the plain as if across wide waters. Animals stirred in their stalls, in pens and bins. A horse stood wide awake in the stable of the absent governor, in what was left of the castle. Horses were awake or asleep in the stable of the *bailli* de Cerisay. Daniel Drouin, the Latin-gifted assessor, was asleep having assisted his wife with his own hands in making a very good dinner, since she was at the extreme end of her nine months; after dinner he had been to the tavern "The Hen" on Henhouse Square for a small beaker of absinthe and some wine in the company of his only cousin, the coach-builder Mathurin Thiboust. He had fallen into bed, but had managed to take off his jacket, waistcoat, cloak, and shoes. The drunken farmer Michel, who took care of Assessor Drouin's little country place and vineyard on the plain southwest of the city, in the direction of Ainsay, was on his way home from Mother Gaspard's inn near the Mirebeau Gate—he had also stopped in at "The Hen." He was half lying in his cart, over which he had put up a small tent. His mule was willing although a bit restless. The large, decrepit wheels creaked, the cart clattered and squeaked, but the sound and his intoxication imbued him with a sense of security. Michel was humming an obscene little piece about the Cardinal's big behind as he was passing the Square of Sainte-Croix and started down the slope toward the Bartray Gate. One who could not sleep that night, because of his deep hatred, was the former *procureur* and royal public advocate Louis Tranchant, who had been forced to retire last year for certain reasons and had then sold his office cheaply to Jacques Poussaut who had married his only daughter, Philippe, soon afterward. Urbain Grainier, the parish priest for the Saint-Pierre congregation, at the same time canon and prebendary at the Church of Sainte-Croix and the foremost priest in the town, was lying next to Madeleine de Brone in her dwelling in Daniel Drouin's house. She slept while he was staring with wide-open eyes into the darkness below the ceiling, listening. His old friend and fellow student, the assessor, was snoring in the dwelling below them. A cart was clattering and creaking across the square and someone was singing a bawdy song. Hoofs were clip-clopping gently on the pavement in front of the church: a donkey or a mule.

Prioress Jeanne de Beaucil was lying in her cell in the house that the Ursuline Sisters had borrowed from M. Frène de Poussaut in the Rue Pasquin; she was entering the borderline between sleep and dreams. She touched her body, mumbled a name, turned over on her back, prepared. A bottle of absinthe was in the chest over in the corner. A wine jug and a beaker filled with white wine stood next to the bed. A crucifix was gleaming in the pale moonlight on the wall above the chest.

The demons climbed down through the chimney in the middle. Nothing definitive happened that night. Neither the teaching sisters nor the serving sisters nor the boarding girls were sufficiently prepared. Asmodeus proved to be the most eager one of the devils; he rapidly stole through the corridors and entered four or five cells and also tried to bewitch someone in one of the dormitories. He succeeded best in the kitchen section with a big strong girl, Séraphique Archer, who was a native of the town and had ended up in the convent after one or two bitter love affairs. She had perhaps lost someone she had been fond of in the upper world of government officials or assessors, where she would never again be able to enter, or perhaps lost him on one of the world's many battlefields. She was very receptive. Sabulon, for his part, was trying very hard

31

with a young girl, Marie Aubin, who was being brought up here but who would never be a nun. This was in a small dormitory with four girls. He touched her and she groped for him in the moonlight; but when he drew closer to her more sensitive parts, she pulled back with a smile, the smile of a girl half-asleep, a smile which may be called roguish. He made up his mind to go back to her another night, when she would be more ready for it, and then joined the others.

The three demons visited about twenty women and made them whisper different names. Eight of them whispered the name of the parish priest of the Church of Saint-Pierre first among all those that were conceivable and possible. Three whispered the name of the former father confessor, Poussaut, but not passionately. Two whispered the name of the present father confessor: Jehan Minet. A few whispered the name of the well-known exorcist and priest Pierre Barrot in Chinon. Sabulon and Asmodeus had rather intimate contact with eight nuns and a serving sister. The most holy of all men's names was whispered by four of them, the name of Satan by a few.

Ashtaroth lingered a while in the shadow in the prioress's cell before he began touching her. She had torn off her linen and he was able to examine her closely. Her head was thrown back on the small and hard pillow. Her hair was very dark, and shiny. Her nose was narrow and straight, but a bit too long. Her lips were full, and very red even now in the moonlight. Her mouth was big, but her features were refined. The corners of her mouth were pulled down in a tragic hunger which was never stilled and never would be stilled. Her chin was small but determined, it showed willpower. Her breasts were flat and undeveloped. With one of his claws he stroked the very white and hot skin. Her shoulders were girlishly rounded and shy. Her back was curved or askew, and her neck was so short that she—at that moment—seemed to be a hunchback. Her left hand rested in her lap. With his clawlike fingers Asmodeus stroked both the outside and the inside of her thighs in order to arouse them more. Her eyelids quivered, the long eyelashes played with a ray of moonlight. Her legs were bent into cramped immobility. The heavy clothes on the straw-plaited chair and on the floor, the coarse black leather shoes, the hood, the rosary, the prayerbook on the brown, low table, and the crucifix on the wall made her look even more naked. She mumbled a man's name.

He heard the same name a while later in other cells: from both the Barbeziers girls, from Sister Agnes, from the Bonpierre girl, from Mademoiselle Escoubleau. They were all young. Séraphique Archer, the serving girl in the kitchen, whispered the name of an angel: Daniel. In one cell he scrutinized a somewhat older woman; she was between forty and forty-two years old and here she was called Sister Anne; but Asmodeus had found out what her name had been as a young girl, and as a very young married woman. She was lying on the stone floor, with a wine goblet next to her. She had spilled wine all around, little shiny deep-black lakes. She was the ripest one he saw that night.

When he opened the door to a cell a little further on, diagonally across the corridor, he had a feeling of reverence mixed with fear. He was standing before Sister Claire, born de Sazilly, a relative of the Cardinal. She was a very dark, thin-lipped, sharp-nosed, skinny, feverishly yearning woman of forty. She mumbled a name. He could have bewitched her immediately but he didn't think it worth the trouble.

*

The plague arrived in April and was more or less over in September. The Ursuline Sisters all stayed indoors and no one died among them, but the demons were industrious and had obtained reinforcements.

*

The Roses

At the end of October—it was still 1632—when many kinds of rumors circulated in the town and the surrounding districts, a government official, Assessor Calvet, let the prioress know that the Ursuline Sisters were welcome to pick chestnuts in his little forest over by Rissay. She gave the offer careful thought before she allowed the participation of some of the boarders and some of the nuns that she considered most reliable. Sister Claire was the leader of the big enterprise. The girls walked out through the remains of the Mirebeau Gate, and when they came to the harvested fields outside the razed city walls, the seventeen-year-old Marie Aubin from around Angers could not adhere to rules any longer. Discipline broke down. In her heavy skirts she began to run down the dusty road; and suddenly she jumped off the road and ran across a harvested field.

"Marie!"

A few of the other girls followed her, running with their skirts flapping up around their legs.

"Marie! M a r i e ! M A R I E !"

She heard them and stopped short, turned slowly and reluctantly and waited ironically for instructions. She was panting; she still had the good feeling in her body of violent motion, her mouth was half-open, her large, healthy teeth were gleaming, she was smiling; she had a wide grin on her face.

"Come back!"

She walked slowly back toward them, looking down and kicking the clumps of grass and sod as if she was searching for something underneath. The other two followed behind, crestfallen and afraid.

"Think of your *dignity!*" Claire de Sazilly said, not as a spiritual sister but as an aristocrat and teacher.

"I just couldn't help myself, Sister Claire," Marie Aubin said, her voice supposedly filled with remorse, but her brown eyes shone, she giggled, she did everything to keep from bursting out laughing.

"We couldn't help ourselves either," said one of the others, Mademoiselle Bonpierre.

"I must report it," Madame de Sazilly said.

"Of course, it has to be reported," the older of the Barbeziers girls, Sister Louise, joined in.

The younger Barbeziers girls, Sister Catherine, usually very quiet, did not say anything either, but she gave Marie a stern look. Mademoiselle Bonpierre giggled loudly and she was not afraid to do it: she was a sister-in-law of a very well known and greatly feared man, M. de Laubardemont, and would not under any circumstances be reported, at least not punished.

Thereupon they all continued silently and quietly all the way to the chestnut forest.

Now and then a chestnut fell down. They had to kick and trample on the yellow prickly balls; when they tried to open them, the needles pricked their fingers. Other chestnuts had come completely open, and the ripest chestnuts fell out, brown and shiny. The girls walked in among the bushes and in the thicket and picket nuts, but the group stayed together. When they sat down to eat and had bread and cheese by the side of the road, they thrust their hands into the baskets feeling the cool, smooth chestnuts run between their fingers. Some of the girls were longing for home, toward the west, toward the ocean. Marie Aubin exclaimed, "Oh, how beautiful it is today! The forest smells so good. One gets an urge to jump and run and laugh!"

"Think twice, young lady!" admonished Madame Claire de Sazilly.

"Yes, think twice!" said the older Barbeziers girl, Sister Louise.

Mademoiselle Bonpierre giggled incredibly loudly, but it didn't matter; M. de Laubardemont, her relative, was a well-known man.

Nor did Sister Louise's voice or Sister Catherine's face indicate any stern feelings just now. There was nothing very stern in the air, about the day, about the city in the distance. Claire de Sazilly wet her thin lips with the tip of her tongue; she was in a jovial mood:

"They look like small—kittens! I mean the shells themselves. They scratch like pretty little kittens!"

"Oh, pretty little kittens, my pretty little kittens!" screamed Marie Aubin, who would be reported in any case.

Sister Claire's unusual gaiety did not subside. When they marched back home, they made a detour past the Bartray Gate, past the Church of Saint-Hilaire, and continued up the hill all the way to the Square of Sainte-Croix; no one knew why. Sister Claire was perhaps curious about life in town and was looking for something to gossip about. And this she got. The parish priest of Saint-Pierre just emerged from Sainte-Croix and walked diagonally across the square to Assessor Drouin's house. He glanced at his breviary and then lifted his head and looked up at the blue sky, or at the windows in Louis Tranchant's house or in Jacques Poussaut's house or perhaps at Daniel Drouin's somewhat smaller house. A white rose stuck out from among the leaves of his book.

The girls observed his powerful shoulders, his erect bearing. He walked very gracefully without losing any of his dignity. Sister Claire slowed her pace. All faces were turned in one direction. Marie Aubin, who would be reported in any case, said in a low voice to Mademoiselle Bonpierre and to Catherine, the younger of the Barbeziers sisters: "Madeleine de Brone lives over there."

Sister Claire, at the head of the group, turned her head angrily.

"Who spoke? Was it you, Marie? What did you say?"

Marie Aubin was silent. She would be reported in any case.

"What did you say? What did she say, Catherine?"

Mademoiselle Bonpierre giggled; she would not be reported in any case. Sister Catherine's lips moved.

"Answer!"

"She said that Demoiselle de Brone lives over there."

"*Marie!*"

They continued down their own street. At its end they
could make out the plain. Along the street there were only
brick walls.

Inside the gate Marie reached down and touched the
wilted white roses along the wall.

"Marie! Keep your hands to yourself!"

They brought the chestnuts into the kitchen, poured
them all on trays, and placed the trays in the sunlight by
the wall in the garden so that the moisture and the worms
should leave them. Marie Aubin was told to go and see the
prioress. Sister Claire was waiting in the prioress's cell.
With tightly folded hands and with tightly puckered lips
she placed herself next to Marie. The prioress was seated.

"What did you say to Sister Catherine, Marie?"

"That Demoiselle de Brone lives in Assessor Drouin's
house on the Square of Sainte-Croix, Mother."

The still young, lean, and (as Marie Aubin thought)
somewhat lopsided woman turned her loneliness-eyes
(precisely loneliness-eyes, thought Marie Aubin now as she
had done the first time she saw those dark eyes, two years
ago) at Sister Claire and then at the crucifix on the wall.
She had dark rings underneath her eyes. It was said that
she was in a period of ordeals and penance and was even
lashing herself.

"Did you mean anything special with what you said?"

"No, I don't believe so," Marie Aubin answered, suddenly blushing.

"Tell me what you were thinking about."

"That they have shouted after her, Mother. That people
say that they have been shouting after her."

Sister Jeanne turned toward the window opening. One of the many carts that always rattled past all window openings in that city, rattled past. Sister Claire's face was like a wood carving furthest inside and furthest down on an altarpiece on a dismal autumn day. No life was to be seen in it (only the eyelids were blinking). When the prioress again turned to Marie Aubin, her face—which Marie now thought beautiful—had changed: as if a violent rage had passed over it leaving behind nothing but dutiful severity and much weariness. She looked at a point in the wall behind Sister Claire.

"One is not supposed to think such thoughts. And if they enter one's mind, one must not tell anyone. They lead to temptations."

"Yes, Mother," Marie Aubin said to the shiny, reddish-brown tile floor.

"You are not to run across the meadow in such a way that your skirt flares up. You are supposed to stay on the road when you are allowed to go out."

"Yes, Mother," Marie Aubin replied and smiled at the floor.

"Now you may leave."

Sister Claire said, "And she has—"

"You may leave, both of you," Jeanne de Beaucil said sharply and turned toward the window opening.

*

The next morning, Marie Aubin told Mademoiselle Bonpierre in the strictest confidence that she had been dreaming about white roses. The curious thing was that she had three thorns in her left hand when she woke up. They pierced her skin and fell on the floor, and she had found one thorn which she showed to Mademoiselle Bonpierre. It was lying there in her soft and slender hand.

Mademoiselle Bonpierre told the younger Barbeziers girl, Catherine, in deep confidence. Catherine had a fit of talkativeness and told her older sister, Louise, with at least

38

ten words and in deep confidence. Right after the morning service in the chapel, just at dawn, Sister Louise wrote a letter to an old unmarried aunt, Madame de Nogeret. The prioress, Sister Jeanne, read the letter and kept it a few days. The older Barbeziers spoke somewhat confidentially about the thorns and the letter to Sister Claire, who immediately was transformed into the Cardinal's relative, Madame de Sazilly, and from that lofty position declared that young girls nowadays dream about the most stupid, insane, and unlawful things. When she was a young girl visiting the Richelieu family in their old castle, which at present was being rebuilt by master builder Jean Rogiers from Tours at the same time that the Cardinal-Duke's new city was taking form, she had at the very most dreamed about single rose petals and other harmless flowers, but never in such a way that the thorns were stuck in her hand when she woke up. These days (Sister Claire said in a less lofty manner and in a milder voice) she dreamed mostly about small, nice animals, such as kittens and puppies and sometimes about foals, and on single occasions about full-grown riding horses, but they were (in that case) always a great distance away.

Séraphique Archer, the tall servant girl in the kitchen, laughed when she heard about the thorns, but later on in the afternoon she became more pensive and sighed so loudly that it was heard in the refectory. Somehow in her seclusion, the unsociable Sister Anne was also informed of the matter, whereupon she opened the door to her cell and shouted down the length of the corridor, "I have experienced that many, *many* times!"

There was no reason for her doing so; the corridor was completely empty. But Marie Aubin heard her shouting and whispered to Mademoiselle Bonpierre that "now the old woman has got hold of some wine again and is dreaming that she is a prioress," and Mademoiselle Bonpierre laughed out loud; she dared to since she was not only sort of related to the prioress, Sister Jeanne, but was also a genuine sister-in-law of the mighty lord Jean-Martin de Laubardemont.

*

The following night Sister Claire had several dreams; some of them were rather gruesome, while others were pleasant. The pleasant ones had to do with yellow kittens and brown puppies and some horses grazing next to a wide river with low-lying shores; but the horses were at a great distance. She also dreamt about roses, many white ones and an occasional red one, and about chestnut picking.

In the chestnut dream she saw the chestnuts still in their shells and she thought that these fruits resembled certain parts of the body, male and female, brown African, yellow Asiatic, and red American bodily parts. Thank God, the roses returned and were the pleasant remnant of what she remembered of the dreams at noon. When she awoke, she was holding three thorns in her left hand. They were just lying there, and they didn't prick her.

3

Grounds for Hatred, or: A Portrait of Pierre Barrot

I

THEY BEAT HIM when he was very little, they maltreated him so that he suffered permanent ill effects. One of his shoulder blades was injured, and his spine was jolted. It happened earlier than he could remember.

His crooked spine was not a hump but a lopsidedness that weighed over him from behind suppressing his body and soul. The defect became one more reason for beating him, especially when he was four or five years old, and two decades later he beat himself. Oblivion veiled much of his childhood. It was forgotten that the royal prosecutor and judge Eusèbe Barrot of Poitiers had torn the boy Pierre from his cradle, shouted something about a bastard, and thrown him to the floor. His mother distinctly remembered that he had fallen, and besides that he had contracted a disease in his back while still an infant. Perhaps the disease had been latent even before he was born. She recalled with melancholic clarity that they had thought the child would die, but a miracle had happened: it didn't die. Furthermore, she and others remembered, his younger brothers and sisters for example, that they had always been kind to him because he was so weak and frail, and in time he would recall the same thing.

41

Along with these memories—of goodness linked to a series of beautiful memories—he had dark ones from the very same period.

He could remember: They beat me. I got the birch rod and the whip. I got the leather strap and the hand slap. I got the clenched fist. They pulled my hair and scolded me. I got all the mordancy and bitterness of their faces and mouths.

But the beautiful memories stayed with him and grew in strength. Two memories might be placed on top of one another like two glass plates containing two different pictures. If one held them up to the light, one would see that none of them or the two together were the right ones.

"My father was strict but just," he said as a grownup. "He managed his house with a firm hand, he was one of the old school. He knew what upbringing was. He was ever keen and determined. That has always marked my character."

And he could say, whenever this matter came up: "Knowledge? Is it so difficult to obtain knowledge? Why do I have so many students in Latin? Just because I know my Latin and my Greek. The teacher woke me up at four in the morning, shook the sleep out of my body, and beat the verses into me with a stick. He was strict but just, and I learned my lesson."

He readily spoke about his parents and about his childhood.

"My father was a state prosecutor and later a judge and I worshiped him. A heart of gold, but no sentimental softness! A splendid fellow! His intelligence was outstanding! He was a splendid conversationalist! He was an excellent host! He was enormously well liked by everyone!

"My mother was an angel, I worshiped her. She too could be strict, but no wonder! When I was sent to Master Guennant's school, I was eight years old and knew both Latin and Greek fairly well, and by then my mother had seven children, four of them alive, and I was the oldest.

42

When they chose a profession for me, when God through my parents called me to do His work, I was thirteen years old, and by then my mother had thirteen children, and seven were alive. I belong to a healthy, strong, and tough family of landowners and government officials, three of us are still alive. Naturally, my mother could not devote much time to me. She was kind-hearted and just, but very strict. They say she had been exceedingly beautiful as a young girl, with an oval, finely shaped face, brown hair and large shining, almost black eyes. A highborn man, an aristocrat and later famous military commander in our war against heresy, adored her and courted her. This story is shrouded in a certain romantic obscurity—in all innocence, of course! Her father chose for her a civil servant of a sturdy civil servant family: my father. I might have become a soldier and a famous military commander too had my back been stronger.

"My parents were, to repeat, strict but just, and were also devout Christians and did what they could for the Church. In their union they had all in all thirteen children, of whom three, as I have said, are still living. My mother died when she was thirty-five years old. My father mourned her bitterly, and when he remarried a year later it was for the sake of the children. I seldom saw my stepmother, since I was staying at the monastery school. She died fairly soon, however; there was no strength in her. She faded away when she was about twenty. She was of a good family and wealthy. She had enough time to bear my father two children, but they both died as infants."

II

He knew:
The devils are afraid of me; I force them to speak.
He made the women open up to him during confession. He could bring out their demons. His soul's longing reached them without his touching them. He called forth

legitimate fear of the demons demonstrating where they were and what they did. On many occasions he forced these servants of the abyss and these tormentors of man to speak: during the interrogation they expressed themselves in Latin, Greek, Hebrew, and at times in the Poitou dialect. He surrounded, locked up, and released the demons, dealt with them as does an animal trainer with his animals, wringing out of them truths about the darkest and most loathsome things, truths that were as close as beads in a rosary. The devils displayed fright as well as trust in his strict but just ways and his skillful and firm touch. He had experience and was widely read when it came to demons and he could argue with those who were skeptical.

In case someone doubted, for example, that in 1491 a devil had entered a convent boarding school in Cambrai and had had intercourse with a girl, Jeanne Pothière, no less than four hundred and thirty-four times before he was driven away and the girl put in jail, he could refer to contemporary protocols, in which Jeanne Pothière's own confession had been put down before she died. Everyone knew that the power of the devils had been great, especially in Spain, during the last few centuries. Pierre Barrot, the canon and exorcist from Chinon, did not have to look far for arguments to use—proofs were found everywhere. And who would dare maintain that the demons' power had lessened even though the times at present were modern and enlightened? Reports were constantly coming in from Italy, Germany, and Holland and countries even farther away. The activity in eastern and northern lands seemed to have increased with the attempts of the mad monk of Wittenberg to betray the Lord and deliver humanity to hell; the demons' exertions assumed huge proportions in all parts of the world and among all races. The Jews, of course, kept to the fore as usual fomenting trouble and disaster. In Rome itself, the Devil and his servants appeared in the year 1554 among eighty young Jewesses who had been successfully converted to Christianity and who lived in a convent. When the girls were interrogated, they confessed that other Jews had lured the devils their way, even though a Jesuit Father, who was remarkably weak in faith, maintained that no human being, not even an Israelite, had such power. When Pierre Barrot read this seventy years later, he shrugged his shoulders and brought out many substantiating examples from Cologne and Savoy: in spite of the fact that multitudes of irreparably possessed individuals were burned at the stake, Satan remained on earth and time and again gave human beings—yes, human beings—the power to do his work. There were many proofs.

But God and the Church fought indefatigably against the Prince of Darkness. In the year 1598, the highly respected Judge Boguet in Saint-Claude in Franche-Comté—the same man who in his old age took pride in having done away with more than six hundred possessed persons—could point to a new victory in his campaign against the Evil One: in 1602 he very calmly put down in his book about witches and sorcerers, published in Lyons in 1603:

"The twelve-year-old Pierre Uvillermoz had been called in to witness against his father; both had been kept in jail for four months. In the beginning the father hardly recognized his child, for the boy had changed and had been given other clothes after his arrest. At the very moment the father recognized his son Pierre, the latter insisted that his father had taken him to the witches' sabbath and had called upon him to give himself up to the Devil. The father explained that he had never attended any witches' sabbath or taken his son to one. He shouted: 'Oh, my child, you are leading us both to perdition!' and threw himself face forward so violently on the floor that they thought he had killed himself. It was strange and pitiful to be present at those meetings, especially since the father was completely broken down because of his stay in jail and wailed and screamed and threw himself on the floor. I still remember that when he had pulled himself together, he told his son in a friendly tone of voice that whatever he chose to say and do to his father he would nevertheless always look upon him as his beloved child. The son did not waver the least but remained intractable in spite of the fact that his words might spell a horrible death for the one who had given him life. But indeed I see God's secret judgment in all this. God doesn't want a loathsome crime like witchcraft to remain undetected; for that reason it is quite understandable that the son was not touched by the sharp sting of Nature since his father had committed a crime against Nature's God."

"That's the way a scrupulous judge should reason," Pierre Barrot said. "At times the Devil will try to trick us with the help of tears. All we have to do is learn how to perceive his temptations and his tricks. And not to forget that no one is safe!"

Not even priests were safe. In the area around Bayonne and Saint-Jean-de-Luz twenty-seven congregations, Basque in particular, were assailed by demons. Three priests were infected and had to be burned as Satan's tools. Pierre Barrot could quote a report rendered by two officials, Espagnet and Delancre, who had been commissioned by Henry IV to handle the case. Delancre had written: "The example of the priests in the area around Labourd shows that false beliefs are not always to be sought solely among stupid peasants and idiots but even among mortals whose calling it is to preach the word of God." One of the priests who were burned, was so old, frail, and obviously deranged that the authorities hesitated; but in the end they decided to burn him too at the stake. Delancre regarded this as useful, since it would give many individuals the courage to inform on others who pretended to be the servants of the Lord. A large number of priests took fright and fled, but they captured some and pressed the truth out of them. At Siboure they caught two, Migalena, who was seventy years old, and Bocal, who was twenty-seven. Both of them were so hardened that they didn't even reply to the questions that the interrogating officials and the specially trained and licensed exorcists put to them. They denied their horrible crimes, and it was impossible to obtain clear proof. They were burned.

The story of the priest Louis Gauffridi showed how justified was Pierre Barrot's demand for firmness. In the year 1609 a sister in the Ursuline convent at Aix—her name was Madeleine—was violently assailed and possessed by demons. She turned to her father confessor and told him that she had been seduced by a sorcerer before she was ten years old. Another nun, Louise Capel, who had experienced something similar, was able to name one of the demons who had harassed her; his name was Verrine. When an exorcism was arranged in all secrecy, the hard-pressed Verrine told them that the name of the leader of the demons was Gauffridi and that he was at the same time the head of all the sorcerers in France, Spain, England, and Turkey. Father Michaelis, a shrewd and skillful inquisitor, cleared up the matter to everyone's satisfaction. The proofs against Gauffridi were conclusive and damning. Everything was clear at once to Sister Madeleine. It was Gauffridi who had taken her maidenhood in a cave in the presence of other persons who had likewise sold their souls to Satan. The nun could also confirm that Gauffridi ate small children. This leader of demons had acted very cleverly. As a priest at the Accoules Church in Marseilles, he had, very artfully through his friendly ways and his erudition, gained the esteem of the other priests. Thus, he had a great chance to become a prince of demons on account of his winning ways, his learning, and his social position.

He was a hard man to break.

When he defended himself before the interrogators swearing by the Almighty, the Son, our Saviour, and by the Holy Spirit, the Holy Virgin, and St. John the Baptist that he was innocent of the sorcery of which he was accused, Madeleine had enough good sense as well as strength to interrupt him with the words: "I understand it perfectly! It is a synagogue oath that you are swearing! When you say God the Father, then you mean Lucifer; when you swear by the Son our Saviour, you mean Beelzebub; when you swear by the Holy Spirit, you mean Leviathan; when you swear by the Holy Virgin, you mean Antichrist's mother; and when you swear by St. John the Baptist, then you mean the Devil, who is Antichrist's precursor and harbinger!" It was obvious that she advanced valid arguments.

But Gauffridi was still hard to break. To help him confess, this prince of demons was turned over to two specially trained monks who kept him awake with questions day and night so that Satan would not find time to think of any shifty excuses. In the end the accused confessed that by his irresistible breath alone, he had awakened carnal desires in more than a thousand women. Pierre Barrot could point to the recorded confession signed by Gauffridi himself, which stated as follows: "Madeleine was seized by a completely insane love for me, and she gave herself to me both during the witches' sabbath and at other times, and I have left my mark on her head, next to her heart, on her stomach, and on her thighs, legs, and feet." Thus the matter was clear, and Gauffridi was burned on April 30, 1611, in the Prêcheurs Square in Aix, after he had been dragged all around the town and exhibited to the people.

Pierre Barrot gathered much testimony on the importance of not losing one's grip but of continually pursuing the Devil and his followers, disguised as they were in all kinds of shapes.

He remembered, wrote down proofs, and collected documents.

In the year 1613, for instance, a number of demons forced their way into a convent (Sainte-Birgitte) at Lille, which they had not visited in six decades. Following the process against Gauffridi, that prince of demons, the girls' vigilance was considerably intensified. Some of them had personally been present at the exorcisms and interrogations at Aix. A rapporteur, J. Lenormand, wrote the following in his "Account of What Happened during the Exorcisms of Three Possessed Girls in the Land of Flanders," which was printed in Paris in 1623: "One could see how some of the girls were possessed by the Devil, how others were mentally disturbed, how others shrank from confession, how some were filled with despair or impatience, others languishing and filled with yearning, how some wanted to die and some were crushed and brokenhearted. The poor girls had hardly entered the convent when they underwent an obvious and dangerous transformation, but as soon as they were again outside the walls of the convent they were already on the road to recovery."

One girl, Marie de Sains, had introduced demons into the convent. During a properly led interrogation, at which, among others, the seventy-year-old Archbishop of Malines was present, she confessed her improper relations with demons with such conviction that three other nuns who tried to deny their guilt, were also sentenced. Marie de Sains was not burned, a fact which Pierre Barrot considered to be injudicious, but was instead locked up for life in the ecclesiastical jail at Tournai. Barrot, who by that time had started to dream of devoting himself to exorcism, was right, as he was to be so many times later: the devils had been encouraged by the mild punishment and immediately afterward possessed another nun in the convent, Simone Dourlet. Other sisters who were involved in the affair could testify that Simone had participated in witches' sabbaths and that she had given birth to several children who were being raised by demons. At last she confessed—to even more than she had been accused of—and eagerly exhorted her fellow defendants to confess too. She was burned; it had been a great success.

III

Pierre Barrot was born in 1595.

He himself had been subjected to demons in a remarkable manner, but they had not been able to get a hold on him.

In the winter when he was seventeen years old his health was so wretched that people thought he was going to die. He lay in bed for two months, but the illness continued even after he was on his feet again. Demons, disguised as women, appeared to him at night. He had visions, not the radiant revelations he had been longing for, but mere glimpses rather of the most forbidden. After much hesitation, he confessed to the prior who didn't seem to think it was very serious however. "Satan is always trying," the prior said. "He is toying with everyone, you just have to stand up to him." One day he called Pierre Barrot in to him. "I have written to your father," he said, "and now I've got an answer. You are going to accompany him on a trip to Paris."

It was an official trip, at the end of April, and it was not to take more than twelve or fourteen days. But Pierre Barrot felt a great deal of unease about his father, whom he had not seen for a year and a half, and also about the journey. Aside from unease there was a feeling of enticement which alarmed him, but he told himself that he would fight this temptation by viewing cathedrals.

Has father came by coach to get him. They had an impressive equestrian escort, six men in all, and traveled via Châtellerault, Tours, Amboise, Blois, and Orléans, where his father had some business, and then via Étampes and Pithiviers, and in this spring of 1612 the road was not without its dangers. And all the beautiful things he saw during the first stage of the journey and the pleasure he took in his father's unexpected friendliness, talkativeness, even high spirits, disappeared in thin air because of what he experienced in Tours, where they took up quarters the first night.

Later on during the years, he put the details together assembling an overview picture of all that happened. The picture might be called "The Devil Makes His Appearance."

The name of the inn was "The Golden Ball" and was located near the Cathedral of Saint-Gatien. It was surprisingly modest in view of the standards set by the judge and prosecutor Barrot, but they put up there since he had known the innkeeper and his wife for a long time. Their party filled almost the entire house. The judge took the biggest room on the second floor—he had to work some during the night and wanted to be undisturbed, he said—and the others were placed willy-nilly. Pierre Barrot was given a small attic room on the next floor up, and he was left to himself for the servant Balthazar wanted to sleep below. Later on in life he saw this as a shrewd plan made by the Devil himself.

They all ate together in the main room with the other travelers, and the innkeeper and his wife helped serve the meal. The innkeeper was small, skinny, with a shrill voice and a sour expression, and he walked with jerky, limping steps; his wife was powerfully built, with black hair, brown eyes, and a glib tongue. She opened her eyes wide and looked reproachfully at Pierre Barrot: "Eat now, young man, and get a strong back!" Everyone grinned, his father laughed out loud. When they began to drink and sing, Pierre felt tired and went up to his room.

He had said his prayers and was about to climb into bed when he heard a great commotion down below. Someone swore and carried on very loudly, and another answered him in an angry, shrill voice. He recognized his father's strong, full-sounding voice and the innkeeper's whining, wailing voice; next came his wife's hearty laughter. Then evidently things got rowdy down there. He thought he could hear thuds as if blows were exchanged, bewildered screams from the maids, and defiant howls. Unaccustomed as he was to the goings-on at an inn, he must have magnified everything in his mind: people were simply noisy. He lay in his bed with folded hands, open mouth, and eyes wide open, listening. Through the skylight high above came the smell of roasting meat, the fragrance of early flowers (he thought), and he felt a fear of the unknown, of the brutal, and of solitude.

There was a lot of noise down in the main room before things finally calmed down. The house and the night became quiet. Far down below in the stairway someone walked with shuffling steps and he heard the rustle of clothing. A door was opened and closed on the second floor. Right after that, or after a while, there was a noise down in the parlor once more. He heard his father's voice, commanding, somewhat blurred and heavy from wine, say something official, definitive, as if pronouncing judgment on someone. Pierre Barrot could not make out the words but he was suddenly and perhaps for the first time in his life filled with a kind of pride. This dark, heavy, and in his circle powerful man who managed to get the noise down, was his father. The tenderness, yes, even love for this man who was so unlike him, suddenly awakened in the air of springtime, the smell of roasting meat, and fear. He couldn't stay in bed, he got up and stood underneath the attic window. He listened to all the sounds of splashing urine and drunken vomiting from the yard below, the steps and the rattling from the kitchen, the distant voices in the main room. "My father is down there," he thought. "He doesn't misbehave; he keeps his balance and dignity; he stands far above all the others, he speaks calmly and in a commanding manner." He wanted to see him right then, and tell him: "I feel safe in your company, Monsieur; God has given me a good father."

He wrapped his cloak about his skinny, lopsided body

and opened the door. It creaked loudly but it was a reassuring sound: it lived, the house was a safe place. He was surrounded by sounds, but they were not the empty, echoing, hollow sounds of the monastery. The sounds of life, and life's eager voices, the very odors of life were in this house. The soles of his feet enjoyed the chilliness of the stone floor. He tried to stand up straight in the dark. All infirmity and crookedness fell off him. He padded silently down the stairs. He shook when he came down to the second floor and had to brace himself against the rough stone wall. His father's voice once again reached him from the main floor, firm and calm, a command: "Now I want some quiet in the house tonight! Remember who I am! Is that understood?"

And the innkeeper's whining, perhaps tearfully angry voice: "Yes, Sir Magistrate, but—"

"Silence!"

Silence.

Light filtered out from under the door to his father's room at the far end of the corridor. "He has a light," he thought. "They have lit a light for him. I'll go into the room and sit down and wait, and when he comes I'll tell him that I'm fond of him, that God has filled my heart with love for him. No, I'll say that I was afraid and felt ill. No, that I am proud that he is my father."

He opened the door.

"Are you there at last!"

The innkeeper's wife was lying on the bed, on top of the bedcover, as on a cloud, naked, spread out, waiting. The picture was to remain forever in his mind; the black, tousled hair, the arms thrown back, the half open mouth, the laughing brown eyes (and then the surprise they registered), the line of her neck, the big swelling breasts with their brown nipples, the plump figure, the hair in her armpits, her crotch in its mad, hairy nakedness. And the wax taper in the copper candlestick on the table gave out a yellow light, softly and quietly, on it all.

He stepped back, closed the door, and shut his eyes. He groped his way up the stairs and was very stoopshouldered and bent. He stood outside his own door, still with his eyes closed, as if that would have helped. He heard his father come from the main parlor and walk with a firm and authoritative step down the corridor. The door on the second floor was opened at the same time that the door to the room downstairs was banged shut. From somewhere in the depths of the house could be heard the coarse laughter of the servant Balthazar.

The following day he sat in the covered carriage next to a happy, talkative, even elated judge who had had business in Tours and who was his father. The innkeeper's wife had said nothing.

*

Paris frightened him and filled him with hatred.

They lived at a nice place which was called "The Iron Cross" by Rue Saint-Martin. Pierre Barrot was from the first morning on left in the care of the servant Balthazar. His father had to attend to much business for himself and others: he had to talk to jurists at the Parlement, visit the prefect of commerce and some people at the Louvre; he had hired a horse, and the innkeeper had got hold of a couple of footmen for him. He was happy and content.

"Take a good look around, now," he said as he rode away.

Balthazar, who was born in Paris but had not been there for a while, started immediately to make arrangements.

"Now we'll take a peek at Pont-Neuf, Monsieur Pierre," he said.

"I want to see Notre-Dame de Paris," Pierre said as peremptorily as he was able to.

"Yes, why not? It's not very far from here."

They walked slowly down the long streets leading to the Seine. The crowds, the smells, the shouting, all the activity frightened and enticed him; it repelled and attracted him.

"This is real life!" Balthazar said. "Don't hang your head now that you've finally come to Paris!"

He didn't answer. The experience in Tours was so deeply etched in his mind that he saw everything through it, and it was always to remain before his eyes. The heavy, dark, dirty houses in the side-streets leaned against one another and whispered about it, and it was there in the women's voices and the men's faces. Paris ought to be torn down, he thought. The people ought to be killed.

What he later remembered of the city? Not that it was large, a wilderness of stone where everything smelled bad, not the gleaming, stinging colors in the light of spring, not the hawkers' shrill shouts and the bustle. But when they got as far as Châtelet, Balthazar pointed out: "And here is the Châtelet prison. There you may be sure, Monsieur, they learn what suffering is. Have you heard about the cells that are called the Chains?"

Pierre Barrot was later to remember the dark walls, the squat towers that served to lock up sin on the inside: they should have been heavier, grayer, taller.

"Ask your father, Monsieur," the servant said. "He knows about it. You can imagine what it's like to sit in a cell like the Chains! I have heard about it! And down below, at the very bottom, there are dungeons called the Butcheries and the Wailing and the Cruelty and the Forgotten Cage and the Spiced Wine Ditch where they stand in water up to their knees and the ceiling is so low that they can't stand up straight! And then there's a dungeon called The Fun's Over!"

Balthazar led the way: he was happy and in high spirits to be back in Paris; he boasted and reviled the provinces.

55

"Over there is the Bastille, Monsieur!" he said. "It is world famous. They also put people in there. And here is the Grève Square, have you heard about that? Here something is always happening, Monsieur. Come here any time and they'll bring someone to be executed. If I had a denier for every barrel of blood that has poured down this square, I would be rolling in money."

He continued to boast about the square, which had three gallows: "Here they have finished off traitors and heretics and swindlers, you may be sure, Monsieur! Ravaillac, the one who put a knife in the back of the old king two years ago, he too came here when he was ripe for it. They gave him some extra treatment first, of course, and afterward they tied him between four horses! And then they pulled, he was tough, but presto! and then he was done! I saw it myself (and now one could hear how he lied). That a man can be so solidly built, I mean so tough and so durable! There was a long cracking sound and he was both long-armed and wide-legged before he was torn to bits and pieces, even though they had four big horses pulling."

"Shut up!"

"But, Monsieur! If you are going to be a priest, you must get your ears used to such things."

"I don't want to hear any more!"

He did want to hear more. There was a void when Balthazar made a sour grimace and kept silent for a while. They stood in the middle of the square; nothing happened. It was a day in spring; there were gallows and the smell of blood.

"Oh, well," the servant said at last, in a melancholy tone. "Paris is really a city where you can have fun and enjoy life if you can afford it. Here is the City Hall. I have visited that building many times. Also with your father, Monsieur. When your father was inside talking with the bigwigs."

"Let's go," said Pierre Barrot.

Silently they walked back up to Rue Saint-Martin and then between the wooden buildings and stores on the Notre-Dame Bridge over to the isle of Cité. He thought the women tried to grab him, they shouted something about his youth and his dark clothes. Perhaps about his bent and crooked figure. One ought to arrest them, he thought. The fun's over. Between four horses.

His recollection of Notre-Dame was later swathed in a brownish gray mist. He stood in the middle of the Hôtel-Dieu Square gazing up at the dark mass of stone but his glance didn't catch hold of it. The mother of churches weighed him down with its great mass. He saw the statues of the kings and of the one the people called the Great Abstainer, the Holy Christophoros. Balthazar had to say something: "That one is called the Gray Lord. That is because he is gray. Shall we look inside a minute, and get it done with!"

"Not now," he said.

They walked back across Pont-Neuf where they had a wide-open view. To Balthazar's great astonishment he wanted to stand there a little while. And from there Pierre Barrot saw most of what he was to see of Paris: the clusters of houses behind them on the left shore, the bridges with their tall superstructures, the walls of the Louvre, the quays being built, the beaches with their sand and brush-wood, a multitude of houses, towers, and church spires. It all passed before his eyes. He felt as if he had a monopoly on God, on Truth, and the Real. He stood in the surge of the bridge's own life and was a steadfast rock upon which a temple was to be built. Later on he never spoke a word about Paris, the way others do. He had seen, he knew, there were pictures of the city within him, memories of sounds and smells. He remembered, but had nothing to say about burghers in wide-brimmed hats and gaily colored clothes, great men in carriages and on horseback, soldiers on leave or on the way back to their regiments, street walkers, magicians, clothes merchants, monks; no, not even about monks and students. It was a life that shone with the glitter of power and seethed with fear and lust; but it didn't concern him. The bells in the towers pealed, banged, rang, voices shouted and cajoled, yelled and implored, persuaded, praised and mocked. He had nothing to do with that. The smell of men and animals, the smell of roasting meat, and of dung, of spring and of water, of profane smoke and holy incense, the stench of squalor, of bodily desires enveloped him; but he was beyond it. He was Pierre Barrot, who defended God.

"Now we'll take a look at the Louvre," said Balthazar.

He didn't want to. The servant accompanied him back to his lodgings. He ate alone in the big room, bread, water and boiled, salted fish, and then went up to his room. There he lay on his back in his bed staring up into the dirty, blue fabric of the canopy. He listened, sounds passed his ears. They did not touch him.

The next day he went to Notre-Dame all by himself. He strolled underneath the high arches, but they only infused greater disquiet in him. He genuflected before the picture of the Madonna near the northern gate, the Cloister Gate, and mumbled his prayers.

They traveled home along the same route: Étampes, Orléans, Blois, and Amboise swayed past in the light of spring. In the inns there were smells of fried meat and women's sweat. In Tours they put up in the same place. He lay awake the whole night in life's most highly scented spring, the Year of Our Lord 1612, and heard the sounds abate down there in the human regions. The room was full of demons. He cast out many of them by the strength of his will, but he could not defend himself against his hearing. Feet padded about in the stairways, clothing rustled, heavy steps echoed in the corridors. He hid his face in his hands and wept over his desire, his fear, his infirmity, and his ugliness.

IV

He acquired the sharp glance, the glance of recognition. He could smell them in the air long before they arrived: in the air surrounding the women. He exorcized demons and that led to his fame.

In the autumn of 1632, following the plague, he met Jeanne de Beaucil, the prioress of the Ursuline convent at L. Its father confessor, Jehan Minet, had spoken to her about Pierre Barrot and she sent a message to Chinon and asked him to come.

"I have heard so much about you and have asked you to come to give me good advice," she said.

They were sitting in the parlor.

She resembled someone he had seen a long time before. She will probably get plump, perhaps fat, as time goes on, he thought in passing and stared at her hairline, at the exact point where her hood covered it. Her bearing was strained. There was something deformed about her neck and back.

"Perhaps I can give you some advice," he said in a drawling voice and tried to sit up as straight in the chair as his crooked back allowed.

"There are, of course, mostly young girls here," she said. "Many of them only stay two or three years with us; then they are to go out in the world. And that's where many dangers threaten them. They are so unprotected against—against demons. So defenseless. Father Minet has told me that you have wide experience in this, Father Barrot."

"Experience does not suffice," he said modestly glancing down at her thighs and her lap. He got an impression of her as a big overgrown girl, soon a middle-aged teenager. There were traces of hunger and greed in her face.

"There are so many dangers," he said after a pause. And

then he looked penetratingly at the rim of her hood: "The Devil knows every pathway to the body and soul of a human being."

She fidgeted with her hands. She couldn't sit still many minutes at a time. She had a certain way of jerking her head and body, and it was not the movements of a busy housekeeper; and her conversation jumped from one topic to another.

"We have a relative of the Cardinal's here," she said.

"Yes, so I have heard."

She searched for something to add to that.

"It is very pleasant for us to have her here. She is very pious. Her name is Sister Claire, born de Sazilly. She is very sensitive."

"Yes?" he said.

"Sister Anne is our oldest, she is over forty. She was married once upon a time. She is very sensitive. She keeps mostly to herself; she is very pious."

"That is nice to hear," he said stiffly.

She didn't ask right out for any kind of advice.

"They are a little restless now," she said.

"You can write me or you can send for me if there's anything wrong," he said.

She is not mature yet, he thought as he was leaving. But he dimly perceived them in the air. They have been here. They will come back when things have matured further, he felt.

V

At times, too often, he heard Urbain Grainier's name. A man surrounded by women. Many women. A priest who lives with a woman, and everybody knows it. A priest who is attractive with an attractive woman.

In the year 1626 he saw her outside his own church in Chinon. He followed her when she crossed the square. He

60

had to moisten his lips with his tongue before he was able to speak to her. He felt dizzy but he knew that his thoughts were exceptionally pure.

"Isn't your name Madeleine de Brone?"

"Yes," she replied and turned her soft, round, astonished face toward him.

He thought it so intensely just then that he didn't know that he muttered it: that she was very beautiful. She said something to the effect that one oughtn't say things like that when one is a priest, and he walked away from her.

She was the most beautiful woman he had ever seen. And although he knew she was a whore, he felt that she was *pure* and that there was inside her a motherly and comradely serenity that no one could disturb and which no demons could shake.

One night soon after he dreamed about her. They were walking across a big bridge, through a throng of people and demons who were howling and through flames that were flickering and leaping up around them without consuming them. They were completely calm. They held each other by the hand. He knew that when they had crossed the bridge, he could rest his head on her full breasts, touch them with his cheeks.

4

Sister Anne

No one could claim that she was a habitual drunkard, but wine had for many years helped her attain strength, courage, and mental balance. She didn't drink every day, only once or twice a week, when she felt the need. And the need varied; at times it was greater, and at times it did not exist. She said to herself, now as she had before, that it was God who allowed wine to ferment. The wine created a wall of peace and quiet around her. Inside the wall she thought soft and clear thoughts that made her hands still and sure and made her voice stay within a good range. On certain occasions the wine would make her voice rise a bit, but never so much that it became shrill and broke—or at least almost never. I have a quieter voice than the prioress, than Sister Jeanne, she thought. She may resemble me on the inside, but my voice is surely more beautiful. She also screams, that we've all heard, that is something that can't be hidden; and if I were to be asked and forced to say something about her during confession, I would be compelled to say she drinks absinthe and white wine (which is bad for one's health if one drinks it to excess) and that she has a very shrill scream. People say that the one we at times call our Mother, Sister Jeanne that is, is beautiful. I was just as beautiful when I was young, and my body, which I never think of, however, was without a doubt much more beautiful. It was not bent. I stay away from white wine, which incites craving and a troublesome thirst. I am calm, I am mostly calm, at rest within myself without anxiety. I don't care about gaining people's sympathy and I do not strive to be considered very holy, very pious. I rest in my unassuming and silent piety, but I do not wrap it around me like a shining cape to dazzle the spectators. If I had made an effort to be ingratiating and smiling at the right moments, I would have had her position and would have been sitting in her room or in the parlor giving good advice without any value and listening to all the gossip that seeps in from without. Then I would not have been tempted to think *these* forbidden thoughts (which I will confess to Father Minet when the occasion comes), no, then I would have thought other thoughts which might also be forbidden.

When her neck started twitching, she had a glass of wine. Everyone knew that she had wine in her cell, but it was never mentioned. She was the oldest, and her neck was twitching. So does Sister Jeanne's, she knew. A few sinews and muscles that are out of joint. During her monthly period she would have a few glasses of wine to help nature along. When in her zeal and with a self-assumed right which no one protested against, she asked one of the girls to come to her for questioning or admonishing, or when she was going down to the parlor to meet someone from the streets or the life outside, she would have a few drinks before and a few afterward. Séraphique Archer, the serving sister, brought the wine to her room and said, "It is at least three years old, perhaps four. I think it comes from Bourgeuil. I tasted some of it. I once worked for a man who knew his wines. He said that Chinon and Veron were better than ours as far as red wines go. The prioress mostly drinks Saumur."

"I only have a small glass of wine now and then; my throat feels very dry once in a while."

"Oh, well," Séraphique said. "It is better than absinthe."

When memories came back to her, she had a small glass

of wine to sweep away or at least alleviate them. Or two or at the most three glasses. They were small glasses and not large beakers. She owned two glasses, one large and the other somewhat smaller, and she had shown them and made confession of them to the late Father Poussaut as well as to Father Jehan Minet, the Lame One. Both had told her: "It is no sin to own glasses." They were beautiful glasses, a remnant of her life: memories that one could look at, hold in one's hand, and lift up toward the light. They had been with her in hard times but were now free of sorrow. She had had four, but two of them, one large and one small, fell on the floor. No, she thought, one of them fell on the wall. The hand was raised by the will of God and the glass, a big one, fell on the wall: through the power of Jesus it broke. It happened during one of her early years here.

Otherwise, the first few years here had not been difficult and the memories didn't come with any special force: perhaps two or three times each spring. She herself had been different then. She could be just as young as the girls whom she was bringing up to become humble, Christian, and educated. She was of their age not only in her ways but also in looks, in her face. She laughed with them and taught them games with nuts and legends about flowers. Later they drifted farther away in their youth, in their duties, in their secrets, into their private middle age perhaps. And the older sisters and the serving sisters didn't open their hearts to her. They had the prioress and the father confessor. For that matter, they never opened their hearts to anyone, she dimly perceived, and she had long ago understood that they had never opened their hearts to her. She resembled the prioress also in the way she frightened them. She seldom used harsh words and only very rarely did she burst into a rage, but she frightened them in that she radiated loneliness. If they confided in her or pretended to confide and confessed something to her, the words didn't come from their hearts. Their confidences were for the most part very decent. They stuck to the form, filling it with suitably innocent content without lying. Sometimes they weren't even secretive: their content was actually just as plain and colorless as the form indicated. Or almost so.

For that matter, one couldn't speak openly without sounding mad, she thought now and then in passing. One can't expect people to open up completely to other people. But during confession? God looks into our heart without need for confession, she thought. He knows without words. He lets our hand throw glasses at the wall and overturn wine goblets, but He won't shatter all glasses or let all wine flow away. He lets the wine grow every year. He makes it a blessing if—as in my case—it is consumed in moderation. He gives us His peace even through His wine.

She tried to help the girls through her calm. She looked at them with her most quiet eyes and used her most quiet voice. She turned slowly around in her chair to face them (she shouldn't have one in her cell; but she had consulted both the late Poussaut and Jehan Minet, the Lame One, and they had approved it.) But she took care not to turn toward them slowly in a threatening manner; she did it in a dignified manner, thoughtfully, slowly like a friend, to put them at ease and give them a feeling of trust. They needed that. I help them through my calm, she thought. For example, Marie Aubin. Marie is sixteen years old now. Or has she turned seventeen? A girl knows nothing. Oh well, what do I know about that anyway? She probably knows about most things. But not the most horrible, that which you never really get through. If I had come through, I wouldn't be sitting here. Marie goes away, Marie will perhaps return. Now we know: Marie will not stay here. In a year or two or three she will be getting a taste of life. Perhaps nothing dark and bitter will happen to her. Perhaps the man will be young and without the smell of old desire. He might smell of newly consumed wine and garlic and roast beef and roasted chestnuts; perhaps he will smell of courtly perfume. Perhaps he has the smell of youth. Horses, the sweat of young men. Perhaps he will smell like the sea. One can tell from Marie Aubin's face that he will not smell like a father confessor. He will probably smell of horses and the sea.

The first time this woman, who is now called Sister Anne, saw the real ocean, wide-open and limitless, was near a fishing village at Les Landes, a small hamlet that King Henry invested with town privileges. She was as old as Marie Aubin is now, or perhaps not quite; she was fifteen years old. She had been permitted to come along with her father on the tortuous jorney from Angoulême via Périgueux and Bergerac, where they had relatives everywhere, and on to Bordeaux, where they stayed a few days, and then straight south toward Bayonne. She remembered the visits to the rich and the poor relatives living in new or ramshackle castles and farms: it was like a fair at which they inspected her and appraised her. The big covered wagon shook and squeaked, the four draft horses were changed or were given some rest at the overnight inns. A saddler's anxious bustle while the rain was dripping on the wagon roof and running down the shiny backs of the horses, a wheel being repaired, a bottle of wine sent around, shouts, and screams. She remembered the coachmen on horseback, the mounted escorts on both sides and before and after, the narrow and bumpy roads leading through the moorland. In the distance or close by there were hills with green clumps of trees, on a bare height stood a lonely cork oak. And warm, sunfilled days when they were swaying forward in clouds of dust. And the ocean. And the Ocean.

They heard it from far off. The Bay of Biscay. When the sun was setting she saw the immense crests of the waves roll softly in toward the shore, and then rise up to become moving green and red walls, crowned with whirling foam—north toward the dunes and Bordeaux, south toward Bayonne and the Basque cliffs—and then, when they

66

got closer: the smell of seaweed and salt water. This was the ocean one day in her early youth.

They stayed with relatives in Bayonne, where she was also put on display. She remembered the chaos, the Basque confusion, the wealth of the noisy house, the silver, the pearls, the polished wood, the music from stringed instruments, the abundance of food, the smells of fish, onions, and fruits. She recalled the picture of the pale lady of the house, her father's cousin, who had been sick in bed for two years, the son who never spoke, only smiled quietly, the two daughters, the older sixteen years, the younger of her own age. And she remembered the mighty baron and government official, going on sixty, noisy, panting, well-fed, guffawing, the father of the family, and a fatherly friend.

A year later the baroness had died. Six months later the silent son was killed in battle. And before another year had passed the baron arrived at Angoulême and made side trips to the farms and castles round about. Everything was arranged by clever hands and she came back with him as his wife. Now my life is over, she thought then. Over and done with, *finito*. But I'll reach the ocean one more time.

She never really did reach the ocean again. They were to stay overnight in Montmoreau the first night. When the happy, loving, and intoxicated man heaved himself over her, she screamed so shrilly that everything else became quiet at the inn. She made herself free of him. She recalled his clothes lying in a heap on the floor having fallen off a chair, the candles smoking in their sticks, a smell of old lust (like the smell of mold in the corners) and of sour wine, belched up from an old man's wrinkled throat.

Her youth ended right there. For two years she experienced old age together with him and his silent, shy daughters. The older managed to become engaged or promised to someone but was never married; the younger never did more than learn a little Latin and Italian. They withered away in noise, pleasures, and wealth. She drank a beaker of wine now and then. When the baron had lowered his bulging eyelids over his brown and somewhat bloodshot eyes, and had forever shut off his official look, she was alone. She dealt with the inheritance to the best of her ability and received willing familial assistance from many quarters. *Finito.*

When everything had been taken care of, she left for Bordeaux to join the Ursuline Sisters. She discovered that she had a calling, and at the same time she felt how the power and temptation of evil through men are great and must at all times be fought with prayer, work, mortification of the flesh, and attempts to forget. She received excellent support from Mother Françoise de Cazères, who predicted that Sister Anne would some day become a prioress herself. She came to Poitiers with the other sisters in 1618, but didn't become their leader. In her stead, the very kind and good Sister Marie de Goffreteau was appointed prioress; she belonged to one of the most distinguished families in Bordeaux.

In 1626 eight sisters were sent from Poitiers to this city in order to establish the new convent. Sister Anne didn't become its head; she didn't even become one of its founders. She thought at that time: It is fair. Once I drank too much wine in the kitchen, I smelled from wine, I spoke very loudly. It is fair. The first head of the convent was Sister Gabriele and the following year when Sister Gabriele, the mild one, was summoned to another position, Sister Jeanne, born Beaucil, took her place. They didn't select me, Sister Anne thought (who was sent here at that time), perhaps I smelled of wine once or twice when I was menstruating or my memories came back to me. And our young Mother Jeanne is unusually capable, yes, really remarkably capable, she is full of energy and enterprise. Although she, just like me, is tormented by dreams, she is very capable. Although she drinks a glass of absinthe or a large glass of white wine once in a while on the sly, she is very capable and right for the position. Although she is a telltale and scolds and plays the hypocrite and pulls her hair and weeps and longs for—yes, what does she long for? the smell and the member of a man?—even so she is very capable. She became our mother, our sisterly mother on account of much flattery during her trial year in addition to her great humility, which she has demonstrated to one and all.

No one can claim that I drink, thought Sister Anne. No sensible person can envy me a thimble-full of Bordeaux or Chinon wine after a toilsome and thought-filled day. I don't bother anyone by doing that; I usually keep to myself and I shall answer to God when the day comes and the moldy life here on earth is *finito*.

She didn't walk into town anymore, even though she could have been given errands and tasks to perform. But on a hot afternoon in the summer of 1630 she walked up to the attic and stuck her head out through the small hatch on the roof. She could see the plain, the towers, and the roofs and a part of the street. Down in Pasquin Hill a priest was walking; she thought she recognized him from the way he carried himself. She climbed down and walked into the garden and stood behind the lattice-window when he walked by. She held the wooden shutter up just enough for one eye. She thought vaguely: He doesn't belong in the cassock; but at the same time she thought the opposite, that he really knows how to wear it. He looked like a slim Italian or a Spaniard. He had a small black mustache and a Vandyke beard just like the Cardinal's. His face was dark-complexioned and hard, his eyes were black, his mouth firm, but the lower lip was that of a soldier who knows of women and their ways. His back, his neck, and his straight shoulders she liked best. She said to herself: This can be appreciated like a picture.

Their father confessor, old Poussaut, died the following summer and immediately began haunting the house. Once she mentioned to the prioress, Sister Jeanne, that if the priest of Saint-Pierre and Sainte-Croix, that particular priest, were not in such bad repute, he could have been summoned as their father confessor. The two women gave each other a searching look. *She hates me because at one time I might have become what she is now,* thought Sister Anne. "Yes, he does have such a pedagogic look," the prioress said. "I have seen him through the lattice-window toward the street," she added immediately. "It was just by accident, a pure coincidence. Actually I didn't see him. It was only a glimpse. But I can imagine what he looks like." "I too have seen a glimpse of someone who might be he," said Sister Anne. The two women once again gave each other a searching look and then averted their glances. *She has dark circles under her eyes,* thought Sister Anne.

Was he asked, or wasn't he? The new father confessor was Jehan Minet, who was called the Lame One here in town. He was a man with excellent family connections. His uncle was Monsieur Frène de Poussaut, who owned this house. Father Minet was canon at Sainte-Croix and rued the fact that the prebend went to outsiders and Jesuit protégés. He was a rather fat but shy man. It was soon discovered that he was afraid of the dark even though he at times took nightly walks in town. That is to say: he was afraid of shadows. If he was in the company of someone, he preferred to walk in the dark. He was afraid of the girls when the sun shone brightly at them, when it was day and the sky was clear.

*

During the weeks that the dead father confessor came back to haunt the corridors, the kitchen, and the cells, Sister Anne felt no fear. After the Lame One, with the aid of a priest from Chinon, had exorcised old Poussaut back into Purgatory, fear and terror came to her in the night. She woke up and lay quietly with a clear head, looking at the grating's brighter square and listening to the silence in the house. Out in the corridor or in the stairway to the refectory and the kitchen a rat was dragging something along; it made short leaps. The leaves were rustling in the linden trees, the oaks, and the chestnuts outside; she heard the soughing of a weeping willow. A beam in the attic creaked. The water from a well dripped, trickled, dripped quickly, drip, drip, drip, trickled again in a staccato rhythm. A drunken, singing, and humming peasant clattered past in a donkey cart, and the sound of the donkey's hoofs echoed between the houses, rose, fell, receded in the direction of the church. In a stable nearby a horse stirred heavily, moved its legs, tossed its head.

During such a silence images came back to her mind. It was easy to turn away from them and get rid of them if she wanted to. She remembered someone who had been young and handsome, a newly enlisted and taciturn soldier who came home to his father, the baron, just to look at her, to inspect, appraise. Swords jangled about him, he smelled of youth. A smile, fleeting, in a young face which attempted to bring forth a mustache and a Vandyke beard not as yet under control, only naively pomaded. A youthful glint from the corner of his eye. Then silence. Then silence. Then this damned silence next to the governor's evil-smelling bellowing. Then this damned silence. A young mouth that didn't speak, a mouth in which the governor had killed all words beforehand. This damned silence.

She remembered it but didn't want the trouble of recalling names any longer. But she remembered the mood surrounding them. Someone's thoughts directed toward her so that she felt it: I want to be with you, sit next to you, and touch you. Touch you, lightly, breathe against your ear.

Out of the silence came dread. Loneliness, she thought, is to lie on one's back in a cell at night and wait without hope. Her clear thought said: Wait like a bird in a cage, wait like a prisoner to be released but all the time know that you wait without hope. This is loneliness: when hope is so weak that you cannot even express it.

Then came the dangerous thoughts and then the fear. In the absence of hope she sought hope, contrary to all reason and all faith and all the low and indistinct mumbling of *niente, finito:* the hope that something would happen so that the grip that Night had on her neck would loosen; that time would reverse its course so that the woman lying here on her bed would suddenly be young again. Yes, so young that she could have jumped off the carriage before it reached the inn in Montmoreau, run away, rush into a forest and hide and then get a totally different life to live.

The first times it didn't occur to her that they were demons. Become younger, she thought. What ridiculous fantasies. To be transformed? What childishness! One night she had to get out of bed and drink a small glass of wine in order to quiet her thoughts. So much for fantasizing, she thought. But the fear and the temptation were mingled within her. Wine is soothing. The thought of the body and its vanished opportunities needed several glasses before it faded away and became nothing—merely a remnant of something turning to weariness and drowsiness.

She was not afraid of the dead. They don't want to do me any harm. She imagined Purgatory to be a station where one gets off, gets a new horse hitched to one's wagon, and is examined by border guards; a longer or shorter period of unpleasantness and trouble, but one doesn't stay there. The faces of her dead ones she could regard at any time without other feelings than a calm, fading sorrow or repugnance and loathing which go away and in time disappear completely. They were not dearly beloved nor intensely hated, they were not threatening or yearning. They were unsympathetic perhaps, but then one could turn away and not have to look at them. The hands of the dead did not grab at her; she didn't feel their chilliness, didn't hear their entreaties and their screams.

She was more afraid of the faces, the eyes, and the words of the living. Glances could tear away the heaviest attire, voices could show that there was knowledge or suspicion of something that was hidden and silenced deep down inside. Voices and eyes would often dissemble but never so well that their scrutiny went unnoticed. Between that which was expressed by human faces and voices and that which their glances couldn't help reveal (knowledge, notions, curiosity, certainty) there was a domain for disquiet, and it was just there, in the interval, that fear rushed in. One couldn't control fear by saying: This is what I feel and why. It was vague. It was not the fear of walking on the rim of an abyss knowing that it is possible to make a false step and fall down and get killed and not the fear of being below a cliff and thinking that a stone may get loose up there unless one holds one's breath at the right moment. No, there was no particular word that she was afraid of, no facial expression or glance that indicated hate or contempt or inordinate arrogance. All of it was vague and impalpable, but it existed.

Perhaps this is how it was: at any minute in this life someone might do or say something, or something unexpected might happen *that would loosen something within her.* What then? She didn't know. Perhaps her hand would be raised against her will and then make a contrary movement? Perhaps her neck would twist to the left when she wanted to look to the right, her legs, her feet walk in the wrong direction, away from that to which she was attracted, toward that which she loathed. Perhaps her voice would change so that the whispering and mumbling far down in her breast would turn to piercing screams up in her mouth.

One night she dreamed that the Devil entered her cell. He was like the pictures she had seen, with horns, cloven hoofs, shaggy hide, and warts. His shagginess glistened from grease and fat. She felt anguish only afterward and mostly because she hadn't had the strength and the purity

73

to be afraid at the right moment. I am damned, she thought when she managed to wake up, I wasn't even afraid of him, and I thought he smelled good.

Spring came across the plain, crept out of the woods; its disquiet was light. The girls laughed a little more boldly, with more wide-open mouths. Their faces were turned toward the light from out of the sky. Sister Claire told as merrily as she could—which is not saying much—about light and gay springs at the Castle Richelieu which she had visited when she was a little girl; there she had been sitting in the lap of the Cardinal's mother. At that time Armand himself had been dreaming of becoming a soldier, a rich and mighty warrior. "Just think," said Claire de Sazilly, "now the castle is being rebuilt and there will be an entire town surrounding it. The power of Our Lord is in it." The girl Marie Aubin said openly and almost loudly that she was homesick, that she wanted to see fields of grain, where the fertile, newly plowed soil steamed and glistened in the quivering sunlight, where things were growing so fast that one could hear them. Yes, she said quite openly that she wanted to see horses and weapons and hear trumpet blasts from the woods at a closer range than she could now.

I would really like to see the sea, Sister Anne thought. It must be beautiful in this kind of light. Green walls of water rising before you, foam like white smoke at the top of the waves, and to feel the offshore breeze with the smell of mimosa in it. Ground-swells, preferably ground-swells. Ground-swells that come rolling in, unceasingly, the water organ, the Bay of Biscay.

One morning those who slept in the dormitory announced that they had probably been visited by demons during the night. Four of the girls had most likely been subjected to very insulting advances.

She wanted to be rid of it, but it was stored up and remained within her. Every time she tried to sort things

74

out and see through them, something incomprehensible projected itself between her and everyday reality confusing her vision; she couldn't see clearly anymore.

The demons came to her three nights in a row.

The first night they came from out of her past. She was rocking in a rattling, creaking wagon across bumpy moorland roads toward the sea. Next to her sat a demon without a face groping between her knees with a cold, bony, rough, and hairy hand. Nails scratched against her skin; they were claws. A hand grasped her neck pressing her cheeks and her mouth down toward the wagon floor. When she woke up (woke up?), when she came to her senses she was lying with her forehead touching the stone floor of the cell. I didn't get up by myself, she knew. I was thrown out on the floor.

The next evening she was afraid to go to sleep. She lay a long time just staring at the bright square of the window opening. Moonlight outside. Memories drifting by like clouds, light and dark. She got up and had a glass of wine, then came a feeling of calm. She woke up by someone tearing at her clothes, and when she struck back her right hand hit her left. Someone is here with me, she knew. Someone is here with me, someone is here with me, *someone is here with me!*

Her heart beat rapidly, the grip around her neck returned. She got up, struck a light with her tinderbox and fell on her knees on the prayer stool in front of the crucifix. The grip around her neck did not loosen. She took a glass of wine. A feeling of calm came after a little while and she could lie down; she was very tired.

The next day she was out in the garden with the girls for several hours, but she hardly talked to them. During the divine services she prayed a long time. She also prayed often in her cell, trying to immerse herself in the spirit of prayer. A few times she stepped up on the stool and looked out through the little window. She held on to the grating and stared straight out across the roofs that were gleaming in the sunlight. Her glance would always be lowered toward the streets, slowly it would arrive there. A carriage was approaching from the city gate. She thought for no reason whatever: that it may be this much talked-about and wanton Madeleine de Brone. She walked down and stood by the lattice-window and opened it quickly when the carriage was right outside. She caught a glimpse of a hat with soft, grayish-white plumes. A woman sat in the carriage and could very well be the talked-about, wanton woman. The carriage continued up the hill; she heard it turn into the square in front of the Church of Sainte-Croix. After that nothing was heard, perhaps it stopped there.

She walked up into the attic and looked out through a small shutter. She knew now that the others were watching her and were wondering what she was doing, but she didn't speak to them. In the corridor she met Sister Claire, who wanted to say something to her, but Sister Anne walked past her without looking up. She heard that the other woman stopped. She stood there listening, of course. Down in the parlor, the reception room, she heard the rising voice of the prioress, Sister Jeanne; it sounded like a kind of screaming whisper, she thought. Father Minet, the Lame One, was there. She gossips and gossips, Sister Anne thought. They gossip and gossip.

Through the shutter she saw a priest walking far down the street. It could be he. Considering his bearing and his springy, even careless step and his way of turning his head to both sides, curious, alert, then it could be he, the one much talked-about. Sister Anne went down to the lattice-work in the gate to watch. In the corridor she met Sister Claire, who said something, but she didn't answer. At first she was all alone in the archway. Then Sister Jeanne was there right behind her. Through the door opening to the parlor there were sounds from the Lame One. She pushed up slightly the wooden shutter before the grating. She heard the somewhat younger woman behind her draw a quick breath. I don't do that, she thought. I am calm, sensible, observing.

It was he, possibly, certainly, probably he, the one who was much talked-about. His cheerful or hard glance (his eyes were black) took in the shutter and the gate; he didn't see them. He was out walking although there was pestilence abroad. He looked up at the window on the other side of the street. He carried his head erect, he was tall and slender, his shoulders were broad and straight. In his hand he held a breviary; a white rose stuck out from between the pages. When Sister Anne closed the shutter and turned around in order to walk into the garden, she saw the prioress's somewhat crooked back—there *was something* about it—in the doorway leading to the parlor, where the Lame One was standing.

The third night was decisive. She perceived four demons who came and told their names. She was expecting them. She heard them slither up the wall and the slate roof and with noisy claws grab hold of iron rods, joints, and cracks in the masonry. She closed her eyes when she heard them come into her cell. They brought with them the smells of spring, buds that burst open, and spring flowers that gave off fragrances, even though it was summer and pestilence. In the gentle soughing in the tree crowns she noticed their whispers. A hand coming out of the darkness grasped her neck and twisted her face toward the window opening, where there was soft moonlight. She was still resisting. I will not open my eyes. I'll get up and have a small glass of wine. I'll turn toward the wall. I don't *want* to.

She closed her eyes tightly. A glance able to pierce this demoniac darkness would see that her face looked like a child's contorted by the tears to come but with its eyes closed, hard, hard, so that there might be a candy instead of a beating. "God, take it away from me," she murmured. But when her lips parted, she felt something slide into her and it was already in her throat, in her chest, in her midriff. Her eyes opened. She saw the rapacious, insinuatingly and cruelly smiling faces in the light of the window opening.

When she awakened from their whispering, from the picture of demons and their obscene movements, when she awakened from their night reality and their night truth, she was lying naked and huddled up like a fetus on the floor. It was early dawn. Next to her lay a wine jug and a glass, both overturned. She lay in a pool of wine and the spilled semen of demons.

5

Daniel Drouin's Protocol (1)

Introduction:

I AM WRITING a secret protocol, a summation, partly in code and with excerpts from my diary, about the most important things that have happened here since the year 1617. Long before that time I had refused to become a rug merchant like my late father, wishing instead to devote myself to that profession, not to say calling, which is closest to my nature, my talents, and my innermost inclinations, namely, that of a government official. I myself am anonymous, that is, I am Daniel Drouin, of course. My diary notes should be looked upon merely as props for my memory. It is self-evident that I keep the most secret things to myself:

The protocol, which is divided into a series of booklets, has been read through, examined, and revised repeatedly. The last time it was examined and put aside was in the year 1637.

Here is the first section with excerpts from the diary.

§ 1

Our city was founded by the Kelts, it is said, and the Romans were here too. It is still a big city, we have 15–

79

16,000 inhabitants, but at one time it was a mighty and powerful city. During the course of the centuries it has played a significant role in the history of our country. This I say without boasting. Now, in the year 1637, the walls and most of the towers and other fortifications have been torn down, with the exception of the dungeon, Nerra. Those who fought most for the city walls and the towers are also gone from the surface of the earth. The religious wars laid waste our area and the land surrounding it. For some years our city was almost completely Reformed. Now the power of the Huguenots is not much to speak of.

Our city is beautiful, and I love it. Here are beautiful houses and beautiful streets to be seen, and we have always had beautiful girls—so beautiful that the well-known and famous François Rabelais, who was born in Chinon, made an amusing remark about this. For women, especially the young ones, are always enticing. I have always thought that our girls are attractive. And so have many others. And it is in my opinion very justifiable to think so. The above-mentioned Rabelais lists four places in our country which he calls "the Devil's tenant farms," full of temptations. Among those he mentions are Chinon and our city.

Louis Tranchant, who for many years was our royal procurator and public prosecutor, is writing the history of the city. It has some bright as well as dark sides. I for my part would prefer to see only the bright ones—such is my nature—but I cannot help seeing the dark sides too, for that is the way I see things.

After the names of Rabelais and Tranchant I will now mention Urbain Grainier's as the third name.

Urbain Grainier came here for the first time in the year 1617. We became acquainted at the time when I attended Jesuit school in Bordeaux. We were about the same age, although he, in many ways, was a more mature person than I was and, I suppose, was even from the very beginning intended to enter upon the life of a cleric. He was the best student in the school and was a favorite of the teachers. I was a merchant's son who in accordance with my father's wishes stayed at the school for some time in order to learn agreeable manners and increase my knowledge of languages so that I later could become what I am: an assessor with the title of councillor, *conseiller*. Grainier and I met quite often and talked a lot together, but he was nevertheless difficult to get close to in my view. He was not uncommunicative, on the contrary, he was markedly happy and unreserved, but at times I was inclined to call him arrogant, although not even now, having seen so much of him that might be interpreted as arrogance, do I think it is the right word.

Marcus Tullius Cicero is the fourth name that I mention here. In the course of time he has become my favorite author. In my work at the office of our *bailli*, our highest civilian official, our bailiff for town and country, M. de Cerisay, I do not too infrequently have the occasion to quote the famous Roman. He expresses everything so concisely, pungently, and clearly. "*Sunt, qui de huius urbis atque adeo de orbis terrarum exitio cogitent.*" "I really mean," I recall having said one day some years ago, "that there are persons here who are working for the destruction of our city, indeed of the entire world!" My colleague at the office, Charles Calvet, gave a start and looked at me in consternation. "That is a dangerous thing to say," he said. "I merely quote Cicero," I replied. "Then do it in your excellent Latin, my dear Drouin," he said, and we both laughed a long time in spite of the serious import of my words.

The words, which undeniably are those of Cicero, could very well have been uttered by a conscientious resident of our city.

I am not a doubter, but I am alert to things. I often say (still quoting Cicero) that it is highly probable that the world has been created for the sake of men, even though I must admit that I have doubted it at times.

Yes, what kind of people is it that work to bring about their own destruction but mend their souls?! In the days when I was a rather witty fellow, up to a few years ago, I would after one or two small glasses of absinthe or a few glasses of wine with my friends at the inn "The Hen," have ventured to say that it is the shoemakers. At that time I was good at making puns. But now my thoughts are heavier. Our own destruction? I recall the bitter struggles between Huguenots and Catholics (I am looked upon as a Catholic myself) that took place here in the course of the years. At the moment there is peace on that front—peace as after a deep, perhaps poisoned exhalation. I suspect, however, that there will be future struggles, quiet or noisy, violent or long and tenacious. If I am still alive then, I want to have the heart and the courage, just like Cicero (on one occasion), to express my wish "to speak on behalf of poverty even if my day will not be long enough."

Thus, Urbain Grainier arrived in our town in the beginning of August 1617. The Jesuits in Bordeaux and Poitiers sent him here; he was one of the ablest among their young ones. It was not at the moment when, as Caesar says in one connection, "*murus defensoribus nudatus est*"—when the wall is without defenders—but the thought of razing our fortifications and our city walls was probably already then lodged in someone's heart. Our walls had not begun to lose their defenders. That didn't happen until six or seven years later. Grainier arrived at a time of relative domestic peace and calm.

He was tall, broad-shouldered (I myself am unusually tall, taller than most people I have seen, but not so broad-shouldered), and his carriage was what one calls proud. He was rather swarthy, his eyes were almost black, he wore a Vandyke beard and a mustache, just like I do nowadays, and made one think rather of a diplomat than of a priest. He was always well dressed, rather on the snobbish side, and was, in brief, a handsome man of twenty-seven. It should also be mentioned that his voice was deep and melodious and that he was an excellent orator, yes, an orator of a very high caliber. He came here as pastor of our Church of Saint-Pierre, and was almost immediately appointed canon with a prebend at our Church of Sainte-Croix thus becoming the foremost prelate of our city.

Our city has had and has several famous men. I am thinking first of all of the physician Théophraste Renaudot, the apostle of the new medicine, the friend and helper of the poor, who fought against unemployment and poverty in Paris through his address offices, his employment exchanges (and his pawnshops, 1637) and useful inventions—an exceptional, richly endowed spirit who lived in our city a long time and is mentioned here because he was a good friend of Urbain Grainier. Then we have Scévole de Sainte-Marthe, the government official, the jurist, the historian, and poet whom all of France, yes, large parts of the civilized world know of and admire. During the religious struggles some decades ago Scévole saved our town from being plundered when the commander of the Catholic army, the Duke of Joyeuse, threatened to regard us—I mean the inhabitants of the Protestant fortress, which our town was at that time—as rebels. With his dazzling eloquence and his patriotic fervor Scévole de Sainte-Marthe succeeded in persuading the duke to spare us, and for that reason he was here called the "Father of His Country," a title which I think he fully deserved. When he was eighty-two years old, this was in the year 1618, he left his positions and came back here to his place of birth and with his family he settled down among us. His house became a center for the city's spiritual and cultural life and he gathered the foremost intellects around him. Among them was our new priest, the young, educated, and witty Urbain Grainier, our royal *procureur* and historian Louis Tranchant, my colleagues, the brothers Calvet, and our *bailli,* de Cerisay, under whom I have been an assessor for a great many years.

§ 2

This paragraph I will dedicate to *kinship,* a subject which interests me very much. Other subjects which I am also interested in are philology—several languages—fiction, viticulture, and the culinary arts.

I will start with myself, as being one of the most poorly situated persons in our city in regard to family relationships. I have no brothers and sisters and only one cousin, which is here considered as being abnormal, almost a perversity. My only cousin is the coach-builder Mathurin Thiboust. Mathurin has been somewhat of a rival as concerns the, in my opinion, beautiful Corisande Dolet and for her sake he has declared that he is a Protestant,—this, in my opinion, is going pretty far as far as one's passions are concerned. My descendants will probably have an easier time of it. Not to have a large family may sometimes be rather convenient, but it can't be helped that there are times when one feels like an outsider.

Louis Tranchant, our *procureur,* to take an example, is better off. He is a royal government official, a learned poet (although I don't think that his Latin and French verses are the most exquisite!), historian and prominent Catholic (my own faith is not among the strongest). He often says, "Do you remember what the Huguenots did to our city in the year 1562? How they plundered, how they destroyed and burned and desecrated our churches and killed the inhabitants?" He is a cousin of the physician René Lannoury, and also of the apothecary Golot, and is thus related to their families. Jehan Minet,—he sticks to the old spelling—one of the canons in the Sainte-Croix congregation, is his nephew, and thus Tranchant is related to the families Minet-Poussaut-Varot-Herseur (our city officer of the watch and chief of police), and they in turn have relatives everywhere—Herseur, for example, is related to Monsieur Mesmin de Silly who is a good friend of Armand du Plessis-Richelieu. And so on and on.

Or the family de Brone or the family Cerisay, or the family Calvet, who is related to the family Renébault, which in turn is related to the de Brone family and the family of the *bailli*. Here I might also mention that when Urbain Grainier came here in the year 1617 he had his entire family with him: his mother (who was the widow of a royal notary at Le Mans), two sisters, and three brothers. One of his brothers is my colleague with the title of *avocat* and *conseiller* in the office of the *bailli*, Monsieur de Cerisay; another brother, François, is an assistant pastor at the Church of Saint-Pierre, and a third, Jean, is a nonconformist pastor in this city.

I have thought of sometime investigating all the family relationships between the residents in our city. But so far I haven't had the time to do it. In the meantime I make notes. But even for me, even though I was born here and have lived here all my life with the exception of the years I attended school in Poitiers and Bordeaux, it is a tangled skein. I don't believe that anyone can keep track of such things unless they make use of some kind of system.

§ 3

Notes made sometime in 1618–19

The conflicts in our city have, of course, something to do with the conflicts and struggles in our country as a whole. Our gracious seventeen-year-old king, Louis XIII, has finally become *king*. Last year some very extraordinary events happened in Paris. The king took all power into his own hands. Concini, Marshal d'Ancre, who has governed our country (misgoverned, many would say) with his spendthrift wife, the queen dowager and queen mother Maria of Medici, during the minority of His Majesty, has disappeared from the stage of politics and from the stage of life. He was murdered, or let us put it this way: he was killed, it is claimed on the orders of the king. I have not yet made up my mind regarding this case—other than that I very naturally am completely on the side of His Majesty. But it cannot be doubted that Concini, this Italian who accompanied our most gracious dowager queen on her arrival in France as the bride of the late King Henry IV, was a scourge fully comparable to the plague and the pestilence. I will now quote a few excerpts from my private diary.

Aug. 15, 1617

"Omnia et provisa et parata et constituta sunt," Cicero says, and it is true to an astonishingly high degree. Everything seems to be foreseen, ordered, and preordained! Louis Tranchant, our royal *procureur,* has been in Paris, and he told me and his nephew, the canon Jehan Minet, about the the terrible scenes in April when the traitor Concini, Marshal d'Ancre, was done away with. He was shot and stabbed in the Louvre, and at night the corpse was carried at the king's command to the church of Saint-Germain-l'Auxerrois, where it was buried with the greatest secrecy. A priest wanted to read *De profundis* but was silenced. The following day, the people, who had every right to hate Concini for having impoverished the country, forced their way into the church, tore up the slabs, put the end of a bell-cord around the dead man's legs, and dragged him to Pont-Neuf. There the corpse, head down, was hoisted up on one of the poles that Concini himself had erected in order to hang his adversaries or impale the heads of those he had had decapitated. Tranchant related that they beat the body with heavy sticks, that is, they flogged the corpse, they put out its eyes, cut off its nose and ears ("and other parts of the body," Tranchant said; his daughters Phillippe and Renée were also listening). Thereupon the cadaver was cut in pieces, yes, Tranchant even claimed that they made fires and fried various pieces and tasted them! It is horrible. I got the impression that Tranchant was more than willing to talk about this, even with a certain

sensual pleasure that I didn't quite appreciate. Our new priest at Sainte-Croix, my old schoolmate from Bordeaux, Urb. Grainier, who was also present at Tranchant's, remarked—in my opinion insensitively and coldly—"that if one gambles for high stakes, one must take the risk not only of being killed but also flayed, dismembered, and fried afterward."—"Concini has gambled. The queen dowager has gambled. The king is gambling now as does his premier minister. Young Queen Anne has not begun her gambling yet, but she will pretty soon," he said. Tranchant, who is a very good friend of his, laughed and pointed to history. Of course he did, it is his hobby. Philippe, one of his daughters, seemed agitated. She is rather pretty, perhaps a little too bony for my taste. I understand she wants to become a nun. But it's no doubt the father who will decide that.

Later in the evening we spoke about the political consequences. For the queen dowager is not the regent any longer. She and one of her new favorites, the Bishop of Luçon, Armand du Plessis-Richelieu, will have to call retreat. The bishop is merely bishop at the present time and is staying near us. The queen dowager is away on a trip. The king is king and governs!

Dec. 1618

Today when I met Ismael Boulliau, who is both a priest and an astronomer, we got to talking about the most remarkable things that have occurred during the year that will soon be over. He mentioned something about constellations of the stars, and we immediately touched upon the most unpleasant thing that has happened in our city. It is most certainly the now nationally infamous episode when Urb. Grainier, our pastor at Saint-Pierre, started a row with our chief of police, René Herseur—or perhaps it was Herseur who first got into a row with him. I was present myself and saw most of what happened.

I don't keep track of ecclesiastical matters more than is necessary, but on one Sunday there was a solemn ceremony at which it was thought that the Catholic government officials (and at present most of our officials are Catholics; it is advantageous) ought to attend. The pastor of Saint-Pierre, the principal canon at Sainte-Croix, Urbain Grainier, was to lead his congregation and others in a procession up to our old castle chapel, Notre-Dame-du-Château. A pulpit had been put up outside the church; the intention was that he preach a sermon there. He thought, however, that he ought to preach inside the church. Our chief of police, René Herseur, opposed it. An incident ensued and U. G. uttered some sharp words. It is true that he didn't (as has been maintained) call Herseur a quarrelsome, loutish policeman, a stupid climber who always dreamed of honors and distinctions, or a fool, but the way he said it indicated that this was what he meant. Herseur waved his big fists in the air and let two of his assistants grab Urb. Grainier; but U. G., who is a powerfully built fellow, tore himself loose, pushed the assistants away, entered the church, and closed the door. For a time it had looked as if there would be a fist fight. Grainier is very arrogant and lacks self-restraint—one must admit that—but on this occasion he managed to control himself. He is tall, muscular, and broad-shouldered, and it would thus be hard to say how such a fight might end.

Now there is a rumor in town that U. G. has seduced or at least turned the head of one of Herseur's cousins, a girl who at present lives with H. It is said that H. wants to marry the girl himself, but she doesn't want to.

Later, at the end of December

Urb. Grainier had Herseur taken before the city court, and he received its support. It is noticeable how the city has been divided into two parties, for and against him. In the more distinguished families much is being whispered

88

about U. G.'s love affairs. Older citizens who have young wives look sour when his name is mentioned. Many younger and middle-aged ladies gather in the church, both at Saint-Pierre and Sainte-Croix, when he is preaching. They say that he is so eloquent, and that is true, of course.

A note from the beginning of 1619

An episode of the most unpleasant sort has occurred here. The priests often quarrel about who is the most distinguished. They constantly make difficulties as to their right to have the use of certain houses and halls, about their prebends and about anything possible that has to do with honors and money. A lake with muddy water, one might call it. In that water swim many kinds of monks, Carmelites, Capuchins, nonconforming priests, agents, and parasites—one never knows where one has them. But let's continue. I have been in bed a few days with a slight cold, and it is my housemaid, Séraphique Archer, and my cousin, the somewhat malicious Mathurin Thiboust, who have told me the story. The other day they had a church ceremony at Sainte-Croix with a procession. All the priests from the neighboring districts had come here. Everything would probably have come off well if we hadn't received a very high-ranking guest, the Bishop of Luçon, Armand du Plessis-Richelieu. He has been banished from politics now, since the regency of the queen dowager came to a sudden end with the fall of Concini, and he now gives his attention to his diocese. At the present time he is at his priorate at Coussay near here associating with a few persons from this city, even with such people who are not pronouncedly Catholic, it is said. He came here, then, and took part in the procession. There was a quarrel between him and Grainier about the order of precedence. U. G. stubbornly maintained that he had a right to the leading position since he is the leading prelate in our town. The bishop was so angry "that he turned gray and blue in the face, and the tuft of beard on his chin jumped up and down as if it was loose and they thought that the monseigneur was going to do something in the pants that he must have underneath his skirts," Séraphique says in her artless way. "He looked as if he had swallowed a Huguenot child," says my cousin Mathurin. But the bishop controlled himself and *gave way!*

The whole thing must have been utterly unpleasant. And imprudently done by Urb. G. It was not with the usual type of prebend-seeker that he was quarreling. For he *is* a bishop!

Unfortunately, I didn't have the opportunity to see the bishop. He is a strange man, an important man, even though he is in disfavor now. But I heard how they shouted and made a lot of noise out in the square.

§ 4

Note from 1619

Our country is torn apart by strife, and one can say the same thing about our city. That is the reason we take such good care of anything that can make us happy, good news and good rumors that make the wine taste better.

At times the rumors from the royal court reach us quickly, at other times they take long to get here. Now I first want to put this down:

During the night between Friday the 25th of January and Saturday the 26th, H. M. the King—according to information obtained from the most reliable sources—slept with H. M. the Queen!

It is supposed to have occurred upon the express request of the papal nuncio and Monsieur de Luyne: they want to ensure the succession to the throne. We didn't hear about it in our town until about the 3rd of February. They say that the king's affection for Queen Anne has not lessened since then, but any result of any real significance has not ensued. (Miscarriage, it is maintained?)

Note from 1620

The Bishop of Luçon is once again in Paris.

I will try to give a brief resumé of what has happened here.

Séraphique A. at the beginning of the year gave birth to a child—a boy—who, however, died almost immediately.

A troublesome priest, the canon Le Mousnier, began about a month ago a quarrel with the pastor of St.-Pierre, Urb. G., and it came to blows. The row is supposed to have been due to a quarrel Le Mousnier had had in the Church of Ste-Croix with the nice old canon Maurat. Urb. Grainier sided with Maurat and made fun in a sharp and caustic manner, as is his wont, of Le Mousnier—even from the pulpit. There was a scuffle, U. G. gave Le Mousnier a good whipping. U. G. is gifted in many ways but doesn't seem to abide by Seneca's rule: "To be the master of oneself leads to supreme power." And Cicero's words about virtue needing plenty of practice, is no doubt still valid.

I will point out something else in this connection, namely, that Le Mousnier has a nephew, René Bernier, who is pastor for the Boutiers congregation in our immediate neighborhood. B. is also of a disputatious nature and tried on one occasion to beat up Urb. G. but he was the one who was given a drubbing. They are supposed to have fought in the sacristy of the Church of Saint-Pierre.

An additional item that ought to appear in my protocol: On a dark night in May or June this year (1620), Bernier was assaulted by unknown persons while on his way from here to Boutiers and was so badly battered that he only with great difficulty could make it back to his dwelling. They have not been able to catch the perpetrators. Bernier now asserts that it was Urb. G. who arranged the attack. What can one believe? Herseur, our chief of police (who is

91

related to both Le Mousnier and Bernier), is trying to incarcerate U.G. But in this he has not succeeded.

Note of June 6, 1620

Today, when I was out at my little country place in order to look at the grapevines and the vegetables, Michel, the local peasant who looks after the place for me, maintained that the pastor of Saint-Pierre, "the woman chaser" he called him, that is, Urb. G., is too friendly in his relations with the Huguenots. I know what is behind it: he helps our governor, Monsieur d'Armagnac, with certain matters and speaks on his behalf with the well-known reformed gentlemen Le Blanc and Goujon. But in such a friendly way that he seems to sympathize with the Huguenots—that is an exaggeration! Michel got the information from someone who had revealed that the canon Jehan Minet and Le Mousnier had said it. I am only noting it here because I have a fondness for the odd and curious.

§ 5

(Worked out in its present form in 1625)

I am careless. I often say to myself that I must take myself in hand and be more thorough and serious when it comes to my protocol. It is being written with the future in mind, and I am thinking of some day leaving parts of it to our procurator, Louis Tranchant, let us say in about ten years. He is—as I perhaps already have mentioned?—our historian.

Here is a comprehensive report from the years 1623–25 with excerpts from my diary:

The wine harvests have not been *especially* good as far as I am concerned. Is it possible that there is something in the air that makes the wine—this sensitive instrument of joy and pleasure!—sad or nervous? Our learned astronomer Ismael Bouilliau, who is canon at Ste-Croix, has spoken about certain spots on certain planets and about irregularities connected with Saturn, but perhaps he was just joking; he knows how ignorant I am when it comes to astronomy.

Last year, in 1624, it was decided to tear down certain fortifications here in Poitou and Vienne, that is, those that have been most frequently used by the Huguenots. Our city walls and our beautiful towers were to be included in the plans for the demolition.

Our good king is still at war rushing from one place to another, and his exalted mother and his exalted half-brothers are supposed to make everything somewhat difficult for him.

To be noted here is the fact that the past bishop of Luçon, Armand du Plessis-Richelieu, on September 5, 1622, was made a cardinal by the Holy Father. To my simple mind it was an extraordinarily well founded appointment, even though I don't agree with His Eminence in everything. It is claimed, to be sure, that the Protestants at the beginning of the last decade had about 150 fortified towns in our country, and for that reason one can, as a loyal subject, understand certain views that Cardinal R. holds—but to raze city walls and towers (as for instance, those of our city) is after all not the same as building up a country. Or is it? Yes, I will, as I said before, not express any opinion.

There are rumors to the effect that the Cardinal's power is growing but that he himself is being influenced by the Capuchin priest Joseph, whose real name is François Leclerc du Tremblay. Whether this influence is good or bad I cannot say. Of course, I hope it is for the good.

The Protestants have made gains. The Peace of Montpellier of October 1622, reaffirms the Edict of Nantes and gives them control of Montauban and La Rochelle. It is said that His Majesty is dreaming of building himself a nice little hunting lodge at Versailles outside Paris. It is also said that the Cardinal has plans of converting his ancestral castle, Richelieu, into an entire city! It would in that case become our neighboring city. In any case, they have sent agents to our town to hire workers for a future big building project. It is said that Jean Rogier, who is the chief of police for the bailiff at Tours, this year—1625—has carried on negotiations with the mason Segeuneau and the contractor Héreault on behalf of the Cardinal. The stones that will be left when our walls and towers are razed, will be put to good use. My position in this matter I will keep to myself.

*

Diary entry, July 1621

Very warm weather. Good for the wine. Have been out there, and Michel has high hopes. (Séraphique A. gave birth three days ago to a girl. The child died right after birth, perhaps on account of the heat. I feel a bit melancholy.)

*

Diary entry, March 30, 1623

Scévole de Sainte-Marthe died yesterday afternoon. He had been sickly for a long time, but in spite of his high age they were still hoping. . . . He had the pastor of Saint-Pierre come to see him. When Urb. G. came, it looked as if Ste-M. was unconscious. But when U. G. sat down at his bedside and took his hand and bent down and mumbled some of Ste-M.'s most beautiful religious poems in his ear, the dying man opened his eyes, recognized his young friend and spiritual guide, and was able to receive extreme unction and holy communion. He entered into eternal sleep a few hours later.

We all feel deep sorrow. Quite rightly we called Scévole de Ste-M. "The Father of Our City" and "The Father of Our Home District." He saved our city from ruin; that we have not forgotten.

94

A few days later (April 7 or 8)

Scévole de Sainte-Marthe has been buried in the Church of Saint-Pierre. All the prominent men in our city and even many from other places were present. Urb. G. officiated. He was so deeply moved that he could hardly speak.

On the 5th—last Wednesday—Doctor Théophraste Renaudot, that noteworthy and strange man, gave a speech in memory of Ste-M. at the City Hall. It was a fine speech, very fine.

Sept. 11, 1623

I am still bewildered from feeling so deeply moved and entranced! I have just come back from the Church of Saint-Pierre where Urb. Grainier held his great memorial speech over Scév. de Ste-Marthe. All the prominent men in the city and many from other places were there. I wore my new suit for the first time. Gray jacket, short, light brown mantle (a modern one, which may be thrown over the shoulder if one wishes), brown trousers, embroidered with our family crest, very tastefully, I think. I also wore my sword, but it felt unfamiliar, I wear it so seldom.

I have never experienced anything like that memorial speech! An eloquence beyond compare! A voice like music! A delivery worthy of the most outstanding Roman and Greek orators! No, I said to myself, it is not true that *murus defensoribus nudatus est,* as J. Caesar wrote on one occasion, our walls do not lack for defenders! The Latin, the French spirit lives among us even though we have lost our Scaevola!

U. G. touched upon Sc. de Ste-M.'s role as the savior of our city. "Gentlemen," he exclaimed, "when you hear the story of this noble deed, don't you then feel yourselves called upon to build in your souls a living temple in memory of Him who acting as the guardian angel of his country and his home district, saved us from the heavy blow that was about to come down on our city? O you, people of our city, every time you see the ivy climb your old walls you ought to remember that it is He, Scévole de Sainte-Marthe, who preserved and saved these walls for you!"

We all cried. In conclusion, U. Gr. recited a poem which his good friend, our royal procurator, Louis Tranchant, has written in memory of Sc. de Ste-M. and there it says:

"Your beautiful name hovers among us . . ."

(I have promised myself to get hold of a copy.)

Yes, we all cried. I still have tears in my eyes when I write this.

Now I really hope that the idle talk and the gossip regarding U.G.'s love affairs will stop. After this almost superhuman performance!

Of course, Tranchant was there with his entire family, that is to say, his son and his two daughters, and with (I believe) *all* his relatives, and there are many of them. There was also our highest civil servant, our *bailli* de Cerisay, and his group of officials (to which I belong). Cerisay, just like the Tranchant family, had the best seats. I sat on a stool next to the younger of the Calvet brothers and right behind Cerisay. Louis Tranchant's oldest daughter, Philippe, looked completely spellbound, yes even bewitched, during U. G.'s speech. Next to her sat Demoiselle Madeleine de Brone. They say she wishes to embrace the religious life. She also seemed greatly moved. She is exceptionally beautiful, with brown hair and round and pretty cheeks.

I must say that it was really a very succesful, yes, a great day!

I am almost completely exhausted from all these impressions, but I am going to take a little walk down to "The Hen." I must talk to my friends about all this!

Nor have they seen my new suit.

In one passage, Cicero has this to say: "It may be that all possible dangers threaten me—but I am going forward to meet them!" And so say I!

96

6

Jeanne

SHE COULD REMEMBER parts of her life, in the same way that one remembers one's life: through a veil of desires, a haze of displeasure, light clouds of hope and heavy cloud banks of fear of what will come after the day that is now.

If she wanted to, she could say, "My parents sent me away. They loved me dearly but they sent me away. Later on I sent myself away, far away from them!"

If we want to, we may say, "How can we at this early stage in the history of mankind—we who have not progressed further than to the atom bomb—get an overview of cause and effect in such delicate interplay and such sensitive material as nerve fibers and souls?"

*

They sent me to an aunt who was prioress in the convent at Saintes when I was ten years old. She wrote to my parents that I was weak, frail, and perhaps wicked, in any event, fickle and strange. I was there five years but was not very happy. My posture was poor, there was something wrong with my back, but now my posture has improved through exercise, and the defect does not show when I am sitting down. My face is beautiful, that is what everyone says.

She might have asked herself (with a manual on the human soul, pressed to her very sensitive nipples): Why wasn't I happy? Was it because I was wicked and made life "unendurable for others"—so say the most callous and this is the phrase of the most persevering—or did I become "wicked" and "unendurable" because I was not happy?—or wasn't I wicked and unendurable? Was it only the others who thought so or wanted to think so because they were jealous of my family and my lineage (among others, I am related to M. de Laubardemont) and because of my many talents or because they themselves were wicked and unendurable?—for that they were in actual fact! They claimed that I had "strange inclinations." I!? The most healthy, with the most healthy yearnings! And who determines what is strange and what is not? They said I was "disorderly," yes, even "wild." What does that mean? That my heart didn't beat as it should have, that I slept poorly and was worried by dreams? Was I unhappy there because of this, or was this caused by my unhappiness?

She became an Ursuline Sister. I want to instruct and teach others about holy life, she could say then. She came to the convent in Poitiers. I wanted to be one of the 11,000 or 111,000 women who call themselves the successors of the greatly blessed Angela Merici. That I have exceptional talents for this has been testified to by many people!

If she could call to us on this side of so many manuals on the life and death of the soul, she might say: During my extremely short novitiate there in Poitiers I was almost a saint. I took care of the most stinking and purulent boils, washed the most disgusting sores. I asked to tend sisters who were scrofulous, who had eczema and were scabby, sisters whose bodies were crawling with vermin and maggots, and I treated them with salves that I myself had fabricated and mixed—this can be substantiated. But was it because I loved healthy, clean, cured, and happy human beings and unhappy ones because they were unhappy—or was it rather that I thrived on their misfortune and liked to see their scabs, their boils, the sores and the vermin, that I enjoyed seeing their suffering and that this was the reason that I wanted to be as close as possible to those who suffered? What is cause, and what is effect? While I was in Poitiers I lost two brothers and four of my own sisters, and that was a long and wide swath Death made with his scythe. My parents wanted me to return to them, but I knew my calling. I took my vows on the eighth of September, 1623.

And what did my convent sisters say about me when I made such great progress with the help of the Madonna and St. Joseph? I can see Sister Claire's jealousy and her schemes, I see Sister Anne's animosity; both of them were older and not so beautiful, talented, and intelligent as I was. What they whispered behind my back is not difficult to fathom.

I cannot see myself from the outside, but can you who have lived after me and live today, see me clearly, see me from the inside? They said that I was capricious and vain and the most unendurable of all and that they certainly would have thrown me out had not my family been so rich and distinguished and with such good connections and had not the convent been so poor. I was helped by the saints in heaven and by the good sense that God in His mercy has given me. When the eight sisters in 1626 were selected to found the new convent here in this damned city, where passions and plagues have since run amok, I because of my schemes (listen well, I say it openly!) became one of them. I have voluntarily admitted this scheming in the long and truthful confession about all my strange experiences and revelations that I wrote for the Mother Superior in Bordeaux. In it I tell about the sins that I have committed—and compared to those of many others, they were, in truth, neither many nor great!—and about all the miracles that I performed when with the help of Father Barrot and Father Minet I was rid of most of the demons that had been conjured up and led by *An evil man,* nor do I forget to mention there the help His Eminence the Cardinal gave me and the help I received from the famous and perspicacious exorcists, Father Trainasse and Father Lacet, who was later on to be so sorely tried. In this document everything is made clear and accounted for and everything is as close to the truth, divine as well as mundane (I dare say!), as a human being can get.

You may say: We know much more now about such things. I can reply that I experienced all this but it cannot be told in full.

*

She arrived in this city with the Ursuline Sisters. They rented an old, decrepit house in Rue Pasquin, below the Church of Sainte-Croix, for a hundred and fifty livres. It was said there were evil spirits in it. The house was owned by a Monsieur Poussaut—du Frène—and a brother of his, an old and not especially attractive canon, became our first father confessor. We carried out our labor of love but were so poor—she would say a long time afterward—that we had to beg. This was long before the Cardinal helped us obtain the other, the fine house, and long before we were suffused with the enduring and—I hope—immortal glory that we were to attain. We were short of money and had no furniture, and when merciful and faithful souls in this old nest of heretics gave us beds, our Mother Superior, the prioress of the convent at Poitiers, decided that we should return them and lie on straw on the floor. (Later, under my strong leadership, things were different!) We were to receive novices and educate distinguished young girls for the life that was in store for them; but no one came. We worked hard for our sustenance, and only through our diligence, obedience, and faith and through my predecessor, the deputy prioress Madame de Fève, the good Sister Gabriele, did we succeed in surmounting our difficulties. I am convinced that we already from the beginning were involved in a struggle against exceptionally aggressive demons.

From the year 1626 on she was a completely changed

100

woman. In this city she instantly became humble and friendly toward everyone, or practically everyone—and I helped our deputy mother, Sister Gabriele; to her I became a true support, a rock, as I would later to many become the almost worshiped and almost saintly Jeanne; and she loved me more than she did any of the others. My face was, as I may already have mentioned, beautiful, the small defect regarding my back and my posture (which perhaps was the work of demons) could not be noticed when I spoke, and people were so captivated by my face and my voice that they forgot about the small defects. I have openly admitted to our Mother Superior in Bordeaux and in the document I have put together to help others that I was not entirely without cunning, nor above ingratiation and truckling toadyism, but it all was, as most people surely know, for a good purpose: to get control into my own hands, a role for which I, by the grace of God, was better suited than most. When Sister Gabriele after a year's work among us here was called back to Poitiers to our Mother there, I was selected, although only twenty-five years old, to become the leader and actual prioress in her place. My humbleness and kindness and my family's high breeding made me the chosen one. I was long in doubt until all my spiritual sisters would ask, even beg me to become their leader. They thought that I was too unassuming and unpretentious even though I was the only one of us who could fill the high and blessed position. I became their spiritual mother the same year that my brother Louis fell on the isle of Ré, where the Cardinal fought against the heretics and the English. My brother died in the struggle against the wonderful Buckingham, who perhaps seduced, or tried to seduce, our queen—the cruel, handsome and profligate Buckingham, whom we all had great trouble to banish from our dreams.

*

The convent and the school progressed under her lead-

101

ership, and when she had assumed all authority she was once again transformed into a scheming, wicked, domineering, haughty, and insufferable human being. The game had been won and the victory assured, she thought. She settled down in the parlor, the conversation room, and received well-to-do pupils, internees, and externees and their mothers and aunts, who came to ask advice and to give advice. There she could feel that breath of the life of the city, the region, and the entire country that came with them, and there she could without any inhibitions be the curious, the inquisitive, and the talkative gossip. Sometimes she would look out through the lattice-window in the gate and see people passing by.

She asked much about the men and the life of men. At times she would ask about the infamous pastor of Saint-Pierre.

She had heard of him: that he was hard and uncompromising toward his enemies and that the women ran after him and that he didn't reject them. She knew that he came from the area around Le Mans and that he had studied with the Jesuits at Bordeaux; they had helped him on account of his charm and his great talents and had obtained for him the pastorate at Saint-Pierre and the prebend at Sainte-Croix.

She had seen him. Later she was to deny it, but she had seen:

His face, his back, his walk, his free and easy movements. He could practically run when he was in a hurry, he could suddenly stop and make quick, impetuous movements with his hands when he met some of his many friends and acquaintances in the street; and she had seen how he could *stride* past his enemies without greeting them; how he could march along like a soldier.

She had heard: that almost the entire clergy in the city were his envious foes, and that he was an excellent preacher and orator. She had heard that he could even write pamphlets and that he was a fine stylist and that his letters were moving if one let oneself be bewitched by his style. She had heard that Governor Monsieur d'Armagnac, his good friend, readily listened to his advice. She had heard that he was vain and that he always stood on his rank and his dignity, that he had seen to it that a priest who had insulted him was reprimanded by the ecclesiastical court at Poitiers in spite of the fact that Bishop Roche-Pozay, an old friend of the Cardinal, was one of his enemies. She had heard that he had won another case against the canons at Sainte-Croix about the right to a house and that Jehan Minet, above all, had been the loser; and she had heard of his row with one of Minet's close relatives, the rich and powerful Monsieur Varot, who was the chairman of the elected council of the burghers.

She had seen (even though she was to deny it): the light that suffused his face one spring morning as he stopped outside the convent gate on Rue Pasquin to look at some small birds hopping about among the rosebuds on top of the wall, while the grayish-black convent cat walked stealthily after the birds almost dragging its belly across the thorns and lifting its paws high in the air. She had seen, or thought she had seen, that his face was neither good nor evil but dark and very much alive and expressive.

She had heard: that he had entered into a very hostile relationship vis-à-vis the royal procurator, Louis Tranchant, who was a relative of Minet's. She had heard rumors, whisperings, and insinuations to the effect that Tranchant's oldest daughter, Philippe, had disgraced the family by running after him and that she had become sick from love and had probably given birth to a child. Through gossip she had learned that the chief of police Herseur as well as the royal advocate, Milouin,—both of them relatives of Tranchant's—had gotten the worst of it in other affairs of the heart.

She had seen—even though it was to be denied—how he walked past with his head held high and how the women turned on the street and looked after him.

She heard herself say to someone she was talking to: I have never seen the person in question, he doesn't interest me.

She had heard: that he had been accused before the ecclesiastical court at Poitiers of never reading his breviary (how could he when he held his head so high?) and of leading a debauched life. She had heard that he succeeded in seducing many women, even inside his churches. She knew that the Bishop of Poitiers, Monsignor Roche-Pozay (of whom someone had written to the queen dowager, Maria de Medici, that he was more wicked than the Devil himself), had given orders to have him incarcerated in the episcopal prison in Poitiers, and there he had sat for two months while morally outraged men seized his prebend and his assets and divided the loot between them; they considered him doomed in perpetuity. But since no one could or would give the names of the women that he was supposed to have seduced, it all came to nothing but hatred. There was no proof. Still, he was sentenced to fasting on bread and water every Friday for three months and was forbidden to perform his clerical functions in the bishopric of Poitiers for five years and in his own prebendary city forever.

She had heard, repeatedly, that Governor Jean d'Armagnac, who continued to be his friend, tried to protect him and that both of them had friendly relations with the Huguenots.

She had seen him in the street (though this was to be denied) right after his return from Poitiers: he was thinner from the hard life he had suffered in prison, but he was just as erect as before and looked everyone straight and searchingly in the eye. The women of the city turned to look at him in the street (she had heard), and when they learned that he was walking by, the girls boarding at the convent would huddle together in the cell openings, even try to climb up and get a good look at him across the top of the wall (she had seen). They always learned when he would come by, she didn't know how. The girls maintained that they wanted to see what kind of weather the day would bring. Older sisters, like Sister Claire, said the same thing, and the almost completely crazy Sister Anne mumbled or shouted: Beautiful weather!

She had heard, she knew, that he appealed the verdict to Archbishop Sourdis in Bordeaux and that his confusing case had at the same time been referred to the high court in Paris, where it was transferred to the court at Poitiers— and before that court several witnesses admitted that they had been enticed and bribed by the enemies of the accused to bear false witness. When the court had had its say, Archbishop Sourdis gave his verdict: complete absolution. And she had heard that Governor d'Armagnac had then advised him not to create any more rows in this matter and not to seek revenge, and she had heard that the Archbishop of Bordeaux had advised the rehabilitated priest to leave town; but she had heard people say that his answer was no.

She had heard it told that he had returned like a conqueror and had made his grand entry through the Chinon Gate and that many were there to meet him with shouts of joy. She had heard that he was smiling and nodding to all sides like a royal personage and that he held his head very high looking like a young man who has won a competition in fencing or in horsemanship. In one hand he was carrying—so she had heard—a twig of laurel.

And right in the middle of all this listening, seeing, and whispering, in the jumble of dates and events that had been thrown helter-skelter, she had perceived, there had been definite rumors to the effect that he had been seen on his way to Madeleine de Brone's dwelling in Assessor Drouin's house on the Square of Sainte-Croix. She imagined it so clearly that she *almost* saw it: how he quickly crossed the square, tall, broad-shouldered, and narrow across the hips, like a Spanish or an Italian nobleman.

Yes, she thought she saw him one day right after their father confessor, the canon Poussaut, had died, and she thought this came to her mind: such an intelligent, powerfully built, and active priest would be very suitable as father confessor for us. He is young, he will be with us a long time.

She had heard: that he had said that his reputation was now so bad that he feared he would be much too popular among the sisters and the girls. She had heard that Madeleine de Brone didn't want him to come to them.

Did she have someone ask him?

This has not been established. Minet, the Lame One, who hated and pursued demons, was called.

*

When she took a close look at her troubles (when she really tried to scrutinize them) in daylight, they looked quite small. At night they imbued her with fear. Such is my life, she thought. Year after year passes by—in God's name!—and I am wilting away. I have taken upon myself a big task, one that makes one wilt.

Marie Aubin climbed around on the roof, and it was certainly not in her dreams. She and a few other girls got up through an attic window. During the interrogation, Marie maintained that they had only wanted to admire the view, to see how everything looked at night and in the moonlight. She sat on the roof uttering something that she thought was the cry of an owl. She said she had done it only to hear what it sounded like.

*

Early one day Jehan Minet arrived. He resembled a little old woman who is slowly getting fatter, as he sat there in the armchair with his soft, round—yes, round—hands

106

folded. His thumbs made circular motions. She recalled the "thumb game": that there was something secretive about it, something alluring which was improper without being forbidden. His feet were pulled in under his chair. His lips were pale and his full mouth was slack, but the muscles around it formed hard knots. There was a sudden gleam in his brown eyes, she thought, and they had a yellow shimmer to them.

"Everyone here seems agitated," he said. "There's something going on here."

"Yes," she answered.

"Something at night?"

She turned toward the window. Stretching her neck, she could see wet slate roofs gleaming in the daylight.

"You have been to Chinon, Father Minet?"

"I was over there," he said. "It was just as bad there."

She could feel the stiffness in her neck (the kind that Sister Anne was also complaining about) as she suddenly, with great difficulty, turned her face toward him.

"And you have spoken with Father Barrot?"

"We talked a bit about it," he said. "It is possible that he will come here."

She turned her face toward the window again. She knew that she should have had just a small glass of absinthe before he came. She could walk up to her cell and have one now if she wanted to.

"We don't have any—any demons here!" she said. "The girls have their dreams—everyone does. All girls do, I would say."

She noticed how his twiddling thumbs changed direction. Now they were circling each other from below and up toward his stomach.

"That remains to be seen," he said. "They are here in town, anyway. Do you also have dreams, Sister Jeanne?"

"Why do you ask me that?"

She turned around compulsively feeling the resistance in the sinews in her neck. Father Minet sat there as before, but he lowered his eyes and pulled his feet still further underneath the chair.

"You said that everyone has dreams," he said innocently.

"What do you dream about yourself, Father Minet?"

His thumbs came to a halt, he moved his feet forward, and lifted his face toward her. His features were slack and expectant. The light-brown beard on this middle-aged man's chin was only down, immature as if belonging to a very young man. His body may be dead and yet full of desires, she thought with a peculiar, sharp phrase which came to her from somewhere. His eyes glistened yellow, a signal. His thumbs hesitated and then began twiddling in the other direction, from above and in toward his chest.

"I dream mostly about flowers," he said.

"I too dream often about flowers," she said able to converse. They talked about flowers. She thought she could mention roses, red ones and white ones; and she thought that her voice sounded genuinely indifferent.

He said, "But are your dreams of roses so vivid that the thorns stay in your hands and lie there when you wake up?"

She said, "I—I dream mostly about lilies when I dream of flowers."

Once again he sent a yellow glance her way. His thumbs stopped.

"Stick to the roses," he said stiffly.

A pause, and his thumbs began twiddling.

"The Devil certainly makes use of lilies, too, Sister Jeanne. Of everything. But stick to the roses. Roses with thorns that stay in your hands."

"I am trying to understand what you mean, Father Minet," she said.

"The Devil is always trying," he said. "In all kinds of dreams."

He spread his arms, placed the palms of his hands

against the armrests, hoisted himself up, and limped toward the door. Before reaching it, he turned around and glanced intently at the edging of her cap. The yellow in his glance was gone, his eyes were shiny and brown. The corners of his mouth were down and loose, his lower lip was pouting. He was standing up straight with his stomach bulging: a round ball investing him with authority. This is how the head of a pedagogical institution stands before the youngest and most insecure of his women teachers.

"How is your Latin these days, Sister Jeanne?"

She thought she ought to stand up. First she placed her fingertips against each other, then her fingers bent and found their way to the rosary.

"I have studied some," she said. "But I am not sure."

"Can you carry on a conversation in Latin? I mean, reply to questions?"

"I am not sure," she said.

He inclined his head, squinted at the floor, and seemed not to be listening, just letting her words pass by.

"Read more," he said. "Practice. I'll be glad to help you with questions. You might as well study a little Greek and Hebrew too."

"I have so little time for studying, Father Minet," she replied humbly.

Suddenly he looked her straight in the eye for the first time during their conversation, actually—she recalled later—for the very first time during their acquaintance.

"At *night* there is always time, Sister Jeanne."

His eyes were once again all yellow. They clung, they demanded. But she perceived the anxious and insecure, the benevolent, father-confessor-like smile around his soft lips. But the eyes clung. It was as if he touched her with his hand, fumbled at her, trying to get his hand under her skirts to touch her skin, the most sensitive and best hidden part of her. She shuddered and lowered her eyes. The door was opened and closed, and he was gone. She was left

109

by the table in the conversation room listening to his uneven steps in the corridor. The walls whispered around him.

Sister Jeanne went up to her cell and took out the bottle of absinthe behind her bed. In a short while the stiffness in her neck disappeared, and her hands were calm and controlled.

*

After the noon service she asked Sister Claire to come to the conversation room.

"I would very much like to know about your dreams," she said. "What do you dream about? For example?"

"Mostly about flowers and kittens. But worse things also."

"What for instance?"

"Demons."

"Ask some of the girls to come and see me, Sister Claire."

They arrived in a bunch, six of them, and Sister Claire was with them.

"Now you can tell me," said the prioress.

"We have told everything to Father Minet," Sister Claire said rather sourly. "We have opened ourselves to him."

All of a sudden Sister Jeanne felt something new toward this middle-aged woman, who smelled of pride and long-suppressed lust: the same feeling she had had about the half-crazy Sister Anne, and it was hatred perhaps. She thought the other one was so ugly, that her eyes were piercing, that the wart on her chin was growing, that her breath was evil-smelling.

"You, Sister Claire!"

"For my part," Sister Claire said holding her folded hands up to her breast, "for my part, I can say that my dreams are generally not very bad. I am so fond of cats, and small kittens come to me at night. In my dreams, you understand. I play with them."

"But it has been worse?" said the prioress and felt a light stiffness in her neck.

"One night it was as if some *person* entered my cell. I had the distinct feeling that it was a demon. I have told Father Minet everything. He too had the same distinct feeling."

"A demon?"

Sister Claire nodded with a certain eagerness which was not quite dignified.

Both the Barbeziers girls had had a similar feeling and seemed stimulated by it.

"That it should happen to *us!*" said Louise, the oldest and more fluent speaker.

"What, Louise?"

"That one can't sleep in peace because of demons! Think of it; happen to *us!*"

"Us? What do you mean by that?"

"She means that it would be more fitting if it happened to Séraphique, who sleeps in the kitchen and cries out at night," Sister Claire said protectively.

"Yes, something like that," Louise Barbeziers said.

The prioress dropped the subject. She could not tell them that this was all loose talk, and besides she was not certain that it was only loose talk. Demons might be able to enter here. The girls were not protected. Except perhaps Marie Aubin.

"You have been climbing about on the roof again, Marie?"

The girl's brown eyes laughed toward her.

"It was as if an invisible hand had dragged me up there, Mother," she said, with a lie which she didn't expect anyone to believe.

Sister Jeanne couldn't continue with her questioning. They were lined up in front of her feeling very hot in their heavy attire. She recalled how it felt to stand like that. And she was afraid to tear something loose inside them. If something is let loose in *one* of them (she thought after a few silent seconds), if something is let loose in Anne or in

111

Séraphique—or in someone else, then there might be an avalanche which no one can stop. If something comes loose in *me*—. And still there was a temptation to find out. Or: the fear of what one might find out was enticing.

"You shouldn't speak so much about it. Our reputation can be hurt."

Sister Claire sent out a new, strong wave of aversion.

"It's already all over town," she remarked.

Sister Jeanne rose and made two steps in her direction. She noticed the irony, the scorn in the other's glance: it was like Sister Anne's had been before, when they were struggling for power and authority.

"Who does the talking all over town!"

Sister Claire mustered all her dignity: "I have the impression that Father Minet is conducting certain investigations—Mother," (she said scornfully) looking the prioress quickly in the eye.

Sister Jeanne felt a stiffening in her neck. If she says another word, I will cry or hit her, she thought, wildly, sharply.

"Good. You may leave."

*

Sister Claire came to her a few days later and mentioned that Sister Anne had apparently been visited by devils and had probably been raped by them. They had not spared Sister Claire either. She was under the impression that they had touched her and had made attempts to penetrate her. Séraphique Archer, who had also been harassed, had possibly all portals wide open to the demons. Sister Claire's eyes had a furious glint in them—or were shining all entranced, it was difficult to say which—when she told about it to Sister Jeanne.

"You must ask for protection," said the prioress. "You must fight with prayer and mortification."

Sister Claire's smell filled the room.

"I have already asked for protection," she said. "I have spoken with Father Minet. This morning."

The Barbeziers girls came to her a little while later. The older one submitted a report which the younger one confirmed by nodding several times. At midnight the cell that they had been given recently for their sole use, had turned almost light. "I woke up first, the light was bothering my eyes," said the older one. The younger one shook her head and said in a low voice: "No, I did." They quarreled a bit about this. The older one talked so much that the words poured out between her big, somewhat protruding teeth, so much that they were standing to their knees in words, thought the prioress, and the younger one shook her head stubbornly pursing her little mouth—with somewhat protruding teeth. The prioress noticed what she had not seen before, that the lips of both girls were thick and creased and purple in color.—"Yes, perhaps we woke up about the same time," the older one said at last. "The light disappeared and we felt that *something* was in the cell. First cold, and then warm. We have a definite feeling that we were subjected to very intimate attempts by demons."

She felt her neck muscles stiffen. But she replied in a friendly and dignified manner: "You mustn't talk so much about it. I think it was a dream. Now you may leave."

Two days later, the slender, dark, peaceable, and soulful Escoubleau girl, who was related to the Archbishop of Bordeaux and of whom much was expected, came to her and said that she had felt so strange during the night. Perhaps it was a demon.

One night they again heard sounds in the attic. In the morning the prioress called in Marie Aubin and Mademoiselle Bonpierre, to whom she was related herself.

"I must warn you," she said. "You make the others worried." ("You make me worried," she almost said.)

"It was as if a strong, invisible hand had guided me out and up into the attic, Mother," said Marie Aubin and tried

113

to smile at the prioress; but Sister Jeanne gave her a frigid look.

The Bonpierre girl looked down, feeling ashamed; one of her feet made a circular motion underneath her skirt: the tip of her shoe was visible.

"Stand still," she said to her harshly. "Answer: you went up on the roof?"

"It was as if I was walking in my sleep, Mother," Marie Aubin said.

"What did you do up there?"

"We were sitting on the trap-door cover by the chimney just looking."

"And you were talking?"

They were silent.

The Bonpierre girl looked askance at Marie Aubin.

"I did the talking," said Marie Aubin. "But not very loudly, Mother."

"What did you talk about?"

They were silent. The Bonpierre girl looked askance at Marie Aubin.

"What did you talk about, Marie?"

Silence.

"Tell me, girl!"

"I was talking about the future," Marie Aubin said trying another smile; but the smile froze on her lips.

"You were talking about—?"

"About how it would be—to be married, Mother!" Marie Aubin said in a mixture of defiance and fear.

"You may leave," she told them. "Tonight your cell will be locked from the outside."

*

That night something was in the attic. And something was climbing on the walls. Something was sitting in her own window opening, waiting for her. She got up and whipped herself and the following day she began a fast for the next seventy-two hours.

114

Seven girls who were sleeping together in the dormitory came to her one afternoon and told her that they had probably been visited by demons during the night. Four of them claimed that they had been subjected to nasty overtures. She did not have the strength to reprimand them. "You must pray and fast," she said. "That is your best protection. Besides that, you should speak to Father Minet."

"We have already done that," one of them, Sister Agnes, replied. "He advised us to confide in you too, Mother."

"Now you may leave," she said.

*

Much later she would constantly think back to:

how good she had been, how wise and provident, how sharp-sighted when it came to ascertaining Satan's games with them all;

and she often thought how clever she had been in obtaining useful connections, how cunningly she had gone about things, and how little she had said during confession without seeming to keep silent or hide something;

and very often she would recall how sensitive and delicate and how deeply unhappy she was and how unjustly they had judged and treated her a great number of times during her childhood and youth;

and at times, following a period of fasting, she would be aware of the strength of the sacred powers within her, and then she understood that she was one of the few elect, one of those who perhaps one day will perform miracles, make springs well forth just by a glance, and make lame ones rise up at a mere word from her ever more sacred lips.

Much of what I have said ought to be written down, she would think then.

When the demons had entered her room, they mentioned their names. The most important one was her secret, and many weeks went by before the others were told this name which she later wrote down or had someone write down in her long confession to the Mother Superior at Bordeaux, in which she said that he

"wanted to have amorous dealings with me, that he incited me with intimate caresses and tried in every way to have me give him that which I in my conventual vows have consecrated to my heavenly bridegroom." I fasted and prayed when the demons had forced me to call out his name at night. I finally let Sister Claire (whom I love dearly) and good Sister Anne (whom I love very dearly) know the name of the one who was tormenting me and them and many others among us; and we discussed this at length and decided to confess everything openly to our greatly venerated and much beloved Jehan Minet. The others fasted and prayed like I did, and perhaps I did it most, and we lashed ourselves, and I did it most.

*

"I think things will turn out all right," said Father Minet following one of his many long conversations with Sister Jeanne.

Her fear, which had loosened its grip on her for a moment, returned. She thought of the absinthe that was waiting. She wanted to turn her face toward the window, but one sinew or other or some power restrained her. She thought: now I am going to scream again just like Sister Anne, Sister Claire, or Séraphique. No, I would not scream that coarsely, that piercingly and unpleasantly. My screams are surely much nicer.

She was forced to look at him. He should have been younger, she thought anxiously. He should not have been lame, he should not twiddle his thumbs. He should not have such a mouth, such pale, fleshy lips.

She smiled at him. My smile is very charming, she thought. But he should have been more masculine, lither, should have smelled differently. He should have smelled of man.

"I can't stand it much longer, Father Minet," she said.

She managed to turn her head. The crown of a weeping willow outside was swaying in the wind. Its long, supple branches were light green.

"I have fasted, I have prayed, I have lashed myself, but they come every night. They beat me. They scratch me with their claws, they prick me with thorns."

"You may continue with your fasting and praying," he said calmly. "Nothing is better right now. Also continue with your study of Latin. I can go over it with you every day, Sister Jeanne."

"I feel so tired," she said.

7

Daniel Drouin's Protocol (2)

§ 6

IT IS NOW many months ago that I last edited and put together my protocol. Now it is spring again and I frequently think of my grapevines. I married in 1625. I lead a tranquil family life.

Much gossip is being bandied about. The *big* piece of gossip, which I do not want to listen to, but which one can hardly escape hearing, mostly concerns Lord Buckingham, who arrived in Paris last year (1625) in order to fetch Her Majesty's sister, Madame Henriette, who has become the queen of England. Buckingham was to stay for eight days and had with him twenty-seven outfits for his own use in his baggage, so he must have counted on a lot of feasting; which there was. One of his suits is supposed to have cost eighty thousand pounds, it was made of white velvet and studded with diamonds. On such occasions one regrets not living in Paris! The prominent diplomat apparently waited on our gracious queen much too eagerly, they say, and therefore he had to leave our country in a great hurry.

What else has happened—? On June 29 this year (1626) His Majesty was in Saumur, quite close to us. He has constant troubles with his brother, Gaston of Orléans. It is claimed that there are all kinds of intrigues, but as a loyal subject I will not express any opinion about it. On August 18 H. Maj. was at La Haye where he met with His Eminence Cardinal Richelieu. On the same day in Nantes the traitor Chalais was sentenced for lèse majesty. He had taken part in conspiracies together with other (highly placed) persons, whose names are not mentioned aloud. Chalais was sentenced to torture and decapitation, but in his mercy the King spared him the torture: a beautiful trait on the part of His Majesty. Completely insane rumors have been spread about Her Majesty the Queen who is supposed to have been involved in the case having conspired against the King and *wished him death* so that she could later marry Gast. of Orléans! There is supposedly great tension between Gast. of O. and the Cardinal.

Many libelous pamphlets are being issued against His Eminence the Cardinal. They ought to be burned—I think—just as fast as one gets hold of them. But one cannot help taking a peek at them. One of those that I took a quick look at (it was called *The Queen's Female Shoe Dealer*— I don't know what the point is here) was exceedingly slanderous. But His Eminence punishes such things seemingly with the words of Suetonius in mind: "Let them hate, as long as they are afraid!" This may be a wise policy. I for my part do not have such an attitude toward events and men, but, as mentioned before, I don't want to get mixed into the higher politics, at least not in a protocol that is intended for a posterity that will judge us all. Several persons suspected of being the author of the above-mentioned pamphlet have already been severely, and I hope, justly punished.

*

What is happening in our city? There are many rumors, above all about the pastor of Saint-Pierre, Urbain Grainier. I will quote some of my diary entries.

*

119

Pages from the diary

March 1, 1626

I have a son! A big, splendid-looking fellow; he weighed almost eight pounds! Charlotte (my wife) is doing very well! Very well!

March 10

My splendid, big, and intelligent boy was baptized today in the Church of Sainte-Croix on the other side of the square by my friend, the pastor of Saint-Pierre, Urb. G. The sponsors were the head of my department, our *bailli*, Monsieur de Cerisay, who very kindly did not excuse himself, and the head of our salt depot, Monsieur Delagarde. I was so moved that I had tears in my eyes. We drank a few glasses of wine, of my *very* best white wine (1619) afterward in our house. Urb. G. was also there, his wit just sparkled. He *flayed* everyone he mentioned, he spared *no one!* Our city historian, our royal procurator Louis Tranchant, ought to have been there, but there is a sort of tension between him and U. G.

March 15

This afternoon I met Poussaut du Frène, who is related to half the city. He stopped, glowered at me, and said, "So, you are a heathen, Assessor Drouin!"—"How do you mean that, Monsieur du Frène?" I answered him in my usual dignified manner. "I have heard that you're not having your newborn boy baptized!" he said. "What do you mean by that, Monsieur Poussaut du Frène!?" I asked angrily but did not look very angry, since he is an important man in our town. He lifted his wine-red nose (there are people who just cannot drink wine in a *sensible* manner) and looked up to the sky as if he expected rain, and said, "Well, you're just letting the heretic and the heathen and the whoremaster Grainier splash a little water on your son, and that can hardly be called baptism, sir."

I didn't reply to this remark but just turned my back on him—although not too demonstratively; I am a peaceful man.

Actually, many rumors are circulating about Urb. G. Still, I do not regret that I had him baptize my first-born son (who is called Daniel after my father, grandfather, and me and Guillaume after Monsieur de Cerisay); it was both a beautiful and advantageous baptism. The fact that I asked U. G. to conduct the ceremony offends perhaps a number of persons. For it is claimed that U. G. has seduced Tranchant's oldest daughter, Philippe, who was supposed to become a nun! She is said to be pregnant! And they say that Urb. G.'s most enthusiastic penitent just now (he is becoming extremely fashionable, in spite of all the talk) is the little sweet and round fatherless Madeleine de Brone. She is related to the brothers Calvet—my colleagues—and to Monsieur de Cerisay.

April 1

Today I heard that Tranchant's daughter, Philippe, doesn't appear outside anymore. She is supposed to be rather big now.

Apparently it was Monsieur Poussaut du Frène who attacked Urb. Grainier one night in January and stabbed him so that he fell and kept lying in the street. They say P. du F. has claimed that U. G. tried to seduce his wife. The most ugly woman in town! She is, to be brutal about it (I am only quoting Michel who tends my vineyard and my friend Antoine, the master mason, who gets to be coarse of speech after a few beakers of wine) very "randy" but has never succeeded in tempting anyone but her own husband. That she did with her money, not with her charms, but he seems to be jealous in any case.

April 3

I was at "The Hen" last night to meet some friends and acquaintances and enjoy a little relaxation; for I have been working hard with certain reports. Once in a while I have a glass of absinthe; it cheers me up and makes me feel good, I have noticed. I sat there quite late, talking with the brother masons Antoine, the little clerk in the city administration, Dolet, master carpenter Petiot, my cousin Mathurin Thiboust, and others. On the way home I felt somewhat tired and walked slowly. My cousin Mathurin wanted to come with me as far as my door, but I said no. In the Square of Ste-Croix I collided with Dr. Fanton in the semidarkness. We both asked the other's pardon and immediately recognized each other's voice. He was just emerging from Louis Tranchant's door—and I thought that it was a peculiar hour for him to do so. We exchanged a few words about the wind and the weather. I really felt quite tired. He took my arm and accompanied me to the rear doorway of my house. It was very kind of him. Charlotte (my wife) was sleeping or made believe she was—the latter she does quite often, I have noticed.

When I entered the dining room and saw that she had put a midnight snack on the table for me, I felt so happy and lighthearted that I began to sing a song. I am afraid that it was a soldier's song that the late Mathieu Archer, our old servant, used to reel off when he was drunk, and I also fear that I sang it too loudly.

April 7

Louis Tranchant and I met at the city hall this morning. He looked tired and despondent. Urb. G. and he don't have anything to do with each other any longer.

Sometime in the middle of June

We are experiencing a heat wave. I have been out at my country place for a few days. The vineyard looks fine; it looks as if this year will be a good one too. My wife and our little Daniel and our maid are still out there. Alone in the city. Last night I heard at "The Hen" that Pierre Milouin, who is a royal government official and a public prosecutor, has threatened to imprison Urb. G. because he is supposed to have seduced the lovely Madeleine de Brone. Pierre M. has courted Mad. de Br. assiduously, is said to have proposed to her and been turned down, but is still hoping. Apothecary Golot, who is related to the Poussauts and to Tranchant, is supposed to have come out with a lot of slanderous nonsense about Mademoiselle de Brone.

July 3

Hurrah! Yes, I will say it once more: *Hurrah!* My wife told me yesterday morning—I have been out in the country to see my family—that she is pregnant again! The Drouin family will not suffer from loneliness in this city in twenty-five of fifty years!

Was at "The Hen" that evening and met my friends. We had a few glasses. The mason brothers Antoine are worried about the future, Dolet made cutting remarks, and Petiot was drunk (he drinks too much). Everyone could see nothing but destruction and ruin everywhere. I can't understand why certain people are so pessimistic.

Walked over to my cousin Mathurin's house. He and Corisande (his wife) now have three children. I told them that I was expecting our second. Mathurin then said that Corisande—she was so lovely as a young girl!—was expecting her fourth. We indulged in fancies a bit and said that if she had a girl this time, then we could arrange something very nice in eighteen or twenty years!

The wildest stories are circulating about Urb. G. Mathurin told me a few of them. U. G. seems to be facing many complications. But it does not show when one meets him. He assists our governor, Monsieur d'Armagnac, with certain kinds of advice, and when the gov. is away U. G. plays the role of some sort of substitute. This is more involved

123

than I can fathom. Together with others they are trying to save our *walls,* that is, to save as many as possible of the turrets and the fortifications from being torn down. For now the old Huguenot strongholds are to be torn down in our country!

Sept. 1

I must hasten to note: Philippe Tranchant, Louis T's oldest daughter—she who at one time wanted to become a nun!—has given birth to a child, it is claimed, even though she has not been engaged to anyone! . . . Of course, it has not been announced officially, it is only being *mentioned* all over town. But her friend and relative, the kind Marthe Le Pelletier, who is not exactly "backward" but is nevertheless "slow-witted" and "good-natured," has "declared" herself the mother of a newborn child *even though no one had any inkling that she was pregnant!* The child—I think it is a boy— is said to have been baptized in a hurry in the Church of Sainte-Croix at the behest of Tranchant! Jehan Minet officiated at the baptism. The father? No one . . .

Marthe Le P. has thus given birth to an illegitimate child. Poor Marthe! She is "confused" but rather nice.

My wife is now quite fat.

The hot weather continues. It may be good for the wine; we will harvest the grapes soon now.

Sept. 17

Last night I was down at "The Hen" and had a small glass of white w. and a small beaker of absinthe in order to unwind, since I have worked quite hard lately with reports of various kinds. Dolet, who is a Protestant—at least in private—told us in his disjointed manner that people whisper around town that Tranchant and his entire family and all the Poussauts and their relatives are now definitely on the side of those who want the walls torn down. Monsieur de Silly, the Cardinal's old friend, fans the flames. They now assert openly (according to Dolet) that Urb. G. has sold himself to the Huguenots, which I, who know him, just can't believe.

But our city is imperiled!

I am of the opinion, just like U. G., that there ought to be a limit to the razing. Our governor, Monsieur Jean d'Armagnac, who is seldom here unfortunately since he must follow the court, is a strong opponent of further razing of the walls. That is also the feeling of my superior, Monsieur de Cerisay, and of my honorable colleagues, the brothers Calvet, and many other prominent men in our city. To us it is not a question, as some people believe, of preserving a fortress for the Huguenots. But if all the walls and fortifications here are razed, our beloved city will be destroyed, defenseless against *everybody* and rather ugly-looking without its beloved turrets and merlons. From a purely esthetic viewpoint, then, the razing is indeed a crime.

Of course, I don't say this in public, that is quite unnecessary, but such is my opinion. Richelieu, the family castle of the Cardinal, is to be rebuilt, in the middle of a new and handsome town. We will no doubt have to supply a whole lot of building material. As a loyal subject I, of course, have nothing against that. I am only interested in my hometown's salvation and future development. I have to think of the future of my family!

At times the thought has occurred to me that I ought to let my son Daniel become a businessman, for example, a rug merchant in Paris. But being a government official is more genteel even though it may be more insecure at certain periods. I seem to have noticed that Daniel has a talent for the work of a government official. He is very determined, but also flexible, I seem to notice. A businessman, of course, can also make use of such qualities.

Nov. 15

Gossip and more gossip! The other night I was down at

"The Hen" in order to cheer myself up with a small beaker of absinthe—I have been working pretty hard lately with probate cases, etc.—and then they were talking about Urb. G-r. and Mad. de B. so that I had it up to here! I heard the most insane theories regarding the affair between apothecary Golot (who is related to Louis Tranchant and the Poussauts) and Demoiselle de Brone: a case of slander. Someone at "The Hen" maintained that apoth. Golot had been *directly bought* by—you'll get the shock of your life!— *the Cardinal!* What nonsense! His Em. the Card. Richelieu does not travel all around the country to buy apothecaries; he has more important things to do. These are the facts: Apoth. Golot has been worked into a state of excitement by Marquis de Chandenier, who for some reason or other hates Urb. Gr. Apoth. Golot has spread rumors about U. G.'s relations with Demoiselle de Brone. This lady has taken Golot to court and accused him of defamation of character. The case went even as far as the Parlement in Paris, where Golot lost "definitively" and was sentenced to pay a substantial fine. But Marquis de Chand. stood surety for him to the extent of ten thousand écus—Golot then took the case to the appellate court but once again lost "definitively." Mad. de Brone, who I think is a charming lady, has received complete satisfaction and ap. Golot is a completely ruined man. Golot, however, seems to be enjoying a good life as usual, and Demoiselle de Brone receives visits from Urb. G. Apoth. Golot has many relatives and powerful patrons, even though I don't believe that he plots intrigues with the Cardinal. But he tries to make life for Urb. G. and Mad. de Brone as unpleasant as possible.

Dec. 2

We didn't get much wine this year, but now that it is just about to turn clear I must confess that I am satisfied after all. I have a feeling that the quality of my white wine is quite good. Now it is raining. Charlotte—my wife—walks around heroically with her big stomach and says that she thinks it will be a boy.

Looked over my notes. Nothing very important has happened in our city, but there is of course some gossiping.

We have received an extra addition to our spiritual domain. Eight sisters from the Ursuline cloister at Poitiers have settled here. They are staying in the old spooky house of Poussaut du Frène in Rue Pasquin, where no one else wants to live. The house is full of rats and other vermin, it is drafty and cold. People have collected money for the sisters so that they can begin their labor of love among us. They are going to open a boarding school for girls of the better classes from the entire province and will also, of course, train novices. Apparently they will accept girls from our city also.

Dec. 5

Have been thinking a bit about the Urs. Sisters. They are facing a difficult winter, the little cuties. A couple of the ones I have seen, are undeniably quite pretty!

Dec. 8

My interest in history is ever present. Ran into Urb. G. this afternoon and asked him about the Ursuline Order. "It was founded by Angela Merici at Brescia in Lombardy about a hundred years ago," he said. "Angela Merici seems to have been a good woman; very early they called her *madre benedetta;* for she is supposed to have performed miracles." I asked U. G. what kind of miracles they were. He couldn't give a definite answer but had heard that Ang. M. stilled a storm while on her way to the Holy Land and that she had turned blind but had regained her sight through another miracle. "People think that she in time will achieve the status of a saint," he said. And right after that: "That is a risk that I don't run!"—I laughed and thanked him for the information and then we talked about

127

something else. We were standing in the portal of Ste-Croix. I thought he looked strained, harried even, though he was just as glib of tongue as usual. Whether his escapades are true—I mean as true as the gossip tries to make them—then he will really have something to answer for when the time comes. But I can't help it: I am fascinated by his charm!

I happened to revert to the same topic mentioning that a few Ursuline Sisters—whom I happened to have had a glimpse of—seemed to be very nice and sweet and would no doubt do much good in our city. "But of course one never knows," I said, "I am often skeptical about such things."—He laughed out loud and took me by the arm: "Really, are *you* a skeptic, Daniel? That is news to me!"— His tone hurt me a bit but I replied with a quote from Vergil which I think was very appropriate. "I am of a skeptical nature, deep down," I said, "and even if the Danaans arrive with gifts of all kinds I am a bit afraid of them!"—Once again he guffawed: "You are one of the few in this city who know the right kind of Latin, Daniel! Why don't you exclaim with Livy: that a prison, a new one, is being built in the middle of the city! *Carcer media urbe aedificatur!*"

We laughed. But my tongue is unfortunately a bit too loose at times and I said, "Many others here also know their Latin! For example, Louis Tranchant!"—Then his face darkened, his laughter disappeared as if a gray piece of cloth had been placed over it. "You are right, Tranchant knows his lesson well," he said. I felt embarrassed, but he avoided a disquieting pause by saying directly and openly: "If they tear down everything they want to tear down in this city, how will you react, Daniel?" I spoke to him quite frankly, since we were alone: "Dear Urbain," I said, (I always call him by his first name when we are alone), "I think that the city would be strangled."— "That's right," he replied, "everyone ought to feel that way."

128

When I crossed the square in the direction of my own door, he called me back. "I just remembered something about Angela Merici," he said. "On one occasion she was lifted up into the air by invisible forces. It happened in front of the high altar in a church, in Cremona, I think it was. She was suspended for several minutes."

Since we were alone I could permit myself a bit of a laugh. He stroked his beautiful Vandyke beard and smiled his most dazzling smile. I don't know to what extent he was just having sport with me. It was perhaps an improper way for a priest to have fun. "Then," he said (in a low voice, for someone was approaching), "there's something else: the holy Ursula had no less than eleven thousand virgins along when she arrived in Cologne, Germany, from England or Scotland. Since that time there has never been that many virgins on this earth all at once."

He said this in all seriousness, but his eyes glittered. I can understand that certain persons, especially married men, but also the unmarried ones, have a low opinion of him.

Dec. 11 (In code)

(Séraphique Archer, who was a servant girl in my house before I got married, has returned to our city. She has been away well over a year and a half. I could of course let the heavy hand of the law come down on her, but—

She is supposed to be extremely—common. With soldiers, etc.

She was a very sweet girl at the time—as a young girl, as a virgin. Séraph.—)

§ 7

(Summing-up 1627–29. Corrections made in 1632.)

La Rochelle fell last year (1628) and there are those who now think that Protestantism has been completely crushed

129

in our country. From time to time I think about much that has been crushed, yes, completely squashed, but which is still alive and kicking. Although La Rochelle was undeniably the strongest fortified town of the Huguenots. The city capitulated on Oct. 28. Its fall is considered a personal victory for the Cardinal.

Many frightful stories are told about the besieged population. They ate cats and rats. The city was literally starved into submission. Afterward more than a hundred persons are supposed to have eaten themselves to death; they could not take food! The last of the resistance forces marched out on Oct. 30: seventy-four French and sixty-two English soldiers. At 3 P.M. the Cardinal made his entry into the city; he was accompanied by the papal nuncio, I don't know the name of that monsignor.

I shall not dwell further on the incidents of the war; I write this down merely in order for posterity to be able to *place* us and our fate in a larger context. The historians will have to do their part!—But the expedition made by our king south to Italy has been a success; that was last year. But our situation, of course, is a rather strange one. As a loyal subject, I don't want to pass any judgment. But we have just crushed Protestantism within our country—I think?—and then we turn against the greatest defenders of the Catholic faith, Spain and Austria! What says our good queen? We can *hear* what many others say about it; but I am not an old gossip.

His Eminence, the Cardinal, is supposed to have declared—in Montauban, which surrendered in Aug. last year: "The springs giving rise to heresy and revolution have dried up."

I wonder?

Undated note:

Things have occurred in our city which are worthy of mention in my protocol.

Minor events may lead to important consequences. One example is the quarrel between Jacques de Chasseignes and Urbain Grainier. It must have started with vanity. J. de Chasseignes is a member of the Royal life guard. He is considered a sort of personal representative of the Cardinal, has good connections in Paris, is a good friend and perhaps a relative of Louis Tranchant, and consequently an adherent of the so-called Demolition Party. He has gone around quite a long time feeling mortified over the position that U. Gr. actually enjoys in our town, and he has spoken very ill of him.

Some time ago, when Urb. G. was crossing our square, dressed in his canon's garments, on his way to the Church of Ste-Croix he espied J. de Chasseignes and addressed him sharply, as is his habit when he is irritated (he has a hot temper); and then J. de Ch. hit him with his stick. Urb. G. very wisely controlled himself—strangely enough!—but soon after he journeyed to Paris to complain to the King and the Parlement. He was undoubtedly supported by his friend, the governor of our city, M. d'Armagnac, who is staying at the court. As might have been expected, U. G.'s enemies took advantage of the situation.

Here are some excerpts from my diary.

March 3, 1627

Hurrah! Another boy!

Was at "The Hen" last night and there I met my cousin Mathurin and my friends. I got home rather late. Today we have glorious weather. All is well with my wife and the boy. All is well, everything is glorious! My head is a little heavy, so I won't write more about the joy with which I am filled.

March 14

The christening did not turn out so bad. I toyed with the idea of asking Louis Tranchant to be a sponsor, which might have been advantageous, although I don't share T's views on the necessity of tearing down our walls and fortifications, but having thought the matter over carefully I realized that I couldn't bypass Urbain Grainier when selecting the officiating priest. Louis Calvet, deputy bailiff, and his brother Charles, councillor, my colleague, were the sponsors. I decided that my second son should be named Charles-Louis-Urbain. I believe that he had an advantageous christening. Following the ceremony we had a glass of my fine white wine from 1622 in our home. U's tongue was sharp as usual. He can indeed be entertaining. But the brothers C-t are just now rather cool toward him. They are related to Mad. de Brone.

Later in the evening I spent some time at "The Hen" to talk with my friends—I didn't stay terribly late. Slow, both happy and thoughtful walk back to my house in the moonlight.

(Notes—in code—undated, but from 1627–28)

The Cardinal is no pillow to lean one's cheek against.

Have been out on—an adventure. Dolet and I met two girls from Saumur, who happened to visit our city.

Thinking often of Sér. Archer—she was so sweet as—a virgin.

Have been on an official trip to Saumur, accompanied by Delagarde, our salt intendant. Since my wife has relatives there, it was perhaps not very—wise.

Charlotte is passing through one of her sour periods.

Was in Chinon together with Dolet. Took care of an inheritance claim. Dol. got dead drunk. I can't recall what happened to me; seem to think that I acted properly and dignified as I usually do. We had some fun. Dolet, however, had bad luck. I show no sign of that kind of disease.

Met Dolet today; he has had a difficult time.

Have heard that the girls—they were sweet—were not of very high repute. I will be more careful from now on.

I often think of Séraph. A. She was so—enticing.

*

Aug. 5

Have been out to my country place, where the family stays on. I worry about the wine—there is always a feeling of suspense during the final month. But Michel is hoping for the best.

As I was riding back to town yesterday morning, Charlotte—my wife—told me that she was pregnant.

*

March 19, 1628

It was a boy. All's well. At "The Hen" in the evening.

March 28

Christening in the Ste-Cr. Church as usual. U. G. officiated. Sponsors: Doctor René Lannoury (who is an influential man in the city) and my coll. in govern. service Césuet (but tension between them and Urb. G.) Still think that the christening was advantageous. Afterward a glass of my white—one of the better ones—25 in our house. U.G. was rather silent, and so were the others. Decided that my third son is to be named René-Julien. In the evening a while at "The Hen."

Aug. 17

Have been out in the country, where the family is at the present time. The grapevines seem to be doing relatively well. As I was about to ride back yesterday morning, Charlotte (my wife) told me that she is pregnant again. I am very pleased with that.

Sometime in Aug.

Have been to Saumur and Chinon.

Notation made in Sept.

Urb. G. has gone to Paris. He has quarreled with M.

Jacques de Chasseignes and with our chief of police, Herseur. Louis Tranchant and Herseur have ridden to Poitiers in a great hurry; it is said that they intend to speak with Bishop de Roche-Pozay, the good friend of the Cardinal.

Sept. 19

As usual, the grapevines are pressed at Michel's. I am not quite satisfied and eagerly look forward to seeing the result. Still, I am quite worried.

My wife Charlotte says that she is not feeling as well as the previous times.

Sept. 22

Can't help thinking about the wine; it often keeps me awake at night.

Besides: there is talk in the town about the new prioress in the Ursuline convent, Jeanne de Beaucil. She is said to have an unequable temperament. She is very talkative, say those who have visited her, is interested in details about local marital and extramarital relationships and connections. They claim that she likes to drink wine as well as absinthe. But things go well for the sisters: many of the high-born young girls in our city are now being brought up by them.

(Notation in the margin: I for my part have always considered a glass of absinthe to be pacifying and stimulating. Not to speak of a small glass of wine.)

October 28

Delagarde and I in Saumur. It was quite successful.

(In code.) Thinking often of Sér. Archer. She was so sweet—then!

Febr. 28, 1629

A girl yesterday. Mother and child are doing well. There may be advantages with girls too.

March 6

Christening yesterday, Monday, in the Ste-Cr. Church. Urb. G. Mme. Charles Calvet very kindly agreed to be godmother. A glass of wine in our house afterward. Urb. G. has a difficult time of it p.t. (The girl was named Charlotte-Louise.)
I was at "The Hen" for a short while in the evening.

July 7

Have been in the country, where I have the family at present. Warm. The vines look promising.

Sept. 20

Charlotte, my wife, told me last night when I came home—I had been at "The Hen" for a while—that she was pregnant. Since I was not sure that I had understood her right (I was a little tired last night) I asked her about it this morning. And so it is. We are now on the way to having our fifth child. I am satisfied with the others, the boys as well as the girl. They are healthy and of normal intelligence. I have punished them with moderation.

Nov. 16, 1629

What a scandal! The pastor of Saint-Pierre, the canon of Sainte-Croix, Urb. G., was arrested yesterday in Poitiers and is now incarcerated in the prison of the episcopal palace—where reigns his avowed enemy, the friend of the Cardinal, Monseigneur de Roche-Pozay!

Nov. 22

My colleague in the profession, Charles Calvet, informed me of some of the details this forenoon.

Urb. G. went to Paris to complain about J. de Chasseignes before the High Court of Parlement, and L. Tranchant and Herseur set out immediately for Poitiers, to the bishop. They have gathered witnesses to all kinds of things. A priest in the Church of St-Pierre, Gervais Messier, a rather somber figure who is possibly related to Tranchant and the Poussauts, is playing the part of informer. It seems that U. G. has given him financial help in the past—which is something that should be done with extreme caution, that is my principle! M-r supposedly alleges that U. G. has carried on "venerial acts" with women "stretched out full length" on the floor of the church! Another witness, the pastor at Basneuil (not far from here), Martin Boulon (who is economically dependent on Tranchant and his son—for he pays Tranchant Junior 70 livres a year for his position), contends that he has seen U. G. perform v. a. with the nice old Mme de Renebaut, who died a few months ago! U. G.'s lawsuit in Paris against J. de Chasseignes seems to have come to nothing. J. de Ch-s too has been to Paris and has probably briefed *certain* persons. When U. G. returned here, Bishop de Roche-Pozay had already written out the warrant for his arrest. It is all very confusing. U. G. has been imprisoned for a number of things that I know he cannot have done. That he is guilty of a bit of loose living as far as women are concerned, that we know—but this! No!

Nov. 23

Ch. Calvet says that J. de Chasseignes is being supported with money from Tranchant's good friend M. Marquis Charles du Valley, who—he too!—at one time was a good friend of U. G.'s. But now they have dinned something into his ears. Calvet furthermore maintains that "they have suborned" two notorious persons of this town, Cherbonneau and Bougreau, "on behalf of the entire population of the city" to accuse U. G. of having "seduced women and young girls, of being godless and of never reading his breviary" and of having "played the role of bishop." (That statement must have been effective!)

Nov. 24

Things are getting clearer while at the same time they become more and more confused! I can't express it in any other way! Just imagine if people would at last come to their senses and stop quarreling! For ours are indeed modern times, with an orderly religion, philosophy, culture, and architecture!

Charles Calvet told me today what he knew. J. de Chasseignes went to Paris, summoned by the Court of Parlement, regarding the case between him and Urb. G. He had already then Bishop Roche-Pozay's arrest warrant with him! There is supposed to have been some awful scenes. The bishop's order to institute a renewed investigation here has made the honorable Louis Calvet, in a fit of disgust, renounce the assignment as the judicial investigator for the civil authorities.

Old accusations crop up again. A pack of hunting dogs has been set loose! Gervais Messier maintains that while hiding behind a column in the St. Pierre Church one day "at sunset" he watched U. G. seduce "women and young girls" on the floor of the church! And Martin Boulon, the pastor at Basneuil, also sticks to his earlier statements. They have testified to this before—Tranchant and Herseur. The canon of Ste-Croix, Jehan Minet, is of course involved in the mess, what else would he be? It seems that they make spurious records and sign anything in order to get U. G.!

Nov. 25

In the presence of examining judge Merrain, Martin Boulon retracted his assertion regarding U. G.'s v. a. with the late Madame de Renebaut. The earlier protocol containing his testimony, which he signed but didn't read through, had been fabricated—forged—by Tranchant and Herseur!

Nov. 26

Ch. Calvet told me today that as soon as Urb. G. returned here from Paris, he traveled to Poitiers in order to place himself at the disposal of Monseigneur de Roche-Pozay. But he was arrested in his lodgings before he was able to do so. At the behest of Tranchant and Herseur. M. d'Armagnac, the governor of our city, is now working in Paris to have him set free.

Dec. 5

Last night I went over to "The Hen" to talk a while with my friends and drink a small beaker of absinthe. I have worked rather intensely with reports, etc., and in the evening I have usually read in my diary and in my protocol and also studied my Cicero somewhat. This, which I would call studious hermit life in the company of my wife Charlotte and the children, has gone on for almost a week. We have rainy weather.

As I expected, Petiot, Dolet, and the brothers Antoine, the masons, were at "The Hen" talking about nothing but Urb. G. and the bishop of Poitiers and Tranchant, etc. I'm beginning to get very tired of the topic and therefore I soon went to visit my cousin Mathurin Thiboust. Corisande, his wife, is rather big now, just like Charlotte. Cor. was so sweet when she was a young girl. She wanted to know whether I knew anything. I am completely fed up with it all! Everyone asks—since I am a respected official—

and think that *I* know any secrets! No, I'm on my guard against talking too much. Mathurin accompanied me back to "The Hen"; we had one or two glasses of wine and I had some absinthe.

When I got home I sat down to write for a while, but there was no continuity in it, which is why it is omitted.

Dec. 26

Among the judges in the case of U. G. in Poitiers there is now also a M. Richard. He is related to Tranchant.

Dec. 30, 1629

Concerned about Urb. G. Here in our city he is already looked upon as sentenced and lost. The chairman of the elective city council, old Varot, who is related to Tranchant and the Poussauts, has begun to pry into U. G.'s economic assets, which surely are not inconsiderable. People think that the prebend will now revert to the party of the Tranchants.

Charlotte, my wife, feels more tired than ever before during a pregnancy, she says. In late autumn like this we are generally close to each other feeling that we belong together. We play with the children. At times I read to her in the evenings, both Cic. and interesting books on the art of cooking and such things. But she usually falls asleep after I have read a few pages.

I go to "The Hen" once in a while to meet my friends.

Received my new suit of clothes today. It was much delayed, one can never rely on tailors. And it is expensive! But I think it turned out quite well.

Note from Jan. 4, 1630

Urbain Grainier was sentenced yesterday by the provincial court in Poitiers to fast on bread and water every Friday for three months; moreover, he was forbidden to discharge his pastoral duties in the diocese of Poitiers for five years and in our city forever. I was at "The Hen" last night. Everyone there felt very indignant about the sentence, which no one considers to be just. It means the ruin of U. G. People are of the opinion that the party of the Tranchants has now won a definitive victory. U. G. is supposed to have behaved with great equanimity in spite of his months in prison! But perhaps he is crushed for good.

Madeleine de Brone (who now rents the upper floor in my house) appears very melancholy, even sad.

8

Madeleine of the Day and of the Night

He stood by the window; he seemed to her a dark figure, carved out of the hot summer. Yes, a figure with a sentence behind him, a sentence above him, around him, inside him, and what she believed and what everyone had to believe: a sentence before him.

His face was leaner than prior to the journey to Poitiers, but the prison pallor had almost disappeared. His hair had touches of gray in it; his goatee had been allowed to spread a bit, his shoulders were bent forward, and his head was not held as straight as before.

His attire was as plain as one can imagine—that of a defrocked or practically defrocked and ruined priest. The black cloth in the long coat was frayed from brushing, but its elegant cut was still evident.

"You are so hard inside that it will make you burst, Urbain," she said.

"What do we know about that?" he said and his very dark eyes were glittering at her. "What do you know about that? What do I know about it? What do we know about my hardness? That I am curious about how hard my hardness is?"

"It's coming soon, I can feel it," said Madeleine. "They talk about it all over town, everywhere, always. Evil

141

tongues have been busy for months, for years. They whisper your name when I walk down the street, children shout it after me. And they shout loathsome words."

He stood in her apartment, in the room facing the courtyard, in Assessor Drouin's house on the Square of Sainte-Croix. In the little park on the other side of the assessor's tall garden wall stood a weeping willow. The gusts of wind flung the supple, green branches upward as when a young girl shakes her hair away from her forehead with a toss of her head.

*

He came to her during the day; at times he stayed longer, she went to him during the night in an unreasonable, useless, unnecessary boldness. These were actions beyond the common sense they accepted so far, but the actions were tied to a firm, abstracted logic. The years, time, his position or her own had nothing to do with this; they were also beyond the time in which lived all the people down in the street, out in the city. The two of them were removed from their time period. "We are floating in the air above time or we are buried together in a hollow, time rolls on above us and does not concern us, Madeleine," he might say; and she answered him with the logic that decided their actions: that she had never thought that love was so long-lasting. She had believed, she said, that love was eternal. But she had not believed that it would last long enough to be envisioned in human years or measured on such a scale. "Ten years," she said. "It sounds improper or banal: a decade. I am a middle-aged woman now, time has passed, our love is not an eternity, no, it is much longer: ten years."

*

They stood next to each other by the parlor window facing the square. The dust down there whirled up by the puffs of air.

142

"They can see us if they want to," she said.

"They like to see us," he replied. "People want to see what they love and what they abhor. The indifferent they don't want to see. The best thing is to be popular; but the next best is to be hated. I mean: if one wants to be noticed. He down there (and he pointed to the floor) would gladly say it in Latin. That is Daniel Drouin's incurable malady. But I am not sure that he would understand the meaning any better because of that."

"You underestimate people, Urbain," she said.

"No," he said. "But I don't overestimate them."

"You don't love them," she said. "That is your malady and it may be incurable. It is easy to teach a child to love people. It is more difficult to teach a man who has been imprisoned without guilt."

"How could I love a herd of sheep other than as a spectacle!" he said. "I can love one of the sheep, two, five, ten, a hundred, if I have sufficient time. I can be fond of beings who are close to me, whom I can touch, long for, miss. But a herd? A mass that is no longer individuals?"

"They are individuals," she said.

"They are individuals who can be changed into a herd and thus are a herd. Who was it that said something about the rage of a herd of sheep? Someone must have said it, since language and the struggle for power first came to man. The rage of a herd of sheep is blind. One cannot love a herd in any way except possibly as a spectacle. One cannot love mankind."

"Yes, one can," she said. "Whenever one recalls that they are individuals and recalls how individuals can be."

"You are my sheep, my lamb," he said.

"I am your sheep, your lamb, your wife before God," she said.

*

It was an act of defiance to stand beside a half-defrocked priest, who as a special favor was lodged in a couple of

143

rooms up by the Church of Saint-Pierre and perhaps would soon be thrown out from there too. His mother and a sister and one of his brothers could still live with *him,* in his looted dwelling, but he didn't want to go back there.— "It is a kind of pride that I call arrogance," Madeleine de Brone said.—"Yes," he replied, "it may be so."—"You don't want to go there and stay there even though you can," she said.—"No," he said, "not even if I can."—"You do want to go back there," she said, "to your things, your furniture, your books, to the redolence of your life. But you don't want to *come* there now. You want to *march* in."

"Perhaps that's what I want," he replied.

It was an act of defiance to stand here by his side, lean out through the open window facing the dusty street, to be seen and to look down when so many looked up at them. When the people down there saw the people above, at this height a few yards above street level, they turned their heads and looked away. They pretended to find out what color the sky had today and whether the church façade was still gray.

"We are their spectacle," she said.

"They get enjoyment but no profit from it, Madeleine," he said. "They get the enjoyment of the agitated curious or the sympathetic curious. They get excited, but it is an excitement that leaves nothing behind in their souls which was not there beforehand, and the kindness that they may feel is shallow and meaningless: it doesn't make them any better, it only prevents them from quickly becoming worse."

"Then it isn't meaningless," she said.

"You may be right," he answered. "But it is a small thing to be right about."

It was an act of defiance against everyone to be standing here, but now everything was a defiance. If they had wanted to hide, that too would have been a defiance.

"Contrary to good taste," he said.

144

"Contrary to my innermost feelings," she replied. "That is much more than what you call good taste."

"Now it's you who suffer from the sickness of arrogance, Madeleine."

"Yes," she answered. "But there is no other choice for me."

"Yes, there is," he said.

"Yes, there is," she said. "But I want to live."

*

It was very much an act of defiance to be standing here early on a market-day. The farmers came in from the plain, in through the gates. The rickety carts drawn by oxen or donkeys rattled and shook on their large, warped wheels up the uneven and bumpy Rue Pasquin, past the Ursuline convent, across the Square of Sainte-Croix, into Rue de Marchands, the Merchants' Street, and toward the narrow marketplace of the poultry sellers and further via the Street of the Butchers to the marketplace for cattle below the Church of Saint-Pierre. They came in through the Mirebeau Gate—or what was left of it!—from the direction of Poitiers or the hills of Châtellerault, through the Chinon Gate—or what was left of it!—or from the east through the Gate of Saint-Nicolas—or what might be left of it—from the direction of Saumur. Perhaps they had things to do at the Capuchin cloister or at the castle (which was being torn down by the order of the Cardinal and, as it was said, for the sake of the domestic tranquility of France, although everyone here believed that it was done to get suitable stone for the giant structure at Richelieu.) Rattling and creaking farmers' carts arrived from the west, entering through the Bartray Gate, which was still standing. The men and the women bowed down low (provided they remembered and there was no muddle with their cart or with the guard) before the picture of the Madonna above the arch between the two round towers. They dreamed of doing good business with the city people, of exemptions from duty, of a successful outcome to their business with the governor at the castle or his deputy or with the *bailli* or with lawyers, notaries, assessors, or councillors or, possibly, of a good blessing by the Capuchins or others. They came, they poured in and were people of a lower kind. But they had ears to hear with, eyes that could see, and there were tongues in their mouths.

When the people from the plains had entered through the gate and encountered the city air filled with more marvelous and superior smells and a more elevated life than their own, and as it penetrated into nose and eyes and mouth, the carts would come to a halt outside the Bartray Church, which had been damaged by the Huguenots. They would make the sign of the cross or enter the church while oxen and mules were resting to gather strength for the balance of the hill all the way to the castle wall and the conglomeration of houses. The peasants looked up, blew the dust from their noses and gaped at the immense, square, many-hundred-year-old Nerra Tower, which might be torn down, that too, but which the governor and the lewd pastor defended against the Cardinal's men. They mentioned no names, at least not very loudly.

Thereupon they continued on their way up to the Square of Sainte-Croix.

"The pastor and ladykiller and blasphemer and seducer helps the governor protect the tower against—well, against whom?" they whispered blinking with shy and bloodshot eyes.

She knew that it was an act of defiance against them and against the entire world to be standing here in the open window by his side. They no doubt recognized her still round and soft face. She had been stared at a lot, glanced at furtively, peeked at. They whispered about the priest's whore who was protected by the powerful; and those who were a bit more powerful than the completely powerless whispered or even spoke out loud, saying that the window

146

up there might be a suitable observation platform when that swine of a priest cheated on her with others, squeezing in some fun in the church in one or two of the ninety-nine ways during a pause in the altar service; or they were whispering that Daniel Drouin's house was close enough so that the whore herself might run over to the sacristy and get what she needed, provided that that devil of a priest didn't have some other woman handy. She knew what they were whispering and thinking when they glanced up.

But they didn't talk only about her. Her name as well as his made a small vein, a rivulet in all the talk that was gushing from many directions across the square in front of the Church of Sainte-Croix. The stream ran all through the city. It was fed from the cloisters, the churches, the administrative offices, and the shops; and also from the plain, from woodlands and marshes, where people were sitting in their miserable, lowly hovels dreaming dreams which were chock-full of experiencing God's word and the priests' interpretations, and dreams that were filled with experiencing pestilence and violent death, of hunger, of lust for power or of their own bodies' desire to be caressed in bed.

She leaned out, past him, thinking about it. I can follow the streams. They chew me up in their mouths, just as they have chewed up others that he has lain with. But I want to be chewed up—if that is the price. And I want to stand here by his side just now.

*

(Summer Night in the Plague Year 1632)

The walls inside Assessor Drouin's house were cool. She held on to the iron handrail and walked slowly, extremely carefully, down the stairs. The wife and children of the assessor were in the country, but the house was listening

147

nevertheless as she lifted the latch and opened the door in the gate on the side of the house facing the narrow street.

The walls, the very stone, radiated heat in the dark. She felt warm inside her cape, underneath her veil. My face is flushed, she thought, my body smells from perspiration. Her glove made a scratching sound against the wall. When she reached the bend further up in the street, she once again had to fumble along the wall in order not to make a false step. If I—at that time—had taken a different veil and had taken the conventual vows, I wouldn't have been afraid now. I wouldn't have been afraid to smell from perspiration. Not afraid of life. I wouldn't have had a life and my hand would not have fumbled along the wall, my feet would not have hesitated, I would not have been his wife.

You are my bride, he told her when he gave her his tract about the celibacy of the clergy. No one can force himself to do the impossible, he had written. The priest doesn't accept celibacy because he loves it but only because otherwise he would not become a priest. If he attempts the impossible, he is exempt from keeping his promise by the very impossibility of keeping it.—She had read it and read it over again and it had changed and it had changed her. So many years! His whore! One ought to know, he had written, that the law regarding celibacy is of the same nature as the law of Joshua and that it is forced on the priests in the same way that Joshua's was forced on the Jews. Since Joshua's law about fasting, which was laid down for all Jews, only applies to those who have strength enough to fast, the decree regarding clerical celibacy should not apply to any but those who possess the ability to abstain—and since God has neither expressed a wish nor instituted a law about the celibacy of the clergy, one will have to agree with the apostle who concluded that it is better to marry than to burn and better to associate with womankind than to perish through continence. "The Lord sayeth: It is not good for man to be alone," he wrote then; and she thought of it now, without finding it comical, yes, without any strong desire. He needs me. But he does not protect me, she had thought at times. I have to protect myself. If I had been in a cloister, he wouldn't have had to show that he can't protect me.

She missed a step and hit the wall with her toe. Oh! she whispered in the dark. Something nasty-smelling had been thrown into the street, perhaps rotten fruits, excrements, it was slippery underfoot and she was close to slipping, to falling in it. Oh! she whispered and stopped short pressing herself against the warm wall.

At the top of the hill someone was approaching with a lantern. The light beam shone above the garden wall and into the tree crowns. The leaves lit up, silvery and withering, silver-green dead, heavy from sleep or weak from thirst: they were waiting for dark, lukewarm rain and got cold, yellow light.

Perhaps they are bringing someone who has died, she thought. Perhaps they are carrying away someone who has been lying dead in the street. I am not afraid of the dead and not afraid of death. Not any more. But I am afraid of the light of the living.

Two night wanderers passed by on the other side of the street. One of them walked ahead carrying the lantern, he walked with a light step, it was a servant. Behind him panted his master, someone who had had a lot of wine to protect him against plague or ghosts and who was now hiccuping helplessly. She saw his fat, unsteady legs and his shoes with silver buckles. She walked toward the men so as not to stand still with her face turned away. She walked fast now, while the light was flooding her. She thought: the light sticks in my mouth. The light brings sweat to my forehead. The light is the plague that catches up with me: the plague I am afraid of. The light is what I slip and fall into. The light is that which cripples my faith that I am his wife before God.

The servant lifted the lantern up high and then lowered

149

it in front of his master's feet. She didn't have time to make out the faces and who they were, but the men could see all of her, the red velvet in her cape, the heavy, warm, green skirts, the Parisian cut to her puffed sleeves. They knew who she was in spite of her veil: Madeleine de Brone, alone in the middle of the night in a city where the plague was still about. Alone in the dark and on the way toward the Church of Saint-Pierre to a priest who had received back all his rights through the inexplicable intercession of Archbishop de Sourdis. On her way to confess? In the middle of the night? Ho-ho, who would believe that!

She could *hear* the thoughts in the head of the fat-legged man. A councillor? A servant of the King or the Cardinal? Someone who tears walls down? A defender of the walls?

If he noticed her at all? Yes, he stopped, turned with some difficulty, she saw his feet turn uphill. In the darkness above his heavy stomach his fully audible thoughts were swimming in wine: She? She who about ten years ago happened to confess her sins to the devilish priest at Saint-Pierre, and then she became neither nun nor wife. Neither Our Lord nor Our Lady got her maidenhead. He didn't receive it any more than many other maidenheads in this town. It went somewhere else, it did.

They disappeared around the corner. Darkness enveloped her with its flowing, sticky, stifling heat. The plague was breathing on the town.

He was waiting for her at the gate, he touched her arm.

"You are brave," he said. "You defy them."

I will never regret one single moment with him, she thought. But perhaps I smell of perspiration.

9

Daniel Drouin's Protocol (3)

§ 8 (Reviewed 1633)

CICERO, WHOM I read diligently at intervals, says that men are caught through sensual pleasure just as fish are caught on a hook, and I am inclined to share his opinion.

For what are we all but fish caught on hooks! And what is it that has made all of humankind, as far as I can survey it, one tremendous catch of fish? Sensual pleasure—or perhaps more correctly: the striving for sensual pleasure!

I write this, however, in full awareness that I myself, Daniel Drouin, am, if not exactly pining, nevertheless somewhat inclined to seek sensual pleasure and to partake of it and to enjoy it to the best of my ability.

What is happening in our country? We are at war and the Cardinal continues to prove himself a great commander. No one doubts that he is a great statesman, not least his enemies. In June 1630 (I am writing my summary with a heart ravaged by suffering in this fall of 1632) the imperial troops sacked Mantua. I recall certain facts: in September the King was very sick, they thought he would die, but he recovered. I still shudder when I think of what political consequences might have followed from that! That the Cardinal in such a case would have been replaced by *another person,* of that we are all convinced.

As far as the events in our town are concerned, I will

151

rely on my diary. I have included a few pages and the future scholar may choose among them at will. A few expressions ought no doubt have been deleted as improper (for I *am* a government official) but after mature deliberation I have decided that this should be a task for posterity. That is, if there will ever exist a posterity with sufficient interest in what has happened, and is happening to us!

A saying of C. Jul. Caesar has often been ringing in my ears over the last years, namely: *The wall is about to lose its defenders.*

Or is it rather that every fortified wall which is threatened will always have its defenders, but that the course of events proceeds on such a grand scale that we—in this our only human life—cannot comprehend it?

Here are excerpts from the diary.

*

Febr. 3, 1630

People talk. Urb. G. walks about town doing nothing. But he shows himself, he is not afraid. At times he visits Demoiselle de Brone, who rents the upper floor of my house. The verdict in Poitiers has not made him a broken man. He pins his hopes on Archbishop Sourdis in Bordeaux and on the governor.

The day before yesterday the wife of the governor gave birth to a son.

Was at "The Hen" last night. Dolet, who had been drinking immoderately, said, "Sourdis! He knows a whole lot about what it is like to be a prelate and not get to marry!" Michel, who takes care of my vineyard, was also present and made a coarse remark, so that Dolet got more grist for his mill and said, "Sourdis knows much about how ladies' skirts are sewn—he will understand Urb. G. better than the Bishop of Poitiers does!" I consider that an almost frivolous remark.

Febr. 10

Charlotte's (my wife's) mood is not the best these days.

I also have trouble with the tailor Beliard, he doesn't do what I *tell* him.

(Notations made in code at the end of February 1630:

This forenoon I was told that Séraphique Archer has ended up in the Ursuline convent as a serving sister. She has been living a little—adventurously these last few years. She was so lovely before—. Thinking of her at times. Memories. What persistent memories they are!

Met Demoiselle de Brone in the street outside our house this forenoon. She looked distressed, and no wonder! Meet her seldom although she lives in my house. Charlotte says that U. G. visits her often, yes, practically every day.

She is a mature, beautiful, refined woman. Has been keeping company with U. G. a long time, in spite of all his affairs. She was lovely as a young girl but she is still very beautiful. With her one should be able to converse, exchange ideas, provided . . .

Actually, I think that the young girls in our town are very charming.

The thought of Sér. A. will not leave me. If she wanted to—I have thought to myself at times—she could now come back to us as a servant maid since she has been rescued from the wild life of the world. She is capable, that I know. She would be good to have around the house during Charlotte's pregnancies—I am not satisfied with our present maid, who is careless and often impudent toward *me!* And Sér. can also—cook! But perhaps Charlotte will not agree to it. Women are so strange, there is no doubt about it.)

March 29

My wife Charlotte yesterday gave birth to a girl. Mother and child are doing well.

April 4

My new daughter was baptized yesterday in Sainte-Croix. Urb. G., who of course has been forbidden to engage in any ecclesiastical activity, could not officiate so it devolved on the oldest canon, Maurat. Godmother, Mme. Rogier, the wife of the doctor. We had a wee glass of wine in our house.

In the evening I spent some time at "The Hen." It turned out to be rather late. Michel, who helps me in the vineyard, was there. He had his mule and his cart with him so I got a lift all the way to my door; then I was fine. Charlotte—my wife—was awake and the smallest children were crying. She breast-feeds them herself. She is in a melancholy mood and cries at times, as a matter of fact: often. I don't really know why, for she did marry rather well.

I'm thinking of my wine. Have planned to expand my little vineyard this year provided Michel will let me purchase a small plot from him. He will probably not turn me down. Naturally, he will not forget that I am an official in the office of our *bailli*.

April 6

Once again there are rumors about U. G.'s case. I know for a fact that U. G. is trying to have Bishop Roche-Pozay's verdict at Poitiers rescinded by Archbishop Sourdis at Bordeaux. His enemies are trying to have him sentenced to corporal punishment by the court of the Parlement in Paris. They refer to a case of some years ago: a priest, René Sophier, parish priest at Baugé, who was alleged to have taken the wife of some magistrate to bed. He was sentenced to hang, but the Parlement in Paris increased the severity of the sentence and had him burned alive. "The jurists around Tranchant are trying all possibilities," Charles Calvet told me the other day.—At the same time it is said that Jacques de Chasseignes is trying to come to terms with Urb. G. (their case has not been finally settled yet), but U. G. has apparently refused to agree to a reconciliation. It seems indeed as if he is still rather arrogant. Is that wise on his part? They say that both Governor d'Armagnac and Archbishop Sourdis, both of whom support him, have asked him to keep completely calm. But will he be able to?

June 8

Have been at my country place a few days with my family, who are still out there. I have bought a small plot from Michel, I'm going to expand my vineyard, and I didn't put any kind of pressure on him, which I give myself credit for. Rode back this morning, since I have been invited to the governor's splendid christening party! Just as I was mounting my horse, Charlotte, my wife, burst into tears, I don't know why. At least, she is hardly pregnant already. However, I dismounted and patted her cheek. I often say to myself and to her—and to others—that I could hardly have gotten a better wife than Charlotte.

June 11

The christening day before yesterday was really a solemn and festive occasion. Governor d'Armagnac's third son was born February 1 but they have postponed his baptism until now, probably in order to make it politically effective and impressive. It took place in the Church of Saint-Pierre. Urb. G., the friend of the governor, was unable to officiate of course, but—if I may say so—they should have selected another priest than that suspicious-looking fork-tongued Gervais Messier! Although I don't know what factors have to be taken into consideration.

His Majesty the King had declared himself willing to be the godfather! He was represented by the Royal Councillor M. Baron Jean-Martin de Laubardemont, who is just now visiting here in connection with the razing; he is the one to supervise and carry it out.

The whole ceremony was without a doubt beautiful and a great success. M. de Laubardemont, who is now honoring our city with his presence, is very tall, almost as tall as I am, about forty years old and, like Urb. G. and myself, he has studied with the Jesuits. He is quite thin, has a long, hawklike nose, small, black, and deepset eyes, a small mouth with pouting lips, and a narrow, very high forehead; he is bald. To all appearances he is nearsighted. An important man. He has conducted several trials of heretics—with good results!—and has been assigned many demolition jobs. He is supposed to be in high favor with His Eminence the Cardinal. He has relatives in our city: the prioress of the Ursuline convent is his cousin and a Mademoiselle Bonpierre is his sister-in-law. Thus he has good reason to take an interest in our city and its problems. It is our hope that he will raze what remains of our towers and walls with a gentle hand.

His energy as regards juridical matters is well known. People quote a saying of his: "Give me a sample of a person's handwriting, and I will get him hanged!" He is undoubtedly an outstanding jurist and government official.

Everyone thought that my new suit was very good-looking. In church I was standing at a spot from where I could see practically the entire ceremony. Afterward we were at the governor's and had something to eat and drink. Didn't go right home from there but went down to "The Hen." Stopped in for a moment at my cousin Mathurin's so that Corisande, his wife, could have a look at me in my suit, but she had already gone to bed. Thinking about her once in a while. She was lovely when she was a young girl. Her confinements have taken their toll. My cousin accompanied me back to "The Hen" where we had something to drink, and after that he walked with me back to my door.

July 30

Have been out at my country place, where my family is now staying. This morning when I had mounted my horse, Charlotte, my wife, informed me that she probably was pregnant already. I dismounted immediately and kissed her on the cheek.

Aug. 18

Urb. Gr. has gone to Paris on account of his lawsuit against J. de Chasseignes, who also is staying there.

Have been out in the country to inspect the grapevines. Everything looks promising.

Aug. 11 (in code)

(Thinking at times about Sér. A. She looked rather attractive, really. So chubby, so healthy-looking—so pleasant—in every way. Perhaps a bit of a wanton. But I was the *first one,* that makes me both sad and also proud in a way. Often wonder how she likes it among the Ursuline Sisters?

Actually, there are many beautiful girls in our town.
Have been to Saumur.)

Aug. 27

Living quietly and all by myself. Nicole, the maid, makes my meals but I have to keep an eye on her. She is by the way a kind person. Good-natured and mature.

Have been sitting at home tonight looking at some new recipes. Got an idea: When I get the time, I will become an author! Publish a book! Have already thought of a title. "A Public Official's Cookbook" or perhaps "A Dreamer's Cookbook" (for I am something of a dreamer). Or perhaps still better: "A Public Official's Rambling through the Culinary Arts." That sounds both matter-of-fact and dignified as well as tempting. And despite the censorship it is possible to comment on certain matters in a cookbook.

Aug. 28

Was at "The Hen" last night and had a few glasses of absinthe (since I have been working rather hard recently on certain official reports, etc.). The lawsuit in Paris between U. G. and J. de Ch. is dragging on. It is too hot now to judge people!

Sept. 8

Today I learned what the verdict was in Paris. The Court of the Parlement remitted the case to the criminal court in Poitiers. It was a victory for U. G., now he will be able to have the case thoroughly looked into. That is, if they *want* to. There was resistance in Paris also. He was put in the Conciergeries; for three days, until M. d'Armagnac got him out.

Sept. 30

Urb. G. has returned to our city. He looked somewhat tired and worn when I met him yesterday. However, his tongue is as sharp as ever. He said: "My enemies were as zealous as if they believed that I was—innocent! Yes, they may even believe it—and then they have to appease their consciences by having me condemned."

I have made a little outline for my book, I drafted a chapter on wine. But then I was stuck. The thought of my own wine worries me quite often; just think of all the diseases that may affect a vineyard or a grape harvest. Some night I am even filled with fear thinking about it.

Nov. 1

Urb. G. had to go to Poitiers on account of the lawsuit. The prosecutor put him in jail for a few days, but U. G. seems to have friends who helped him get out again. *Here* in our town there is great commotion right now! Many people who have testified against U. G. have retracted their testimony. Gervais Messier, for instance. They claim that they have been lured, suborned, and threatened by Tranchant and his cohorts.

My wife is rather big now.

Nov. 20 (in code)

Great things have happened in Paris! On Sunday the tenth Queen Dowager Maria de Medici attempted with the aid of the Minister of Justice, Michel de Marillac, and others to *overthrow* H. Em. the Cardinal! Don't know any of the details yet. In any case, the coup did not succeed. (It turned out to be a day which is already being called "The Day of the Duped.") But it must have been very close. What then would have happened to all of us! And what will happen now? The Cardinal's power is supposed to have increased. I haven't taken a definite stand yet. He is of course an outstanding politician. In any case, I am loyal to H. M. the King!

Notation made in Dec. 1630

Urb. G. has stayed temporarily in a room in my house— it is actually part of Mlle. de Brone's apartment. People talk a lot about this. But both of them are mature, middle-aged persons. And she who is single—despite her large family—and well-to-do (I should think!) should be able to open her door for any one she wants! Even for a priest without a congregation at present!

Yesterday U. G. traveled once again to Poitiers. He is to be put back in jail for some time. But many of those in Tranchant's camp are scared!

Jan. 2, 1631

A new year which I sincerely hope will be a good one for all of us! Everything is well in my family. We take such pleasure in our children, they are all healthy, happy, and I believe talented. Hope that the next one will be a boy. It is always better to have boys, but I have nothing against girls; moreover, through one's daughters one can establish good and useful family connections.

At "The Hen" a short while last night to meet my closest friends, Petiot, Dolet, the brothers Antoine, and Charlot, and then on to my only cousin, Mathurin Thiboust. We talked a bit about the polit. and military situation. The past year was on the whole a good one even for France, I believe.

(Notation in code): The Cardinal fooled his opponents. It was Sunday, November 10. The Queen Dowager had tried to outmaneuver him, but the King stood fast. His Em. the Card. is now stronger than ever, they say. He is a controversial person—also in our city. It cannot be denied, however, that he is an outstanding personality. "A constructive spirit," someone said here. (But *our* fortress and *our* walls are no more! Although, as I said: he is an important personality.)

Febr. 20

It was a boy! Am very pleased. My wife seems to be rather tired; perhaps she ought to rest for a few years. We already have a *whole flock* of children!

March 1

My new son was baptized yesterday in the Church of Ste-Croix. Maurat officiated at the christening; he is Urb. G.'s good friend and a fine man. I had asked the deputy manager of our salt depot, Laporte, to be the godfather. We have a little to do with each other—in our work—and I believe it was a good thing to ask. It is not quite clear to me where he stands in the struggle about *our walls*. On that question he keeps his own counsel. But, like me, he is angry at the Tranchant party since their manipulation with false witnesses, etc.—After the christening, we

160

enjoyed a glass of wine in our house. (I got out—the white from '27). Went to "The Hen" in the evening. We had so much to talk about so I got home rather late. I had on my new outfit, which I had not used since the christening of the governor's son. It looks exceptionally good on me, they all say.

March 15

Urb. G.'s case is never at a standstill; they are busy with new investigations. Was at "The Hen" a while last night. They talked about Urb. G., who is in town. He is now staying in a small flat up by the Church of St.-Pierre, but he visits Mad. de Brone often, yes, every day. I hear him singing up there once in a while. Charlotte, my wife, says that it often sounds as if they are having a merry time up there. But he is not allowed to officiate at any church ceremonies.

The Ursuline convent seems to be a hotbed of gossip of the worst kind. "They get all charged up," said the unballanced Petiot, who at times, especially when he is inebriated, expresses himself in a singularly offensive manner. "It is the fluids in them," he said.

Their father confessor, old man Poussaut, who once upon a time tried to whip Latin and Greek into me, is supposed to be in poor health.

(Now and then I think of Séraphique A. How is she—among—those who are "charged up"?)

May 26

This morning I found out about the decision of the court at Poitiers. All the charges against Urb. G. have been dropped! Bishop Roche-Pozay's ecclesiastical verdict vis-à-vis U. G. will certainly stand, but the civil court gave the Tranchants a real slap! They failed in their attempt to have U. G. hanged or burned! The verdict fills me with a sense of deep satisfaction.

161

July 22

Have been out at my country place, where the family is staying. I think our city has never been as hot and dusty as it is now. All the dust from all the demolition settles around one's heart!

When I was to ride back to the city yesterday morning, Charlotte, my wife, informed me that she was pregnant. I am rather pleased with that. The vineyard out there seems to be shaping up very well. The soil is excellent. Have given some consideration to asking Michel whether I can buy yet another small piece. It might be good to own land now that the family is growing in size.

July 30 (in code)

The Cardinal punishes. Marshal de Marillac—the brother of the fallen Minister of Justice, who was imprisoned for treason—is now a prisoner at Verdun.

It is difficult to fully understand our politics.

Aug. 1 (in code)

Thinking often about how Sér. A. is doing among the Urs. Sisters.

Have been to Saumur and Chinon—on an official trip together with Laporte, the vice manager of the salt depots, who is quite a jolly fellow. Success.

Aug. 22

Read the *Gazette* with great interest, the newspaper that Dr. Téophraste Renaudot has published in Paris for the last three months. All polit. events seem to be at closer range. Or: closer? In any event, interesting reading. One seems to be able to detect the exquisite style of H. Em. the Cardinal in certain articles.

Sept. 3

Now I am worried about the wine! We are soon going to reap it, but it certainly looks poor. And I am not satisfied with Michel, he has a weakness for wine and drinks quite a lot when he has the opportunity, that is, when he is in town and gets away from his wife. And that is too often, in my opinion. The other day, some rogues from Richelieu—the Cardinal's new city—tricked him into exchanging mules with them. That he was tricked into it is quite clear, now he is mortified. I often wonder how he takes care of my vinyard when I am not there to supervise things. This ought to be looked into with some care!

Nov. 23, 1631

A great day! My friend, our pastor at Saint-Pierre—our canon at Sainte-Croix, Urbain Grainier, whom I have always thought highly of in thick and thin, *has been reinstated in all his ecclesiastical rights and duties.* The Archbishop of Bordeaux, Monseigneur de Sourdis, who resides in his abbot's diocese of Saint-Jouin-des-Marnes, has annulled the judgment of Bishop Roche-Pozay at Poitiers! U. G. was at the bishop's and heard the decision himself.

He—U. G.—made a *triumphal entry* here. He rode in through the Chinon Gate (or what is left of it!) yesterday afternoon and in one hand he held a sprig of laurel! The people greeted him with loud cheers! Those who witnessed his entry found it impressive as a spectacle; though others think that the entire thing was too grandiose, simply overdone. Now people ask themselves: What is Bishop Roche-Pozay saying to all this—and Tranchant and Herseur and Jacques de Chasseignes!!!???!!!

Notation made in Oct. 1631

Louis Tranchant has resigned from his position as royal *procureur!*

The scandal involving the false witnesses against U. G. was *too* much.

He has sold his position—at a low price, it is being said—to one of the Poussauts, Louis Poussaut, on condition that the latter marry his daughter Philippe. Which has taken place. I was not invited to the wedding.

It should be noted that a number of our most outstanding—Catholic—citizens have written to Bishop Roche-Pozay at Poitiers and have requested that they be excused from having anything to do with Urb. G. concerning baptisms, funerals, etc. They have received dispensation, naturally! Both the Calvets, Louis and Charles, were tricked in some way into signing the petition. Now they are saying that they are sorry, that they let themselves be persuaded in a weak moment.

(1632)
Jan. 2, 1632

A new year. What will it bring me and all of us?

Yesterday my wife Charlotte and I and the three oldest children visited my only cousin, Mathurin Thiboust. Mathurin has some white wine which I—with no little vexation—must admit is superior to mine: a Saumur wine from the year 1624, a sort of present that he was given by Corisande's Huguenot family.

After Charlotte (who is big and heavy these days) and the children were sent home, Mathurin and I walked over to "The Hen" to say hello to those of our friends—childhood friends!—who might be there. We discussed the resumed lawsuit between Urb. G. and Jacques de Chasseignes. It is possible that it may go either way. It is generally held, it seems, that U. G. carries matters a bit *too* far. Both our governor and Archbishop Sourdis at Bordeaux are supposed to have asked him to calm down now that he has obtained redress. But he wants them to acknowledge that he is right *on every point!* Is that possible? Can a man

164

ever be in the right—permanently? But he is stubborn and (I must admit it) arrogant.

Febr. 24

It was a girl. My family is getting to be quite large! All the children have survived! The mother and the newborn child are well.

March 1

My new daughter was baptized yesterday in the Sainte-Croix Church. Urb. G. officiated at the christening. We had—after some doubt—invited Madeleine de Brone to be a sponsor and, in a way, godmother. Afterward we had a glass of wine in our house. U. G. was very pleasant and told some (rather risqué but witty) stories and we laughed heartily. Dem. de Brone is really a very charming woman, attractive and intelligent. Mature, seems to be firm in the flesh. U. G. has aged somewhat, graying at the temples. But neat and well-groomed as always. He is now living in his old apartment up by the Church of St-Pierre, with his mother, a sister, and a brother.

Was at "The Hen" in the evening and had some wine with my cousin Mathurin and our friends. Michel (the farmer who takes care of my vineyard) was there, drunk as usual. We discussed politics—rather heatedly, I seem to recall. Got a ride with Michel, who had a mule and a cart along, all the way to my door, and afterward everything went well.

Notation made in May

A plague in the city. My family, who is staying in the country, has not yet been infected. They say that Urb. G. displays a great deal of courage.

*

Nov. 7, 1632

Haven't made any notations in a long time.

Haven't had the strength, unable to pull myself together.

We were visited by the plague from April until September.

Many people died.

We lost our four oldest children (three boys and a girl) in addition to the next youngest (a boy). Charlotte, my wife, who is pregnant again, and I always feel very sad when we think about it.

Nov. 24, 1632

Exorcisms of devils in our town. Some of the Ursuline Sisters are possessed. Those of us who are among the more prominent officials in town are at times called in as witnesses. I was there today and saw the horror of it all and couldn't refrain from making a remark which, to all appearances, was greatly appreciated by the more sensible among the spectators. I expressed some doubt that the Devil—the way he appears—is fully conversant with Latin.

Otherwise, I feel very melancholy.

*

Dec. 30, 1632

Soon the year will have come to an end. Thought of putting together a political resumé but haven't been in the right mood. There is much that weighs heavily on me. In May, when the plague had already arrived, Marshal Louis de Marillac (the brother of the former Minister of Justice) was executed in Paris for high treason, in October the Marshal-Duke Henri de Montmorency was executed in Toulouse for high treason. Some time in November, King Gustavus Adolphus of Sweden was killed in Germany. There may be some connection between these events, but I don't have the strength to try to discover it now.

166

The exorcisms of the devils in our town are going on under the guidance of Pierre Barrot from Chinon and the canon Jehan Minet—he who is called the Lame One.

At times I feel a certain weary calm. I seem to think I am a river which eventually will reach the ocean. But what will I do in the ocean, I have no business there. That's the way I feel at times.

*

§ 9 (In its present form since 1633)

There is a phrase that is often ringing in my ear, it was uttered by Caesar, when he says somewhere that the wall has lost its defenders.

Just like Cicero did on one occasion, so have I done on many occasions during the last several months. I have accused myself of being listless. It is my duty to continue writing this protocol as long as I can hear, see, survey a situation, and be a witness.

What is happening in the outside world the historians will no doubt deal with. But what has happened here in our town I can note down for future use. And for me it is a diversion, which at times may be tinged with bitterness, I mean when the memories hurt.

Urb. G. won his lawsuit against J. de Chasseignes but it wasn't a real victory. The verdict only strengthened the hatred that those on the side of the Tranchants feel toward him. Governor M. d'Armagnac as well as the Archbishop of Bordeaux, Monseigneur Sourdis, advised him to move away from here. But he stayed, perhaps to continue the hopeless: to defend our walls. And perhaps for the sake of Demoiselle de Brone. He was very courageous and didn't spare himself during the plague. Was that due to his hardness, I have asked myself. At any rate, his enemies calmed down a bit when death struck us all and didn't care whether we were Catholics or Huguenots.

Already before the plague—which lasted from April to September last year—there were rumors circulating to the effect that the prioress of our Ursuline convent together with some other Ursuline Sisters, among them a relative of the Cardinal, were possessed by demons. No one talked about it during the time the plague was raging, but this past autumn the rumors were revived. The authorities have ordered that exorcisms take place. I myself, in addition to some other officials, attended as witnesses and spectators. My superior, our *bailli,* M. de Cerisay, wants to get to the bottom of this matter; like myself, he takes a skeptical view of the demons. A priest from Chinon, Pierre Barrot, is assisting the father confessor of the Ursuline Sisters, the canon of our church, Sainte-Croix, Jehan Minet, to incite and exorcise the demons, who, it is said, have been dispatched by or take orders from—Urb. G.!

U. G. is also accused in certain circles of having brought about and caused the plague. I can't believe any such thing.

Charlotte, my wife, expects to give birth again in April. I am very worried about her. We are very close now.

*

Notation made on April 7, 1633

It was a boy! Mother and child are doing well.

April 14

Christening today in Ste-Croix. Urb. G. officiated. Asked Charles Calvet to be a sponsor. After the christening a glass of wine in my house. In the evening I read to my wife, who is still very weak. I read some meditations about death and birth which I have written down for my projected book and which I think are quite successful. We both shed tears. When she fell asleep, I went down to "The Hen" for a short while to meet my friends.

August 26, 1633

I am alone in town with one of the maids. We are—it seems to me—in an ever-lasting cloud of dust, on account of the accelerated demolition, which M. de Laubardemont supervises with great energy. The last of the small towers is now practically level with the ground. The profile of our town has indeed been lacerated. I can hardly manage to speak when our city wall is the subject.

Have been to the country (my little family is staying there). Try to be with them as often as possible. The wine harvest looks, if not exceptionally fine, then at least reasonably good and I hope for the best. It is being somewhat neglected on account of what happened last year.

Charlotte, my wife, is now pregnant.

Visited "The Hen" last night and had a glass of absinthe. My cousin Mathurin and other friends were there. We got to talking about the plague; we talk about it quite often. Mathurin and Corisande—his wife—lost three of their children (the two oldest boys and a little girl), Antoine, the mason, lost one child, his brother Charlot lost his wife and all his three children, Petiot lost his wife and one of his children, Dolet lost his mother and brother. I think Petiot drinks too much. We talked for a while about politics, but not with any great interest. Many people think that our city is completely ruined and doomed on account of the dire combination of plague and demolition. Voices among us have turned silent, no one is fighting on the walls.

I went home early, my heart felt heavy. Mathurin saw me to my door. We talked about our children, about the living ones and those who are dead.

10

Deployment

IN BRIGHT DAYLIGHT, while the city was resting in the
dust not yet dispersed by the rain and the plague was
coming to an end, Father Barrot came marching across the
plain, on paths through leafy woods, through sand and in
the haze of parched clay.

He himself, wizened, unable to perspire, wore his cere-
monial robes and raised the crucifix up high as he stood in
front of the crumbling, the disappearing, and forever
doomed Chinon Gate with his retinue: those who believed
in his powers of exorcism—the worried and curious ones.
His was the task to drive the demons out of the women's
bodies. Father Jehan Minet came to meet him accompanied by three Capuchin Brothers. The Lame and Fat
One perspired profusely when he hobbled toward the
Crooked One. Drops of sweat seeped into the corners of
his eyes and his squinting eyes were covered by a film of
dust.

*

Philippe Poussaut, née Tranchant, who had recently become a mother, sat by a window of her husband's, the
Royal Procurator's, house on the Square of Sainte-Croix,
watching the listless and comical procession pass on its way
down to Rue Pasquin. She shivered and was aware that
autumn had arrived.

The famous words that Assessor Daniel Drouin, weighed down by many sorrows, uttered on an autumn day in 1632, were these (which he later gladly helped circulating):

"There is a devil who is not *congru!*"

Some people will say quite rashly that the word *congru* means well adjusted or suitable or appropriate. We, however, understand immediately that this is wrong, since Drouin's observation would then have been unnecessary. Devils and demons are in no way whatever adjusted or suitable or appropriate—no more than diabolical persons: their nature or the water in which these fishes are swimming is inappropriate, their breath and their behavior, especially in regard to women, are and have always been among the most unsuitable and inappropriate ever. What Drouin meant with *congru* was what we today would call *grammatically correct.*

When Dan. Drouin exclaimed:

"Voilà un diable qui n'est pas congru!"

and his words were noted down by another assessor who helped him bruit them about, he didn't mean to express a demand that devils should behave correctly, for such a demand is unreasonable, but he wanted to display his knowledge, a result of his school years and his reading, and give his listeners an idea of his intellectual endowment. *Correctness*—and the playwright Molière would show that he was right a few decades later—in this connection had nothing to do with clothes or with manners but instead with grammar. Drouin simply maintained that the Devil and his retinue didn't know Latin, a contention which in view of the situation was a bold one.

One doesn't have to be a demon in order not to know Latin. There are also many almost saintly individuals and a countless number of less saintly ones (although not demoniacal) who don't know that language either. There are completely honorable and besides talented persons who are unable to say one coherent sentence in this ancient

171

means of communication. *But* a devil should be required to master a fluent and flawless Latin and further the chief dialects of Hebrew and Greek, and among the living languages—besides Spanish, Italian, and French, which are obvious choices—at least the one spoken in Scotland.

I make note of this so that the reader, if he wishes, will get a background for evaluating Daniel Drouin's courage. His remark, which was later spread abroad but curiously not distorted (unless we distort it now), essentially expressed—in an appropriate form—his doubt as to the existence of the Ursuline demons. He had more courage than we have today: we don't dare to express such a tremulous or affectedly confident doubt.

*

In October they had moved the exorcisms, which could not be kept secret any longer, to the Saint-Hilaire Church, down by the still-standing Bartray Gate. The exorcists had elicited the names of six of the demons who lived or, to put it more correctly, were housed for certain purposes within Jeanne, the prioress.

The rumors circulating in the city, recently laid waste by the plague, were so wild and many individuals were so indignant (with the sensitivity that comes in the wake of sorrow and plague) that the matter received more publicity more quickly than one had counted on.

Counted on?

Today some scholars say that the hand of a Higher Power could be perceived in the channeling of these events. Yes? No? But here on this little point in mankind's past, everything gives evidence that a cardinal's finger was raised and pointed.

*

Things often went well for the demons in church. But they also encountered resistance. The *bailli*, M. de Cerisay, a tall, middle-aged government official with a chin indicating willpower behind his pointed beard, requested that the case be open and public enough to be examined in detail. He demanded that those Ursuline Sisters who were most grievously possessed be isolated from their usual exorcists for a time so that other experts, practitioners approved by the civilian authorities, could step in and give juridical proof that they were bewitched. Nothing came of it. The pastor of Saint-Pierre, Urbain Grainier, could make as big a row as he wanted to: the sanctity of the convent protected the demons' actual work from outside view. Any demonstration of their diabolical activity in the women's bodies was for the time being completely dependent on the decisions made by Father Jehan Minet and Father Pierre Barrot.

What one saw: glimpses of frenzied demons on display before a rather numerous, relatively distinguished, at times frightened, at times curious and amused public.

The women had been brought here from the convent on Rue Pasquin and they had been placed on six mattresses on the stone floor by the high altar.

The most important person, Sister Jeanne, the prioress, lay in the center. On her left side lay the Cardinal's relative, Sister Claire, and to the right of her lay the older Barbeziers girl, Louise. The sorrowful assessor Daniel Drouin, who had been called in as a witness, had the impression of a carefully planned table setting. On the right—seen from Dan. Drouin's observation post—next to Sister Claire, lay the younger of the Barbeziers girls, Catherine, and on the left, next to Louise, lay Sister Anne, who according to the rumors had been especially hard pressed to drive coarse devils out of her cell. A short distance away from her, but rather in the background, in the shadows and correctly placed as far as the table setting was concerned, lay the serving sister Séraphique Archer showing much alarm from the very beginning.

They had been brought here to be observed and over-heard. The rumors about them had been replete with hor-ror and magic power. The Devil and his henchmen had selected them and had settled in their bodies and were speaking through their mouths. When Daniel Drouin heard the obscene words from the mouth of the unfamil-iar Séraphique Archer, the girl whom Capuchin friars and Ursuline sisters had captured for themselves and for the Lord, his reaction was not astonishment at first but a sense of shame both personal and entirely impersonal.

Deeply shocked, he looked at her a long time. She had changed considerably. He thought and feared now that the Séraphique he had known a long time ago was merely an outline of this woman, made with a light and nimble touch; when the clear and distinct picture was completed, it was not the same hand that had held the pencil. She had changed. She had been, he thought while shuddering at the brutality of the expression and the truth inherent in it, used to the utmost. Long, muddy, and rough roads had brought her far away from the girl he had known in his youth, the soft, trusting person with whom he had amused himself in the pitch dark in the back yard and during siestas out in the vineyard.

He had a fleeting knowledge of her later life, and we must firmly believe that he desired to help her. That she had been a whore he would not admit for the sake of his peace of mind, but his thoughts formed word combina-tions approaching the concept of a woman of ill repute, as for instance "victim of a false step," "itinerant existence without a thought for the morrow," "inner rootlessness"— and so on.

He was standing in the church behind his superior, the *bailli* M. de Cerisay, and the civil prosecutor, Louis Calvet, who was the *bailli's* right-hand man, and his brother, As-sessor Charles Calvet. Next to the tall Dan. Drouin stood the unbelievably tall, sturdy, and big-footed Scotsman Duncan, a Protestant who for many years had been a physician and teacher in Saumur. Consequently, Assessor Drouin had to control himself. But what he saw first and what he thoroughly assimilated as outline and as dreadfully finished pictures was Séraphique.

It was repugnant, even loathsome, to watch her twist and turn in the grip of the demons at the exhorting, arousing, and commanding shouts and cries of Jehan Minet and Pierre Barrot. Daniel Drouin thought of a stubborn donkey (and the thought stung him) which has had so much of a whipping that in the end it decides to trot off every which way. He knew of deplorable facts. She had run away from her servant's job when he was about to marry Charlotte. He had heard that she had kept company with a soldier and that she soon had exchanged that soldier for another. He could have had her jailed as a runaway but he had desisted. He had heard that she changed soldiers quite often and exchanged simple soldiers for simple clerks, but he felt certain that the latter didn't converse with her in Latin. She had stayed away from the city a long time and returned and was this: lost, lost! Later on, when she had become sufficiently lost, she was sufficiently converted to end up as a charwoman for the Ursuline Sisters, and the kneeling position, which she had already then assumed, had helped her reach the possibility of salvation and blessedness.

Did she recognize him as her glance was roaming unsteadily and her eyes, which had once shown such innocence, were now turning around in their hollows? Did she scrutinize the witnesses, face by face, seeking his? Or did she merely see a mass of witnesses, black, brown, and red shapes, the *bailli*, the priests, the government officials, and the burghers? A tall assessor, he stood among the secretaries and the notaries.

Besides, her demons tugged her all over the place on the straw mattress, pulled up her skirts, made her howl and scream and tried to make her vomit. But what did she see? Daniel Drouin, whose judgment just like most judgments was utterly subjective, thought he noticed in her some degree of satisfaction at being able to perform and play a role. But in the beginning he had great doubts that some demon—be it ever so shrewd and stubborn—would manage to speak Latin through her mouth. As the demons nevertheless did so, nothing could check the embittered philologist in his breast. I do not want to use the word incorruptible. For no human being is. Desperate firmness, embittered learning are the words that I want to use about his position in this matter.

Vis-à-vis the prioress, Sister Jeanne, he was less restricted. Here the examination and the censure could be more unimpededly objective. Sister Jeanne de Beaucil was no Séraphique Archer. Her features were purer, nobler if you will, and her hands were sensitive these days, not being used as much. There were no doubt inner similarities. She and Séraphique played two leading parts this rainy October afternoon and the others were their chorus. The leader and the servant resembled each other to an amazing extent in behavior and general rhythm and strangely enough also in the wretched Latin that the demons spoke through their gaping, shrieking, spitting, and cursing mouths. It was, quite simply, a Latin without depth, in a painful way reminding Assessor Drouin of the stuttering and jerky language that the late Father Poussaut had systematically whipped into and later whipped out of the first and second year Latin pupils in the very same town and its environs about three decades ago.

It occurred to him: I believe that old man Poussaut is really haunting the place!

Now it started to come out. Séraphique's stomach, chest, and neck twitched, it was in her throat, it came out of her mouth.

"Dibbolicka! Dibbolicka!"

The lopsided Father Barrot from Chinon looked displeased, disturbed:

"Speak, demon," he said quickly.

"*Diabolica!*" she cried. "*Diabolica—rosa!*"

"Yes, yes, yes," said Father Barrot impatiently bending over Sister Jeanne who was lying with her eyes closed, ready to start another obscene writhing of her stomach. Father Minet stepped closer to where she was lying, he waited and watched, tensely but respectfully: it was his work that had cultivated the field and sown the seed. One of his shoes squeaked. His hands were folded but he rubbed his palms against each other so that a faint, smacking sound could be heard. His hands perspire a lot and he eats a lot of garlic, went through Assessor Drouin's mind.

"*The other one!*" cried Séraphique. "*The other one!*"

"Yes, yes," murmured Father Minet without looking at her.

The other one—namely Sister Jeanne—now displayed much writhing of her stomach. Sallust writes (thought Daniel Drouin) that many people have derived much enjoyment from their body in the most unnatural manner, or at least contrary to what nature has intended, whereas the soul has merely been a nuisance and a burden. As mentioned above, Drouin was standing next to the tall and strong Scottish physician and teacher Duncan from Saumur. The assessor hid his hands on his back underneath his coat; his fists were clenched. He was looking at the prone figure in the middle, Prioress Jeanne. She must have been beautiful as a young girl, he thought, with another soul she might have been beautiful even now. Yes, beautiful but not sweet or attractive. That she had never been. One would hardly want to have anything to do with her. Her skin must be like a scratching, chafing hair shirt, her private parts like the mouth of a pike. Her eyes have probably always had an insane look.

Father Barrot, the highly reputed exorcist of demons,

stood stock still for a moment—a statue of decaying wood—waiting for what was to be lured out of the woman's mouth. He was listening, but his ear was also straining to hear M. de Cerisay's remark. The *bailli* had just asked when the demons intended to leave Mme. de Beaucil, when they could be regarded as having been driven out and when the prayers, threats, shouts of entice-ment, and authoritative commands would finally have an effect.

Sister Jeanne writhed violently in the grip of the demon. She panted and a cooing sound was emitted from her throat—a murdered siren call, thought Daniel Drouin. She stuck out her long, narrow, red tongue, but it was pulled, quickly and lizard-like, back into her mouth. She had long, narrow, very white teeth, her front teeth were slightly protruding. They closed together with a snap, and with a grinding sound. If her tongue hadn't been so quick, it would have been bitten off, no doubt.

It should have happened a long time ago, thought Daniel Drouin.

The very next moment he found this a cruel and unjust thought. Her tongue should have been paralyzed instead, he thought. Her whole being should have been paralyzed since birth, even in her mother's womb; the seed from which she had grown should have been dead—or never ejected from a man and never received by a woman's womb. Actually (he thought a moment later) that is an equally cruel thought.

As a spectator among many, chosen among many who had been chosen, in a group of mostly silent witnesses, he felt hostility toward her from the very first. He wasn't im-mediately aware of the cause, his own *causa animositas,* but behind it was probably his discomfort regarding Séraphique Archer's present situation. She should never have been allowed to leave us, he thought of her who was now shrieking from a modest place over in the corner. And afterward came one of his more ruthless thoughts:

Séraphique should have kept on as a whore for soldiers and clerks. She should have kept it up. She shouldn't have been seduced into this abomination!

Disconnected words, splinters of words, tufts of words came out of the mouth of Prioress Jeanne. The demons were working. They were busy acquiring within her a place with suitable acoustics for practicing their voices.

"Cras mane," it murmured.

The demons promised to stay until early the next morning. Daniel Drouin caught the word "the priest" and this *sacerdos* could only refer to one certain person. *Pactum!* cried a demon through her mouth, and this diabolical pact bound her firmly to the unfathomable, the loathsome, and longed-for—or to longing itself to be bound by a pact and to the longing to be set free.

Finis or *finit?* The end in any case. Daniel Drouin suddenly felt (with a kind of compassion) her weariness, her unsympathetic weariness. Did she mean that it was over now or that the demon had stopped tormenting and calling her or that she of her own accord had stopped cursing the priest—or that the thought of *sacerdos* and *pactum* and *rosas* no longer made her wild and frenzied? He saw how the beads of sweat on her temples trickled into the black, greasy tuft of hair below the edge of her cap, glistening on her downy upper lip. Was it all over now?

No, it was not all over. Did the Devil lie in order to take a breather while getting new strength deep within Prioress Jeanne? It is possible. Right after the brief interval as she was resting with her eyes closed and as Séraphique Archer had been silenced or was waiting for new signals, the prioress started to roll from one side to another. A body in heavy seas, a pendular movement in which her heart was alternately the heavy burden and its sudden relaxation. The muscles in her face were moving uncontrollably. Daniel Drouin saw a quick, bright, beautiful smile shine forth between two grimaces of disgust. The smile passed rapidly over her face, yes, it seemed really beautiful to

179

him, and then it was gone and drowned immediately in her distorted features. She was pale, against the ashen gray and against the deathly blue. Then came new surges of blood, and her skin color changed to a mournful, solemn, or angry violet rapidly turning to red and rosy pink. Then the paleness again, then the gray, then the violet in a rushing play of colors limited to a few but distinct tones, a stream of speckled shadows. And everything was connected and closely related to her groans, gurgling sounds and tongue protrusion and to the insomniac creaking of Father Barrot's shoes, to the rumbling in Father Minet's stomach, with his smell of sweat and garlic and with the smell of incense and the noises from the assembled witnesses: coughing, shoes scraping, and low or hissing whispers.

Duncan from Saumur murmured a word in Daniel Drouin's ear.

Outside it was dusk, it was drizzling. The noise from the carts leaving the city, the shouts from the Bartray Gate, the light clatter of the donkeys' hoofs and the dragging thumps of the horses' hoofs became distant and muffled.

"Adora Deum tuum, creatorum tuum."

Barrot's hoarse, harshly commanding voice. It was a phrase, an introductory remark, but it sounded so uncalled-for just now to ask her or her demons, above all the cursed Ashtaroth, to worship their creator. They waited and could see the answer emerge from her throat. Once again she was pale blue and at that moment the word "shroud" was formed in Daniel Drouin's brain.

"Adore te!"

The words were flung out very distinctly from her mouth. Barrot looked quite taken aback in this moment of great disappointment. He held out his hands as if to keep back the words. Daniel Drouin noticed how many of the witnesses were also taken aback: they were the Latin scholars; and his own grammatical soul was for some seconds a conflagration of vexation. He took a quick step

180

forward jostling his colleague, the younger Calvet, and stepped back slowly. The Scot Duncan touched his arm. His broad face was one big grin.

Did she worship Barrot, the mad or evil exorcist? She means Grainier, thought Daniel Drouin and of course all who could understand. If the Devil wants one to believe in his presence, he should not make such glaring linguistic blunders, thought Daniel D.

Barrot had to save the situation.

"*Quem adoras?*"

This was in order to help her, that is, the demon, and Father Minet translated it loudly for those witnesses who possibly hadn't understood: "*Whom do you worship?*"

Then the Devil made another mistake. Through her mouth he said much too distinctly:

"*Jesus Christus.*"

It was on that occasion that Daniel Drouin made his oft cited remark:

"There is a devil who is not *congru!*"

In a rage, yes, a *rage!* it burst out of him. One must also believe that in his rage he felt the pure, light joy of the know-it-all together with the annoyance of the man who knows grammar. All eyes were turned on him (this one time) and long afterward he remembered Minet's staring eyes and Barrot's icy, oblique glare; yes, D. Drouin had the somewhat insane feeling that the glance of the exorcist had hurt its back and was limping and like a drill twisting into the object of its vision.

Some of the witnesses tittered. The *bailli*, M. de Cerisay, and Louis Calvet, his closest man, for whom this October performance in the Bartray Church had been especially arranged, laughed out loud. Prioress Jeanne opened her eyes. Daniel Drouin noticed the awareness in them and saw dimly her fear: a schoolgirl who has made the wrong answer and will get poor marks or a note to her parents.

Séraphique Archer had received a signal, her demons started in:

"Dibbolicka! Dibbolicka!"

Daniel Drouin thought just then that he was conducting a struggle with Barrot not merely concerning the souls involved, as for instance that of Séraphique Archer, but to a high degree the very knowledge of Latin. He knew how the question ought to be phrased in order to help Prioress Jeanne and the demons: one only had to turn it around. It was as easy as feeding good children, although she was not being fed applesauce and fruitcake but devils and so violently and brutally that the food stuck in her throat. Duncan again touched his arm, clutched it, and when he gave the Scot a furtive glance, their eyes met. The Protestant physician and teacher from Saumur listened and blinked. His long, broad chin looked like the heel of a shoe, the little goatee was surrounded by gray stubble, his lips were moving. He was about to say something. His long, narrow nose was wrinkled from its tip to its root and the gray hairs which stuck far out of his nostrils began to quiver with every excited inhalation. He stood there like the Edict of Nantes itself. His light, watery eyes were staring under the dark, thick eyebrows that almost grew together, his eyelids were blinking and his pupils were contracting as if hit by a strong light. His broad forehead, which was creased both lengthwise and crosswise in an oddly searching and wild way, showed both irony and anger; and the black tufts of hair bristled as if the Scot had stuck his head into a whirlwind. These were observations that without being elicited by his curiosity merely flowed into and filled Daniel Drouin. Duncan remained silent, his wide mouth was tightly closed: now there would either come an angry shout, a snort, or else he would bare his long yellow horse's teeth in a smile at the same time ruthless and compassionate, an honest but bitter grin.

Barrot carefully phrased his question and now his voice sounded less hoarse:

"Quis es quem adoras?"

Here she was given much help: who was the one she

worshiped? But either (thought Daniel Drouin) the Devil would make fun of the grammarians or else the frightened, confused woman, driven into a corner, would merely grasp at words so as to get an answer that led her closer to an end, a *finit* or *finis;* she snatched at one of the forms and got hold of the vocative:

"*Jesu Christe!*"

A poor answer, useless in a final examination. If the demon Ashtaroth who had been tormented so persistently with questions and up to now had managed to get along with vague statements and definite hints, if he made fun of the spectators, the listeners, investigators, and officials, then the joke had fallen flat. Everyone was now thoroughly tired of him. Poor Latin, thought those who knew it. That time he really missed the mark, thought several who noticed the expressions of those who knew and guessed what the words meant.

"Louder!" shouted someone farthest to the rear.

Barrot craned his neck, pushed his chin forward together with his asymmetrical body, his warped chagrin. He was the teacher who really had given his pupil an opportunity and she had frittered it away, hadn't comprehended what was most simple and easy. For the sake of appearances he just couldn't give her a box on the ear on the day of the final examination. He said quickly:

"The possessed one said: *Adore te, Jesu Christe.*"

*

Here the protocol and the interpretations flow together in a smell of mildew and lust. We who now go through them with a listening ear cannot grasp any more truth than that there were demons in that city on that rainy evening. They didn't exactly come up from the underworld that people believed in. They were tired and obstinate, and Barrot, a much tormented and therefore tormenting man, pulled their ears and their legs trying to make them talk in an entirely special way. We cannot dis-

183

cuss his belief objectively, nor can we determine its strength, but we have no difficulty in perceiving the driving power behind it.

Dust and rain, even snow have settled on these protocols. We ourselves will have been earth and rain and snow many times before they have parted with their entire content, every seed and smell and drop of their truth. Many wars have already passed over them, they have been hidden and forgotten underneath ruins and sufferings *that have always been of greater current importance.* The parchment and the paper have been folded and then unfolded and in the creases great age has been collected. We cannot assert that we can see the demons. Nor can we deny the possibility that someone saw them clearly right there or that someone will see them clearly in the future.

The attempts and the renewed attempts, the rearrangements, the changing facial expressions and the different postures of the women, the men, the witnesses, and the victims seem distant and flow together into a prolonged and confused séance, lasting several months, even years of exorcism.

The questions and the answers had a purpose which one couldn't see very clearly just then (oh, yes, someone could!) and which one cannot say at present that it is clearly seen. Not by us with our heavy load of crimes and sufferings. One can dimly see a tower: it is still standing and it is called The Square Tower. There is a glimpse of castles and fortifications, if one looks hard one can see them even though they have now disappeared. One may hear hoofbeats that recede into the distance or get closer. Snorting, almost worn-out horses trembling when they come to a halt, panting, perspiring, muddy or dusty riders who jump down from the saddle, rolling, coming down with a thud from the saddle, or eager or anxious messengers who vault or crawl up into the saddle. Finely or carelessly cut pens scratch down meaningless—at that time

184

meaningless—words and phrases that were of decisive importance—at that time of decisive importance—which historians will sift or poets stare at without comprehending them.

Changes.

Mortar comes loose slowly and falls down from a surface made a long time ago and the stone underneath is graying, crumbling, or is getting darker. Forests sway as they rove across hills and plains: a wave of forests receding a few yards toward the south or toward the north, gnawed off at the edges where the peasant's axe and hoe penetrate for a generation or two. Later, in a movement that we with our limited view, our time-conditioned shortsightedness believe is immobility, the forest rolls, surges, or slinks back for a generation or two when the axe and the hoe have fallen out of the old man's hands;—a forest that buries, absorbs, and changes both man and hoe, before it once again pulls back when new roving fields and meadows drive it away and want to take its place in the plains or on the hills of Touraine, Poitiers, Vienne.

But in this shadowy course of events we can at times clearly see Daniel Drouin's tall figure, his sloping, not very broad shoulders: his well-kept, yes, as we now would say, foppish attire, his unwarlike official's sword. We can see his large, somewhat protruding brown eyes and behind them we perceive his curiosity, his knowledge of Latin, and a certain measure of other knowledge. A man who keeps his own protocol and therefore reads protocols with close attention, a witness we can use.

The words in the protocol vary, from precisely recorded babbling, like Séraphique Archer's "dibbolicka," "dibolka," and "diabolica" and the constant references to *The Other, The Other* by her other women longing for men, plain women, sanctified, or sexually inhibited—to Prioress Jeanne's at times almost automatic replies to Barrot's, Minet's, and the other exorcists' and conjurers' often perfect questions as to whether she was possessed *ex pacto magi, aut ex pura voluntate Dei,* through alliance with a sorcerer or solely through the will of God.

Prioress Jeanne was The Other, yes, in this situation she was, just as in the convent, the first and the most important, the permanent abode of demons and of fear for a long time. From her six demons made excursions to the bodies of the sisters and the serving maids who had been placed in a row here. Clarity came through her, she showed the direction and was during these hours a fine instrument. When curious or seriously inquiring witnesses asked questions and dropped a few words showing that they had gone to school and were up on the knowledge of the time or that they were interested in further moral or juridical clarity, then Barrot, the tireless pursuer of demons, immediately posed a new question that wedged itself in between the one he already had asked and the one an outsider had intended to ask: a direct question to which most of them knew the answer but which nevertheless had to be asked:

"What magician is that? What sorcerer is that?"

*

They had reached the source, the cause of causes. The question affected all the women who were lying there. Sister Claire on the prioress's left drew a deep breath and at once the older of the Barbeziers girls, Louise, did the same. The younger Barbeziers, Catherine, who was lying next to Sister Claire, whined like a little dog and showed that her demons had not gone to sleep, and Sister Anne, who lay beside Louise, on the outside, started rolling and moaning. The serving sister Séraphique opened her mouth to make a "diabolicka" howl, but Father Minet quieted her by saying, "There, there, there!" sounding both like a strained and friendly appeal and a harsh command.

186

"Urbanus!"

It is believed that the exorcist had promised the highest official in the town, the *bailli* M. de Cerisay, that he could ask a few questions all by himself, but that promise was broken.

"Who?" cried Barrot.

"Grainier," replied the demon through the mouth of the prioress, so remarkably softly and with so little hatred that it became a plain assertion.

Finally M. de Cerisay was given an opportunity to try out his Latin. He was taunting and skeptical and one can definitely claim that he conversed with the demon Ashtaroth, who was on duty, with that amiable irony with which a man of his type, powerful but enlightened, converses with a helpless enemy who may become dangerous if allowed to grow. The questions and the answers flowed easily into one another.

"Where is the sorcerer from?"—"From Le Mans."—"Which diocese does he belong to?"—"That of Poitiers."

It all happened so peacefully, the women were calm all of a sudden, languid, when it had been said.

The calm lasted a while.

*

The days become blurred. They tinge the protocol with their gray fear or leave behind narrow streaks of light. The scenery, the background, and the women's faces are changed somewhat, the features are made clearer or are smoothed over. The voices rise and fall through the clash of arms and deathly quiet, they can be heard despite the rustling of paper, scraping of feet, and the squeaking of shoes. Like a well preserved scream, a scream of hatred, may be perceived the exorcist Pierre Barrot's outburst one afternoon, right now, at this moment, exactly as it was perceived by Daniel Drouin:

"I would like to see you tortured for the glory of God

187

and that you give your body to the Devil for him to torture, the way Our Lord gave His body to the Jews!"

*

Those who were already convinced that four to six demons, all of them known by names, had penetrated
Prioress Jeanne through the sorcery of the priest Grainier,
those who realized how necessary it was to protect the
wives and sexually mature daughters of respected citizens
against the seducer from Le Mans, and those who gradually through impulses from higher quarters had arrived at
the opinion that the castles, walls, and fortifications of this
city ought to be razed—those who believed in this triad,
now adhered to it even more firmly. The others, on the
side of Governor d'Armagnac or those who were Protestants or only curious, were frightened, downright and de-
liberately scared and perhaps uncertain; but most had
their belief strengthened: the party of the Cardinal
wanted to kill a man in their city.

Prioress Jeanne sat up—was thrown or pulled up, someone asserted. Her hands were groping about aimlessly,
one could only see the whites of her eyes, her mouth was
wide-open and she screamed:

"I want to be free! I want to be free!"

Her face, a moment ago pale and tired, was darkening
to rose-colored, red, violet. She was perspiring and her
nose was running. She was groping for something invisible
in front of her and then placed her hands on her stomach
as if she had a cramp. They were helpless and could do
nothing but nevertheless it looked as if she was feebly trying to fight against a kicking fetus. Then the strength returned to her hands. She tore her kirtle open revealing
her naked, white stomach, her private parts and places
where demons are staying, wander about, and penetrate.
She twisted her body and the groping but not feeble hands
pointed to areas where the digested food and the used or
superfluous juices leave intestines and canals. Her convul-

188

sions showed an obscenity the like of which had surely never been seen in this room (it now served as the chapel of the convent) and hardly ever in the entire city. Through the formal wording of the protocol, this picture of it emerges: mentally disordered woodcuts in a rough style. When two very attentive Capuchin friars forced her to lie down again and another one tried pulling down her kirtle and Father Minet dawdlingly, *much too dawdlingly,* threw a red piece of cloth like a diabolical underskirt over the lower part of her body, she or the demons within her offered resistance. Through her tense facial expressions, across all the creases in her face grimaces of joy and weeping streamed as if an invisible hand—surely there were invisible hands present here—wrung and kneaded strange figures from her very elastic facial muscles.

The Latin poured with the saliva from the corners of her mouth. The words came in bubbles of spit, cascades of broken grammar, torn and wildly mixed remnants of what she had learned by heart. The demons didn't wait for Barrot's questions. They asked questions themselves, or fragments of questions, and the replies followed in a series of bits and pieces, two, three, four words in a row like links in a broken, scorched, in many places rusty chain: *Quare ingressus—Urbanus—rosas—pactum—Jesus Christus—cras mane —Urbanus—Jesu Christe—es in corpus—Urbanus—hujus puellae—sacerdos—adore te—propter praesentiam—Urbanus— tuum—*

Barrot was at first satisfied, later he felt uneasy. He had started something that he couldn't stop all at once. It was as when little boys set fire to a small and quite harmless wisp of hay right next to a big hayrick: suddenly everything is consumed by fire. He demonstrated, he feigned a kind of self-assurance but his limping was more mobile, his face was more tense and his hands were shaking when he extended them toward the demons. His questions were clearly formulated, and when she no longer tossed about so violently his words reached the Enemy:

189

"Why have you penetrated into this young woman's body?"

"Young" sounds like an exaggeration, thought that day's Daniel Drouin, the diligent, stubborn witness who had not yet been banished or been refused admittance.

The answer was late in coming, it was far to go to reach bottom. She was lying still now and Barrot could hold the monstrance against her forehead. One may possibly imagine that partial truth or perhaps the entire area of truth that also existed within her, was lit up.

"Because of your presence!" she replied.

The bitter taste of surprise on Barrot's tongue. Some laughed out loud, among them the *bailli,* M. de Cerisay, and both the Calvet brothers. Daniel Drouin smiled slightly until again he heard Séraphique Archer's coarse, broad guttural sounds:

"Dibbolicka! Dibollic . . ."

whereupon his face froze.

Yes, Barrot was like the man who, intending to have a drop of wine that he knows tastes good, by mistake has lifted out the vinegar bottle (it is always standing next to it in the cupboard) and still tries to look as if he really did get good wine in his mouth.

Into this came—with the caustic humor which not only mankind can display but also the animal world—a cat.

Its appearance is historically true. The protocols, the manuscripts, the printed notes may indicate some doubt as to the position of the cat in this play for fire and death and on such a big stage as this one—but it was there and all the reports agree: it was grayish-black.

Unusual sounds were heard and in this moment, so sensitive to sound, they were perceived as coming from the underworld. Perhaps Séraphique's scream had frightened the cat or it may have been tempted to come out by certain fumes and smells or by groans that sounded like miauws. In any case, there was the cat. One witness asserts that it first appeared in the antechamber, where it had come in through a chimney flue. It slipped quickly through the room, wholly visible to the human eye.

The séance was not interrupted but took another direction, turning into a cat hunt in which were combined zoological, psychological, historical, and demoniacal interests. The men were running, jumping, stretching out their hands, or grinning. The squeaking of Barrot's shoes was heard above Minet's heavy breathing, and echoes of many political and religious trials of heretics throughout the world seemed to reverberate. Finally someone got hold of the cat. A Capuchin friar held it with his hands protected by his cowl, the way one tries to hold a burning piece of wood. Barrot made a motion of command, which indicated respect for the one he was just then in command of. One might think that the cat was an Ashtaroth or Asmodeus changed into flesh, fur, claws, and spitting. The priest held the monstrance over it guiding its continued journey to where the prioress was lying, and placed it there. He sprinkled some holy water on both of them and then stood there waiting.

What was he waiting for?

That the cat was going to speak French or Latin and admit who it actually was.

The cat miauwed at the monstrance, blinked its eyes at the holy water, and started lapping up the drops. It observed attentively the signs of the cross and became very quiet when it felt the nice demonic warmth of Prioress Jeanne underneath. She herself lay with her eyes closed but in the eyes of the other possessed ones was lit the light of reason. Séraphique Archer's mouth was at first agape in amazement but all at once the red-cheeked girl began to laugh. Sister Claire, who had been quiet for a long time, spoke up and there was a measure of friendliness in her voice:

"But there is our pussycat!"

After this occurrence most of the participants thought

191

that the exorcism, the spiritual exercises of the day, ought to come to an end. The prioress was still lying immobile, with the cat on her chest. She lay there with her eyes shut seeing nothing of the external world, but her lifted right hand softly stroked the cat.

This would have been the end of it. Just at this point there was a possibility that may be called the human or— why not—the feline, the catlike, the final note, the sign that the end has come.

The potential of the smile. The play has come to an end, the spectators begin to get up from their chairs, applauding or displeased or merely with passive indifference replacing their earlier curiosity toward that which had occurred. The cat had shown that it was not a demon in disguise and with the ability to speak but in fact a cat.

The infinite potential of the smile. With the hidden resources which animate cats as well as human beings, the secret weapon which recent Western or earlier Eastern humanity has always retained as a possible solution to certain situations, namely with the smile elicited to oppose fanaticism, and superstition raised to dogma, the cat had subdued Barrot and Minet. Certainly not vanquished them completely but stopped them at a significant moment. If King Henry IV, so greatly missed by many, had been alive now in the autumn of 1633, he might have sided with the cat and resolved it all with a roar of laughter, this being the guess of one who has no claim to guessing correctly. Henry's son, Louis XIII, did not know how to laugh, at least not in any life-affirmative way, and the Cardinal, who at times smiled his thin, dangerous, acid, or sentimentally appealing smiles, was especially untalented when it came to laughter: his laugh lacked the necessary fullness. The spectator sneer, the official laughter of this locale, and Daniel Drouin's Latin-charged assessor smile sufficed at the most to create a pause. That's where we are now.

192

On the other side of the pause . . .

life with its wealth of variations, as history shows, held yet another potential in reserve.

Presumably awake and no longer totally possessed, the prioress Jeanne who had been lying quietly on her bed while being swayed back to the normal world, what we are inclined to call normal, everyday reality, swayed away from the obscenity and absurdity of the immediate past, began to move, and prepared to get up. She expected a request or a command from Father Barrot. Nothing was heard. Barrot looked for one more sign of finality, or for a renewed, better vantage point. He expected temporarily stupefied Ashtaroths and Asmodeuses to revive and help him. As when a prudent army commander, a strategic talent, is planning future battles in the very middle of the skirmish which he is losing because of tactical errors which he is aware of, so did Barrot plan the next offensive, the next regrouping of his forces. The moment was lost, but not the day.

The day too was lost, however. Marc Duncan made it a completely ruined day. For the seventh time the physician, teacher, and observer from Saumur and Scotland loosened his grip on Daniel Drouin's arm, lifted his square chin so that he looked even taller, more powerful and scraggy, and stepped forward next to the *bailli*, M. de Cerisay, and the Calvet brothers. He said:

"Would it be permissible to put still another question to the spirits and demons of whose presence here we have been informed?"

His stately appearance, his harsh although correct pronunciation, the foreign intonation in his voice, made the silence still more oppressive, a silence that ought to have been shattered by laughter. One could hear the rain dripping outside, as it had been dripping one day after another, but now the drops were more hesitant. The candles on the chapel altar smoked, one of them had burned

193

down to within a half inch, the other one had a few inches left. The cat blinked at Duncan and the spectators and purred.

Father Barrot looked up at him at a slant and then at Minet. Father Minet nodded, a mistake that was probably due to astonishment. Then Barrot nodded too:

"Please go ahead."

"Gentlemen," said Duncan, "it is well known that the Devil appears in all countries in the most varied shapes and that he converses fluently in all living and dead languages. Yes, his knowledge of languages spans even small, local dialects. I therefore request permission to interrogate Ashtaroth, who, according to my information, is still residing in Madame de Beaucil, in my mother tongue, in Scottish."

The prioress's lips moved. Barrot looked for a way out and when he in his confusion stepped half a pace forward toward Sister Jeanne's bed, his lopsidedness was most noticeable. He opened his mouth, his thin lips were completely bloodless, and he was still groping for words when she spoke herself and said:

"You are much too curious, sir!"

The Latin mechanism within her was set going:

"Deus non volo!"

At that Daniel Drouin raised his invisible red pencil and put a checkmark in the margin:

"Deus non vult!" he corrected her, and this was his second direct contribution in the month-long debate.

But she had already translated it to the wording she had in mind:

"God does not will it!"

Louis Calvet poked the *bailli*, M. de Cerisay, in the side and the *bailli* nodded to him; and then Calvet said:

"You have the regulations for exorcisms at hand, Father Barrot. If you take a look, you will find that one of the most important signs of genuine diabolical possession is, *primo:* that the Devil and his demons speak all foreign

194

languages absolutely fluently; and, *secundo:* that they know how to look into the past and what is most secret and to ascertain things that happen at a great distance from them and—"

But Barrot had had time to collect himself. He made, figuratively speaking, a jump right over the cat and the catlike and was now standing with the monstrance in one hand and with the other hand raised in an episcopal, yes cardinal-like, perhaps even popish pose: ready for battle.

"The Devil knows Scottish too!" he shouted. "Be sure of that! He knows all languages, but right now *he doesn't want to* speak Scottish!"

"You interrupted me, Father Barrot," Calvet said curtly. "You violate agreements. And I thought that you somehow could give commands to the demons; that's what you are famous for."

"The demons don't want to speak Scottish now, sir," said Barrot sourly; he was a man who had been put in his place.

"What about Hebrew?" Marc Duncan suggested.

"He doesn't care for Hebrew either, right now, monsieur," Barrot replied gruffly looking askance at Father Minet, but Minet had his back turned and was of no help.

Marc Duncan straightened himself up a little more, which indeed was possible, and once again stuck out his square chin. He was angry and the tuft of beard at the tip of his chin quivered:

"*How do you know that, Father Barrot?*"

"*I know!*"

"Then you ought to know whether he is used to miauwing instead of speaking Latin," said Duncan with one of the broadest and most yellow-toothed smiles appearing between the years of 1632 and 1634.

Bailli M. de Cerisay nudged Louis Calvet lightly in the side and Calvet also raised his goateed chin:

"And the clairvoyance and that which is generally hidden, Father Barrot? Do you also have power over that?"

Barrot got the opportunity to make a smart repartee:

195

"The Devil knows about the most hidden things, my good Monsieur Calvet," he said. "If you so desire, sir, I shall gladly order him to tell about all your sins. He will answer immediately and in a loud and clear voice."

Tittering. Someone looking at the floor. Another one scraping his feet.

"Oh, there's no hurry," replied Calvet laughing heartily, but not without some uneasiness.

At that moment Barrot was on his way back.

"I won't be stubborn either," he said and it sounded like an act of kindness on his part; and perhaps it was.

And Daniel Drouin?

He was very likely filled with thoughts or at least formulas and formulations. Just as other witnesses, called in or unwanted, he felt that the end of all this, which perhaps was still quite distant, had to do with blood and fire. He probably thought of Urbain Grainier who just then had a certain invisible authority in this city while the governor was away. Where was he, why wasn't he standing here defending himself, why did he turn his broad, straight, arrogant back to them letting new walls, which would be surrounding himself, come into existence, be built, and grow? Were there any demons within him? Or did he fight somewhere on the outside and by other means than with a red pencil à la Drouin in the protocol, a forefinger à la Drouin in the Latin grammar, irony à la Calvet, questions and sneers à la Duncan, nudges and winking à la de Cerisay? Did he sit perhaps in the governor's domicile, not yet torn down, reading letters with assurances from M. d'Armagnac that the prison tower had been saved from demolition, and giving Madame d'Armagnac good advice, or did he sit in Daniel Drouin's own house holding the hand of Mlle. de Brone?

*

What finally happened in the evening of this day of exorcism was merely an exercise prior to the next round.

Barrot had succeeded in salvaging something, perhaps the next encounter, and the defeat he had suffered vis-à-vis the cat and Duncan was suddenly no real defeat but only an episode tainted by a shadow.

One may gather all the available protocols into a bundle and turn the slow, month-long process into one single day of demons, ending with rain. Before the assembly of witnesses and prime movers dispersed, the demon Ashtaroth accompanied by the demons Asmodeus and Gresil forced his way into or out of the woman who had been tormented the most and was lying there a body of lust and anxiety, a soul in agony and in bewildered flight. They expressed themselves in brief phrases as when one bell answers another but the sound following every beat of the clapper is abruptly muffled.

Barrot raised both hands demanding silence. He summoned the demons. Prioress Jeanne once again started throwing herself back and forth, like a prisoner in chains who wriggles away from the lash. Her mouth opened, gaping wide, her eyes rolling in their cavities, from every side revealing the inflamed whites, with streaks of blood; and she *screamed.*

The magic of her movements infected the others, and when Sister Claire and Séraphique Archer responded with similar screams, they all screamed and began tossing back and forth. Father Barrot tried to give Sister Jeanne Holy Communion, but she fought it and seized hold of the monstrance with hands like gripping claws. He had to tear it away from her. She stuck out her long, thin, red tongue like a panting, exhausted dog. The documents state that he succeeded in giving her the Host but that she made an effort to spit it out: so profound was the loathing of the demons for that which is sacred. When Barrot wanted to push it in with his fingers and press it down her throat, she tried to vomit, and then he gave her some water. She had a fit of coughing, and when that had subsided she fell back on her bed and lay quiet for a short while. Her face was

197

sweaty, her hair sticky with sweat. Witnesses have said that she drank three mouthfuls of water.

Meanwhile the others were groaning, gasping, and rolling back and forth, and Sister Anne and Séraphique Archer were letting out wild shrieks.

Again silence, so that one could hear the squeaking of Barrot's shoes.

"Through which pact have you managed to enter into this woman's body?"

Sister Jeanne's demons answered through her mouth with the same words that the prisoners of war and the slaves of the rulers of Rome were apt to use when nailed to the crosses along some Via Appia—the cry of thirst, the eternal cry for water:

"Aqua!"

Daniel Drouin was probably the only one present who was thinking of crucified prisoners of war even though he had not been endowed with much imagination. He was also aware of the dryness in his mouth, the same kind of dryness in the mouth and the throat that sets in when one sees foreign foot-soldiers marching on the roads on a hot summer's day, or when specially commissioned troops tear down the fortifications, the old ramparts and towers which have infused one's hometown with life. He swallowed, moved his lips and the muscles in his neck and throat in time with the prioress's and he was not the only one to be doing so.

"Who brought the water of the pact?"

"Magus," she replied. "The sorcerer."

"At what hour?"

"The seventh," she answered, and that was just now. But he asked anyway, in this game between crashing, yes, crashing, bells, whether it was the seventh hour of the morning or the evening.

"Sero, that of the evening," replied her hoarse, croaking evening voice.

"How did he enter?"

"Janua," she answered, and Daniel Drouin thought of this word: the gate, which could be one of the gates of the body as well as of the convent.

"Who saw him?"

"Three," her voice replied.

They went away from there, singly or in small groups. Some of them hurried away, bent forward in the rain, to reach the inns before the *aqua* of heaven had given them croaking, coughing evening voices. Others walked away slowly, since autumn rain falling on their town didn't matter now.

Daniel Drouin walked up Rue Pasquin. Afterward he couldn't remember who had accompanied him. Perhaps Charles Calvet or Marc Duncan. He thought of the plague and the children. And he recalled that he stopped by the Church of Sainte-Croix, under the arch of the portal. There was a light in Madeleine de Brone's window on the second floor of his own house on the other side of the square. The old rug-dealer's store below was dark but he recalled a time when light filtered out through the shutters. He thought of how life might have been in this town without demons and without the plague and without the hands that tore down walls and moved people from one place to another. When he entered his courtyard through the side gate, the rain poured down, more noisily than he had ever heard it before, in the weeping willow on the other side of the garden wall; a few gusts of wind penetrated that far. There was a friendly light in his own dining room. Out in the courtyard he recalled—in his sorrow, his longing for the dead children—once again Séraphique, rather fleetingly. The memory vanished like a mild breeze in the autumn evening, a fragrance of youth, gone forever, a sort of bitter happiness in the dark.

PART II

The Story

11

Waiting and Dialog

A NIGHT IN the fall of 1633.

One candle had almost burned itself out, and when the wick at last bent down toward the puddle of wax, he took the candle snuffers from the pewter bowl and waited. He snuffed it out when the blue flame began to flicker. The burnt wick remained in the hollow of the snuffers, its tip still glowing. The smoke stung his nose. He reached out and put out the other candle. The room was dark but some light entered from outside. It came from an undetermined source flickering above the crucifix on the wall, shining with faint gleams on the dark table top, at the edge of the pewter bowl and across the worn leather of the armchair. He dropped the candle snuffers into the bowl. The tip and the blades made a dull scraping noise against the pewter.

The chair creaked when he got up. The thick bast soles of his slippers dragged across the worn and polished floor. He opened the window just a bit listening for footsteps outside. He heard the rain, a slow, fine, inexhaustible autumn rain on roofs and streets. Aside from that, the city was very quiet. It slept, the houses slept. Madeleine, who was not coming to him tonight, slept or lay awake. I wonder whether Louis Tranchant is sleeping now or is at a jolly party, he thought. How he sleeps—if he sleeps. The thought was unpleasant, he turned away from the window listening into the house. He thought he could perceive how his brother was sleeping—restlessly—in his room, how his sister was sleeping—restlessly—in hers, how his mother was sleeping or lying awake in her rooms on the other side of the house. How the church over there was sleeping or was waiting and at rest. How the plain all around lay beneath the rain sleeping or keeping vigil and waiting for loud human voices.

How the dying towers, the collapsing walls, the remains of the past kept vigil and slept.

How the books, what was left of them, those he had got back, were sleeping. He touched the backs of the books with his hand. On the other side of the room, near the door, he perceived the mirror surface. He imagined that he saw his own picture in it against the brighter window opening and thought—fleetingly—of the curse that his appearance had been.

He turned toward the window and listened. Some one was approaching from the depths of Sainte-Croix: heavy tramping wherever the street was paved. He tried to make out whether the person was limping. When the sound reached the Street of the Butchers he realized that there were at least two persons. Did the right one have some kind of bodyguard? But the footsteps died away and were not the right ones.

Madeleine would not be coming tonight: she knew. He reached out and felt the rain drops. We have been living in a hell, but I don't regret anything. Or? Nor does she regret anything. She ought to be here tonight, I want to touch her.

One night long ago, he didn't want to count the years, the Tranchant girl was standing outside here calling his name. He had leaned out of the window that time to tell her to be quiet. If he wanted to he could still hear her footsteps as she finally walked away. A young girl, a virgin no more, with a fetus in her womb. The paved part of the street started at the corner of the Street of the Butchers.

Did she slip right there? That part was always slippery with blood, clotted blood, which was never washed away, and the smell of blood and entrails. It happened that someone forgot about the remains of dead animals and not stepping carefully in the dark would slip and fall. The blood of oxen, of cows and calves, and sheep's blood were powers in the darkness obstructing people on their way. If one slipped and fell, one would at least get spots on one's coat.

Someone walked past the church and the corner of the Street of Saint-Pierre. The pavement outside responded. He could make out a moving figure. Its feet were in a hurry. A human being on the way home or fleeing. Frightened? One might while away the waiting time with completely unnecessary questions. "You are always asking questions, Urbain," Madeleine had said at one time, "but you never listen very closely to the answers and you yourself don't reply to questions put to you."

A human being in the darkness: now merely the sound of the steps remained. A man on the way home to surprise his wife?—or someone who just had been close to being taken unawares by another man? Testicle and vagina, the play, the desire of lips and thighs. Someone who was filled with love, with passion? With fear that it might be discovered or that it had been discovered? Or someone who wanted to discover with anxiety and anger: anxiety because there might be something to discover or because there was nothing to discover, a fear that wrath would be unfounded and changed into absurdity; anger because of the absurdity? A hunted one? It could have been me ten years ago or five years ago or fifteen years ago, he thought. Me? No, it was different. How different, then? Well, different. For that matter it is always different.

One night he opened the church gate for himself and for her. They entered. He held Madeleine by the hand, they stood in front of the high altar. The old stone work in the walls was so sensitive that their thoughts reverberated. Their whispers were like an ocean in storm, like volcanic eruptions and landslides. "I shall marry us, my beloved," he said. "Now you are my wife." If he wanted to, he could recall the trembling of her hand, feel it across distance and time. He could remember what she whispered to him and what he tried to answer or did answer. He wanted to remember it now, clearly and for a long time, he wanted—now—to be moved by it always because it gave him strength. He wished for tears. The raindrops on his hand, he now thought, ought to be my tears. I wish for tears, they give strength. Purely egoistically and coldly (he smiled at his thought) I wish for a feeling of indignation that will give me tears. Tears make me a better man than I am. When I cry I am a better man than when I am silent or tell the truth or smile. I want to be good. I want to remember that which makes me good. My beloved, my beloved, he whispered at the rain, beloved, beloved, we are the only ones who can know, about that night, and no one else will ever know more than we once knew! Our love is to know that we knew: it is the two of us standing here in darkness with boundless courage! No one will ever enjoy life upon this earth more than we did then! No one! And with us it will be forgotten.

Someone, or perhaps several were walking up from the town, they were three. A lantern was carried ahead; it made the darkness more impenetrable, shinier: it made the drops of water glitter. In the rain it was a ball of light, a rolled-up ball of a million fine threads. The lantern was swaying in a steady hand. Both the shapes following behind had put their coats over their heads. There was a splashing sound from a puddle, the light danced across the ground, someone missed a step.

I can smile here in the dark facing *the danger,* he thought. If they could see me now they would think that I was in league with the Devil, indeed that I might be Satan himself. Now he smiled even more broadly, his laughter was as audible as the rain: They believe that anyway! I "give the women flowers during the night!" I "give them flowers," I come to them "per flores" and rape seventeen dried-out or still moist virgins! I am the head of the entire demonological catalog, from Ashtaroth, Asmodeus, Behemoth, and Gresil! I give women flowers during the night and they give me back thorns and dry twigs during the day. Shouldn't that be called being ungrateful?

He remembered something, the glimpse of a memory quickly fleeing, hovering with the lantern shining on a puddle and disappearing with the desolate and yet comical sound of stumbling steps, of wet shoes, of curses at the puddles, the rain and the city: he recalled Théophraste Renaudot and his medicines that cured everything. The physician, the genius whom he had met several years ago and who now wanted to be a director in charge of the poor in Paris and the publisher of *The Gazette*, the Newspaper where among other things could be traced the tremors or the steadiness in the Cardinal's forefinger. Renaudot, the tall, pointy-nosed, talkative, and controversial friend of humanity and savior of men.

Polychreston! Twenty-five kinds of medicine in one single formula! Ambergris—rosemary—hypericum—figs—iris; nutmeg and pepper, anise and angelica, burnet and others. The philosopher's stone changed into mush and ointment, pills and drops that became the chemical and botanical cure-all of humanity for the root of mankind's sickness, which was now attacked at its very base; the enemy of coughing, gout, melancholy, colics, dizziness, paralysis, perhaps the plague, perhaps even death.

Perhaps of possession?

Then the smile disappeared; its brief existence had come to an end.

He pushed the window up a bit. Down there the right one was coming. He heard him gush out of the Street of the Butchers, and here, with the memory of the comical events still close, with a remnant of the humor through which he used to look at most things, even the most serious—yes, above all, the most dangerous—he thought: It is the ending of a catalectic verse, always the ending, where the last metrical foot is incomplete, the step never completed but implied, the one that sneaks past, an incomplete dipody.

The Lame One crossed the little square diagonally. He covered his head with his coat and stopped in front of the gate, waiting. Perhaps he was surprised when it didn't open by itself with the playing of music? And when there was no light in the window? He took a step or two into the street and looked up. All his movements were discernible, a visible lump of darkness. Finally, he said in a low voice: "Grainier?"

He let him wait a little while longer. He would be sitting here soon enough. He closed the window and groped his way across the room. The floor creaked loudly. He struck a light and lit the piece of the candle left in one of the sticks and put it back on the table. He assumed that his mother, his sister, and his brother were listening behind their respective doors. He wasn't in a hurry, far from it. The very hatred, the feeling of disgust, was a sort of restful satisfaction, a good and safe hunger that may soon be satisfied in combat. He walked slowly down the stairs and before he opened the gate he closed his eyes and breathed deeply:

"Come in, Minet."

*

The Dialog Begins

They were sitting across from each other at the table with the light between them. I will give him the opportunity to show his face, thought the one who had been waiting. And he will get the chance to see mine.

"I understand that you haven't come here to confess your sins, Minet," he said.

208

Canon Minet had already placed his fingertips together and his thumbs started moving. He looked askance at the wet coat hanging from a hook next to the door and dripping down on a tiny carpet. He has fine rugs, thought the canon. He is still wealthy.

"No."

"Nor have you come in order that I should confess my sins to you, Minet? Have you?"

"I can't answer no to that question."

That is the way one of my results looks, the other one thought when he saw the canon's short, fat thumbs at work. I am not to blame for the color of his eyes, his lameness, his smell of garlic nor the smell of mold and sweat about his body. And yet I have shared in his creation. Or is he a creature without a creator?

"You want to take a look inside me, though, don't you?"

"I'm not looking forward to the sight, Grainier," said the canon. And he thought: So that's the way he looks at night, the way the women see him. Or almost like that. His voice is like honey at times and like bronze, his back is straight also when he is sitting down even though he had a hard time of it in the bishop's prison. He is forty-three years old now. He takes good care of his hands so that they will feel pleasant when he touches women.

"No, the sight doesn't make me very happy. You know what I think of you, Grainier. What I have always thought of you."

"You have hidden it rather well for many years, Minet. Since the year 1617."

"In the year 1626 I told you who you were, Grainier."

He didn't answer. The canon was right. He told me then, and he remembers all the facts. He has been collecting facts and is right as far as that is concerned. But he is not right in actuality. He collects facts and soon he will have added others. It is curious how facts sound so convincing, how convincing they are in and of themselves. One thinks: data, facts, truth. He need only mention them to make them into arguments. One listens to facts, one drowns the truth in facts.

"I am sure you can even say what day it was, Minet."

"Yes."

"It's of no consequence. But you feigned friendship for me until—let us suppose—1626. Now you can say: I have always behaved as if I were his declared enemy. With the exception, of course, of a few years—for the sake of the good cause. Those few years turned out to be amost ten."

"Nine and a half," said the canon.

His thumbs stopped short to reverse their direction, he looked up, awaiting more questions. He can wait a bit longer, thought the other.

"You are no doubt wondering why I sent word that I was going to pay you a visit, Grainier?"

"No, I'm not wondering about that at all. I have expected it a long time."

"But you must be wondering what I am going to tell you, what I am going to ask you, Grainier?"

"No," said the other thinking to himself: He can wait, he can sit there waiting and imagining that I am playing some kind of game with him, figuring out some clever tricks.

"You arrived in our town in the year 1617," said the canon. "You've been here sixteen years now."

Numbers again. No one can deny that I came here in 1617 or that I have been here sixteen years. If he enters it in a protocol, they are irrefutable numbers. What is 17 deducted from 33, messieurs? With an overwhelming weight of truth the answer will give the result of 16.

"I trust you haven't forgotten to deduct the months that I was locked up in the prison of the Bishop at Poitiers thanks to you and Tranchant?" he said.

His thumbs emphasized his remarks:

"You came here in 1617. The Jesuit fathers in Bordeaux sent you here. In that quarter it was felt that you would be—successful."

The other man was waiting. He is not going to mention that I was rather good-looking and that the girls liked to have me act as their father confessor. He is not going to mention that I converted many Huguenots. He is even less likely to suggest that I was a great success and that I was received everywhere with open arms. He is not going to say that people liked to listen to me.

"You managed to worm your way into the better families around here," said the canon. *"You had your plan all ready!"*

The other one drew himself up from his watchful, somewhat hunched-up posture, placed his tightly folded hands on the edge of the table and with head held high and very straight back, he leaned forward facing the canon:

"You know very well that I didn't 'worm' my way in anywhere, Minet. People wanted to meet me in those days. They wanted to hear me preach. They also wanted to hear me discuss various things."

"That makes no difference."—The canon's thumbs paused in their movement.—"That doesn't make much difference, Grainier. When one takes in the whole situation the way I am able to now, one can see the plan very clearly. I can prove my contention with numbers and dates."

"I believe you really can do that, Minet."

"One might almost claim that you already from the very first moment wanted to destroy our city, Grainier."

"Why only 'might almost claim," Minet? Don't your numbers and dates and proofs suffice as valid evidence? You do know the facts? Put them to good use. You know that I have wanted to save the fortress walls and the towers from demolition. You know that the very existence of our town depends on the walls being allowed to stand and that the walls are not going to be allowed to stand, that the greater part has been torn down already."

211

"The fortress was a great asset for the Huguenots," Minet said. "The stronghold of the heretics, which you wanted to protect. So that they could stick it out here and corrupt the city."

The other man smiled at the canon: without cordiality but also without cruelty.

"So that's the way your plan looks," he said. "The fathers in Bordeaux sent me here in the year 1617 so that I could worm my way into the distinguished families and prevent the walls from being razed in accord with a decision that was made in the year 1622 at the earliest, and which the Cardinal did not put into effect until five years ago—and this the fathers in Bordeaux did merely in order to help their adversaries, the heretics, in this city?"

"This is merely dialectics," said the canon having observed his thumbs.

"No, it is your own argumentation."

"It is dialectics."

"In your hands it is a lethal weapon, Minet. In my mouth it is an attempt to dig out the truth from under the heap of lies made up of quite correct numbers with which you are now busy building a pyramid. I am to be buried underneath the pyramid. Isn't that so?"

Now both thumbs pointed outward and downward at the same time. Minet's chin rested on his chest, he had stretched his legs into a more comfortable position and was looking at his wet shoes.

"I am also seeking the truth, Grainier," he said. "You mustn't think otherwise."

"You are seeking truths that may help you, Minet. That is the kind that every one is seeking. It is not unusual. That's the way it is. But you are not seeking any other truths, for you have no need of other truths. The bravery of truth seeking ensues when one seeks truths that fall outside one's own need for them. You turn your back on the unnecessary truths. Instead, you want necessary facts that resemble truths. The supervisor of the razing and royal commissioner Laubardemont said once: 'Show me three lines of a man's handwriting and I can have him sentenced for heresy, high treason, or whatever.' He also meant to include: arson, the seduction of nuns, the prevention of urban destruction, or the spreading of the plague. And now you have Laubardemont here. Tonight he will give his big dinner, and tonight the decisions will have been made. Or: the proofs assembled. Or—? Do you want me to provide you with his biography?"

"You don't need to describe His Majesty's representative to me," said Minet. "You don't need to waste time on evasive maneuvers. We can stick to the facts. To your role as Governor d'Armagnac's secret counselor and deputy. To your role as the guardian of morality in this city. To your own biography."

"Is it to get my life's story that you have come here now? To enjoy it from my own mouth? No. But to make it."

"Yes, partly for that reason, Grainier. And in order to make certain things clear to you."

"Do you want me to guess?"

"That is not necessary," said the canon and for a brief moment looked him straight in the eye. "I want to give you a chance, Grainier."

"That I believe. A chance to enter posterity? Like the priest from our city that the canon Minet had burned?"

"I don't understand?"

"No, not quite perhaps. Not yet. It is lucky for you if you don't. But you know at least this much, that you already, publicly, have mentioned the name Gauffridi—the priest who was sentenced for witchcraft at Aix more than twenty years ago. A colleague of us both. Yes, a colleague of ours, of yours and mine and Pierre Barrot's from Chinon. A priest."

During the pause, the thumbs were twirling.

"There is certainly a striking resemblance between you

and him," said Minet, squinting up at him.

"Yes, that's where you have arrived with your logic: a striking resemblance. An astonishing resemblance between the two cases. Why don't I stand up and say: Doesn't Minet's case show a striking resemblance to Gauffridi's? Both of them priests! No one can deny that!—Now listen, Minet: every 'case' is at some point 'strikingly similar' to all others. At some point. If one doesn't look for *that* point, one is not compelled to know that it exists, and then one may claim that no person's 'case' resembles another's. But if one is looking for the point, one can easily prove that anyone is like Louis Gauffridi in a certain way, from a particular angle. It was raining on Gauffridi, it is raining on me. There you have all at once a resemblance that is striking, Minet. It rained evil spirits on the good sisters in the Ursuline convent at Aix twenty-two years ago, and it is raining evil spirits on the Ursuline Sisters here. That is a fact that you are acquainted with. You can say with a completely clear conscience: The case of Grainier resembles in a curious way the case of Gauffridi. Both are priests and both have been accused of turning demons loose on Ursuline Sisters."

"The resemblance is quite remarkable," said Minet.

"Certainly. It is raining on me. I am a priest. The nuns are possessed. You only have to select from a big pile of arguments against me. And you readily select some. You select the argument Gauffridi and select the ear into which you whisper it. As to the rest you are only a human being who hears and sees all that the others think they see and hear. You are not inventing lies. Your conscience is clear."

"Once again, what you say is merely dialectics," said the canon, in an unexpectedly calm voice. "But you are right in saying that I have a very clear conscience. You are just now defending yourself so zealously with dialectics because I have told you some unpleasant truths. The only way you can escape my truths is through dialectics. You know that you are an unnecessary, useless, and harmful person in our city."

"At the very moment I tried to prove how unnecessary and harmful you are, I would be giving you another argument which would be a proof of what you are saying," said the other man slowly. "You would maintain that I twist and turn unwilling to face the truth about myself. Perhaps you think that that's the way it is. You can obtain many proofs to this effect—since you already believe it. And merely this that I defend myself you construe as a half confession of my guilt. Guilty of what? Of that which you have a thousand arguments and proofs of: *of everything!* From a certain viewpoint, every human being is, or may become, guilty of all that is evil. It is only a question of placing oneself at the proper lookout point in order to get the desired angle."

The canon twirled his thumbs for a moment or two before he all of a sudden and resolutely sat up straight in his chair becoming a man who no longer was lame: the upper part of his body was long and dominating, his plumpness gave him a sense of authority. After a slight pause, the thumbs continued at a slow rate of speed.

"I have not come here in order to discuss humanity with you, Grainier," he said. "Humanity rests in the hand of God."

Pause.

"Do you deny that, Grainier?"

"No, that I can't deny."

"Do you deny that the Church is God's consecrated instrument and that the priests are its representatives?"

"I am not able to deny that."

"Do you deny that if anyone injures the Church, then he injures God?"

"God cannot be injured, Minet, that you must know? Human beings can injure one another, that we know."

"You're being evasive. You are afraid to say what you

215

think. Do you deny then that he who injures the Church injures God?"

The canon once again gave him a quick and searching glance. Just then he looked as if the entire Roman Church had been entrusted to his care—not for a long time, only very temporarily, but *just now.*

The other man leaned back in his chair. His long, narrow hands (well cared for! thought Minet) lay on the leather armrests. When the candle flickered because of his slow movement, shadows passed over his long face like a smile.

"You are much too elementary, Minet," he said. "I thought you had read more and that you weren't that elementary. I thought you had developed during the last ten years. I hope your feet aren't wet? I don't like opponents who have wet feet and sit here catching cold. It's no good wearing soaking wet shoes. Would you like a glass of wine?"

"No," said Minet after a slight pause, sinking back in his chair, the upper part of his body looking shorter.

"Then I want to listen to my biography right away," said the other man. "That shall be my punishment for the way I spoke just now: to hear it from your own mouth."

The canon decided on a direction for his thumbs and did it conscientiously.

"Shall I start with Scévole de Sainte-Marthe?" he said. "The way you deceived him?"

"He was my highly respected friend, Minet. One of the finest men I have ever met. You shouldn't talk about him, above all not you, Minet. You are desecrating a dead man. You are raping his memory. You are slobbering on his coffin."

"You wormed your way into his home," said Minet. "*Now* one can see it all clearly. You needed a cover for what you were doing nights—with our women. You tried to have a hand in everything. They made you pastor here

216

at Saint-Pierre after Father de Laval, and when you came here you had practically your entire family with you: your mother, your three brothers, your unmarried sister. Can you deny that?"

The other one didn't answer. He was staring at the candle, got up, fetched a new one, lit it, and placed it in the other candlestick. Everything in the room stood out more sharply. When he sat in his chair again, he saw that Minet's face had taken on color and radiance.

"You can't deny it," said the canon with a note of triumph in his voice. "You can't deny that your brother François has become first curate at Saint-Pierre, you can't deny that your brother Jean has a parish here in our city and that you helped place him here, you can't deny that your brother René is an assessor in the office of the *bailli,* your friend M. de Cerisay. Can you? Nor can you deny that your helpers in Bordeaux didn't take long in obtaining for you your prebend in the parish of Sainte-Croix? Can you deny that? No? Well, there you have my little truths, Grainier!"

"Minet," said the other one leaning forward and trimming the wick with the snuffer, "I can expand my biography so that you will have a background for the little truths. You may regard it as boasting or an attempt at subterfuge but I can tell you that I was born in the diocese of Le Mans forty-three years ago, that my father was a royal official and that I was so clever and bright that my uncle Claude—who was quite famous, did you know that?—brought me to Saintes where I first attended school, and afterward I came to the Jesuit fathers in Bordeaux and there I was a very good student."

He threw the snuffers into the pewter dish and sat up straight in his chair:

"I can give you more background information. Should I say that I was goodlooking? You will think that it sounds worldly but when all is said and done it was God who created me like this and one ought to be pleased over His work, isn't that right? But go on, go on!"

"Nothing is easier," said the canon. "Your boasting alone now proves who and what you are. As soon as you came here, you sought out the right people to know—who could help you to greater power. You forced or wormed your way into the house of old Scévole, for there you would meet the right people. You had trained your tongue, it was smooth and it fooled them. They considered you witty and learned. You made fun of the monks, who hadn't received your theological education. It was easy. But in fact you blasphemed against both the Holy Father and God."

"Above all, I fell out with your family, Minet."

"My family had to defend itself," said the canon. "It still does against all kinds of importunate strangers in our city."

"Yes, it's your city, isn't it, Minet."

"Yes, it is my city, Grainier."

"It has become *mine*," said the other. "And now you want to harm it and take it away from me. You want to destroy it thinking that you and your family will find happiness in the ruins."

"We want to defend it," said the canon. "Against seducers and their demons."

"It is my city now," said the other man again leaning across the table. "I have fought for it and that makes it my city just as much as your family's. I am proud of fighting for it."

"Yes, you cannot hide your arrogance."

"No," said the other, "I neither can nor will I deny that at one time I was so arrogant that I gave myself precedence before the then bishop of Luçon. But I was within my full right as the ranking priest here and he was only prior at Coussay."

"He was a bishop and now he is a cardinal," said the canon.

"Yes, he is the Cardinal now," said the other one.

"Yes, he is His Eminence the Cardinal now."

"And Laubardemont, who is giving his big party this evening and tonight—why aren't you there?—is his, shall we say, tool."

"The commissioner plenipotentiary of the King and his deputy," said the canon.

"And the Cardinal is razing the fortifications here in our city and is building his own city with stones from here."

"You have always had a subtle tongue," said the canon (and now he enjoyed his own candid simplicity), "and I don't want to discuss the matter. But the fact is that His Majesty with God's help, and I acknowledge also that of His Eminence the Cardinal, is tearing down the last strongholds of the Huguenots and the heretics."

"I don't want to go further into what the stones are to be used for," said the other man. "Nor how the officials and artisans here are to be made use of—since so many of them have helped tear up the soil they themselves are standing on. Is it possible that Cardinal Richelieu's city has a need of inhabitants?"

"You are very subtle," said the canon again relishing his simple candor. "Shall I go on with your biography or have you had enough?"

"Go on, it interests me," said the other. "Perhaps it will help me."

"In regard to what, if I may ask?" said the canon.

"To get an overview, Minet."

"I will gladly help you with that, Grainier," said Minet, and once again the upper part of his body seemed to increase in length. "Do you want me to tell you about the Tranchant episode?"

The other man also sat up straight in his chair. His hands were at rest, at first he clenched them, then cupped them over the armrests. His chin with the black glossy and well-groomed pointed beard—the "cardinal's tuft" it was called here and in other places—pointed upward, he looked at the ceiling.

"Please go on," he said after brief hesitation. "It will be fascinating to hear your version direct from your own mouth. I don't begrudge you the pleasure. Or, to be absolutely honest: I do begrudge you the pleasure. But please go on. You—."

12

Deliver Me from This Fear!

DANIEL DROUIN WAS not invited to M. de Laubardemont's grand dinner until the very last moment: before
noon the same day. He didn't regard the invitation as a
sign that he had suddenly been raised to be one of the
most important men in the city. During the hours he was
busy getting dressed, the thought came to him time and
again: They need witnesses now and that is why they have
invited me too. One always needs witnesses who are
thought to be weak. Do they think that I am weak? We'll
see about that!

He was wondering who would be coming and about
what they would get to eat. In the afternoon, when he
finally considered himself ready, he walked into the
kitchen to see his wife Charlotte. He walked about with
great care in his fine clothes. Their small children, the
youngest ones, were crying in the bedroom. They always
want food, he thought. That is good, it shows their will to
live.

"Now we have fair weather, Charlotte," he said. "It's so
nice outside that I'll take a walk and get some fresh air.
There's nothing wrong with the children, is there? They're
crying?!"

"No," she said. "But are you leaving so early? Are you
worried about something?"

"A breath of fresh air never hurts," he said. "One can't

leave parties like that until the most distinguished guests have departed."

"Are you nervous, Daniel?"

"Nervous, no not quite!" he said more impatiently than was usual. "It isn't *that*. But there is something ominous about all of it. And I guess I was invited at the last moment instead of someone who was prevented from coming."

"Someone who dared be prevented from coming," she said.

"Now, now!"

"Assessor Drouin looks fine," she observed sagely touching his modern jacket, his fine cuffs, and full-cut trousers. He put on his short cloak and put his hand on the rapier hilt, stood at attention. "Assessor Drouin," she said, "he who has been invited to His Majesty's commissioner, the famous burner of people and demolisher of cities M. de Laubardemont! Daniel Drouin, my fine husband!"

"Pshaw! Stop that kind of talk," he said stroking her round back and her stomach, which was getting round again. "You know how one feels about it."

"And how the Governor and how Madame d'Armagnac feel about it, Daniel. D'Armagnac will slip away as soon as Laubardemont is here. Will there be ladies present? Has Madame d'Armagnac been invited? Do you know?"

"I'm wondering above all if *he* has been invited," said Daniel D.

"Grainier?"

"Exactly," said Daniel D.

"Then Tranchant can't come," she said.

"I'm leaving now," he said bending down low to kiss her on the cheek.

"Imagine how far the son of an ordinary rug-dealer can get in this world," she said looking up into his face. She walked back a few paces inspecting him from top to toe. "You should have had a servant and a coach, Daniel. Or a nice carriage at least. The streets are so muddy after all the rain. You are a fine-looking assessor, Daniel."

He drew himself up and let her admire him.

"My pet," he said. "You are married to a fine fellow who knows foreign languages, has some money, a couple of houses, a vineyard, and is strong enough to give the Devil a real knock on the snout."

They both laughed. The maid standing over by the stove giggled. The children's screams sounded like music.

"Daniel," said Charlotte Drouin and took a few steps toward him, "it is dangerous to get on the wrong side of those—over there! Of them and their demons!"

She laid both hands on his breast.

"I'm not the kind who bows and bends," he said. "But I know how to act when invited out."

"Why have you been invited, Daniel?"

"So that it will look like mixed company," he said in a serious tone of voice. "They want some neutrals to be there too."

"Daniel," she said with her hands on his breast, her fingers touching the fine, gray cloth. "It is dangerous! To me it is like—like the plague!"

"It *is* like the plague," he replied not looking her in the eye.

"It smells of death, Daniel!"

"It stinks of death, beloved Charlotte," he said. "There is howling death around it."

"Be careful, Daniel," she said, with her forehead against his breast, with the marvelous cloth against her forehead. "And—don't come home so late—and—and don't drink so much, Daniel? I will be awake and waiting for you with something good. We will keep it warm for you. Daniel?"

She looked up again, pushed him away from her.

"Go now, otherwise I'll be nervous too. Are you afraid? No, forgive me, I know that you are brave. Go now, run, you don't have much time, it takes at least five minutes to walk over there and you have only a little more than two hours to make it in!"

*

223

With long strides he walked across the square and turned the corner into the Merchants' Street, which was very crowded. He had to greet people, many looked at his attire, and he could see what they were thinking. When he passed the tavern of "The Broken Wing" he heard his name mentioned in the semi-darkness inside. I am well known, he thought, they know that I am a man who speaks up when it's necessary.

He crossed the Square of the Poultry Dealers and looked in through the open door of the inn "The Swan of the Cross," which was owned by the mother-in-law of his colleague Champion. A few soldiers could be seen in the main room on the bottom floor; two of them sat by the stairs leading to the second floor, one was loitering by the door to the kitchen, two were sitting on the settle on the right with small wine glasses before them. Daniel Drouin pulled his head back. This is where M. de Laubardemont was staying. He was to give his splendid dinner in the big room on the second floor.

Assessor Drouin lifted his glance to the row of windows. M. de Laubardemont had the entire second floor so that *it should appear as if. . . .* It's a fine building, thought Daniel Drouin lowering his glance; he turned around and walked slowly across the square. There, on the other side, lay his favorite tavern, "The Hen."

"Drouin!"

He looked down through the door opening. Inside, in the semi-darkness, sat the narrow-shouldered and skinny Petiot on a stool below the oaken counter, and on the bench right across from him sat Antoine, the foreman of the masons and bricklayers, broad, heavy, and short-bearded, and Cerisay's clerk, the well-kept and half-drunk Dolet.

"Come in for a while, Daniel."

He hesitated. All three were Huguenots and so was the innkeeper. Just now it wasn't the best thing to be with

224

Huguenots, not at this moment, on this particular day. But he walked down the three steps and over to them.

"How fine you look," said Dolet and felt with his thumb a corner of his coat. In the light from the outside his closely shaven cheeks had already taken on a rose color.

"Going to a party? To the party?"

"Yes," answered Daniel Drouin looking around. Petiot quickly extended one foot and pulled a stool over to him.

"Sit down!"

"What are you doing here so early in the day?" said Daniel Drouin.

"We're sitting here thinking," said Dolet. "We're thinking about the future and about the honor you're doing us by sitting down with us *here,* as finely dressed as you are. Are you going *there?*"

"Yes," said Daniel Drouin and sat down.

There was a smell of sweat and dirt and on Dolet a hint of perfume. In the corner underneath the lattice window facing the street, a man sat staring into a tin cup which perhaps was empty. Daniel D. thought he had seen him before. From the kitchen came the sizzling sound from roasting meat and the grating sound of a spit. There was a smell of roast pork. He looked into Petiot's dark eyes and winked at his childhood friend.

"Who is that over there?"

"The one over there," said Petiot in a loud, almost screeching voice, pointing with his thumb. "Do you mean that fellow?"

They turned toward the lattice window. Dolet smiled scornfully, the restrained smile of the intelligent intoxicated man. Antoine stared with his pale eyes. He shrugged and it seemed as if he had just lifted an ox or a big boulder.

"He is a spy," said Petiot, as loudly as before. "He's sitting here spying on us. In case we say something about the

225

Cardinal. Whom we admire so greatly! Whom we almost worship! Isn't that so, Dolet?"

"Sure-sure. He is our god. We *love* him!"

"We would kiss his behind if we could only get at it through his skirts," said Antoine.

"Keep quiet with that stuff," said Daniel Drouin glancing furtively at the man in the corner, who had looked up and was listening.

"His name is Pantaleone and he is a Genoese," said Petiot. "Now, you Juppitter over there, clean your ears for now we're going to do some talking, my friend!"

"Keep your mouth shut, you damn'd carpenter," said the other one without looking at him.

"This time he came here with His Grace Monseigneur Baron de Laubardemont," said Petiot. "He is going to help him hunt devils. We know the fellow, he's been here before."

"The dirty swine," said Antoine.

"Be quiet now," said Daniel Drouin, "and I will drink something light with you."

The innkeeper, a blond man from the north, appeared in the door to the kitchen, smelling of roast pork.

"What would you like, Drouin?"

Daniel Drouin immediately felt more at ease; he stretched his long legs, removed his plumed hat which he placed carefully on the bench below the counter and stroked up his thick brown hair.

"First of all, go easy on the garlic—not stingy but just enough, Albert. And don't forget that you'll get heartburn and an upset stomach from too much pepper."

"It is to help the thirst," said the innkeeper, grinning.

"Secondly, I would like to have a small absinthe," said Daniel Drouin.

"Red," said Antoine and put his glass on the counter.

"White," said Petiot. "No, red, it gives you more blood. In case you're forced to sacrifice a pot to the Devil now that Laubardemont is here."

"Keep quiet with that nonsense," said Daniel Drouin.

"Absinthe," said Dolet. "A big one."

"You big lout over there, what do you want?" said Petiot.

"Shut up, you damn'd carpenter," said the man in the corner without looking up. "Red."

"Write down carefully everything we say, so you earn your wages," said Dolet.

"And don't forget what we're thinking, you louse," said Petiot.

Antoine turned his face toward the ceiling, his broad beard stood out like a stiff brush. He wiped his left eye with a corner of his shirt, smoothed his mustache, and drank.

"Daniel, you are a learned man, why don't you tell him to go to hell in Latin."

"I'm that learned too," said Dolet.

Daniel Drouin drank, he was feeling much better in spite of the man in the corner. The tiny fear was almost gone.

"Absinthe and crap," said Antoine. "Red has always been good enough for me. And for my father and grandfather and my—the Devil only knows—for my grandmother."

"What were you sitting here talking about?" asked Daniel Drouin.

"About the workmen here who will soon be as badly off as the clerks and the minor officials," said Dolet.

"Worse off!" said Antoine. "As for the clerks, they can be loaded on a cart and driven to the Cardinal's new city over there. Then their living is secured. The workmen won't be treated with that much consideration."

Dolet stared at the man over in the corner, drank from his glass, and said:

"Note it down correctly, Pantalong."

"Shut your mouth, scribbler," said the Genoese with his hard pronunciation and didn't even look in their direction.

"Masons build," said Antoine. "They build cities, at least they did so in the past. Scribes and clerks write to make cities disappear and they want the masons to help with the razing. Just a little scratch of a goosefeather and then masons show up to tear things down! When everything is torn down, we masons may as well go hang ourselves. Or let them burn us alive in the public square. Unless we want to trudge over to the Cardinal's new city with stones from this city in our hands. —Write down what I'm saying, Pantalong."

"Keep your dirty mouth shut," said the man without looking in their direction.

"Cut out that stuff," said Daniel Drouin.

"And the carpenters—," said Petiot in a shrill tone of voice. "The only ones who'll be able to support themselves in this town the next few years are the lawyers and the monks and the whores. The whores especially can look forward to a fine future here. Just think of all the soldiers arriving here who feel peckish."

The innkeeper who had taken a look at the roast pork, was again standing in the door to the kitchen smiling his fine smile which took in every one.

Dolet emptied his glass and waited to have it refilled.

"The whores—," he said.

Séraphique, thought Daniel Drouin to himself. He stood up from his chair, fished a coin out of his pocket, and took his hat. He put it on his head with great care. They observed him in silence.

"I'll have to go now," he said.

*

Daniel Drouin stopped on the corner of the Street of the Butchers, turning things over in his mind. The best method, he reflected, is to think of something else more pleasant. In the past one could use the method of conjugating Latin verbs in order to get away from unpleasant

228

thoughts. It is just like counting imaginary running woolen sheep when it is difficult to fall asleep. But there's always of course a goat bleating among the sheep or a lion roaring or the Devil himself and then you're horribly awake at once. I thank the Lord that I always sleep well, he thought with feigned piety. Cicero says: *Hunc mihi timorem erope.* Yes, deliver me from this fear. What fear? *I* don't feel any fear, do I? I am standing here in my own city and it was a good thing that I had a little absinthe. Absinthe always makes my head feel so clear.

There was the smell of a slaughterhouse in that area. The street was still wet from the rain, although the afternoon sun was shining down on it. Some fellows were shouting loudly and boisterously while hoisting up a heavy steer's carcass in the middle of a wide gate. The noise reverberated as if it came out of a funnel. Daniel Drouin looked down at his shoes. Antoine had accidentally kicked them with his wooden shoes which were always muddy. I can rub it off against my stocking before I walk up there, he thought. But then my stocking might get dirty?

He looked up and down the street and at people who hurried past. Someone greeted him, he nodded back. I wonder what they feel and think? That one is a Catholic. That one there is a Huguenot, I know for certain. The one over there—

Two small boys came running, they were trundling a hoop. He quickly jumped aside and pressed so close against the wall that his back was touching it. The hoop brushed against the lower edging of his coat and hit the wall just at the corner and fell to the ground with a clanking sound. The wooden hoop was covered with filfth and the blood of animals. The boys' bare soles made a squeaking sound against the cobblestones. He looked at his coat but discovered no spots.

The thirteen or fourteen-year-old son of the notary Béliard was crossing the square and seemed not be in a hurry. He waved him over to him.

229

"Jean, will you see if I have any spots on my back. I bumped against the wall."

The boy first looked up at his face to see if he was drunk; when he had taken a good look, he immediately became more courteous and attentive.

"Yes," he said. "I'll brush if off. It's only a small white one."

"Thank you," said Daniel Drouin. "Why aren't you in school, Jean? Weren't you in Poitiers? Or was it with the Jesuits in Bordeaux?"

"In Poitiers," said the boy. "My father had me come home."

Jean's face closed up. Daniel Drouin became interested. "Why did he do that?"

"I don't really know," said Jean. "Good-bye, I have to run along."

He was in a hurry and started off at a trot—all the way up to the gate of the slaughterhouse. There he stopped to talk with someone inside the archway.

"Don't really know," thought Daniel Drouin having crossed the square and now standing at the top of the street leading down to the Chinon Gate. "Don't know." Of course he knew. If Béliard starts out as a Huguenot and later becomes a convert, or at least a semi-convert, and enters his daughter in the school of the Ursuline Sisters and sends the boy to the Jesuits in Poitiers—but then takes the girl out of the Ursuline school and lets her stay at home and then brings the boy home from Poitiers— then—then *something has happened, then someone knows something!* "Don't really know." Humph! But I know, my friend. Your father took your sister Louise out of the Ursuline school when the Devil possessed the prioress in earnest! Many of the fathers here did the same! But he doesn't want people to think that he who was almost converted again is almost not converted any more, and he doesn't want the Huguenots to believe that he repents! He

230

doesn't want people to ask *why* so that he has to think of a *because*. It is truly very confusing.

He took one step down the street, two, looked around, some one said hello and he greeted him back. Is Béliard afraid of something? he was thinking.

He took fairly long steps. The sun was still so high in the sky that it shone into the street, he had it at his back.

*

Where the street again divided in two, he stopped and hesitated outside his cousin Mathurin Thiboust's entrance gate, which also served as the entrance to the inn "The Golden Apple," which had a stable inside the yard. A horse was neighing. Someone quite close was singing in a low voice, he could make out the words. It was annoying to listen to them.

An unhorsed closed carriage was standing outside the inn stable. In another part of the yard there were another stable and Mathurin's smithy and carpenter shop underneath a roof sloping down from the brick wall of the neighboring building. Three unhorsed peasant's carts with high, narrow, and warped wheels, a plow with an iron-tipped share, and a donkey cart covered with a kind of tent made of rough cloth were all standing in the yard. Inside the carpenter's shop lay a yoke for oxen and wheels that were to be repaired. There was a smell of horse manure, soot, and freshly cut wood.

He walked across the muddy yard on the cobblestones, which served as the boundary between the coach-builder's property and the inn, and looked into the forge. Some embers and a little smoke were still there, it smelled warm. He pulled at the bellows, which sighed and creaked. A few puffs of smoke were emitted, followed by thick smoke, with sparks flying from it. The handle he held felt so friendly, the big wooden ring was so familiar.

"Hello," he said.

231

The singing stopped.

"Hello, Mathurin!"

The coach-builder came out through the door of the house facing the street, smoothened his brown full beard with a steady hand and stroked the tips of his mustache. He had evidently been sitting down to a meal. Behind him were seen his wife Corisande's thin face and the nine-year-old girl and the seven-year-old boy who had survived the plague.

"Is that you, Daniel! Come in!"

"I don't want to disturb you," said Daniel Drouin, when they had made room for him. "I was just passing by."

They were eating mutton and chestnuts, the food smelled good. The children slid into the bench on the inside of the long table. It was standing straight out from the window. At the ends stood armchairs for Corisande and Mathurin. Daniel Drouin always recognized the chairs when he visited them: they had been made by his grandfather.

"Sit down," said Corisande. "You may leave now, children."

They looked askance at their father.

"Let them finish eating," said Daniel. "I didn't want to disturb you."

"They have eaten more than enough now," said Mathurin smiling broadly at the children. "You'll have to stuff yourselves with more later on. Get going now.—They put away as much as monks and priests," he said.

The children folded their hands and murmured something but kept on giggling. And they stared at Daniel's attire while sliding out of their seats.

Corisande said: "My, how nice you look, Daniel! Are you—"

She interrupted herself, her face darkened.

"Is *that* where you're going?" said Mathurin.

"Yes, I have to, as a government official."

Brief silence. The smallest child was whimpering in the

other room, Corisande opened the door to the room, looked in, and returned to the table.

"But sit down, Daniel!"

Mathurin was sitting in the armchair by the window. Daniel took Corisande's chair with his back to the hearth. He kept his hat in his lap until Corisande carefully picked it up and took it into the other room. He rested his hands on the wooden armrests, so worn, so old, a generation or two, and he sat there and felt at home with this wood.

"I heard you singing, Mathurin," he said. "I heard you way out in the street."

The coach-builder's white teeth were gleaming, half hidden by his beard.

"The children wanted to know the words," he said. "Would you like some wine? Corisande, bring our glasses."

She brought two stemmed glasses from the cupboard, took a jug from the side-board and disappeared.

"We haven't had the wine from my wedding out since you were here last," said Mathurin.

Daniel Drouin was touched. He felt that he would soon give expression to his feelings. They would talk about their boyhood, as they always did. But first he wanted to finish what he had started.

"It isn't such a good thing for you to sing so loudly, is it, Mathurin?" he said, bending closer toward his cousin.

"You mean about the Cardinal?" grinned Mathurin. "He can stand what he gets and he needs it too!"

"There are so many ears, Mathurin. Spies everywhere. What kind of carriage is that one out in the yard? Almost as big as a coach."

"Coach, oh no!" said the coach-builder. "But it has always had fine people sitting in it."

Corisande was back from the cellar with the jug and filled their glasses. Mathurin held the glass carefully in his big hands. When he drank, he closed his eyes, Daniel felt like doing the same. It was a full-bodied, rich, golden wine, from Saumur.

"Do you know Marc Duncan, the teacher and doctor at Saumur, the Scotsman? He doesn't dare show his face here any more, do you know that?"

"I have heard of him," said Mathurin and held his glass in both hands. "Sounds intrude this far, too."

"And extrude, as I said," said Daniel and wanted to warn him some more. Soon they were going to talk about their boyhood, it was just the right day and the right moment for it. Do you remember when we visited grandfather? Do you remember when I was here working the bellows for your father and didn't want to go to school any more? Do you remember the summer I was staying home from Bordeaux and we were out in our vineyard doing mischief? And when we stole off to Saumur and they thought we had enlisted in the army? He would soon start talking about it. Such talk always made one so calm and full of confidence. But first he wanted to finish what he had begun, otherwise there would be a gap somewhere.

"Yes, sound *is* coming out from here," he said. "I heard you from the street, every word of it. Do you think it is a good idea to teach your children that he h'm—h'm—has such a big—h'm—h'm—to sit on that there's room for an entire nation, the entire French nation, underneath it?"

"Take it easy with that h'ming of yours!" said Mathurin laughing again. "Both you and I know that we're all sitting under the Cardinal's behind. You ought to know it better than me, since you're sitting closer to the hole where the fine smoke is coming out."

The silence had to be broken once again.

"It may be dangerous to sing things like that too loudly, Mathurin!"

"Nonsense!" laughed his cousin. "You never change, Daniel. Of course it may be *dangerous!* Everything is dangerous these days. But no matter how dangerous it is, *those people* are also singing it, and they bellow much more loudly."

"Who are 'those people'?"

"The ones who arrived in what you thought was a coach but is only a small junk wagon—oh well, a big dung cart, one might call it. The ones who are staying at 'The Golden Apple.'"

Mathurin carefully put down his glass so that he could make a motion with his hand in the direction of the yard:

"Everyone in town is singing it. It is only Tranchant and his party and the crazy Ursuline Sisters and their devils of priests and exorcists and you who are not singing it. For you're not singing it on the sly, are you, Daniel?"

They laughed. In a little while, we will talk about our childhood and youth, thought Daniel Drouin. But first—

"Who are they, Mathurin?"

Mathurin's smile disappeared.

"They came with Laubardemont, the great butcher. They are tools, some of them are dressed like gentlemen. Very competent. But the soldiers who are with them sing a piece about that fellow also, and that is a good thing. At the end it says that the man who exorcises devils should start with himself first. Or that he should change to the butcher's trade right away and not make so many detours around courts and protocols of inquiry. So there's plenty of singing without my help!"

They could laugh again. Now we can talk about our childhood days, thought Daniel Drouin. But first—. It is peculiar that as soon as you start discussing serious topics here in this town, someone will use the word "ass" (he thought with a feeling of embarrassment) and then they mean the Cardinal's behind. It is probably a—h'm—makeshift measure. For if they said the harsh words that I use only in my own mind and in Latin about *murus* and *hunc mihi timorem erope*, it would be even more dangerous. The Cardinal becomes more human if one likens him to an ass and says that he takes a cr-p and f-s people in the throat or that his large—h'm—organ has been waved in front of the noses of the court ladies for so long that they have yielded at last. But if you take Cicero and turn one of

235

his quotations against His Eminence, then the human aspect of His Eminence's person will disappear and only his *deeds,* as we know them today, will be illuminated. Mathurin and Antoine and Petiot and Dolet may argue that the Cardinal is a big—hm—piece of shit—and that he covers the entire country with his cr-p, etc., but that makes the Cardinal seem more human, perhaps more popular even. He goes to the privy like everyone else, you have something in common with him. You have some contact with him even though it is by excrements. But if I say that—no, I'm not going to say it. Now we're going to talk about our childhood, but first—.

"Mathurin, answer me frankly: what is everyone thinking in the city?"

"Thinking? Do you really want me to give you a frank answer?"

"You must answer in a way that suits you, I'm not asking for more," said Daniel Drouin.

Mathurin lifted his glass, but when he saw that Daniel's glass was already empty, he put it down and filled both glasses. With his index finger he removed the drop left on the rim of the jug and licked his finger with his tongue; and with his thumb he wiped up the drops that had been spilled on the table and then he stuck his thumb in his mouth and sucked on it. Daniel Drouin saw the movement of his hand, his respect for the wine. I am very fond of Mathurin, he thought.

"To your health, Daniel!"

Mathurin lifted his glass very carefully.

"I've been thinking of you a lot, Daniel—of what you told them about the Devil's Latin. If you want to know what people around here are saying about the Cardinal, I'll tell you. They are saying that he is a real stinker. Or that he has made the king into a beggar and a stinker and a pisspot. And that he wants to get at the Jesuit Grainier for the reason that Grainier hasn't fawned and groveled enough and because Grainier doesn't want the city to be destroyed more than has been done already. And they say that Minet wants Grainier's prebend at Sainte-Croix and at the same time wants to get back at him for something in the past. And that the prioress at the Ursuline convent and some of the sisters, one by the name of Claire who is related to the Cardinal and one whose name is Anne and several others and among them one I think you know— Séraphique Archer who was a maid in your house at one time—that they have gone stark crazy for want of men whom they are longing for. And that Tranchant has not forgotten that his daughter gave birth to an illegitimate child, which Grainier is supposed to have fathered. And that the Gray One, the Cardinal's Gray One, Father Joseph, wants to help the Capuchin monks here to power and glory, and—well, do you wish to hear more?"

Mathurin lifted his glass, no, he *tore* it up from the table and drank vehemently. Daniel Drouin took care to drink something also. He's getting himself all worked up, thought the assessor. Now we'll have to talk about our childhood soon. He held his thumb and index finger around the stem of the thickset, bluish-colored glass. It was empty.

"It's an exceptionally fine wedding wine this here, Mathurin," he said slowly. "It's twelve—or thirteen?— years since Corisande and you got married?"

"Thirteen," said Mathurin with another broad smile.— "But that doesn't prevent the Cardinal from being a stinking pisspot and Laubardemont from being his supreme executioner. Now he has gotten the scent of this city, Daniel!"

"I can remember it like yesterday when you got married," said Daniel Drouin.

"Yes, you did join us even though we weren't so popish," said Mathurin (a bit drily).

Daniel Drouin took off his coat. He heard Corisande's footsteps; she had been standing by the hearth listening. She took his coat and carried it into the other room. He put his elbows on the table in order to sit more comfortably.

"Mathurin," he said, "do you really mean that you walk around in this town feeling *afraid*? There is no reason for that, is there?"

"Well, what do you think?" said the coach-builder; he straightened up in his chair and kept his eyes glued on his cousin. "Soon you can't trust a single human being here. I for my part don't even trust—"

"Mathurin!"

"Yes, Corisande," he said looking glumly and angrily toward the stove where she was standing and making signs to him.

"Don't talk politics now," she said turning to the pots on the hearth.

Daniel Drouin turned his head a little more and looked at her narrow shoulders. She had really been nice-looking when she was a young girl, he thought. Now she looks worn. It couldn't be all that fun to be married to—

"Don't you trust *me* either?" He first addressed her back and then turned toward Mathurin and looked him straight in the eye.

His cousin winked at him and carefully raised his glass to his bearded mouth. He smiled, but quickly averted his glance.

"To your health, Daniel," he said and drank and filled his glass once more.

"To your health, to the health of you both from the depth of my heart," said Daniel, but he only took a sip of the wine. I have had too much wine now, he thought, and then one shouldn't get into discussions. Words may slip out that one will regret later. The depth of my heart may have sounded a little exaggerated to their ears.

He sipped a bit more of the wine. First he's yelling and singing so that he can be heard all over the square, and then he says that he can't trust a single man in this city, he thought. That doesn't tally. No logic to it at all. I don't give a damn about it. I want to talk about our childhood, about our youth. About things that Corisande can listen to. But first I ought to ask—

"Oh, Mathurin," he said, once again placing his elbows on the table. He held his glass with both hands, between his fingertips, tilting it one way and then the other; when he noticed that it was empty, he put it down—"There's no logic in anything you're saying," he said. "First you're singing about—h'm—about all possible parts of the body and organs that a—h'm—certain person possesses and—well— you understand—and you're singing so loudly that I can hear it way out in the street. I recognized your voice. And then you say that you can't trust anyone. Now I want to tell you that even though I won't assert directly that I enjoy the words in the song they still—h'm—appeal to me—in a certain way. I am on—the right side, you understand! But my position—well, you understand, don't you?—makes it so that I can't use such words myself. It wouldn't be proper. It would sound unnatural and affected, and far-fetched. But—"

Mathurin laughed out loud and Daniel thought he heard Corisande giggle. She shouldn't do that, he thought. But she probably had to giggle and snigger instead of laughing out openly as she used to—now that she has lost three front teeth. She who laughed *so* much when we were young. Young? Have we become old now? But first—

Mathurin poured more wine in both glasses.

"No, no more now," said Daniel Drouin. "You know that I have to go *there*. It's not such an easy thing to do, you know. For I am compelled to show up. But I'm going there to listen to what they're saying, to investigate and to scrutinize their faces."

"Daniel," said Mathurin. "Let's drop all this. May I tell you that I sing at times in order to prove to myself that I'm not afraid at all. That sounds queer, doesn't it? We'll drop it. To your health!"

"To yours and Corisande's very best, well deserved, and

from all points of view desirable health and good fortune!" said Daniel Drouin in a serious and solemn manner before he drank. "Now I have to leave. But—you know: we belong together. We belong together."

"I know, I know," said Mathurin and got up from his chair. His broad face was beaming with friendliness, his teeth were gleaming.

It was nice to have a glass of wine in all simplicity, thought Daniel Drouin; standing up, he looked very tall in the low-ceilinged room.

"You must come and visit us soon," he said. "Make it some Sunday. Then we can walk up to the old ramparts or even drive out to my vineyard, provided the weather is nice. We can sit in my cottage out there and think about—think about—about next year's wine and eat and drink something and talk about how things were when we were young."

"Daniel, you never change!" said Mathurin, warm friendship tinging his voice.

They were standing outside the door facing the courtyard. I ought to say something about his work, thought Daniel Drouin. Otherwise he might think that I came here just to show off my fine clothes.

"You are really elegant in your new suit!" said Corisande when she gave him his hat and coat, and he thought he heard a note of genuine admiration in her voice.

"You always have your hands full," Daniel said to Mathurin.

"I'm going to build you a coach before the Devil takes all of us!" laughed his cousin.

"What's this going to be?" asked Daniel when they were standing underneath the overhanging roof of the carpenter's shop.

"A shaft for the ox cart, and it is to be put in place now," said Mathurin. "The farmer's waiting."

It would soon be twilight and the mood that goes with it.

"If I had time, I would help you," said Daniel Drouin

looking down at his clothes. "Then I would have taken off this finery and helped you."

"Yes, you never change, Daniel!" said Corisande.

"It's Michel out in your vineyard who's having the shaft fixed," said Mathurin. "He was here this afternoon to pick it up, but it wasn't ready yet. But he was so afraid of those over there (he pointed at the inn on the other side of the courtyard), that he didn't dare leave his mule with *me,* even though he's known me since I was a boy! Can you imagine that: *afraid! here!* in my courtyard!"

"That is ridiculous," said Daniel Drouin.

"And now of course he's drinking up the entire mule," said Mathurin.

They turned their faces up toward the darkening sky, all three laughing out loud.

"I think there will be more rain tonight," said Corisande.

An evening with rain on fine clothes, he thought.

"Now I'll have to be off."

"Good luck!" said Mathurin warmly. "And say a few words once again!"

"Words?" said Daniel Drouin.

"Yes, say a few words on the town again. Like the ones you said about the Devil not knowing Latin. We were proud of being related to you then. It's just the kind of words that are needed, you see!"

Daniel Drouin stood up straight becoming even taller underneath the darkening sky.

"I'm not as afraid as you may be imagining, Mathurin," he said with dignity and force. "I'm not afraid to speak up when it's necessary. But you've got to give thought to what you're going to say. With great care, so that it will have an effect!"

"That Daniel, he never changes!" said Corisande, and the three of them laughed out loud.

241

13

Dialog with Pictures

THE THUMBS CONTINUED TWIRLING. He is weaving a net, he is working on something to entangle me with, thought the other one.

"I can, for instance, say something about the case of Philippe Tranchant," said the canon. "She is a relative of mine."

"Please go on, Minet," the other one repeated.

*

I am the miserable woman Philippe Tranchant—for two years the miserable Philippe Poussaut, for as everyone knows I have been married for two years to the royal procurator Louis Poussaut, who is also related to me. My age is now thirty-one. Seven years ago and six and five and four and three years ago they looked upon me as a whore, but of course I am not. I am only the miserable girl Philippe Tranchant, now Mme Poussaut, and I am related to the entire city and the entire city knows everything about me.

My father protected me for many years. Now I am protected by my husband, who made me his wife to get the post of procurator cheaply when my father had to leave it. But they know everything. I was once the happiest woman in our city, in France, and in the world. In my happiness there was the unhappiness that I saw coming while I was happy, and that made me perhaps feel even happier. I don't know. But I was on an island called Happiness and I was not completely blind. I knew that the ocean surrounding me was called Misery.

He came to our house often, to the house on the square in front of the Church of Sainte-Croix where my father is still living, across from the house where my husband, our royal procurator, my esteemed spouse and I live with our entirely legitimate child, our little living child who was born last year and baptized by my cousin Jehan Minet in the Bartray Church. Yes, the man whose name I don't want to mention came to our house often, my father's house, and there were scandals surrounding him. My sister Françoise, who is now married to the esteemed physician Guillaume Roger, and I were hostesses in the evening, for our mother had died before that time. Father received all prominent persons in his house and he said it was useful and good for us to be present, we would get to be better known that way, and people had a chance to see how capable we were or might become as wives and mistresses of a household. We often talked with Father about our mother and Father said that there was never a better woman in all of Poitou. The late King Henry had once cast eyes on her and Father always said that the king had done it with respect and deference.

*

"You forced your way into this respectable house," said Minet. "Among these decent people. You spoke ill of the rest of us behind our backs and you made sarcastic epigrams about us in our presence, but toward Tranchant and his daughters you were all subtle learning and mild sunshine. But we saw what you were doing, we were observing you."

*

Father said that we shouldn't worry about all the gossip. Our family and all our relatives make up a hornet's nest of gossip, said Father. The apothecary, the physicians, the aldermen and the priests in our family—they are all of them great gossips, he said. They can't live unless they get to gossip and whisper and be envious, he said. The stories about the priest at Ste-Croix and St-Pierre are concocted with malice, said Father. He himself felt happy and proud to have such an acquaintance, even friendship, and he thought that a learned Jesuit was really needed here among all kinds of dirty, ignorant, and fawning monks. The Church will profit from learning and from priests with good manners, said Father. And he felt happy himself to have actually found a man in our town with whom he could talk about poetry and history. "We are both as children in the house of Scévole," said Father. "I feel as if I am his older brother," he would say at times.

*

"We were watching you, we knew," said Minet. "We were unlettered and comical from your viewpoint, from your very learned and haughty viewpoint. We uttered no witticisms and we couldn't be as eloquent as you were when Scévole de Sainte-Marthe died ten years ago and a funeral oration was to be given. We weren't so elegant either, we natives, we didn't bother to perfume ourselves or take care of our hands like a lady-in-waiting. But we had hearts in which there was room for justice!"

"And a little more," said the other man. "There was room for something else besides."

"And we had eyes that saw," said the canon. "Many eyes. Tranchant was blind to your little game, but we saw it!"

"You saw more than there actually was to be seen," said the other man. "All the time you saw what you wanted to see, and nothing else."

*

When my younger sister Françoise was married to Guillaume Roger, Father said that this was not quite the right order of things, for I was the oldest, but he also said—and then he was joking with me—that I was no doubt saving myself for something even better and nicer. Yes, I had at times thought that I would save myself for Jesus Christ and the Holy Virgin, but he didn't mean it that way, but instead like this: that if a girl is the oldest daughter of a high-ranking royal official she shouldn't throw herself into the arms of the first man who comes by; in such a case she is one of the select and is to be *placed,* he said.

*

"You ruined the girl," said Canon Minet. "We saw you, we can bear witness. And perhaps you forgot that I was her cousin, that we were many cousins, many uncles and many nephews who saw you and who were watching you. You enticed her to come to you before she could be placed. You ensnared her with eloquence and poetry, with flowers and sorcery and you played both Demosthenes and Apollo, you quoted from both Cicero and Lucian. You captured her in your net but we saw, we watched the game you played with the girl."

"You know nothing about this matter," said the other one coldly.

*

He was the one I always wanted to see and always to be near. Father made suggestions regarding a husband but I said that I wanted to wait some time yet. Others made suggestions to my father, but I wanted to enter on a different path where there were darkness and happiness. I wanted to give myself to Jesus Christ and the Holy Virgin in order to be near him in spirit. I could see in his eyes that he wanted to be near me and when his hands touched me, I was near him.

*

"We know, we saw, we watched!"

"No, you know nothing about it, Minet," said the other man and now his voice was cool no longer. There was a kind of eagerness in it, an eagerness to make an appeal, he wanted to persuade, to convince.

"You cannot wriggle away from the facts, no matter how clever you are, Grainier," said the canon.

*

My father said that he couldn't understand what was wrong with me. All the people who came to visit were winking and whispering—and their pauses, their interruptions, their silences! And their lustful desire! My cousins showed their desire for me too! Some said sarcastically that I looked happy, others wondered what was wrong, I looked so unhappy. They asked whether I was the one they had seen one night on the way to the castle and the Church of St-Pierre. They asked whether I had made a habit of going to confession in the nighttime. Others asked why I never went out any more but always stayed home.

*

"That was the hardest blow suffered by any man in our town," said the canon. "Do you realize what it means to be a royal official and a procurator and have a daughter who—."

*

It seemed as if Father was withering away. He became so thin that his clothes were hanging like bags on him. His face, which had always been so round and rosy, looked as if scorched to rough, gray stone. He didn't ask how I felt but he asked if I realized how he felt it, and perhaps I did. I was fond of him, I am still fond of him. But I couldn't see through the darkness and didn't know what would happen to me in the end. I only knew that I had been very happy and had then become very unhappy. I hardly told my Father anything. But I remember shouting to him out of

246

my darkness. I shouted that he shouldn't kill and shouldn't hate and that I didn't know whose fault it was or whether it was anyone's fault in the end. I shouted and he heard. I shouted that I was prepared to take my punishment now and the punishment afterward and that I knew nothing about the fault, the sin, and the shame. Then Father stiffened. He had raised his hand to strike, but he didn't strike me. He is still standing like that. Behind his hardened movements I can see his hardened soul. "Wait," he said. "I am a royal official and my name is Louis Tranchant. Wait," he said. "That day is coming," he said.

*

"A day is coming for you too, Grainier," said the canon.

"You know nothing about this!" said the other man. "You have no right to talk about it. You too were one of those who tormented her, who are perhaps still tormenting her!"

"She is a close relative of mine," said the canon. "We know, be convinced of that! And a day will come for you too! It is near."

*

No, I wasn't allowed to go out any more. Doctor Fanton came by in the evening after dark and felt my stomach. Father stood next to him and looked at me. He shouldn't have done that. I am still very fond of him, he is my father and he always used to be so kind and cheerful and full of fun. My sister and I helped him copy documents about our city when he was working on its history. I was allowed to make a fair copy of Father's poem to the memory of Scévole after Scévole had died, and I was allowed to copy Father's poem of thanks to—to the Orator when the Orator, The Wonderful One, had given his famous funeral oration over Scévole de Sainte-Marthe. But Father shouldn't have been standing there asking Doctor Fanton about things while Fanton was examining my stomach. I

247

wasn't alive then. I died. I sat. I was. I wasn't alive, I only existed as something and in *that something* there was something else that Father would rather have taken away. He asked Doctor Fanton about that and I heard it although I was dead and didn't exist. Doctor Fanton's answer was No. He didn't express it in words. He looked at Father and shook his head. Then Father went into his room and prayed. Late in the evening he was with our relative Canon Jehan Minet and confessed his sins, his temptation, his wishes, his sorrow.

*

"I experienced it at very close range," said the canon. "As you know, she is my cousin. Her father has, as you know, great confidence in me."

"I don't doubt that what you are telling me was experienced intensely by you and that you tried to participate at as close a range as possible," said the other one calmly. Again his hands were resting on the leather armrest.

*

I could hear how the city was whispering. In my heart I heard everything. I wasn't allowed to be seen standing in the window either but I stood there anyway behind the draperies. I saw people I knew and people I didn't know cross our square and enter the Church of Sainte-Croix, I saw them at the market in the square, townspeople haggling about the prices and farmers coming and going and buying and selling and shouting and gesticulating and haggling. I heard the voices rising from the cobblestones and the mud in the street, from the stalls and the carts. I saw the tall Assessor Drouin, who as long as I can remember has always lived in the house diagonally across the square, standing there gesticulating and quoting something in Latin. I saw our *bailli*, M. de Cerisay, and Father stand there conversing and Father would now stand most of the time with his head down hardly listening to what people were saying to him. I saw the pomp when some distinguished or powerful man visited our city. I heard them speak and laugh in our great hall, I heard someone sing. But I never again heard the voice of the Orator in our house. From the window I could see him walking across the square, alone or in a procession. And I saw Madeleine de Brone enter the church many times. I saw her most often. I remember that I thought I was very happy once upon a time that had now come to an end and was gone, a time when I walked across the square and into the church and was very happy.

*

"You know *nothing* about all that, Minet!"

"I know what I need to know and a little bit more, Grainier. You had even at that time begun to seduce, bewitch, and destroy another young woman in our city. Shall I mention her name?"

*

Was a child born?

I don't know that any longer, I am Mme Poussaut and have my own child with my husband, who is the royal procurator in our town succeeding my father who was forced to resign and to sell his office because of harassment. Our child was not baptized in the Church of Ste-Croix, but we received episcopal permission to have it baptized in the Bartray Church. My cousin, Jehan Minet, who is canon at Ste-Croix, officiated at the baptism.

But was a child born *then,* long ago?

No, I don't know that any longer. Did it come out of my body as the last way station of my youth, the last stop before dusk already sets in, the last resting place, the most bitter one, before I drifted into the darkness where I am now?

Marthe Le Peletier came to our house late one evening to fetch something that perhaps was mine and not hers, something that was His and mine and had not been blessed and never really could be properly blessed. Marthe the good—just like the saints are good—could in her poverty provide a wetnurse for the child that she had fetched out of the night to make her own, but she waited too long to have it baptized. I stood by the window watching her cross the square and I saw how two city guards stopped her and forced her to go back home. I knew that Father was standing behind the window, making sure that everything was done the way he had directed and arranged. I saw how people gathered in the square, talking and waiting. I saw the guards returning with the good and courageous, bewildered and self-sacrificing Marthe Le Peletier, and I saw her carry a bundle in her arms, and in it was something that perhaps was not hers. I could hear them shouting at her, that it was time to get the whorechild baptized now. I heard them laugh and whistle and mention names, and if I had wanted to I would have heard the good Marthe Le Peletier sobbing, but I didn't want to hear anything. I saw my cousin, the canon of Sainte-Croix, Jehan Minet, by her side. I saw them disappear into the church and the guards following them as witnesses, perhaps as sponsors. You women who have had a child in your arms and have called it yours, you women in the poems that we used to read in my father's house, and you women in the poems, the speeches, the books, and the cities that will exist long after all of us here in our city and in Vienne and Poitou and Touraine and everyone on the other side of the plains and the vineyards and the forests and the mountains and the oceans are gone, you women in a distant future when all of us here are dust, as fine and as suffocating as that which is spreading over us when our walls are torn down today and tomorrow—you will no doubt understand what I felt in my breast and in my belly, in my heart and in my limbs, you will no doubt understand my silent lament at that moment! I saw in the year of Our Lord 1626, and it is now more than seven years ago,

Marthe Le Peletier, the quiet, silent, compliant, slow-witted and friendly, who before was my good friend, my poor but very close confidante whom I will never meet again, the self-sacrificing and saintlike woman and yet later horribly possessed by demons from Saumur, carry a child out of the Church of Sainte-Croix here in our city, and it had been baptized in her name by my cousin Jehan Minet and registered as her child in the baptismal records, and this name will remain in our archives until fire and time destroy it.

*

"You thought you could escape, Grainier. But we saw, we remember, we were witnesses!"

"Yes, you saw the advantage and the opportunity, Minet. You saw to it that processes were started against me, and when you lost one you immediately started a new one. I was never to enjoy a minute's quiet, you thought. You wanted to drive me out of town. But it was not because you thought the gossip was true but it was in order that you yourself would receive the prebend of Sainte-Croix and in order that you would get hold of my economic resources. It was in order that you would obtain my reputation, the good part of it, of course, and that you yourself be regarded as a witty and scholarly orator. —Yes, wasn't it because you wanted to obtain my nature, my bearing, and my appearance?"

"We wanted to rid our city of vermin," said the Lame One.

*

They all gathered in our house; Father was the leader. I have never seen him as lively in all his inner petrification and have never heard his voice echo so loudly in our hall as it did now when his spirit had become numb and his smile had been extinguished. It was in our house that the Party was actually formed and I could hear the resolutions

251

and the accusations, the true ones and the false ones, trickling through the stone walls like the moisture in musty cellars, creeping like vermin, waiting silently like spiders. I could see it come out and disappear in the cracks like watchful lizards and then stick its head out again and again. Father's party lost its law suits against him—the Orator, the Hunted One—he who was accused of having blasphemed, exceeded his authority, and not having submitted to the Right Reverend Bishop of Poitiers but instead appealed to the Archbishop in Bordeaux and to M. d'Armagnac, our governor. They accused him of attempted murder of another priest, they tried to dig up old matters to hold against him and among the diggers were my relative the apothecary Golot and my relative the physician Lannoury and my relative the chief of police René Herseur and my relative the canon Jehan Minet and other relatives of ours and their relatives and friends.

*

"You took advantage of every opportunity that came your way, Minet. Many lies have been uttered in this city in your time and you yourself have worked hard to help the lie."

"There are verily many reasons for accusing you, Grainier," said the canon. "Didn't you worm your way into the confidence of many people? Shall I mention one name: René de Brone. He trusted you so much that he left his daughter in your care when he prepared himself for death. Is that a lie?"

"On the surface, it is not a lie," said the other one. "But you know nothing about this either."

"Quite enough, Grainier. We see, we hear, we understand enough. We can listen and think. We have been observing you. We saw how you ingratiated yourself, how you feigned the fatherly friend even though René de Brone's daughter was a mature woman. We saw how you tempted her."

*

They claimed that he tempted her father first so that Councillor de Brone left his daughter in his, the seducer's, hands when he knew he was going to die. But I, the unhappy and at times very sharp-sighted Philippe Tranchant, who is now Madame Poussaut, sat in my darkness knowing otherwise. Madeleine and her sisters were often with us when he whose name I will never mention again, came to our house, and it took long for me to be forced into my isolation, and I know that Madeleine de Brone was not despoiled or bewitched by him the way they claimed, but that she was *drawn* to him and wanted to go to him with her eyes wide open. It is so long ago that one almost cannot believe it, and when I see her enter the gate of Assessor Drouin's house on this square where I and my husband also have our house, I'm always thinking: that woman is much older than this I sitting here and watching. He remained with her, they say. Pierre Milouin, who is a royal official and a relative of hers and even of us, wanted to marry her, but she said no many times. Milouin would come to my father's house in the evening, and now he is often visiting my husband's house and is a zealous member of the Party. At one time he tried to kill the one they call the Seducer. I heard Milouin's loud voice through the walls of my father's house.

*

"Quite enough," repeated the canon.

"You have mentioned the name of Gauffridi," said the other. "You have collaborated well with the Party. You have brought Laubardemont here, or let me put it this way: you have enticed him to come here by help of the word Gauffridi and with the words 'sorcerer' and 'despoiler.' But you yourself are not going to his party this evening, tonight, so that it will look as if you are outside all of it. You are pressing for fire, aren't you? Why have you come to me?"

"I have come to warn you for the last time, Grainier,"

253

said the Lame One. "Henceforth you will not receive any more warnings—from us."

"I know that you are pressing for fire. But you are in doubt, you are hesitating. You are afraid of burning your own fingers. You are afraid of burning your soul."

"I have come to warn you and not to listen to your dialectical skill," said the canon. "I suppose you intend to try to prove that you are a saint and that we are the demons."

"I know that you are the demons," said the other. "I know that you want power."

*

I who am sitting in the darkness in my husband's house can only listen and look out through the cracks in the walls, through the lattice-work windows in my prison tower. I cannot put together all that I hear and see to arrive at conclusions and timetables. The special commissioner of the king, M. Baron de Laubardemont has come here once again. He is not staying with us, as he did last year, nor with any other prominent family in our city, not even with M. Mesmin de Silly, who is the confidant of His Eminence the Cardinal, but instead at the inn "The Swan of the Cross." Father and Silly and my husband and Herseur have been to see him and he has visited Father evenings and I have heard that everyone has been there. I don't know what words were said but the meaning of their words is trickling through the stone walls in our house. Simone, who is our maid, says that she has been told by the maids in my father's house that they are busy gathering wood for a big fire. Simone, who came to our town from other towns where she saw bonfires and stood very near and shouted I don't know what, always knows a whole lot. She talks and talks and in my darkness I even have to laugh at her words. She says that the wood for the fire is to be gathered in our square, the Square of Sainte-Croix, and that is where the disgrace will be burned out of our city's body. That is why M. de Laubardemont is here. I can sense through the walls that one of the driest logs for that fire is named Catherine Hammon, who was a chambermaid for the mother of our king and who accompanied that queen during her banishment which beggars description and has never been fully explained to anyone. And I know and feel, as does everyone else know and feel, that that fire is going to burn away my disgrace and that Father in his boundless love of my honor and the glory of the name of Tranchant and for the sake of the true and pure faith and for the sake of his deep hatred by no one quite comprehended—I know and feel that Father is one of those who carry most of the wood to the pyre and that he carries it night and day and that the fire which soon will be lit in our city (which we all love so dearly and will love even more dearly when all the walls of heresy are torn down) will burn me clean and will give me a new memory where nothing of the past will be left—

*

"I might perhaps take the occasion to mention another name, that of Catherine Hammon," said the Lame One.

"You might as well mention it," said the other one. "I was waiting for it."

"Could it be any pleasure for you to hear her name?" asked the canon.

"You might as well mention it, Minet," repeated the other. Erect and calm, he sat there, his voice sounded brighter, there was a kind of cheerful irony in it.—"I can stand hearing it," he said. "Didn't I say that I was waiting for it?"

"We have found out a number of things," said the canon.

"You must have performed another and very efficient job of digging," said the other one. "You have been spinning and knitting with great zeal. I can imagine what your net looks like."

255

"Net?" said the canon. "We investigate, we observe."

"A net of threads and moles' galleries underneath our city," said the other one.

"I don't care for your subtleties," said Minet and his thumbs were spinning around, he was sitting quite comfortably.

*

I, the unhappy Philippe Tranchant, forsaken by almost everyone and now advantageously married to the present royal procurator, sit in my darkness and I listen and observe. I know everything about Catherine Hammon. She came back to our town when everything had collapsed for her in almost the same way as for me, I who am so unhappy and so sorely tried. She was a chambermaid for our gracious queen dowager Maria de Medici, later deported at the king's command, and she has a sister, Suzanne, whom the demons at the Ursuline cloister have attacked and possessed.

I am lying on my bed, waiting. I don't know for what. I am not always longing for the future, where there are blood and fire and more darkness, and not always for the past, where there were happiness and afterward unhappiness and darkness.

I can see a fly moving on the ceiling, making strange figures, angles, triangles, in sudden turns, an autumn fly in my husband's house. It is as if it bounced against invisible walls and turned sharply before dangers that I cannot see, the invisible which I cannot comprehend but which does exist.

I am thinking of Catherine Hammon, who returned to the city where she was born, our city, when the queen dowager had waged her struggle with the Cardinal and he had won and the queen dowager, the mother of our king, had to go away or flee. Catherine Hammon walked around in our city and was a glib talker and beautiful and proud of having been in the service of the queen dowager, and with her wit and her beauty she opposed the Cardinal. This was in the year of grace and unhappiness 1627, and then she often met *him,* the Orator and the Great Preacher, whose name I don't want to mention except by his initials, that U. G., who some day will be completely nameless and unknown to me. Catherine Hammon went to him for confession and if they did something else together I don't want to know it. Her sister is now with the Ursuline nuns and the news has trickled through to me that she is possessed by demons and that the demons accuse the U. G., who is more and more disappearing from my memory, of being the prince of the demons and their leader in this part of the country, in all of Vienne and Poitou and all of Touraine. To me, however, these things are of no significance. At present I am mostly interested in the fly which is still in my room even after the long and dusty summer of demolition making the most curious figures in its flight. It is confined between invisible walls which only I, the witness, can fathom. Once the man whose name I have forgotten, uttered words that I have also forgotten, and they were words I can recall if I so wish, about all those who are confined behind invisible walls. I am not of course. I am at home in my husband's house on our square. I am lying on my bed, resting, but if I want to go out for a walk in the wet streets be it daylight or dark no one tries to stop me anymore and no one dares say an impolite word to me. What they used to shout after me I have forgotten. When I at times walk about our beautiful, famous, and historic city (for it happens that I do that, when I am in the mood for it) then it is to prove that I am not shut in or hiding from human eyes or have any reason to stay away and cover my face. When I cross our square I don't think of the words they shouted after me and whispered around me before but I am thinking of fires, of flames, of wood for the fires and the flames. Even now I am thinking of this while lying on my bed quite willingly watching the curious flight of the fly. Tonight the king's commissioner is giving a big dinner, a decisive and fateful dinner, in his temporary residence at the "Swan of the Cross," and my father and my husband and many others have been invited.

*

"We now know who wrote the very obnoxious, insultingly foul and mendacious libelous tract, the stinking pamphlet entitled 'A Letter from the Queen Mother's Chambermaid and Caretaker of M. de Baradas's Shoes,'" said the canon. "We know about you and Catherine Hammon. You haven't forgotten her, I am sure. At any rate, the Cardinal has not forgotten that it was the nastiest and most mendacious of all the nasty and mendacious libelous pamphlets about him."

*

I am gliding away from what is soon about to happen, I am not really the cause and I have no real responsibility, I am only the unhappy Philippe Tranchant, Poussaut being my married name.

The plague had come to our city but it didn't touch us, the demons are here, but they haven't touched me. But the sister of Catherine Hammon is one of the most exposed of the Ursuline girls and she has often mentioned the name that I will never mention again except perhaps at times by his initials.

When the demons came to our beautiful city and assaulted the prioress, Jeanne, as well as Sister Claire and Sister Anne and Sister Agnes and a serving sister by the name of Séraphique Archer, they didn't forget Catherine Hammon's sister. Father has said that this is to the good and that he believes that the demons possess a very sure political instinct for what is a valid argument and for what is of no value clerically or in law and theology. It has seeped in through the stone walls of our house that M. de Laubardemont has spoken with His Eminence the Cardi-

258

nal about Catherine Hammon's letters and other writings, when he was in Paris in order to again try to convince His Majesty and His Eminence of the importance of having the big square tower also torn down, in spite of what our governor, M. d'Armagnac, maintains, namely that not all the fortifications should be completely leveled. M. de Laubardemont is now in possession of a power of attorney, which he has read aloud for my father and my husband. It has leaked through the stone walls of our house into where I am lying letting my thoughts wander and touch all my misfortunes, that M. d'Armagnac's letter to His Majesty is worthless and will not at all be able to help preserve any of the walls or towers and that M. de Laubardemont's power of attorney is the document that is a real value in these difficult times, when so much has to be torn down in order to protect us all against dangers. And in order to obtain this power of attorney, which is now conclusively to save our town from being a nest of heretics and an enemy of the King and the Cardinal, M. de Laubardemont in his wisdom, his foresight, and his great political and adminis-trative ability and talents, has informed His Eminence that the worst libelous pamphlet that has ever been written against His Eminence came originally right from here and from Catherine Hammon (whose sister is at present sorely possessed by demons) and that the woman by the name of Catherine Hammon, just mentioned above and previously referred to several times, is merely the supplier of mate-rials and the cover signature for the just mentioned writ-ing and that the real author and instigator in all proba-bility, bordering on certainty, is the man whose name I never mention but who—

I, the unhappy one who is in everyone's thoughts in these documents and in this evening and night in this our historic city, am unable to stop observing the fly circling underneath the rings of light in the ceiling in this room in my husband's house where I am now resting and thinking about things and events of the past and trying to look into

259

a future when I can walk about in this our beautiful city and carry my spotless name Philippe Tranchant, Poussaut being my married name—

*

"It has been established that you are the real author," said the Lame One.

"Who has established that, if I may ask?" said the other man, and his voice sounded a nuance less confident.

"We have established it," said the canon Minet.

The other man stood up, reached for the candle snuffers and put in a new candle, and in a short while their faces could once again be clearly seen.

"You have done much careful preparatory work, Minet," he said when he sat down again. "You started out so well with all the pinpricks of envy, with all the slander, all kinds of small and big law suits. Once you thought you had me and then I sat for two months in the bishop's jail in Poitiers and you succeeded in having me sentenced to never again perform as a priest in this city. The archbishop in Bordeaux rescinded the judgment, but you started in again, and again, you never tired."

"Those are all your sins that are festering out, without end, again and again," said the canon. "You're trying to wriggle out of it with dialectics, but the sins are still there and we who see and hear and oberve are also there. Your arrogance hasn't been able to help you either."

"Then came more preparatory work," said the other man, who hadn't been listening to Minet's words. Again, he bent rather far forward trying to catch the canon's eye:

"I'm not complaining, make note of that, I'm not complaining but I feel a need to determine what is happening to me, what is happening to life on the whole, and what is happening to the Church and to God."

"You should watch your mouth more closely," said the Lame One.

260

"You prepared Barrot at Chinon, Minet, and that was easy, he was ready and receptive. His nature is such, just like yours. You prepared long and conscientiously the demons which you claim you have found among the Ursuline Sisters. One of the best prepared ever is the prioress. And now you are preparing a huge bonfire. But you are going to burn your fingers. You see, I believe in what truth can do. I won't maintain that I am *good* or even *just* by nature, but I believe in the power of truth. You have prepared everything very well, but you will burn your fingers, Minet."

"You yourself have prepared everything that's going to happen," said the canon giving him a brief, open look.

The other man extended his long narrow hand (so well kept, thought the canon hatefully) toward the pewter dish and the candle snuffer. He carefully trimmed the candle, which had burned halfway down. The other stump lay in the wax, smoking.

"Actually, you are quite right, Minet," he said. "I have prepared everything myself. Don't think I'm blind to that. I too have possessed arrogance and a lust for power, though that is a thing of the past, I believe. No, I don't know, I haven't faced the final test. I have helped myself to too much from my life. I don't mean that it is wrong to help oneself to much of life. But I forgot that every bit of honey you get on your tongue, is taken from a flower. But why do the flowers have honey if it is not to be taken? Or— I can put it another way, and, mark it well, not for *you!*— that every tiny bit of sweetness one gets is taken from someone else who may be standing right next to one not getting anything. That's how simple it is in reality. Too many have been standing by the side watching, knowing that they will get nothing of the most secret, the finest. Will you give me an honest answer to a question just once, Minet?"

"I haven't come here to answer questions," said the Lame One. "You know very well why I am here."

"But still," said the other one and now there seemed to be a trace of anxiety in his voice. "But still?"

"I'm not here to listen to questions and to answer them!"

The other man suddenly leaned hard against the back of the chair. He threw the candle snuffer in the pewter dish, it made a clatter, the tips made fine gleaming scratches in the pewter. His hands pushed hard against the leather of the armrests, he stretched his long legs so that his shins touched the beam underneath the table, he turned his face upward and closed his eyes.

It was a play and yet it wasn't: it was a performance but not for anyone present or not exclusively for the one present. An observer of statues, of saints' images or of illustrated works depicting eminent personages from history might have thought that he was sitting model for his own portrait and that he didn't want the one who was now depicting him with chisel, brushes, or in his memory, inwardly, to create and take along with him an ugly picture without falsifying and lying; that any other picture than the one of this very moment would be left with posterity as incorrect or as a caricature. Besides, with this picture before his eyes or in his memory, a picture perhaps never drawn on paper or canvas, never formed in stone or wood, the observer or admirer of pictures portraying human beings or historical and current events would be able to deny that his stance just at that moment interpreted his inner self, his true nature with its spiritual, psychological, and perhaps moral content.

It was a play, but an unassailable one. It was not fraudulent but a reproduction, a synthesis of his personality. It was morality in rehearsal—strictly speaking without an audience—and it was also the art of seduction before a certain public. His pose comprised the desire, in the absence of real and wholly satisfactory witnesses, to charm, to impress, and to move even the one person who happened to sit in front of him radiating hatred and exerting himself to radiate contempt.

"I'll ask you this question all the same, Minet," he said peering at the canon. "Do you really believe in the demons at the Ursuline convent?"

The thumbs kept on twirling.

"Descend to our innermost depths, Minet, and ask and investigate. No, you will not do it. You will continue to believe in demons, it's easier for you and it will make you more secure now to believe in the demons than to doubt their existence. If you didn't believe, if you could and wanted to force yourself to doubt their existence, then you would be the most unhappy man in the world. In the situation in which you now find yourself you are possibly at certain moments one of the happiest men in the whole city. That's how badly off you are."

The canon took his time answering him.

"I have come to warn you, Grainier," he said. "I'm not here to listen to your linguistic virtuosity. We see, we know."

"*No!*" said the other man. "*No!*"

He rose from his chair, took a few paces about the room and stood facing the door with his back turned to the canon, he walked back, sat down as before and assumed the same pose.

"I have often thought about the situation in which a judge finds himself," he said. "It is not an easy one. A judge isn't any more a free man than is a prisoner; he is less free; he is the prisoner of the one he is judging. There are supposedly judges who are in the service of the people and not in the individual service of princes and rulers. They have the weight of the entire people behind their decisions. But not even they are more free than are judges who serve tyrants. The situation of the judge is always a tragic one—unless he possesses the kind of uprightness called blindness, the narrowness of mind which will only follow the regulations, the law, and nothing else."

"I don't want to listen to what you are saying," said the canon. "But I cannot help hearing that you are referring

263

to His Majesty's commissioner M. de Laubardemont or to His Majesty himself or to His Eminence the Bishop of Poitiers, your and my spiritual father, or perhaps to His Eminence Cardinal Richelieu."

"You don't understand what I'm saying," said the other man. "You don't understand what I am talking about or even that I'm talking about *something*. I assure you: I am not referring to M. de Laubardemont, who is always—you know that well, don't you?—very courteous and friendly toward me and who has several times invited me to dinner. Nor am I thinking of His Majesty the King or His Eminence the Cardinal-Duke Armand du Plessis-Richelieu. You are listening to the tone of my voice? If you wish, I can say what I just said in a different tone of voice. Do you wish that? No, we won't bother with that."

"I am not listening to you at all," said the canon.

His thumbs were still; they would soon change direction.

"Therefore," said the other one. "Therefore: what I can say about M. de Laubardemont, about the King and about the Cardinal in this connection is that they too are prisoners. What I meant with the situation of judges is quite simply this: it is far from easy."

"I'm not listening too closely to what you're saying," said the canon; "but I notice that you are looking for loopholes."

The thumbs resumed their rotation.

"I don't read proscribed writings," said the other one. "But I have—like you surely must have, Minet?—heard of Copernicus and the mathematics teacher from Padua, Galileo Galilei, and their contentions about our earth. One Father Sizzi wrote already in 1611 that their view contradicted Holy Writ and the Dominican Father Caccini attacked these views in the year 1614. It took a year for Galilei to be called to Rome. Cardinal Belarmino and a Father Seghizzi asked him in the name of the Holy Father to renounce his heresy. Another writing by Galileo Galilei appeared, however, in the year 1624. I have not read it of course; there is a wall between him, who may be a heretic, and me who am a faithful servant of the Church. But I know that he exists. And I know that they *right now,* Minet, *right now* are considering what sentence to impose on him. It has been delayed. They haven't been able to decide whether he is a heretic or not. The judges' doubt has lasted almost twenty years! Can you conceive of that? Every judge who passes judgment also pronounces a sentence on himself—and it is passed on to posterity. We are afraid of posterity, no matter what we are saying about it and no matter how we pretend to express our indifference, even our contempt of what it may think. Most often we deal with posterity with a kind of masked respect, thinking possibly that it will be wiser than we can be—we make a condescendingly elegant bow in its direction but deep inside we feel fear toward it. Yes, perhaps fear. It is for that very reason that you have come to me tonight, Minet."

The thumbs were twirling very energetically.

"I have told you that I have come to warn you, Grainier. To give you a chance."

"You have come to give yourself a chance," said the other one. "To get it from me. I don't intend to give it to you."

Minet stood up, the other one remained sitting. The canon's shoes, which were still wet, were squishing as he took two steps toward the door: one long and one short step. He was almost standing in darkness.

"You could leave town—*quietly,* Grainier," he said.

He spoke with an effort, it might be a game or due to fear.

"You may have a few days to arrange it," he said. "Four, five. All of us are not involved in this, but some of us. We can give you six days at the most. That is the furthest we can go."

"You want to avoid passing judgment," said the other

one and remained sitting as before. "You want to be let off from being judges. It is you yourselves that you want to give a chance."

The canon limped a few more steps toward his coat.

"Then you intend to fight?" he said turning toward the light.

"Call it what you like," said the other one. "I'm staying here, I'm sitting here, my hands are hardly moving. Call it fighting, if you like. If you knew anything about me, you would realize that you are not giving me any chance at all."

"A chance to live," said the canon.

"The chance to run away, what kind of chance is that?" said the other one. "The priest Grainier who is dead anyway—even if he gets as far as the New World. The priest Grainier is in any case still here with *that* which is his person, his living or dead person. *One cannot run away, Minet!* My life is that which I have lived, not a future. The future isn't life, it is nothing until it has become a past. In the past there will always be judges, always new judges. The future is at most a hope, but what happens to that hope we know nothing about. I hope I will be judged leniently by it. Don't you too? And if my judgment is made more lenient, then yours will be more severe. You know that? *One cannot run away, Minet!* In a way it is a source of strength to realize that. You can't run away either—even though you want to. And how could I, who *don't want to,* be able to do it? If you have demons inside you—and I believe you do—then they will come with you. If I have something evil that I want to run away from, then it will follow me. And death will accompany us. He will always accompany me and you and every one."

The canon stood with his face turned toward his coat, he stretched out his hand to take it.

"But there is something before death—something worse, Grainier!"

"I understand," said the other man. "You mean torture. Are you afraid of torture?"

The canon didn't answer, his hand had reached the coat.

"It only lasts a few moments, Minet, a few moments, a short while. Or: a moment outside time. And the torture is an experiment. It is of interest. One may observe those who do the torturing, one may play a game with oneself, the one who is tortured, and wonder how long *they* can keep it up."

"I have warned you," said the canon in the direction of the coat. "You have been given a chance."

"Minet," said the other one, "you haven't given yourself any chance. The Cardinal has his chance. He wants to save the state, France. He wants to make the country into one firm unit and do away with anything that can cause trouble. He has a program; and if one has a program, then one has a chance, a fixed point, something that seems capable of defending and excusing everything one does, *everything*, provided one does it for the sake of the state, the country. Everything! One appeals to posterity's judgment with results and not with morals—yes, provided one has a program, which is consistently followed, and succeeds in one's undertakings. The Cardinal has his chance, but his emissary Laubardemont has none, for he is an instrument of a lower and more brittle kind: an instrument without any other program than to be any kind of instrument every day, every second, every *now*. He is the visible hand, and if it is covered with blood, people will notice it and point at it. And you don't have any other chance than that of the instrument: which is hated because its deeds are not great enough to serve as an excuse for anything. One doesn't hate God but perhaps the stone that falls on one's toe by the will of God. The stone will be remembered. Posterity will remember such stones with hatred and loathing even though it was God who allowed it to fall. You will be remembered *thus* and that is the reason that you will not have a very good chance. I can tell you why in a different way: you will be remembered *because* there is no love in your life."

The canon suddenly turned around, he was holding his coat in both hands. He took two halting steps across the floor, the light fell over his face. There was hatred in his pasty features, in the thin stubble, and fear.

"You—!" he said. "You will be remembered as—the Devil! You are not a human being—you are—"

He turned toward the door. There was a squishing sound as he pulled the wet coat over his shoulders. The other one rose, grasped the biggest candle, which had almost burned down, and held it high.

"I will light your way out," he said.

The canon limped ahead of him in the corridor. He hesitated at the stairs before slowly walking down. The other one remained at the top of the stairs with the candle raised high before walking down after him.

"I'll close the door after you."

When he got back up again he placed the burned-down candle on the table and opened the window a bit. The Lame One crossed the square with the coat over his head as protection against the rain. A lump of darkness in the other darkness. When he reached the corner of the Street of the Butchers, the squishing footsteps were louder; his limp was very marked.

14

Fear and the Intoxicated One

Wʜᴀᴛ ʜᴀᴘᴘᴇɴᴇᴅ ᴛᴏ Dᴀɴ. Dʀᴏᴜɪɴ? He walked down
toward the Chinon Gate thinking of various things. His
walk was as it should be, steady, and his head as it should
be, full of thoughts, and he greeted people he recognized
and at times lifted his hat in a big or a small sweep of his
arm.

Bells were ringing in the twilight. The cross-streets
north-south were already dark. I will just have time for a
little air, he thought breathing in deeply, a little air to get
my head completely clear, my tongue rested, sharp, and
fine, my repartee quick and to the point. Those are the
things that are noticed. And I do have a reputation for wit
and for saying the right word at the right time. That kind
of reputation should be taken good care of. I will have just
enough time to get down to the gate and back to Sainte-
Croix—and possibly—have a small and stimulating absinthe before I—

The city walls had been torn down on both sides but the
gate towers and one of the low, round towers were still
untouched. Perhaps they were to be left standing. The
Bartray Towers further toward the west would perhaps
also be spared. It is very kind of them! he thought with
extreme irony. What generosity, gentlemen, what nobleness, what true urbanity! Those words I shall remember,
he thought. Gentlemen, I think you ought to tear down

the entire city—isn't the risk *too* big otherwise? That's the way, he thought. Concentrated. The nail on the head. Then: a brief pause. I lift my glass, take a sip and—talk about something else.

"Are you standing there counting the cobblestones, Daniel?"

He looked at the unshaven cheeks and the square-cut beard. It was the face of the mason foreman Antoine although a few years younger: his brother Charlot.

"Is that you, Charlot?"

"Oh my, Daniel, how fine you look! But I knew that already."

"In this town everything is known all over before it happens," said Daniel Drouin.

"I just stopped in at 'The Hen' and Antoine and Petiot were sitting there," said Charlot.

*

It was getting dark around them. Down at the gate a candle was lit in an aperture.

"Yes, I'm going there," said Daniel Drouin. "But only as an observer, those are also needed. Are you still working with your brother, Charlot?"

"We're razing," said Charlot, yawning. "We're tearing down as if we had the Devil at our heels."

"It's certainly no fun to see our city being destroyed," said Daniel Drouin, using the same words and tone of voice as most people did.

"No," said Charlot, indifferently. "But you make good money on it."

"Our city," said Daniel Drouin dreamily. He felt himself moved by his own tone of voice. "What are you yourself now, Charlot? In relation to faith. How do you stand as regards the new era?"

"The new era?" said Charlot. "Has a new era started?"

I must express myself more clearly and in a simpler way, thought Daniel Drouin.

"Do you think that the Cardinal is a big. . . ?"

He bent forward and whispered the word in Charlot's ear.

"Of course he is a big ass!" said Charlot in an unnecessarily loud voice.

"Don't speak so loud," said Daniel Drouin. "You know that the city is full of spies."

"I talk as loud as I want to in my own city!" said Charlot. "What was it you wanted to know?"

"Charlot," said Daniel Drouin, "believe me or not: I have forgotten what it was! But we could have a drink somewhere and then I'll probably think of it again."

They walked in the semi-darkness along the partly razed wall toward Mother Gaspard's little tavern by the Mirebeau Gate at the corner of Gate Street. Daniel Drouin thought of something:

"Charlot, what I wanted to ask you just now was in which camp you're standing. Your father was a Huguenot and your mother was a Catholic, or was it the other way around? Where are you now?"

"Here!" said Charlot. "On my own two feet. Where are you standing, where are you sitting, where are you lying, where are you hanging—if one may have the impudence to ask!"

It was said in a brusque tone of voice. I must think of just the right words, so that he doesn't misunderstand me, thought Daniel Drouin.

"I am an official," he said. "I must look after my business in and between both camps. And I have a certain sympathy for certain persons in both of them. This is my attitude. It is self-evident and clear."

"I think it resembles a mixture of horsedung and chicken-shit," said Charlot.

"I think you're exaggerating!" said Daniel Drouin.

*

They walked through the gate and across a yard filled

271

with junk and rubble and where it smelled from a stable and a tannery. The tavern was not very big, more like a hole in the wall, but it could accommodate an incredible number of people. Old Mother Gaspard, with white hair and wrinkles and much fat, sat underneath the lamp behind the counter supervising the service and shouting whenever necessary; and that was quite often.

The noise suddenly abated—and silence surrounded Daniel Drouin's splendid outfit. They stared at him, curious and suspicious: laborers, a few city guards, artisans, clerks, and peasants.

"Step aside there!" shouted Mother Gaspard. "You, Jean, and you, Michel! Let the honorable assessor get a seat!"

"Don't trouble yourselves," said Daniel Drouin affably; "we're leaving right away. We're just having a glass of something or other."

"Here, monsieur assessor!"

A grinning, red, bearded face was turned up toward the light; the odor of manure and sour wine felt like a blast against his face. It was Michel, who used to tend his vineyard.

"Is that you, Michel!"

"Yes, it's me, monsieur assessor," said Michel hitting the table with his big and dirty fist. He tried to get up, but it was too crowded.

"Just sit, Michel, sit."

"Yes, here I'm sitting," laughed Michel. "The assessor must excuse me, but here I'm sitting! I can't get anywhere. And now it's starting to rain."

Daniel Drouin heard the rain lash against the roof and the yard. I'd better wait till it's over, he thought. Now he was sitting squeezed in between Charlot and another fellow, a fat, heavy man, who seemed to be mute. Here I'm sitting, he thought, but it mustn't be for long.

They were served white Saumur wine, in a much too big tin beaker standing right in front of him. Four fellows, staring silently, were sitting right across from him, on the bench on the other side of the table. He recognized two of the faces and nodded to them. Michel was squeezed between two others at the corner.

"These fellows want to buy my mule, but I'm won't sell her," said Michel once again pounding the table with his fist. "I'm not a fool selling mules. They want to take her along to Richelieu's city but I have said that she is with me and she's going to stay with me. For that's the way I am, you see!"

"Well, well, Michel," said Daniel Drouin in a friendly voice.

The others stared at him in silence while the noise in the room was getting louder.

"Are things progressing in the Cardinal's city?" he said in a friendly tone of voice to the man facing him.

They looked at each other.

"Oh, pretty well," said the fellow sitting at the end of the bench.

"But this city is finished at any rate, mark my words," said Michel and hit the table with his dirty fist.

"But it's nice of them to leave the gate towers standing," said Daniel Drouin with fine irony.

They stared at him.

"What?"

"I mean," said Daniel Drouin and tried but didn't manage to recall some really coarse expression, "I mean, they ought to tear down the entire city all at once, and be done with it!"

His words were received in silence. The men looked askance at one another and down underneath the table. Daniel Drouin noticed how the quiet suffused the entire room. Mother Gaspard sat on her high stool behind the counter, staring at him. The one who recovered first was Charlot.

"Oh, you surely know how to joke, Daniel," he said. "You haven't changed since the old days."

"Is he joking?" said Michel, his eyes blinking.

"He's only joking," said the fellow sitting at the end of the bench.

Their smiles returned, tentatively. I have to do better than that, thought Daniel Drouin. Choose the right words.

"I think that the one—h'm-h'm one doesn't like to mention by name is a—a cowardly—h'm-h'm," he said. "A very cowardly ass!"

They stared dubiously at him, until Charlot began to laugh. Then they all laughed, not quite sure at what. They had more drinks.

"You all know that it was Daniel Drouin who said that the Devil doesn't know how to speak Latin!" said Charlot. "He was the one!"

He pointed with his thumb. They comprehended something but still had their doubts; and anyway, one shouldn't mention the Devil by name in such a wanton manner so close to Rue Pasquin where the Ursulines were residing.

Daniel Drouin had another drink.

"Now I have to leave," he said. "I'm really in a great hurry."

"It's pouring outside," said Michel with a snigger.

He listened. Yes, it was indeed pouring down. They ought to become fully aware of where I stand, he thought.

"What generosity!" he said. "What urbanity! What nobleness!"

"What?" said the one sitting across from him at the end of the bench.

"Imagine, they leave the gate towers standing!" said Daniel Drouin. "In them could—for instance—mark it well: I'm only saying for instance!—four or five who are—who aren't of the right faith, I mean—well—there they could hide and threaten the entire city!"

Silence surrounded him, it poured down outside.

"That Daniel, that Daniel," said Charlot, but he didn't sound very sure of himself either.

The others were silent, staring and waiting.

"I mean—the city is suffering a great injustice," said Daniel Drouin slowly and distinctly.

They remained silent. He emptied his glass and they poured more wine. He felt that his palate was dry, as always when he drank too much.

"But now I have to leave," he said when the glass was empty.

He stood up, there was nothing wrong with his legs. I should have expressed myself more succinctly, with more clarity, he thought. I'll stop in at "The Hen" and have an absinthe before I continue. He gave the serving girl a coin. Charlot remained sitting on the bench, he had moved further in, yawning repeatedly. The fellows from Richelieu's city were just staring.

"I have to leave too," said Michel. "I have pretty far to go, and now I will at least have company part of the way. If the assessor will allow a simple peasant to walk with him?"

Michel's legs were not very steady, and he took hold of Drouin's arm.

"As soon as I get started, I can move about pretty fast," he said. He pointed with a shaky hand: "Just think, those fellows wanted to buy my mule from me."

"Thank you, Mother Gaspard," said Daniel Drouin in a firm voice, turning toward her. The others moved aside looking at him in silence. They don't know what to think of me, he thought. They don't trust anybody.

Darkness outside, downpour. The tavern boy helped Michel get his mule out of the stable. They were cursing volubly. Daniel Drouin walked across the yard, he managed well in spite of the lot of rubbish lying about, and he thought that his coat would keep him dry except that it was somewhat too short. But that was the fashion. Fashions were not created in the rain but underneath roofs and were intended for large halls, castles, and great banquets. He walked up the street, his feet saying swush-swush. Behind him, he could hear the hoofs of the mule clip-clop in the darkness, and Michel's voice talking to the animal.

"Come now. Come on now." The hoofs clip-clopped again, it took a few steps. Then: "Come now. Come now, you damned mule. Come now, sweetheart."

There was light in a few windows in houses on Pasquin Hill. When Daniel Drouin had come pretty far up the hill, he heard Michel shout to him:

"Assessor Drouin!? Assessor Drouin?! Don't leave me now!"

He stopped and felt at least a bit irritated. I can't take care of drunken peasants, he thought resolutely. I have more important things to do. I'm in a hurry and a bit late already.

"Monsieur assessor, monsieur assessor!"

He walked back down the hill. He felt that his head wasn't completely clear, but there was nothing wrong with his legs.

"What is it, Michel?"

"She won't walk any more, assessor. Everything went fine until we came to this spot but now they have loosed the devils on her."

"Damn it," said Daniel Drouin, "what an idea to drag along a mule right through the city like this!"

Michel was standing in the uncertain light from a window without shutters high up on a wall, breathing heavily and smelling of dirt and wine and sweat.

"The cart is at the coach-builder Thiboust," he said, "but I didn't want to leave the mule with him because of the tavern and the strangers. For the tavern was full of Laubardemont people, see. I felt more secure taking her with me. As soon as she is in front of the cart, she knows her duty, see."

"What do you need help with then?" said Daniel Drouin, mollified.

"If the assessor could pull, I will give her a kick in the behind."

Daniel Drouin pulled at the halter. The mule resisted.

"Now I'm pulling," he said. "Give it a push."

276

Michel kicked and pushed and shoved, but the mule just stood there.

"When we get past this spot, it will be easier," he said, "and then I won't trouble the assessor any more. It's just this spot right here."

"What spot?" said Daniel Drouin, resting.

"God protect us! This one here!" said Michel and his voice was full of fear.

Good God! thought Daniel Drouin.

They were right in front of the gate of the Ursuline convent. The yellow walls gleamed in the darkness.

"They're holding back!" said Michel.

"Nonsense!" said Daniel Drouin, but not in such a loud and firm voice.

"Yes, they're holding back," said Michel. "If the assessor will be so kind as to pull, then I will try once more in the back."

The mule didn't want to, it just *stood* there.

"No, they're holding back," said Michel on the verge of tears.

"Who are holding back, then?" said Daniel Drouin calmly and in a dignified manner, but he knew it full well.

"Those over *there!*" said Michel. "What a damn fool I was when I didn't take the other road straight up to 'The Hen'! I was a damn fool. But the whole city is just as damn crazy as I am. It's worse than the plague."

The plague, thought Daniel Drouin. The children. The plague.

"No," he said with sadness and bitterness. "Now we'll make another try!"

The devil take it, he thought, if it is impossible to get the mule past this damn gate! They were lying inside the house of course possessed by devils spreading it to people and animals. It wasn't inconceivable that the entire district was saturated with demons.

"Give it a real push and I will pull, Michel!"

He pulled at the halter strap. Michel was able to push

the mule a foot forward, but it moved back immediately to its starting point as if its rear end had become elastic. The mixture of rain and dirt made the street slippery, he began to slide every which way.

"Push with all your might, Michel!"

Daniel Drouin slipped and fell. His left leg slid from under him and knocked against the mule's foreleg and the animal fell to its knees. It half covered him and he felt its hairy neck and its wet muzzle against his face.

His clothes!

"Good lord!"

He had hit his hip and his right elbow. He sat while the mule struggled to its feet. Michel sat behind the animal.

No broken bones, thought Daniel Drouin, but he felt a pain in his hip, in his behind, in the elbow. He was back on his feet again, Michel was almost up, and the mule completely so.

"You should never defy the powers!" said Michel and his voice showed how scared he was. "That's what I have always said!"

"Stop that kind of nonsense talk!" said Daniel Drouin. "Now I'll have to leave."

He felt his elbow and his thigh. They were sore. If only the cloth is not torn, he thought. The material was smeared with the dirt in the street, but he couldn't find any rips in it. The seat of his pants was wet. In his eyes he had tears of indignation.

"Now you'll have to manage by yourself, Michel. I'll have to leave."

"Please, dear assessor, please my dear assessor!" pleaded Michel. "I think she's getting a move on now! Yes, I believe that *they* got scared (he whined in a fearful voice) I believe. . . . But look, it is just as I said!"

The mule had really gotten a move on and started off of its own volition. Daniel Drouin held the halter strap in his hand and walked ahead, ascending the hill in long strides.

The mule's hoofs went clip-clop and behind them Michel was panting and puffing.

They moved at a fast pace all the way to the Square of Sainte-Croix, which was now empty and dark. There Daniel Drouin let the halter strap go. He was perspiring and breathing as hard as Michel and he thought he smelled just as bad as did Michel.

"Now I've had enough of all this!" he said.

*

Daniel Drouin bent backward, stood firmly with his legs apart, and could take it all in: there was a light behind Madeleine de Brone's shutters. She is sitting there pondering and mulling over things, he thought.

He peeked through the crack in the side gate and noticed that there was a light on in his own kitchen. He heard voices, it was Charlotte and the maid, and the smallest child was screaming. It's bedtime for all of us, he thought.

He lifted his hand to get hold of the latch, but he still hesitated. He heard Michel guiding the mule across the square, its hoofs clattering against the paving stones. Now they had entered Rue des Marchands, they were evidently doing all right. His hand dropped.

He fumbled at his clothes. Wet, dirty spots on the sleeves and the upper parts of his trousers. And on his back and on his knees. He again reached for the latch but then lowered his hand. He turned away from the gate (with a sense of shame, some people might think) and walked away. Now he was in the middle of the square, now he entered Rue des Marchands. It was drizzling.

*

When he arrived at the coach-builder's gate he could hear that Michel, the mule, and Mathurin were in the courtyard.

Michel was telling in too loud a voice about how the Devil had tried to prevent him and Daniel Drouin and the mule from getting past the residence of the Ursulines in Rue Pasquin. He, the courageous Michel, and Assessor Drouin had been cursing so volubly that the demons had immediately let go their hold and had fled, and all of it happened so quickly that they had been lying in the filth and mud without knowing how they had ended up there. They had slipped or—which was most probable—they had been knocked down by a strong, invisible hand. There was no doubt that Satan himself had been the cause of it and—

Daniel Drouin stepped into the area lit up by shafts of light from the inn's kitchen, the coach-builder's open door, and the lantern in the wagon shed. It was easy to walk there.

"Here comes the new devil exorcist himself!" said Mathurin.

"Yes," said Daniel Drouin, and while he was walking toward them he took great satisfaction in noticing that his legs were steadier than they had been for a long time. "I happened to slip," he said. "And now it's high time I get *over there*—you know—but I first wanted to see if my clothes are all right."

Corisande stood in the doorway:

"Daniel, come inside! Where in the name of the Lord have you been!"

They surrounded him, even the children, his cousin's children with their parents.

"I happened to slip," he said.

His clothes were looked over in the coach-builder's parlor. His sword was in good condition. His coat, trousers, and shoes were covered with clay and filth. His cuffs were soiled from sweat, wine, clay, and grime, his hat had been lying in the street, the plume was broken. But they couldn't find any tears or rips anywhere in his clothes.

"Sit down!" said Corisande.

He felt a bit tired while she rubbed gently with rags, water, and a soft brush. She turned up his cuffs.

"I only went for a little walk," he said. "And then I met Charlot; we had a drink together and talked for a while. And then I was going to help Michel up the Pasquin Hill with his mule and then I happened to slip."

"Yes, so I see!" said Corisande rubbing more forcefully with the brush. The children laughed and he heard Mathurin telling them to be quiet. Michel was standing in the doorway, staring with a foolish smile on his face: he looked stupid and dirty as always.

"There!" said Corisande (a little starchily, he thought). "Now you can go home to Charlotte and show her how you look!"

"But don't you know I'm going to—Laubardemont?" he said.

"That's out of the question!" said Corisande. "It's too late, anyway. You left here three hours ago."

"Good Lord!" he said.

"Go home, Daniel," she said. "Be a good fellow and go home."

"But I *have to* go there!" he said. "At least show my face."

"It's completely out of the question," Corisande said very firmly. "Mathurin, you'll accompany Daniel home."

"I can drive him home!" said Michel with a laugh. "For now she's moving again. They've let go. And she's as strong as a horse."

Daniel Drouin rose to his full height; his head touched the beam in the ceiling. He was not angry, not quite, but he felt offended and a little annoyed.

"Corisande," he said, "I'm a government official and I know my duty."

"Your duty is to go straight home, Daniel!" she said.

"Corisande," he said very calmly, "I peeked through the chink in the rear gate. I was about to go in. But I deliberated and hesitated. Charlotte was up, waiting—with something good to eat, I imagine—and the children were awake—and she will ask me about all kinds of things to which I won't be able to give a clear answer. And I am a little—very slightly, by the way—but a little tired in my head. That is the first thing I want to mention. The other is the fact that I have been invited to the party as a government official, I have the responsibility to represent my office. I'm not just anybody."

"Pooh!" she said. "You have as low opinion of that mass murderer as any of us. Just go for a walk and get some air before you go home and go to bed. You can tell Charlotte that you slipped and fell. And that you returned home because the party would be a very dull one. And that's no lie. Isn't that so, Daniel?"

Daniel Drouin tried to make himself even taller, but was unable to do so.

"Corisande," he said. "I am a bit annoyed with you in spite of your great helpfulness. You are urging me not to lie but to withhold the truth from someone. You know what I think of that. I'm not a cowardly wretch, I usually speak up and say my piece. But now I'm yielding to superior force. Thank you for your kindness."

She put her thin, worn hand on his sleeve.

"Daniel, Mathurin is going to walk you home," she said.

"I can drive him," ventured Michel, "for now she's moving again."

He walked ahead into the courtyard where the mule was standing by the new shaft.

Daniel Drouin paid no attention. Besides, he noticed that Michel was staggering. Drunken peasants, he thought. As soon as they get a glass or two of wine they get as drunk as swine. They have no intellectual resources.

*

Mathurin held him by the arm. This is just like the time we were young, he thought. They stopped in the middle of the Hen House Square. He noticed that it was raining

282

heavily again. There were many lights to be seen, both down in the tavern and in the upper story of the "Swan of the Cross." The windows up there were wide open. From the chatter, the noise, and the laughter he realized that the party had been going on for quite a long time. He wondered what they had had to eat and what they were drinking. I can find out more about that some other time, he thought. I ought to be sitting there speaking my mind. Fighting with the weapons of the spirit.

"Mathurin, I'll drop in at 'The Hen' and have something to eat, for I'm very hungry. Later I will go *up there* and say what I think. That's my duty."

"You're crazy," said his cousin.

"We'll step in at 'The Hen' and have a bite to eat, and that's all!" said Daniel Drouin.

"Daniel," said Mathurin, "you're crazy. Think of Charlotte who's sitting home and—"

If he mentions the word "tears" I'll get angry with him, thought Daniel Drouin. He said:

"Now we'll go inside, for I am hungry, haven't I pointed that out? And Albert knows how to make a good meal if you keep an eye on him and keep him away from garlic and salt. That is: not too far away. But you do need to keep an eye on him."

*

Antoine, Petiot, and Dolet were still sitting at the same table, together with a few others. A great number of people were sitting around the counter and the other tables. The only thing that had happened was that Daniel Drouin had gone for a walk just when it got dark and the rain started falling on the city and the plain.

Dolet moved over and Albert brought an extra stool. Daniel Drouin stretched his legs and breathed in the odors.

"You got tired of it?" said Dolet. "How were things otherwise?"

"Albert," said Daniel Drouin, addressing the innkeeper, "Mathurin Thiboust and I would like something to eat. What have you got?"

"Didn't you get any *food* up there?" said Dolet, and Petiot who was quite drunk mumbled something like it. Antoine stared hard at him, he had an evil look in his bloodshot eyes.

"Keep your mouth shut," said Mathurin.

"Take it easy, Dolet," said Daniel Drouin.

He downed a small glass of absinthe and Mathurin stuck to white wine. Daniel could feel how his head cleared, high up, right underneath the top of his head. I know what it was, he thought very lucidly. I was afraid to go there. Consequently I am a cowardly person? That doesn't seem to be true. I am not afraid.

Albert had a fried chicken for them. Daniel Drouin saw how Antoine, the big glutton, was staring at it with his bloodshot eyes and kept swallowing and it touched a sympathetic chord: he ordered one more. They ate, it smelled good, it filled one's mouth and belly. They were sitting there together and were friends in a safe and secure world where everyone knew everyone else. It was a good world— if they could only change a few details, could move about or put out of their minds some of the figures high up and in the distance behind the curtain of rain and night.

"This feels all right," he said.

"Is it true that you didn't get any food up there?" said Dolet caustically, while gnawing on a chicken wing and then licking his fingertips.

"I want some bread!" said Antoine and kept on chewing. "Albert, bread!"

"Albert, wine!" shouted Petiot. "Red wine for me!"

"Here there aren't any demons and things that prevent you from living and enjoying life," said Daniel Drouin.

"Daniel," said Mathurin, chewing slowly and savoring it, while taking a sip from the new wine. "Daniel, we'll have to leave very soon. Don't forget that."

"It looks very good," said Michel, standing in the doorway. He stepped closer, and stood behind Daniel. "Can you imagine it let go so suddenly. All at once! As if they were scared!"

"I'm not scared," said Daniel Drouin and noticed that there was now red wine in his cup. "I have decided to go up there and tell them off."

He turned his head.

"Sit down, Michel. Have something to eat!"

"Don't forget that we have to leave right away," said Mathurin.

Albert came in with more fried chicken.

"Are you going to say it right out that you didn't get anything to eat?" said Dolet. Even though they were all in the friendly world of mankind, Daniel Drouin thought it sounded malicious.

"I didn't go there," he said. "Not because I was afraid to go up there. But I went for a walk instead and thought about things. I'll soon go up there and tell them what I think."

He looked up, his glance took them all in. He took another drink.

"What shall I say? There's much that I can say. That the devils don't know Latin, that I have said before, so that has been said. But here are other things to be mentioned. Should I say that—"

He was thinking very clearly: his thoughts were all in good order inside his head and his breast. Now they were listening. Mathurin gave him a nudge but even he was listening.

"Should I address him like this: Monsieur de Laubardemont, Monsieur Baron de Laubardemont, it's beginning to smell of fire and blood wherever you go? We don't like the smell of blood in our city. Shall I say something like this: Monsieur Commissioner and Baron de Laubardemont, you want to slaughter both Armagnac, our governor, and Grainier, that's what you want—but you are not

285

able to slaughter the Devil for then you would have to commit suicide, since he's living inside you! Should I say that? How does it sound? For he's living inside you, Monsieur de Laubardemont. Or should I say it like this: Every single human being here *believes* that the demons have arrived here only because the Cardinal—"

"*Daniel!*"

Mathurin squeezed his arm and shouted into his ear:

"Daniel! *You must go now!*"

"I'm not a timid person, don't ever think that," said Daniel Drouin. "I'm staying. Urbain Grainier isn't a timid person either, no matter what you say about him! He's doing the same as I: *he's staying!* The Cardinal—"

"*Daniel!*"

His head felt just fine. His thoughts were arranged the right way, and he could visualize just what he was going to say immediately, in a little while.

"I am not an easily frightened person," he said, "that you all know. And I can't stand it any longer. I can't stand doing like some others, walking around keeping silent and mumbling a bit. I'm going up there to say that—"

"*D A N I E L !!!*"

*

This happened to Daniel Drouin on a rainy evening in the year 1633:

He was sitting in a tavern with some good friends; they had something to eat, something to drink, and were exchanging thoughts about current events and about things that had happened or were happening in their own city. The light from lamps and candles enveloped them. The kitchen odors and the smell of people who had sprayed perfume on themselves and from people who had taken care of animals in the course of the day, the smell of people who broke wind or were belching or burping surrounded him, together with the noise and the chatter. And outside, it was raining.

286

He threw a chicken leg into the wooden bowl in front of him. It bounced up, jumped out of the bowl and slid along the table which was already slippery, making another grease spot there. He placed his palms and his forearms on the table and was leaning on them when he rose from his chair in order to really say what he planned to say up there in a short while. Then his elbows slipped a bit, the stool he was sitting on also started to slide, both his own legs and those of the stool, and he tumbled to the floor.

"I didn't hurt myself," he said, sitting next to his cousin Mathurin's feet. "I can stand all right," he said when they had helped him up. "I can stand by myself. Let go and you'll see."

They didn't want to let go.

"Let go and you'll see," he said, stressing each word.

Then Michel who was standing on the right, let go. It was done thoughtlessly or shrewdly, perhaps as an experiment or for some other reason, for Michel was not quite sober. He let go, and then Daniel had to throw his long arms around his cousin and childhood friend Mathurin. His legs collapsed, he was just hanging there, but the coach-builder kept his balance.

"Now I'm going to—," said Daniel Drouin.

He was not going to at all. Michel and Mathurin led him out and someone followed with his new, but still fine-looking hat.

"His sword is completely bent!" cried Dolet.

"The carriage is ready, sir," said, hiccoughed, and grinned Michel, that damned peasant, that ill-bred drunken ass, that terribly superstitious country hick.

"I'll reprimand him when I get a chance," thought Assessor Daniel Drouin. "I'll take up his case and discuss it with myself before I take any action according to—according to—according to the thoughts that the case evokes in me as a wine grower and government official. A carefully considered reprimand won't hurt."

287

"Keep your mouth shut, peasant," he said in a rough tone of voice.

"But your carriage is all ready," said Michel, grinning. "And now she's moving, it has let go."

"I urge you most earnestly not to comment on this present matter," said Assessor Drouin.

"In any case, it has let go in her," said Michel and was not afraid.

His insolence is due to his drunkenness, thought Daniel Drouin.

They helped him, rather one ought to say: they loaded him onto the cart. He also gave a hand, fully conscious that he could walk, sit, think, and speak. He was sitting in the straw and the twigs underneath the taut canvas as in a tent, even like a Roman battle commander in his army camp in Barbaria, and the rain was pattering on the canvas, it was night, and he was about to give the order to storm the fortress. He said very clearly:

"Go home to Corisande, Mathurin, and tell her that I managed by myself. All my decisions stand firm. I'm just going home to rest a few minutes, then I'll go up there to really speak my mind. They listen to what I say. For I'm not timid."

"I can follow you all the way home," said Mathurin, blinking because of the rain.

"Mathurin," said Daniel Drouin, "you are my cousin, my dear relation, my playmate, the friend of my youth, my confidant. But now I can manage by myself. We'll have to talk about our youth and what we had in common some other time. Now I can manage very well by myself. I don't want you to accompany me home. That will have to be some other time. Right now I don't want anything of the kind."

"Daniel," said Mathurin, "remember what you are going to say to Charlotte! That the party was not very enjoyable and that you slipped."

"Get going, Michel!" commanded Daniel Drouin.

Michel climbed up in front, sat underneath the canvas top, bringing his smell with him. He held the reins without getting himself or the animal entangled in them. People from the tavern helped to get the load moving. The cart started off with great difficulty, the wheels started to turn.

"She's completely over it," said Michel, turning his head toward Assessor Drouin. "When she wants to, she's as strong as a horse."

Daniel Drouin saw the rectangle of light, the door of "The Hen." The tavern owner and Mathurin were standing there with some others, they were shouting and waving to him, and bawling out a song. He moved further in under the top and leaned against Michel. He sat comfortably. Safely. He was able to think about things if he felt like it. And he didn't feel like vomiting, no need to at all. He might do it inside the gate of his house, as usual, or perhaps before that, in the street. He might cross the square and support himself against the church wall. Or, he thought, against the house of that damned Poussaut or against the damned house of Louis Tranchant, the procurator who had been dismissed. He didn't decide on any of this now. He would see how things would turn out.

When they had just entered the Rue des Marchands he closed his eyes. The donkey's hoofs slipped and clattered, the cart rattled and creaked, wailing about the city, mankind, and life. The world isn't as bad a place as all that, thought Daniel Drouin. Actually, many people are kind to each other. Cicero says—. Well, what does he say? *Quod benevolentia fit, id odio factum criminaris.*"

"What did you say, sir?"

"Your contention is that whatever happens on account of kindness is the result of hatred."

"I?" said Michel. "I've been silent the whole time. I haven't said a word in a long time."

"I was thinking of something else," said Daniel Drouin without opening his eyes. "I was thinking of the powers and of mankind. Of happiness and peace. I was thinking

289

of—. Say, Michel, I want to take a trip into the country."

The raindrops were drumming against the canvas top, water was dripping down his neck.

"What did you say?"

"I want to go out to my vineyard," said Daniel Drouin very distinctly but without opening his eyes. "Don't think I'm afraid of the city. I have no fear. But I'll go with you home, and tomorrow I'll take a look at my vineyard, my now leafless vineyard, I will rest my eyes on it, and take in my impressions. That's what I've decided."

"We've arrived at Sainte-Croix now," said Michel sleepily. When he was done yawning, he explained further: "The assessor is to get off here. I'll help."

"I'm going to my country place and my vineyard," said Daniel Drouin.

"I'll be glad to help the assessor all the way into bed," said Michel. "I'm not very drunk."

Daniel Drouin didn't reply but he could rise up enough to vomit outside the canvas top without any trouble. Then he sank back in his seat and sat there as before. His head felt unusually clear even though his eyelids were sleepy, just like other parts of his body. The cart had stopped, it waited, hesitated, moved forward again. He's happy to get company all the way, thought Daniel Drouin. I'm not afraid of anything. Neither of Charlotte nor of— something else. I'm especially not afraid of—something else.

The cart rolled down the hill.

"Now we're by the Bartray Church," said Michel.

Daniel Drouin didn't bother to answer: He thought: In the Bartray Church the demons are creeping forth between the thighs of the womenfolk. They stick their heads out from the hairy forest. He thought: In a little while, if I feel strong and sober, in a little while, I'll ask Michel if he has any womenfolk at home. If the maid is all right. If I feel in the right mood.

290

"Now we're at the Bartray Gate," said Michel yawning in between the words.

Daniel Drouin heard what he said but he disdained to answer. He could have answered if he had so desired. The Bartray Gate, he thought. They will leave it alone. They won't tear it down. His thoughts continued in this vein, firmly and clearly: I'm not one who's afraid of anything.

15

His Name

THE POSSESSED WOMEN were lying on mattresses in the convent chapel. Father Barrot said that this was a renewed attempt. One might regard it as one more exercise, a necessary effort to be made by *every one* (he said) so that a way out would be prepared for the demons and a final release would occur.

The lights were burning in front of the picture of the Madonna, and the smoke, mixed as it was with incense, was so thick that some of the women were coughing. A cloth screen had been placed in front of the window opening; she could see the bright square from where she was lying. As usual, a cart creaked and squeaked on the hill outside. It was a beautiful autumn day with a clear sky.

Father Barrot bent over her. Minet stood somewhat closer to the door. He didn't join in with any questions just then but merely listened and learned. It occurred to her, for only a moment, that the demon who wanted to enter her or already was there in order to drive out other demons, was named Barrot. He wanted her to be released soon. It was expected. She had to open her mouth and say or shout something so that the chain of voices would be released, to run on and rattle: a chain of shouts from throat to throat. They were waiting for her.

"Sister Jeanne, you must let them reply!"

The thin, boney, gray face came closer. The

crookedness of his back made him look like a corkscrew. He bored himself into people.

"You must give in and let him speak," he repeated. "Don't offer any resistance."

His face came still closer, she noticed his smell. Today he had been chewing garlic. His clothes smelled of perspiration, even though he was unable to perspire; it dried up. Shoes were squeaking far out on the stone floor.

"You can say it again. Can't you say it again?"

She whispered yes.

"Try to understand what I'm saying."

"Yes," she whispered. "I am trying, but it is so difficult."

"Listen closely to me. I am saying: Why have you entered into the body of this virgin? Now answer."

"Because of hatred," she answered and her train of thought was once again unbroken.

"No," he said. "I am asking the question and you must reply with my clear answer. Why have you entered into the body of this virgin? I am going to ask it in Latin: *Propter quam causam ingressus es in corpus hujus virginis?* And then you will answer clearly and in plain words. God wants plain words. Jesus Christ wants plain words. The Holy Virgin wants plain words. Saint Joseph wants plain words. The enemy, think of the enemy! Now say the plain words."

"Because of wickedness," she said dully.

"No: because of animosity," he said. "Remember: because of animosity."

"*Causa animositatis,*" she said and remembered.

"That is right. Now I'll ask you: Through which association, through which pact. Remember the words: *Per quod pactum.*"

Something was released inside her. Suddenly she could answer clearly, radiantly, fragrantly, sensually correctly:

"*Per flores!*"

He bent one knee and was now crookedness without end, a crooked garlic smell, she thought and shuddered. His shoes were squeaking far out on the floor. She could hear how the others were breathing in, breathing out, holding their breath, were moving, waiting.

"Now listen carefully to what I am saying," he said. "We have to go by the rules so that you will be set free and obtain peace and redemption. Listen and translate my questions and all your answers—so that you will know them later, so that you will follow the rules. *Quales?* I'm asking: *Quales?*"

"Which flowers," she translated. "Which flowers."

"Now you answer yourself," he said.

Once again this sensual pleasure. One might want to die at a moment like this, she thought, feeling tired. Right now.

"*Rosas,*" she replied.

*

He had slid away but she could hear his voice.

"With three thorns, remember that, Sister Claire, with three thorns. That's what you have said, that is the truth: not four or two but three. Satan tries to confuse you, but remember that there were three thorns that pricked your hand when you woke up, Sister Claire. Listen, Sister Anne, there were three thorns. There were three thorns, Séraphique. Listen carefully, Sister Catherine, it was three thorns that pricked you."

She closed her eyes and gray, speckled light flickered underneath her eyelids. Shattered light. For long she saw a light gray, almost white, oblique square. Then the light turned red and then the darkness set in. She was breathing calmly and looking into it. She heard the shoes squeak and go away and had a strange and comical but not very laughable thought which also contained some fear: that the shoes went away with him and with Father Minet. She would be free. Shoes were walking away with prison guards. But the fear was to stay behind, and she was left alone with it, without any help. He was in the shoes, and then they walked away with him and she had been abandoned. She wished they were closer.

She heard Sister Claire's brief, clear, confident replies and Sister Anne's mumbling. His voice: "You must tell me the name of the one who sent you the roses, Sister Claire; you must be silent now, Sister Anne. Séraphique, breathe through your mouth, you are making a wheezing noise in your nose and it is disturbing." Now Sister Claire's doubts appeared: "I can't. I can't find it." "It's not you who are talking, Sister Claire," was heard from the remote garlic smell, from the remote squeaking of shoes, from his remote-close smell of perspiration. "It is the demon who is speaking. But you must let his voice come through your mouth so that we can know the terrible truth. I am going to start over again: *Quis misit.* Translate: Who sent them—"

Who sent them? thought the prioress, Sister Jeanne. *He sent flowers to us, to me!* Did he? I can't stand it any longer, I will have to mention his name! Far away she heard Sister Claire—that freak, that freak!—mumbling and hawking. Would she mention his name right now—she, the loathsome, ill-smelling, shriveled-up freak? No, she thought, I am not the one calling her a freak, she is not a freak, it is a demon within me who calls her a freak. She is my sister. No, I am her spiritual mother. It's not I who want to mention his name, it is the demon Ashtaroth within me who will shout it at them. It is the demon who has tempted me to think of him and drag us away from our Saviour, Jesus Christ, my blessed king. It is I, no, it is *my* demon who has the right to shout the name, the beloved, the cursed name, it is *I* who have the right to utter the name!"

"Say it now!" said Barrot, far away.

Now I am going to say it, thought Sister Jeanne, it is my demon who will say it!

"*Urbanus!*" she shrieked.

*

When she heard the squeaking of his shoes approaching and perceived that even the heavy perspiring that was Minet hobbled close, how Sister Claire swallowed saliva, and how the others opened their dry or moist lips and murmured the name again and again, she felt a kind of joy: I was the first one! It was through my mouth!

She opened her eyes, and there was unexpectedly much light in the chapel. She glanced furtively to both sides. The girls were lying as before and nothing or almost nothing except the intensity of the light had changed. Barrot's face was right above her and next to it she saw Minet's round, flabby one. His forehead was covered with beads of perspiration. She saw the gleam in Minet's yellowish-brown eyes. The tip of Barrot's tongue showed between his thin lips: he was panting.

"Is he talking now?"

The demon retained his grip around her neck. Again she closed her eyes and struggled with him.

"Is he going to speak now?"

The bright, lopsided square turned dark. If I can get some sleep tonight, I may be able to get out of it. Bright rays were flickering through the dusk. A sunset with parts of the day remaining. Up in the mountains it may stay a long time after it has gotten dark in the valleys, she recalled.

They could walk through the forest along a path up in the mountains. In the evening, the valley lies in deep shadow turning to dense darkness. A candle is lit down there, making a reddish-yellow dot in the bluish-black and the dark green and around it the darkness is even denser. Yes, Jeanne, it is evening. Up here there is still light. A lizard is rustling in the dry leaves of chestnut and beech, which have retained the sun's warmth. Yes, Jeanne, it is evening. It is in Italy. Such is the evening in northern Lombardy, at Angela Merici's long ago. Yes, Jeanne, it is evening and your lover is with you, the man Jesus Christ or someone with another name. Yes, Jeanne. He is holding her hand saying Jeanne, which is her name, and he is not saying Sister Jeanne or Mother Jeanne. She whispers his name in return. Now, soon, he will touch her. Soon, he will put his arm around her, it moves upward, moves slowly up toward her right breast. Her breast is lying in the hollow of his hand and is like a bird in its nest at night. His other hand covers her left breast—the way mine, Jeanne's hand, covers mine, Jeanne's breast. It slides downward; she feels the voluptuous pleasure from the hand, which becomes that of her breasts and her waist and her thighs.

"*Urbanus! Urbain!*"

When she opened her eyes, the room was very bright. The faces of both the exorcists were close to her own; and with the light came their smells and their sounds.

"We must let him finish talking," said Barrot. He commanded: "Let him finish talking, Sister Jeanne!"

*

She tried to turn her face toward Barrot. Her mouth was full of saliva. She wanted to spit in his face. She felt it running out through the corners of her mouth, froth, dribble trickling down her throat. But the grip on her neck held her head firm.

"You must rid yourself of him, Sister Jeanne!"

I'll never be rid of him, she knew. I'll never get rid of them.

"Say his name!"

"*Causa animositatis!*" came from her mouth, it was sputtered out.

"Say his last name!"

"*Per flores!*"

"Say his last name distinctly!"

"*Rosas!*"—and she felt the saliva foaming about her mouth.

"Say his name once more!"

O your name, your sweet, your beautiful, your kind and exciting, your delightful, your beloved name! O your beloved, your delightful—your name which is within me! I am not going to say it, my lips won't let it pass, the demon within me will not be allowed to say it!

"*Diabolica!*" The shriek emanated from her throat and from her inner being. The others moaned and stirred a bit. She heard Sister Claire's voice coming from the bed beyond Sister Catherine's as a shrill, ringing echo: *diabolica!* Further over, far on the other side, the girl Marie Aubin repeated, mechanically as during a lesson in school, without any fervor, from duty, rapidly, hastily: *diabolica!* Then was heard a shriek—stored up, fully ripe, an emptying of dammed-up sounds that are released, a gathering of sounds collapsing into a heap: *diabolica!* It was Sister Anne, and in Sister Anne's shriek was intermingled Séraphique Archer's howling.

She tried to enter farther into the darkness but the shrieks and then the silence kept her awake and in the red. Someone in the row of women—we are seven or eight or ten, she recalled—wanted to get up but Minet came limping over and must have pushed her down. Without thinking of the girls she knew it: Marie Aubin.

The creaking of the shoes was in her ear. The smell of garlic and the smell of perspiration became thin tapeworms creeping into her nostrils. The one side of her neck was moist from dribble. The whistling in her ear from the pressure when she clamped her jaws together, became louder: her molars were pressed together with annoying firmness but the saliva was still trickling out at the corners of her mouth.

"You, the representative of Satan, Ashtaroth, answer me!" Barrot commanded.

They didn't walk in the mountains. His cupped hands were gone. Instead of Lust it was the Claws that caressed her breasts and tore at her side.

"*Say his name!*"

"*Urbanus,*" she replied in a firm voice without opening her eyes. She felt satisfaction at giving this answer. She had

298

understood his question correctly. She thought her pronunciation was good. Again, her jaws were firmly pressed together.

"Say his last name. Listen carefully: *Dic cognomen.*"

Again it was difficult. Soft hands, and sharp claws, touched her. The demon wanted to let the name cross her lips, through her throat, from her inner being, her abdomen, but she resisted. If I resist, I will soon be able to turn my head and spit in his face. She got further into the red and toward the dark green. She came toward the bluish-black, through the forest and up toward the mountains where a streak of this day was still left. They walked in an even rhythm, gliding easily forward with straight backs and strong thighs. They stopped and stood at the important moment of beginning repose. In one of his hands lay her right breast as in a bird's nest. His other hand moved away from her left breast and dropped, slipped, glided down toward her thigh, in between her thighs, they had no clothes on.

"*Dic cognomen!* Repeat his last name! *Dic cognomen*"

When he wanted to put his warm hand between her thighs, up in the mountains, where there were no other people, where no one could see them, where the evening was mild and it was still light—when she felt the hand come near her, Séraphique Archer, who was lying near the door, cried out:

"*Dic—dibbocka—dibbolicka*—oh, now he's coming, now he's coming, now he's coming!"

She glided into the red darkness, she lay in dark-red consciousness. Barrot's and Minet's shoes creaked loudly as if they too were gasping.

"*Keep quiet over there!*"

Séraphique Archer's demon fell silent. There was a sound like tittering coming from somewhere. Marie Aubin, she thought. The world was perfectly clear and the grip on her neck was tight. She was being guided, and that gave her a feeling of security.

*

In the clarity of this brief moment she could look at everything in a logical manner. She understood that the Devil in the most cunning way imaginable had assaulted her through a priest of the Church of Saint-Pierre and Sainte-Croix in this city during a period of weakness while she was struggling against her body. This was as clear to her as if she had just read it in a book which had been fully approved and blessed by the Holy Father himself in Rome. It seemed clear to her that the Devil had turned the priest's coarse desires toward her and that the desires had contaminated her body. As long as she did not recall the priest Urbain's back, shoulders, and his hips, which she officially never had seen, or the name Madeleine de Brone, the logic was perfectly pure, ruler-straight, and clear.

During this brief period of great clarity, while she felt as tired as after sexual release and during the hurried over-view which she now took of her life (not with thoughts but with a feeling of surveillance) she saw how she, one who had been called by God, had been wandering on a hard and difficult path up through her childhood, through schooling that had been forced on her, through her struggle against lust and desire. She saw how she had learned to love the most seriously wounded, the injured, the infected, and evil-smelling. That love made her more courageous than all others and it enabled her to nurse and look after the most scabby, lice-infected, and evil-smelling people with a bravery and a ruthless self-sacrifice, which may only come about in connection with being one of the chosen. She felt as if she had invented Christianity. Yes, she had—according to this lofty, straightforward logic—invented it. She could not formulate the logic behind it in words, but she experienced it as a distinct feeling. She knew in this peculiarly long-lasting and concentrated moment that she was a saint and that she had to make great sacrifices in order to have it confirmed. She was a saint who hadn't yet been able to carry out her mission and then die and be beatified and later become holy and venerated. Her spiritual reach (she felt) was greater than that of any other women she had met and who were living on the earth at the present time and even a bit greater than that of the virgin Jeanne d'Arc (who was burned in Rouen) and the blessed Angela Merici and Teresa (of Avila) and also that of the saintly Ursula.

Within this extremely concentrated and clearly illuminated circle of time, while she was lying with closed but sharply seeing eyes and with her thoughts and feelings perfectly clear and surpassing everything that was insignificant, and within a logic which was luminous and perfectly valid and satisfying, she saw how straight her path had been in its essential features without unnecessary and improper dialectics (which conjurers and exorcists might make use of, provided they wanted to). How uncompromisingly it had led from the novitiate at Poitiers and further ahead in a difficult world where she always got on the wrong side of everyone on account of the wide scope of her personality and her enormous demands. She saw how she was being led by a secret agreement with God, which was never written and yet firmly binding and straightforward, and how she had been in the immediate proximity of the sainted Joseph, the earthly husband of the Holy Virgin. She perceived in repeated, continuing clarity how straight her path had been through the novitiate and the suffering, the stinking, and the vermininfested to her present situation; and in this state of clarity she understood that these were points in the series of stages and stations perhaps just now embarked on, which had been selected or were soon to be selected for her.

She looked into the past and saw clearly how she became one of the eight women who founded the Ursuline convent in this city. She saw how, through and beyond this, in a period when she no longer knew any peace but genuine cunning and tenacious pushing ahead, she was lifted up and in spite of her own protests was called upon to head the convent to hold the chair of prioress and spiritual mother. She was still there. She was the one who governed (although severely assailed by demons), an omniscient or practically omniscient, deeply feeling and sentient, clearly seeing and wisely counseling mother. She was still that. At the moment she didn't see in detail the stations further ahead but she could imagine them; and in suffering but also in the exercise of influence and power she was to wander, be carried, soar on to the last stage: Sainte Jeanne, a holy maiden from Saintonge in France.

In this extremely brief moment of clarity, which was merely an interval between two squeaks of Father Barrot's shoes, she comprehended the higher and spiritual aspect of her situation.

The word *comprehend* is not used here in the sense that she thought through her situation, from the past and into the future. To *feel* is the correct word for that kind of assurance. She felt how he whose last name she was to mention soon and whose position within the church, in life, and geography she was to talk about in distinct and intelligible Latin words, had desired her and had tried to prevent her from ascending to holiness by tempting her away from this holiness. He tempted with masculine beauty, with the overpowering, fiery, dark glance he was said to have, through the reputation he had gained of taking delight in sensual pleasures and of having the power to force all women onto their backs and to take their maidenhead, provided they still had it. Yes, he tempted with his reputation for possessing great masculine sexual power underneath the clerical robe and by having such a voice and such a glance that they weren't aware in him of God or Saint Joseph, the husband of the Holy Virgin, but instead the tempting, passion-inciting, and experienced seducer, the man who knew much about women's passion

302

and wanted to share it or transfer it to himself or transfer his own into theirs.

She *comprehended* with exceptional although brief sharpness that he was an obstacle to her own fulfillment, as he at the side of the governor was an obstacle to the complete leveling of the fortifications of the heretics in this city and thus of the extermination of heresy in the entire country and the whole world; one of the obstacles which delayed or completely prevented the razing of the defense fortress, the towers, and the walls of the heretical crowd. He had not cared for her in any but that devilish way: letting her watch him through the small lattice window in the gate or from the windows or the small window-openings on the roof. It was to cast a furtive and thus rather shameless gaze that he tempted her through his mere reputation. He had declined to become her own father confessor and that of her spiritual daughters and her protegées; and his lure was so great that she dreamed of being allowed to confess her sins to him.

She had *also* seen very clearly that he walked past and left her unnoticed because she was not perfect as a woman. He went to other women who were younger and spiritually inexperienced and bodily, if this were possible, even more virginal and unsullied from play with the most secret—or to women who were more experienced and were rewarding in that respect: experienced females who possessed great knowledge about the art of lying underneath a man. Or he sought out females who were so young and soft that they could give him greater pleasure than she herself could give him, and in their simplicity and lack of a higher calling they would derive a greater passion from him than she herself would obtain if she—no, it would never, never happen!—were to be with him.

She realized that he was an obstacle. In this moment of clarity he was The Obstacle. Yes, he was the walls against which she scratched with her nails to no avail: the walls *that she didn't know if she would want to surmount* or that she wanted to surmount in spite of the fact that her will was a great sin that had to be atoned for (and thus a great sacrifice, from which one might derive useful knowledge when wanting to approach greater holiness).

More could be said about this clarity which she, of course, did not formulate or even put into thoughts or words. She *was* in the clarity in the same way that someone drunk with alcohol or drugs is in a state of clarity, which liberates him from time, inessentialities, and inhibitions. She remained in that state, just as the genuine or the spurious artist may be in a state of intoxication, that of creativity, the ignition of the self, or the extinguishing of the self.

She was there.

We—afterward—may claim that it was the solution of the failed genius, the solution of the false, emotionally intoxicated, emotionally messy, dreadladen and therefore the solution of the superficially sure and superior genius. Or that of the stupid fool, the narrow-minded but mad one. A zealous but hunted human being whose blood has been given a few seeds of talent on its journey from the heart to the other vessels, seeds that secrete poisons of possession.

What do we know about her?

She was possessed.

This was her strongest, most genuine, most profound consciousness.

She was possessed.

*

"Dic cognomen!"

When she twisted her eyeballs, raised her eyelids letting the red darkness fall away from them, she saw the vault of the ceiling above her. There were two vaults that came together, two eyelids of stone that prevented the light from entering. Below them, the incense was floating in impure clouds. If she lifted her glance even higher up and

304

turned her glance backward on a slant, she could make out the tall, wilting candles in front of the picture of the Madonna. Within the range of her glance were the shadows of Barrot and Minet. If she looked sideways, she could see the sisters, her spiritual daughters. They were there, perceived through the corner of an eye. On the far left, but so high up that the picture was reflected in both of her eyes, was the window opening, the oblique square covered with a gray piece of linen.

A moment of calm. Right now I am here. She felt calm in her isolation from the past, which was now trembling away from her like a distant light, and from that which is yet to come, which was trembling in toward her like a light that glows out of the far distance where she herself would presently be. A tiny shadow flickered on the ceiling, a moth that had been awakened by a voice and which now in its immediate future was to choose one of two paths: either toward the bright window opening, where she saw the narrow shadows of the bars like a laced pattern against the gray linen cloth, or toward the candles on the altar in front of the picture of the Madonna.

"I repeat: *Dic cognomen!*"

I ought to know everything, she thought. My superior ability has made me always able to understand everything at once. I have also been able to count my demons even during the greatest of suffering, during the most upsetting internal and external pain. They are seven. It is I, Jeanne, with the fine intellect, who has counted them.

Then Barrot shouted. It sounded like the orders of a commanding officer during an attack at night with the enemy within earshot; a command said in a low voice and sounding like an entreaty:

"*Asmodeus! Leviathan! Behemoth! Isacaaron! Balaam! Gresil! Aman! Answer me!*"

She could feel how they began to stir. The clarity fell away, the plain and the true became intangible.

"*Answer me!*"

305

The clouds grew denser underneath the ceiling, the eyelids of the vaults were blackening stone and cracked plaster. The candles were smoking. The moth flitted toward a light which might be freedom or death. She heard steps out in the street, they were heavy burghers' shoes or heavy or light clerical shoes without creaking, without garlic smell, without the smell of sweat, young bone pillars, young, strong feet—out in the street, down the street, past and away. The demons obeyed the call stirring like a fetus within her. First, those on her left side, their claws searched for her heart. Then those on her right side, they wanted to stop her breathing. Those who were in her diaphragm wanted to make her vomit, and the one down in the round barrel of her stomach working along the lower paths wanted to compel her to pass water or let out wind or faeces. They will stay within me forever if they are not allowed to speak through my mouth. If they are not allowed to borrow my voice for words, they will get out along the other paths, by the other methods.

Then I will be lost.

"Answer! Dic cognomen! Answer!"

Then she said his name.

Or: didn't say it, it was an answer that the principal demon, Asmodeus, was forced to give to a question by Father Barrot, the outstanding conjurer and exorcist. She didn't say it, it was said. The instrument was her throat and her lips. *I don't want to!* she thought while the voice was speaking. Now he is lost, cut from me, never again will I be able to know how we wander up from the red twilight, up into the mountain in the evening, alone. Never again will I feel how he touches me saying my beloved, my beloved, my Jeanne.

The one who screamed the loudest was Séraphique Archer. It sounded like a roar.

"Dibba-bibba-bolicka—Grainier! G r a i n i e r! G R A I N I E R! G R A I N I E R!"

Later on—right afterward, coinciding with this—came those of the others. Five, six voices screamed the name: hatred, longing, hatred again, longing, crushed hopes, imprisonment, the certainty that he would never come to them and touch them except in their own dreams: longing-hatred.

Sister Claire's voice, so dry that it resembled the creaking of a shoe:

"Yes, it is he!"

Sister Catherine or Sister Louise with a voice so thick that it was a stammer:

"Yes, he, he is the one!"

Sister Anne's piercing shriek:

"Oh, it's he! Oh, it's he!"

And her own lips that moved.

Barrot was gasping above her. When he breathed out, it sounded like running a pin through a hog's bladder: pip.

"Keep quiet all you others! Listen!"

I am playing the main role. I am the leading character, she thought.

"Dic qualitatem! I repeat and translate once more: Tell me his title!"

She tossed her body back and forth a few times. The demons inside her tried to stretch up her arms and part her thighs while her neck still remained in their hard grip. They spoke even though they didn't want to. They were forced to say who he was. She cast about for the word they soon were to say: priest. Such an easy word. A felicitous word that gave her relief. They said it through her chosen mouth:

"Sacerdos!"

She heard:

"Oh!"

One of the women got up suddenly, she heard running

feet, light, shy, frightened, away, toward the door. And the creaking shoes under a heavy priestly body. The smell of garlic and of sweat settled like clouds under and around her. She could see whom they wanted to hold back.

"Marie Aubin!" shouted Minet.

The door was wrenched open and shut again. She heard the running steps across the stone floor out in the corridor.

She sat up. The others were already sitting up on their pallets. The straw rustled drily. The stiffness in her neck was gone. One of the candles in front of the Madonna had been burning faster than the other one and there was a yellowish-brown lump of wax on the candlestick.

Barrot went over to Minet. He had folded his hands around the service book. His eyes were half closed and there were red splotches on his gray cheeks. His mouth was a straight line, but the line was nevertheless a smile. Séraphique Archer turned her empty face toward him. Her mouth was wide open, her thick, red lips gave her a slack expression. Her nostrils were unusually large or seemed to be. Slowly and awkwardly, she folded her big and worn work hands.

Sister Jeanne, the prioress, thought, worn-out and matter-of-factly: The girl's nose is clogged. Despite her large nostrils, her nose is clogged.

Sister Anne's face was pale and closed; she sat staring at her feet. Sister Claire looked *sated*. Both of the Barbeziers sisters sat with their mouths open; not as wide open as was Séraphique's mouth but it looked much more dignified. They had more beautiful hands. But their mouths were rather wide open.

16

The Background of the Story and Its Core

Iɴ ᴀ ᴄɪᴛʏ in southwestern France, the following happened in the late autumn of 1633, more accurately during the night between December 5 and 6.

*

But first some background reflections:

The First Minister of King Louis XIII, the Cardinal and later also Duke Armand du Plessis-Richelieu, had on account of certain circumstances sent his authorized representative, Commissioner and newly appointed Baron Jean-Martin de Laubardemont—"messire Jehan de Martin, seigneur et baron de Laubardemont, de Saint-Denis-de-Pile, Saint-Georges-de Guesboin et autres places, conseiller du roy en ses conseils d'État et prémier président en sa cour des aydes de Guyenne"—to this city on earlier occasions in order to lead a process in the desired direction and see to it that a decisive and irrevocable judgment be given.

Apparently involved were witchcraft and heresy, the seduction of young women in an Ursuline convent and also in the city, but in actuality it was an expurgatory action.

The Cardinal, who at a great distance and at times at closer range followed the course of events through his confidant, Father Joseph, known as the Gray Eminence, was not above believing in witchcraft and demons. When on his deathbed he is said to have been asked whether he forgave his enemies, he supposedly answered that he had no enemies and had never had a feeling of enmity against any one but the enemies of the State. Throughout his entire life he retained his childhood faith, that is: he believed in demons. Besides this belief, as a subdivision of it, he had an insight into how superstition and even genuine faith may be utilized and exploited in the service of the common welfare—for example, in order to strengthen policies which in spite of their force need and have always needed the support of all kinds and by any means: the policies which depend on one single person or upon the security and protection of a small group of persons.

The Cardinal was at this time, at the beginning of December 1633, forty-eight years old. He was to live several more years, dying precisely nine years after the night that is now to be described. He left behind a great legacy. We might think that it was bad or good, that it was a mixture of both, that it was filled with incidental or planned and coolly executed cruelty, with farsightedness, with narrow-mindedness, blood, death, building up and tearing down. But we cannot deny that it was a great one, whether we say that it was as great as Nero's or as that of Augustus, Erasmus, or of Luther, the Medicis or Savonarola. It was of great dimensions and its after-effects were so long-lasting that we still notice their traces.

He built fortresses for the future, wherever he thought it was necessary and tore down fortresses where he thought it was unavoidable. In this important city, where our story is taking place, he and his followers thought it necessary to tear down walls, raze fortresses, and despite the Edict of Nantes, make it impossible in the future for a reformed population to rise up against the absolute Catholic and royal power which was his dream.

He wanted to raze the walls and towers of this city. The decision had been made a long time ago and was strengthened by the long-drawn-out siege of La Rochelle, the strongest fortress of the Huguenots, which fell in the year 1628. The demolition in the city of our story had in the main been completed by 1631–1632. But while they were being planned and carried out, there went on a partly silent, partly open, and vociferous struggle between those who wanted to raze and those who wanted to keep the ancient walls. The line between razers and defenders cut vertically through the entire population. It has been established that the Huguenots were usually on the side of the defenders, and that the most fervent and obedient Catholics were on the side of the razers. There were also Protestants who for opportunistic reasons, because of fear or loyalty to the royal power, refrained from protesting, and there were Catholics who thought the razing was unnecessary, even uneconomical and harmful. What those in favor of razing hoped to achieve is not quite clear. What the defenders feared is obvious: the destruction of the city. Not only because it would become defenseless against external enemies but also because it would lose its face, its beauty, and its animating force.

In this matter, the Cardinal struck hard.

Some say that he did it blindly and without considering the uttermost consequences. Others maintain that he—as always—acted on the basis of cold calculation. We do not know for sure. What we do know is that Father Joseph, his adviser during this period of strife, which lasted from the end of the 1620s until long after the walls had disappeared, visited the city at least three times: once before the beginning of my story, in the year 1616, when he founded a Capuchin monastery here; once during the course of my main story; and once some time after this story may be considered to have ended. His role was obscure, but it was nevertheless an important role. The clenched fist that most clearly represented the Cardinal was Jean-Martin, Baron de Laubardemont.

We ought to take a close look at this man's face and character.

He was tall, bald, full of energy and ruthlessness, an able government official, cunning, stubborn, enterprising, and extremely obedient vis-à-vis the powers that governed him: the internal and the external powers.

The external powers were the Cardinal and the monarchy. The internal powers were his demons: the desire to shine, to live well, to command wherever he was not forced to serve, the desire for riches, power, and excitement, the desire to gamble where he could win and where the odds of losing were small and insignificant. His liking for intrigues should perhaps be alluded to, but this desire was mixed into all facets of his character as a means, a way out, and a game. He was a relatively powerful but not very significant person. He was afraid to lose, and this infused him with a force that was immediate and direct. We also know that he didn't survive, that he couldn't be saved: he is wrapped in a shame which no one will ever be able to wash away, his bones rest in shame, his memory cannot be honored by anyone.

As one of the Cardinal's most effective representatives, he conducted processes against heretics, witches, and sorcerers. He did good work tearing down fortifications. He was given the task of tearing down the stronghold and towers and defense works of this city.

In this respect he was faced by two powerful antagonists who were not Huguenots. One was Governor Jean d'Armagnac, the other one was the priest Urbain Grainier.

D'Armagnac was murdered by his former valet about a year after the end of this story. Urbain Grainier—

*

312

The Night between December 5 and 6, 1633

She asked him not to put out the light. "I want to see your face," she said. "Tell me what happened, while I look at your face. Give me your hand. Place your head on my arm. We can lie like this and imagine that we are old, that life will soon be over, and that it doesn't matter from which direction death will come."

"To me you are very young," he said.

And he thought that such words cause amusement. One ought to express oneself with more despair, ought to enjoy one's own despair. His lips touched her earlobe, it was so soft, he touched it with the tip of his tongue. Her head fell back on the pillow, she closed her eyes and murmured that his beard tickled her neck, it was not unpleasant. This might be called a mildly comical situation, he thought. And so it would be if I didn't love her. Then it would be a game that we couldn't bear. Then we would really be old. Soon my desire for her will be aroused and then everything will be serious, he thought.

"Do you think that this is a farewell, Urbain?"

"I don't know," he said in her ear. "How would I know that? And what do you mean by farewell? What is a farewell to us? If you believe in divine justice beyond all theology, then we will be allowed to meet again no matter what happens to us. Meet again, again and again."

"We could travel far away."

She opened her eyes and turned toward him. They looked into each other. I cannot tell her that going away is meaningless, he thought once more. We would lose the youth that we still have, and would not get a new one. We would be a fleeing middle-aged couple and nothing else. Our love now is *danger*. The name of our love is *the danger*: I love her faithfulness now, the chances she takes on account of me and she still loves the priest in me, the one who has not been defrocked, she loves the man who was young and proud and witty and handsome, the one who

313

fights back. In a foreign land our bodies would be left—in poverty—in drudgery—perhaps in prosperity—but only our bodies. This other which also binds us together now and is our love, would be gone, passed by, something that we once experienced together and which made us flee in order to grow old or die together. Only two bodies and between them that which is past. Later there will be hatred? Or not hatred. Not loathing either. Perhaps not loathing. But a feeling of distance. And I would never again be able to triumph, the flight would never be justified. We would save our bodies and then there would be nothing more.

"We would be able to live so happily," she said. "We needn't suffer any want. We would see many new things, castles, churches, landscapes with mountains and seas, animals, new people. We could live quietly in some corner of the earth where there are no envy and slander and war. We could be together without worry, Urbain?"

"Yes, Madeleine," he said.

He lifted his hand and touched her cheek. It was round, soft. He let his fingertips wander across her forehead from one eyebrow to the other and from the roof of her nose up to the hairline. Her forehead was smooth, the skin was still taut. His fingers were fumbling around in her hair. His palm was pressed against her soft ear. Her head rested in it, helplessly, trustingly, submissively. He touched her chin and her throat. He let his fingertips brush against her lips, they kissed his fingers. In the now subdued light he saw the contour of her body beneath the cover. Her fragrance, the fragrance of the newly washed, mature woman and the perfume from her breasts and her stomach and her sex he felt to be above and around them, together with the smell of clean clothing and the autumn air that was wafted into the room this night. He thought: that when she awakes, when she is awakened, then my body will begin to awake, my desire for her will awaken, and then we will have

314

drifted past the problem. Then we will have found a solution and the happiness of being together. Then we will again have come closer and later we will be led farther away from each other, farther and farther away—toward loathing—toward more loathing—toward more and different deaths—and then we will be forced to seek each other again and come even closer to the loathing which forces us to seek each other more and more—

"Yes," he said, "that might be a solution—to travel farther and farther away—farther and farther—"

He thought he saw a path now: farther and farther away, and not a farther away which was better and freer. The first day of flight, the first way station would give them freedom in full measure. Then they would be everything they could ever be just once, one solitary time. Later on:—farther and farther away from the past, from the walls that were coming down, from the whisperings and the threats—farther and farther away until it had completely disappeared—and farther and farther away—into the loathing and out of the loathing farther and farther away into the loathing and out of the loathing and farther and farther into the loathing—farther and farther—

"It is passing across your face, Urbain."

"What is passing across my face?"

"Our journey," she said moving her head and craning her neck. Her glance was roving from his forehead, she looked him in the eye, her glance rested on his mouth.— "Our journey passes across your face, one can see our flight in it, our future also. You don't want to go away?"

"I do, Madeleine. I want to travel farther and farther away with you. I don't want to have a past, no future. I want the here and now."

"You want opportunities to dominate in some way or other," she said. "That has always been written in your face, and it hasn't disappeared."

"Now I want your happiness, Madeleine."

"I know that too," she said. "You want happiness for me, but you don't believe in it. You don't believe any more in our chances."

"I believe that we two can give each other more than any other people on this earth," he said.

It sounds perfectly ridiculous to say it now, he thought. It is correct, it is the truth, it is the blood's own truth, the truth of the body and the soul. But it cannot be expressed. We can feel it but not say it.

"That's the way it is, Urbain."

Why is she saying that, he thought. She should not have said that now. She should have spoken of power, about my desire to dominate her for a few minutes and my desire to have her touch me while I am touching her.

"Touch me, Madeleine," he said in her ear.

She closed her eyes, he closed his eyes and waited. Her hand came, and he murmured: "I like you touching me." She answered in a low voice, "I like to touch you." His hand rested on her breast with his fingertips touching her nipples. I want to, he thought and closed his eyes more tightly, I want to, I want to. She pulled back her hand, it lay listlessly on the cover, a disappointed woman's hand. She didn't open her eyes. He let his hand rest on her breast, a despairing, anguished man's hand. They heard the sounds outside. Steps. A gate was opened and closed, the owner of the house, Daniel Drouin, had come home. She turned away from the man's body, so slightly that it was hardly noticeable, it was more intention than action. He let his hand remain where it was. He put his lips against her cheek, they brushed lightly against it.

"You mustn't cry, Madeleine. You must wait."

"Put out the light, Urbain."

When they were lying in the dark, the sounds seemed louder. Daniel Drouin walked across the yard, slowly, unsteadily. Stopped and relieved himself. They could hear

316

what he was doing out there. It took some time and sounded like a horse. Now he was done. His steps made an echo in the front room. A door. He walked through the kitchen, stood there poking about in the stove, perhaps he was looking for something to eat. He walked across the floor, stopped, perhaps he was tickling the maid, under her feet or between her knees. Now he was in his parlor. They could follow all his sounds. He sat down in a chair but right after got up and walked over to the cupboard. He placed a cup on the table. He walked over to the cupboard once more, the cupboard door was creaking. Back again. Perhaps he was sitting there writing and drunk. They waited; that is what they were doing: waiting. After a while the man down there got up. They heard him bump against something. Now he was in his bedroom. The voices were loud, but the words were like murmurs up here. The assessor talked, told about various things, while undressing. He moved a chair to place his clothes on it. They heard how he crashed into bed. They heard that he was in a hurry with Charlotte.

Afterward the silence buzzed in their ears.

"Don't cry, Madeleine," he whispered with his mouth close to her ear. He pressed against her, stroking her cheek.

The man down there was snoring.

The frame around the satiety and the silence down there.

"I love you, Madeleine," he whispered. "I love you. That is why I am here. That is why I am like I am. I feel afraid for your sake. You mustn't cry. I will come to you. Soon I will be with you. My spirits are heavy. It makes me feel unnerved. But soon I will be with you."

He turned over on his back. They were lying with arms and hips pressed close. He looked up into the darkness trying to have everything fall off him, to have the day fall off him, have his years fall off, get rid of everything that stood in the way. She is young, he thought, she has never

317

known a man. We are in a time long ago. She is young, no one has touched her.

He thought of all the passion that had been flowing toward that female body lying at his side. All the male yearning over many years, all the women's envy of this body so full of love were still here, surrounding it. When he touched her again, she didn't reply, made no motion in return: there was an endless submissiveness close to indifference in her motionlessness. He had never before been so lonely with her. She loves me and would do everything for me, he thought. But now she is far away from me and I am slipping far away from her even though I want to and she wants to be closer and closer.

"I will come to you soon, Madeleine," he said in a low voice. "There is so much weighing on my mind. I can't make any decision. I know that I have to fight, to defend myself, but not how. To stay here is a kind of defense. To flee is a kind of defense. To advance toward them and attack is defense and struggle. And all the time it is a question of our life, mine and yours. I am not afraid of losing mine. No, don't think that I want to lose it. I am afraid of pain—perhaps—but not of death. I am not afraid of losing my life but of losing yours. To destroy your life more than it has already been destroyed."

She did not reply and did not move.

"I know that I am lying even now when I speak the truth, Madeleine," he said. "I am still vain, want to shine and be a hero. I want to boast. Now I am boasting to you and you are aware of it. I speak about love and do not give you any. I am boasting. And you are aware of it. Are you aware of my boasting?"

He groped for her hand, held it, it was warm and soft, but it didn't answer him.

"Do you know what I am thinking of now, Madeleine? Of the many who have desired you. That the only one who won you was I, someone unworthy, and that I am being

318

punished for it. That the very knowledge that so many have desired you is inciting and unnerving."

These are the wrong words, he thought. The word unnerving is unnerving. The word fear makes one frightened.

"When I saw you the first time, I knew it was going to be you, Madeleine. Other things, others came between. But later it was us two. And has not been anything else. I don't look upon it as blasphemy, as an offense against God. I was handsome and you were beautiful and are beautiful. You are the most beautiful of anything that is in my heart and in my eyes. I love your hair and your eyes and your skin and your fragrance, and your voice. I love the way you move about, your dignity, your mature body. I love your cheeks and your hands. When I was in prison, my desire for you was strong even while I was starving and freezing. When the rats ran across my face and the moisture dripped from the walls in the bishop's prison in Poitiers, I felt desire for you. Not hopelessness and despair and hatred—but desire for you, longing for you. I wanted to get back my honor and my ecclesiastical position and power in order to reach you and be with you."

He might have said that there were lies in this too, but then he could have answered himself that not everything was a lie. He searched for new words for her ear. His hand lay on her breast, the warm, soft pillow, and she lifted her hand interminably slowly and placed it on his. She is helping me from love, he thought then, but in her love there is compassion. The past is nothing to her now. Nor does it mean anything to me.

He whispered in her ear: "We are here, because God exists."

She did not reply. I have said it so many times in the past, he thought. It is the truth for me but it is a lie because

319

I have said it so often. It doesn't reach her innermost being any more.

"We are together here because God exists," he said. "I must believe that God exists. I cannot possibly believe otherwise. The man whose name is Galileo and who has been taken to court, he has another possibility. He has the possibility of mathematics. Of mathematics—Are you listening to me, my love?"

She pressed his hand to her breast.

"I can seek help from the Christian experience, if I so choose," he whispered. "That may give strength and justice to the faith that I hold on to: in Holy Church. If I take one step beyond, I do it in accord with the will of God, I can tell myself. If I take another step in order to prove that the first step was correct, then I do it in accord with the will of God. But there is the boundary, which perhaps is mathematics. If I take another step beyond, I will plunge into an abyss between faith and knowledge and then I am lost. Although no one knows the outer limits of God's will. If I believe in God's purpose with it all I am still protected: I can believe in his just punishment. I cannot think any further. I must believe: He makes no mistakes. But Galileo is aided by a mathematics that I do not master. My ignorance is what aids me. I don't want to search for more knowledge. His mathematics might perhaps be my salvation if I am exposed to danger. I mean: if I wanted to go further."

Her hand was lying as if dead on his.

"I am afraid," he said, "that is why I am speaking about this. I can still say: We are together and I love you because God exists. There is courage in my fear because I *must* believe that God exists. I have no theoretical possibility to feel doubt."

He lifted his hand when she took hers away. He put his cheek close to hers and felt his eyelashes touch her eyelashes. He kissed her eyelids, the tip of his tongue touched them. He kissed her hairline and her ear.

"It is you and God who make me hold out," he said. "I cannot leave you nor can I leave God. I can fuse you together at certain moments, now, into that which gives me security and love. I am equipped for that. That far I am equipped. But if I leave God, I will be lost, thrown away, wasted, without any footing. You I cannot leave, then I would be annihilated. May I confess my sins to you, Madeleine?"

He waited for her answer. I place the burdens on her, he knew, I want to use her as my shield, and she knows it.

She didn't move but she whispered against his cheek, so softly that it was merely a thought that he perceived in her breath: *continue speaking.* He understood it that way and felt remorse and anguish for having enticed her into making such a reply. He touched her breasts, he stroked them lightly, he felt her nipples brush the skin of his palm. He touched her waist, let his hand rest on the soft area below her heart. He felt how it beat irregularly. He felt as if he were paralyzed. If she touched me now, it would come, he thought.

"I will soon come to you," he whispered so softly that he hoped she wouldn't hear it. "Soon. You must have faith. You must have faith in my body."

"Yes," she whispered back, but it was not an answer.

She is not indifferent, he thought, she is paralyzed by the words, she is waiting for silence, for silence within me.

He lifted his head from her arm, she lay on his.

"You have made confession to me, deeply and candidly, on one single occasion," he said slowly and again lay on his back and spoke into the darkness. "You confessed that you had sinful thoughts. You spoke of everything to me with great candor. I answered that your thoughts were not sinful, that your desire was not a sin, that God had given you the thoughts and desires. I lied. I didn't believe it at that time. No, not then. Later I have arrived at that belief. It was a lie that was changed into truth. I lied that time."

She didn't stir.

"You mustn't cry because of this, Madeleine. We are far away from that now. Was it a sin that time—an abiding lie—then we are already lost. We have repeated it so often that it isn't a false step made rashly but instead a sin that was committed consciously—if it was a sin. Now I know that it wasn't a sin except that it was hidden. The sin cannot be with God. It may be with the Church. But it isn't a sin with the Church either. It is only a mistaken rule that priests cannot marry. I officiated at the ceremony when you were wedded to me, you are my wife before God. But my sin was that I believed that it was a sin when we performed the wedding ceremony ourselves, when I wedded you to me. Now I don't believe it was a sin. But when I asserted that we were guiltless *then*—then I lied. I didn't believe that we were guiltless. I believed that we were lost. Do you hear my confession? Do you accept my confession, my love?"

She whispered a low yes, but he could not tell whether she felt indifference or warmth.

"I lied because I was afraid," he whispered into the darkness. "And the fear gave me the courage to strike to all sides, to attack my enemies and force them back. Fear gave me the courage to hold my head high. I had to choose between defeat in shame or triumph in pride. I felt contempt for everyone except myself and you. I could be agreeable and witty and engaging just for that reason. Now it is otherwise."

"Tell me more about it," she whispered.

She also wants to go through it, he thought. There is no other way for us.

"You are wise and warm," he whispered. "I kiss you, my love."

She lay still as before when he brushed her forehead and cheek with his lips. Her lips did not respond. "Do you still love me?" he whispered although he knew. He waited with his mouth above hers. He heard the sounds outside and the assessor's snoring below. He heard steps passing by.

"Yes," she whispered, but her lips did not respond to his. Her very being drew away from his.

"Now I am not afraid any longer," he whispered into the darkness and again they were lying shoulder to shoulder. "I know that we are on the side of God. He will not judge us for what we have done. I am without fear. But when the fear disappeared, my pride, my strength, also disappeared. I cannot attack any more. I can defend myself by not giving ground, by standing still and by waiting and confirming that I have the courage to wait and bide my time. But I don't defend myself by attacking. If I say: God is with us and still take flight—then I will deny Him."

He waited but she did not answer. He lifted her head, her head rested on his arm.

"Receive my confession, my love," he said bending his arm, moving her head closer to his, putting his cheek against her hair. "I hope. I don't know anything of what will happen to me, but I hope. I lied just now about my fear. There is still fear in me, but I close my eyes to it."

She did not reply. He touched her eyelids with his fingertips. They were closed.

He lay back; he felt as if he was sinking deep down and far away from her, although he felt her neck in the crook of his elbow. He tried to sense his own body, his genitals without touching them. He felt the desire in his abdomen, in the small of his back, the desire to move but not the strength.

"I must confess before I come to you," he whispered. "You must listen closely. You must know."

"No," she whispered, "I don't want to know everything."

"The women came to me," he said, turned toward her body. "I hungered for them, for their fragrance, their movements. I was such a good student with the Fathers in Bordeaux just because I wanted to get away and get to know Women. I came here filled with hunger. The women of this city gave me their hand and drew me toward them. I didn't want that. I wanted to draw them to me. I sought virgins and found them. Beloved, I remained with you, but before—"

In the silence they waited for each other to continue.

"I don't want to know everything," she whispered.

"What are they saying now?" he said into the darkness. "That they felt desire as soon as they saw me. Yes. It was my own desire they encountered. Many whose faces I do not recall, whom I never touched and never felt any desire for, encountered my desire—and now they are encountering my desire for you, it is found in my face, in my body. What are they saying now? One: that when I had given her Holy Communion I looked at her so intensely that she felt a sudden and violent love for me and began to shake all over. Another one felt the same way when I held her hand. A third one claims that when I looked at her, she became as if paralyzed and followed me into the church and lay down underneath me in front of the high altar."

"Don't say any more about it," she whispered. "I don't want to hear any more about it."

"Beloved," he whispered. "I didn't touch any of them. I don't remember them. The ones I touched and remember they remain silent. The ones I approached halfway, hate me for not having gone the whole length."

She whispered: "There is a hatred of women in you."

"No," he said in a low voice, "but I chose, I didn't let myself be chosen any more after I had matured and knew what women were like."

"Oh yes, there is a hatred of women in you," she whispered.

"Yes, perhaps there was a hatred of women in it," he said into the darkness. "But you must listen to me. There was desire all around me. They wanted me to become the father confessor of the Ursuline Sisters and the young girls. I wanted to. I declared to you that I didn't want to.

But I wanted to."

"You wanted more virgins, Urbain," she said in a louder voice.

"I don't know," he whispered into the darkness. "Perhaps I wanted to test myself: not to touch. Perhaps I am lying when I say it. I don't know. Perhaps I wanted ever stronger temptations—in order to be able to resist. I don't know. Perhaps—"

He sought her lips, she turned her head away. Why do you do that? he thought. Why do you do it although you love me? Why don't I know more about you?

They lay still. He took his hand away from her body.

"Say it," she said in a low voice, into the darkness.

"It is a confession, Madeleine. I open myself to you as much as I can. Perhaps I wanted to be their father confessor in order to be near them, so that they could tempt me, so that I could feel a desire which I constantly, always would turn toward you, constantly, always—"

He waited.

"If I had become their father confessor, perhaps I could have saved everything," he said slowly. "I think I could have protected them against the demons."

He waited.

"You mustn't cry," he said against her ear. "It is a confession, you are my mother confessor, my beloved. I have to use the coarse words for you to get a picture of what is happening now among the ones possessed by demons."

"I know that," she said into the darkness. "But you give way to it, you are hiding in it now. You believe that you are the one who could have saved them. Perhaps you are lying yourself into it now."

"Beloved," he whispered, "listen to me. It has been whispered into my ear that the one who is called Sister Claire has been lying on the floor in her cell with the crucifix between her legs and tickled herself with it while shouting my name."

He waited.

325

"Is it over now?" she whispered.

"No," he said in a low voice into the darkness. "When I heard it, I felt a certain kind of satisfaction."

He waited.

Her silence.

"A new power," he whispered.

Silence. But through it and after it he heard her cry. He brushed his lips across her eyelids and sought the tears under her eyelashes, but there were no tears.

"Beloved," he whispered. "I am beyond all that now. It was a temptation to feel that way. It was the feeling of power that grows when one loses his power: when one becomes hated, just when one begins to fear being hated. It is over now. It was fear. I am not afraid any longer, not much. I don't think I am afraid any longer, I am lost in their eyes, I am hated because I am lost and I am saved because I am hated. Yes, saved because I am hated: that gives me the strength I have and when I am aware of that I am not afraid. Go on, cry. I am on the side of God because I confess to you."

Silence. He waited.

"I accept your confession," she whispered. "I am receiving it within me."

She turned her face toward his. He waited. Her body followed, he felt her breath, her warm, fragrant breath against his cheek, a mild womanly scent that swept over his eyelids.

He waited.

"Then you don't want to flee?" she whispered.

"No."

"Then you want me to stay."

"No, not like that," he said, his mouth close to hers. "I want you to go away, so that you will be safe. Later you may come back here. If I am away, you can still stay with your friends here. Then you will be close to that which was I. Then you will be close to that which was mine and yours, which was ours. But now I want you to go away. Early tomorrow morning. I have tried to arrange it. Don't wait any longer."

"Then it is farewell, Urbain?"

"I don't know, my wife," he whispered against her eyes. "Perhaps I will win out. If so, this is not a farewell."

"My husband," she said.

She changed position, turned toward him, her hand sought his body. There was a feeling of security in her movement, expectation in security.

"Do you want to talk more about it now?" she whispered. "My love, my husband, do you want to talk more about it now?"

"They have warned me twice," he whispered. "First through Minet. Then came a message from the chief of police in Chinon. Laubardemont is in Chinon just now."

He waited.

"They cannot harm us," she whispered. "They will never be able to do us so much harm that our love, our marriage, becomes meaningless. Do you think so?"

"No."

Her hand moved toward him. She came toward him with much security, with gentle trust. He touched her breast when he felt his member filled with great passion. She touched it, she changed her position, she guided it toward her when he bent over her. In this peace, in this deep calm she felt him come to her, and she opened herself, touched him, guided him, he came to her.

17

Daniel Drouin's Protocol (4)

§ 10 (In its present form since 1634)

I OFTEN SAY to myself that I ought to apply greater concentration to my ongoing protocol. Especially now afterward, when I can see all that has happened to me (and all of us) condensed and in one single large picture which may be a fresco, and yet a picture that can be surveyed in a few minutes or a few hours.

When I consider it carefully, however, I arrive at the conclusion that it isn't a summing up that I am striving for. It is the variation within the course of events I want to stress. It is the nuances. The entirety will go down in history, of that I am convinced. But my breath, my gasps, the small gestures of my closest neighbors and friends and enemies will not go down in history in any other way than by drowning in it. To preserve important nuances, as they are reflected in my own breast, I regard as a kind of lifesaving.

Cicero speaks in one place about his illusory hopes and about thoughts that are of no use. But I think—with a respectful bow to Cicero's shadow—that all the thoughts I think serve some purpose. That is a further justification for these present notes.

*

Notes from the autumn of 1633

The wine has had me worried. Fortunately, it looks as if the quality this year will be relatively good. But there is little of it in our area; it is supposed to be better up by Saumur, and also at Chinon.

Monsieur de Laubardemont is here. Something is about to happen. I can always tell beforehand.

Nov. 1, 1633

Have been ill, a bit out of sorts, and stayed in bed three days. I am now getting better and am able to sit up and write.

I was invited to M. de Laubardemont's dinner party, which he gave for the most prominent citizens of our town at the inn "The Swan of the Cross." I felt very uncertain as to whether I ought to go or not. I did get myself ready in the afternoon and put on my new suit, but when I was all dressed, in good time, my uncertainty became so strong that I decided to go for a walk in order to think things through. Why is M. de Laubardemont here now? I wondered. Our city's towers and walls may be razed even though he doesn't personally see to it that every stone is torn loose.

I was thinking of these and other things during my walk. I visited my only cousin here, the coach-builder Mathurin Thiboust, and Corisande—his wife—whom I have always thought highly of.

They greatly admired my new suit.

As I continued my walk, I ran into the master mason Antoine's younger brother, Charlot, who is also displeased with developments in our city. We decided to go to Mother Gaspard's little inn where I haven't been in many years. The inn was full of people and most of them recognized me. We had a few small glasses. I had by then been seized by such a great aversion at the thought of M. de L.'s invitation that I had almost decided not to go. When I left

Mother Gaspard's inn in order to walk home (and simply let M. de L.'s party go hang—which certainly was a courageous thing to do considering that I am for all that a relatively high-ranking official), I walked along Rue Pasquin up toward our square. Then it happened that someone called me. It was Michel, the peasant who helps me in my vineyard. He had been at Mother Gaspard's and was rather inebriated—in the manner of simple peasants. Now he was coming up behind me with his mule. His wagon was in for reparation at my cousin Mathurin Thiboust's place. Being afraid that his mule would be stolen (there is a lot of riffraff in our city these days) Michel dragged the creature with him everywhere. But the animal refused to walk up the Pasquin Hill, that is, *past* the residence of the Ursuline Sisters. I betook myself immediately down to Michel and could only establish it as a fact. I don't suffer from exaggerated superstition but the occurrence made an uncanny impression on me. The mule refused emphatically to move. In the prevailing darkness (there was a light only in one window in the proximity) Michel was standing there and was, I suppose, very much afraid. I calmed him with a few words and then helped him to *pull the animal* past the "dangerous" spot. When we had succeeded in this, since we are both rather powerfully built men, I stumbled and hit my elbow against something as well as one knee: my hat dropped likewise to the ground and my suit was of course soiled. I therefore didn't continue on my way home, as I had intended, since I didn't want to disturb Charlotte—my wife, who is pregnant—by coming home so suddenly and too early. Instead, I walked back to my cousin Mathurin in order to brush my clothing (it had started to rain again), and when that was done, Mathurin and I went to "The Hen" (where I, incidentally, had stopped in earlier that evening), and we sat there talking with our friends and having a bit to eat; for I had become hungry. For a moment I played with the thought of going to M. de L.'s party and say a few words which might have reechoed throughout our city, but upon further consideration I desisted. I am now rather pleased that I did. One oughtn't unnecessarily make a lot of noise and take needless risks. After a while I took my leave and got a ride to my door with Michel, who had now got his wagon back from my cousin Mathurin. However, during the ride to our square, I decided to accompany Michel to my country place.

When I came back from the country, I felt unwell and have been sick in bed for three days. I feel a certain unease over not having shown up to M. de L.'s party. Since I am a government official, it was perhaps my duty to attend. Have tried to find out whether M. de L. expressed any displeasure over my absence, but none of those whom I have asked, know of any such thing.

*

Nov. 20, 1633

Have been doing much work recently with reports, etc., and when I felt a bit tired and depressed last night, I walked over to "The Hen" in order to meet my friends and have a small glass of absinthe.

We chatted about the present situation. They wanted to know what I knew. For rumors are circulating to the effect that a few of the Ursuline Sisters, Sister Claire and Sister Anne, have behaved in an extremely peculiar way during exorcisms of demons in the Bartray Church. Sister Claire is supposed to have accused herself of having wanted to kill Urbain G., whom, she is supposed to have said, she is in love with and has had intimate relations with; and Sist. Anne has accused Our Lord of having given her lustful desires and also the prioress, Sister Jeanne, for having pressed her to make false statements. As regards the prioress, it is said that she on one occasion has expressed remorse over all that she has stated about Urb. G. but that she has later changed her story again. A girl by the name of Marie Aubin has fled and is now staying with her parents in Saintonge, and the latter do not want to send her back as long as the Ursuline Sisters are possessed by demons. To all appearances, the prestige of our city has been lowered, which pains me deeply. Father Barrot, who is supposed to have been barred from exorcising demons in our city, is now doing the same in Chinon, and the possessed ones in that city are accusing Urb. G. of the same crimes as the possessed here have accused him of. Our possessed ones are now being dealt with by a new exorcist, Father Lacet.

They wanted to know if I knew anything interesting. I was very careful since intruding listeners are to be found everywhere. The sense of being secure has disappeared. I recalled that Urb. G. a few times—at night—has visited Madeleine de Brone who lives on the top floor of my house on the Square of Ste-Croix. This I told in a low voice (and in the greatest confidence) to my cousin Mathurin. He only laughed and said that "the entire city knows that," or words to that effect. Later, Mathurin accompanied me to my door, we talked about the old days, about our youth and childhood—

At times I think of Séraphique A., who is supposed to be truly possessed. She was really. . . . She was attractive, to put it in a few words. And now she is one of those who are most gravely affected—!

Nov. 23

Have decided to stay at home a few evenings in order to read and go over my notes. Be close to my children. And Charlotte does her best in the way of our meals: our maid is also clever in this regard.

Charlotte seems at times to be somewhat melancholy and she cries easily. She doesn't blame me for anything (and actually she has no reason to blame me) but her eyes are not happy. Perhaps it is caused by her pregnancy? For women act so strange in that situation! I comfort her and tell her that I am very fond of her.

November 26 (In code)

Thinking of Sér. A. quite often.

Have been on an official trip to Chinon together with the head of the Salt Depot. . . .

Cicero says about old age that every age has its own desires and purposes. I suppose that I will be a very harmonious human being if I reach an advanced age. Such is my nature despite the disquiet which sometimes takes hold of me and despite the sensitiveness that I am often aware of.

*

Nov. 29

I was at "The Hen" last night and met my friends and had one or a few small glasses of absinthe in addition to something else.

Petiot, Dolet, and Charlot, of whom the two last-named stayed remarkably sober—for once!—walked me to the entrance of my house. We talked partly about what is happening here and partly about loose women. We walked along Rue Pasquin past the residence of the Ursuline Sisters. Petiot maintained that he could feel such a strong resistance in the air that he could hardly walk past. He really had some difficulty, but my guess is that it was because he had been drinking! I happened to stumble when I was going to show them how Michel and I had dragged the mule past the building. We walked arm-in-arm up the hill—it was mainly in order to support Petiot. I couldn't help mentioning the name of Séraphique A. I feel very sorry for her and am curious as to how she is doing. At the exorcisms of demons—which I don't want to attend any more!—one doesn't get a clear impression of how the girls *really* experience it.

At the Square of Sainte-Croix we gave a cheer for U. G. I don't know why. It was an imprudent thing to do, since both Louis Tranchant and his son-in-law, the royal procurator, live on the square. My wife, who was awake when I got home, claimed that she had heard the shouting. She considered it possible that Madeleine de Brone and Urb. G. had also heard them (provided that the latter was visiting the former's dwelling at that time).

*

Dec. 8, 1633

Things are really happening! My hand is shaking when I write this and not the way it shakes after late hours with friends, etc. It is shaking on account of my inner agitation which I am not able to control!

U.G. was jailed yesterday morning! Not by our own local guards but by policemen having arrived from Chinon!

Yesterday, I used part of the day and evening to learn about the details. Charles Calvet said that U. G. had been warned beforehand. M. de Laubardemont, who had made a brief visit to Paris, returned on the 6th, that is, two days ago. He arrived quietly, however, stopping over in Chinon. He had with him a very important document. Ch. Calvet lent me a copy. It is the most wide-ranging authorization one may imagine. It had been drawn up at a council held in Ruel on November 30 in the personal presence of H.M. the King.

I can only report as follows: M. de Laubardemont has been given complete authority to institute a process against Urbain Grainier "and all others who are found to be accomplices and involved, and to pursue the matter until final judgment without having to take into consideration any kind of opposition in the form of remittal of the case or of Grainier's *defense*. . . ."!!!!!! "His Majesty orders all governors, viceregents in the provinces, all city and rural bailiffs, all royal military commanders or their deputies, all judges, all mayors and councillors". . . . etc., etc., to comply in every way and in all circumstances with the commands and wishes of M. de Laubardemont in this matter . . .!

Now it is M. de Laubardemont who decides whether there are demons or not!

— — —

My hand has been shaking again.

But I am a very strong man. I have seen and experienced things which I can't even confide to a diary like this one.

But when I transcribed the copy of the warrant for Grainier's arrest that is now in M. de Laubardemont's possession, my pen would not obey me and my handwriting (which is usually considered clear and distinct, even beautiful) became almost unreadable.

*

Dec. 9

Urb. G. had been warned. It is said that Guillaume Aubin from Chinon, who had been ordered to arrest U. G., warned him in the evening of the 6th. Urb. G. thanked him warmly but is supposed to have said that he relied on his pure conscience in everything that they might accuse him of and that he didn't feel he had any *real* reason to flee.

I have been mulling quite a bit over this *"real."*

They arrested him in the morning when he walked out of his door on his way to the Church of Sainte-Croix in order to officiate at early mass. G. Aubin stepped up and bowed to him when he arrested him. All U. G.'s enemies in our city had gathered in the Square of Sainte-Croix outside our house. U. G. took it very calmly. People came running from every direction. I was not fully dressed but we were standing in the entrance to our house and could see and hear what was happening. Most of the people were evidently on U. G.'s side and were jeering those on the side of the Tranchants. Charlotte, my wife, stood next to me with tears in her eyes. She too wanted to shout but I explained to her how inappropriate such a demonstration might be. For I do hold the position of a government official. I put my hand across her mouth, very gently, using no force at all, while she quieted down. She was a little offended with me because of this. For she is pregnant. I myself was of course very indignant but kept cool as usual.

Have learned several details. They at first planned to take Urb. G. to Saumur—keep him under arrest *here* is out of the question!—but it seems that Saumur was considered too close to our city. They give some thought to the mood of the people here. U. G. has friends and they might hit on the insane idea to—yes, do what? M. de Laubardemont instead ordered the leader of the city watch, Jean Poucquet, to take the prisoner to the castle at Angers, where he is now staying.

*

Dec. 12, 1633

They are digging into U. G.'s past again. They have of course made a search of his living quarters. Ch. Calvet, who is my source, tells me that M. de L. has personally taken part in the snooping. They are supposed to have found U. G.'s piece about the celibacy of the clergy and a pamphlet attacking the Cardinal, which U. G. is alleged to have written. (I think both papers make very interesting reading.)

Have had much to do—reports, etc.—the last few days, and last night I was at "The Hen" to meet my friends. It is actually a risky thing for me to spend some time there but I can't stop doing it although my oldest friends and my only relative here are Huguenots. Think I can notice a certain reserved feeling toward me on their part. But they know me, of course, and they know where they have me— I should think!

Earlier in the evening I was at the house of my cousin Mathurin Thiboust and his wife Corisande. Cor. was surly toward me saying a few things which I don't find necessary to put down here. In short: it pained me. But in order to smooth things over (I guess) Mathurin got out his best white wine, which really was exquisite. I myself have nothing better at this point. My hope is that I will in time. Well—we spoke about things happening here and I gave a sort of apologia for my equable way of behaving. Finally—influenced by what I had said—Corisande indicated that she was aware of my exposed position even though she couldn't always approve of my "prudence." We were friends again when we parted.

Mathurin accompanied me over to "The Hen" where we sat a while carrying on a discussion with the others. Sharp and I must say rather imprudent words were uttered. For I know what M. de L.'s letter of authority really involves!

Mathurin accompanied me to my door. On the way we talked about the old days, when we were children and young fellows. "If only these damned walls had never existed!" M. exclaimed when we touched on the dispute over our walls and fortifications. I replied that we do defend them and that they have protected our city many times and that they have protected our parents and *us.* "They attract demons our way!" he exclaimed. "Now it is demons who tear down our walls!" I maintained that the walls had always provided good protection and that he as well as I had opposed their demolition. Then he replied with a few words that seem peculiar to me. "Nothing can protect man against men," he said. He stopped short and cried in a loud voice, yes, he shouted: "No, nothing!"

His words can only be explained by his having had something to drink.

*

Dec. 22, 1633

I believe that the world is turning blacker. This mood could also be due to the fact that it is late autumn.

Urb. G.'s mother and brothers and many others are

working to have him get out. Mad. de Br. ought to move away (this is the general opinion here) but she is staying on in our city. Our maid who fetches her food and makes her meals now, says that she eats very little. It is a pity—in circumstances like these good food is very important as a source of strength; yes, also at other times. She stays inside the house all day but steps out in the evening to meet her friends. Urb. G.'s mother has (with the help of his brothers) composed long letters which she has addressed to M. de L. She is fighting. She is trying to challenge M. de L. and his witnesses. I suppose that M. de L. only puts the papers aside. He has his letter of authority. We who can read documents know the significance of it.

Last night I was at "The Hen." This takes a great deal out of me—I mean: that which is about to happen in our city.

*

Dec. 30, 1633

The year will soon have come to an end.

As far as our city is concerned, it has been filled with significant events.

U. Gr. is still imprisoned at Angers. They are investigating his entire past—which has been investigated so closely before!—and are snooping for something that can be used against him. The old testimonies against him are to remain in force. Even though they were given under duress and through perjury.

My heart is apprehensive. I should perhaps act in a more determined manner than I do and voice my opinion (which, however, all my friends *know*) more clearly. But when all is said and done, I am a government official.

U. G. is sitting in the castle of Angers in one of the cells in the dungeon on the west side, from which there is a view of the Loire. I visited the castle of Angers once and remember that I found it especially unpleasant to have a look at the cells and the persons who were staying in them.

When I left my office yesterday afternoon I was tempted to walk right over to "The Hen" to meet friends. But I overcame the temptation. Instead I went for a walk along the remnants of our walls—from the Bartray Gate to the Chinon Gate.

It seemed to me that the demons were sitting on the rock piles shouting at me. I thought I saw the walls fall down under their weight. The walls, which no longer have any defenders. Or do they?

It occurred to me that I ought sometime to sum up and present the entire case.

I got into such a gloomy frame of mind that I went home right away. Charlotte, my wife, noticed how melancholy I was and took pains to make a very good evening meal. She had bought sweetbread, which I love.

While we were eating, we conversed in a sorrowful mood. Charlotte cries so easily now. We talked a while about our children's future. She felt some anxiety about their fate in the insecure world in which we live, but I calmed her with a few carefully considered words about the inherent strength of growing things and the increasing enlightenment and humanization.

Later in the evening I visited my cousin Mathurin Thiboust and when I had been sitting there a while, Mathurin and I walked over to "The Hen." Petiot and Dolet were there but not Antoine and Charlot, whom I would have liked to meet. They are said to be moving to the Cardinal's city, where there is a need for masons.

Mathurin accompanied me to my door and that was very nice of him. We talked about our youth and about our children—the dead ones—and about the future. I said—as I had told him earlier in the evening—that all the documents ought to be collected and lie there bare and revealing to the eyes of the future. He thought that I should collect all the facts known to me in the case that is uppermost in the minds of all of us, with the correct dates, etc. I replied that I had already given it some thought.

He made a curious remark (he is somewhat of a philosopher even though he lacks higher education): "Now that the walls have been torn down, the view is more open." I answered: "Our city is not as well protected, isn't that what you mean?"—"I mean that the sight is frightful but one can see farther," he said.

I asked him to come inside with me. We sat in our dining room and had a glass of my best white wine. At times we could hear Mad. de Brone walk back and forth upstairs in her bedroom. We spoke about it, in as low a voice as possible. I showed Mathurin some of what I had written in my diary lately, they didn't add up to many pages. He appreciated my ability to present things clearly, I recall. I am sorry to say that we sat there a long time, and we had a few more glasses. I don't know when he left. I was rather tired and fell asleep but this morning I was lying in my bed anyway.

18

Exercise in Silence

(*Urbain Grainier's papers from 1634*)

Can I now at the age of 44 look into that which desires to burn me in this city which has become mine? Seventeen years—from 1617 until this spring of 1634—it took me to get where I am now. And in spite of this long time I have not yet learned to comprehend what has happened to me.

I am sitting here in the custody of the couple Bontemps, on the top floor of a house, in a prison which they have furnished just for me. My colleague, the canon Jehan Minet, owns the property here in Rue Pasquin, opposite the house of the demons. When they came to get me at Angers, they brought me here. The windows were blocked up with bricks; I get only some light through a grated opening—enough to tell the day from night. They put iron rods across the stove opening so that I couldn't escape that way. They also splashed holy water into the stove. I was given no bed, only straw on the floor. There are rats here, as in all old houses in our city.

Guillaume Aubin came to get me. He was very friendly. Many people were friendly. Canon Pierre Bacher was friendly and helpful.

Things were not difficult for me in Angers. My mother was allowed to send me paper and other things, at least some, and even though the entire large, heavy, and old castle pressed me down with the weight of its age like a grave for someone still alive, I had hope.

On February 4, the man, Laubardemont, who is tearing down the walls and is tearing me down as a brick from the wall, came to Angers on a visit. He had a few of his aides with him. They were to interrogate me. I refused to reply to certain questions. He showed me a copy of the manuscript "The Celibacy of the Clergy" and asked whether I admitted that I was the author. I answered yes. He asked if this manuscript had been written for Madeleine. I answered no. He stayed until the 11th.

*

I now realize that I will not have time to write my autobiography. If I am to die soon, I will have time for many things. If they let me go free and I am able to go away (it is my dream to go away) I will not have time to do it. This sounds like a paradox, but if I die now, soon, one will be forced to read my notes about the motives with greater attention and then perhaps my autobiography will emerge from my papers. All words will have a greater and deeper meaning, because they are definitive and cannot be touched up with additional proofs or proofs to the contrary, additional explanations, additional facts. In this indistinctness, the reader I hope to have in fifty or a hundred or three hundred years will have to grope toward the clarity that I myself cannot achieve. He will have to find his way between that which is suggested, through the extensive, dark areas between the kinds of information that we now call facts. On that road one will reach the truth about me, for there is nothing else to reach—in the end.

Nothing in the future can bring me down if I am already condemned and nothing can set me free if the accusations are confirmed as true.—I mean: if one finds that confirmation within oneself. The truth will appear, and then this, these intimations, will become my grand autobiography. If they let me go, these notes will become meaningless: for they assume the man who is writing them is soon going to die. Without that assumption the pages will wither and fade. If I die, all the facts surrounding my death will become my autobiography: they will sharpen the forcefulness of my words now. When I am dead, the words are irrevocable and must lead to the truth about me. Yes? No?

*

The Motives: The Walls

Old man Bontemps comes in with the food:
"Here you are."
I have known him a long time. At first an unimportant man, a verger whom one would pass in the street without noticing. Now he is my warder and a significant fellow around here. He is old and, strangely enough, lame. I have encountered much lameness. His nose is swollen from too much wine, his puffy cheeks always have a noticeable layer of grease. His eyes are big, bloodshot, without a firm glance. He has tufts of gray hair in his ears and nostrils. He is aware of my smell (which must be repulsive now) the way I am aware of his (his smell is repulsive) and he is aware of my words the way I am aware of his (repulsive). He remembers every word I utter. His wife runs over to the Ursuline Sisters to report. In this way they create truth and facts around me.
One day he said:
"That's what you get for your walls."

*

They are not my walls. If I look into my heart, my mind, and my wishes, there is nothing left of any walls there. Once I said: They must not tear down the walls and the towers, it is unnecessary. The city's walls are beautiful, I

343

said to myself, our towers (for I looked upon the city as being mine) are beautiful. It is unnecessary to tear them down.

My feeling for them was not deeper.

Now I defend, here and as the loser, the walls which I do not love and do not believe in and which do not tell me anything but that they were and are walls around a city. With my body and all the organs of my mind and soul, I, the vanquished, the one soon to be vanquished, defend the walls. I became an obstacle to those who wanted to raze them. But if they had examined themselves, they would have discovered that I was no obstacle—or only a small obstacle. They have not examined themselves.

Bontemps is saying: "Here's your food, that's what you get for your walls."

*

My mother, my brothers, my friends compose long letters in which my entire "case" is gone over. For all the attacks against me in the course of the years have been rejected by courts, both ecclesiastical and civilian. The facts have been killed. Now the facts have been revived on the lips of perjurers. When my brother René was in Paris in order to have the Parlement take up my case and investigate all the facts, he was arrested. When the proofs in my favor were given to Laubardemont, he tore up the papers.

*

One day I was visited by five men who called themselves physicians; they examined my body. They pricked me with needles to see how I would react. They wanted to find out whether my demoniacal power might make me insensitive.

They found demoniacal signs on my body. They examined my anus and testicles. It was very painful.

Those who called themselves physicians were led by my enemy, Lannoury, who is actually a physician. The others were barber-surgeons, apothecaries, quacks, and charlatans. Some of my future judges were along. They all noticed demoniacal signs on my body. I stood naked in front of them. The old Bontemps woman stood staring in the doorway. Downstairs (they have some city guards on the bottom floor to keep watch over me) it was quiet: they were listening.

After I had screamed, the silence was even deeper.

These are facts about me.

*

What is moving in the light and in the darkness? Processions between the churches where demons are being exorcised, where people are conjuring, shouting, accusing; they are raging like Barrot and Minet, they are waiting like Laubardemont—and the women are the victims who are screaming that I have given them flowers and thorns.

My weak eyes cannot see but I can hear the echoes. Paper is rustling, they tear up, hide away, and burn paper; and they produce paper. The demon Asmodeus has written a letter to Prioress Jeanne. People are whispering, women are shrieking.

And the rats are gnawing.

A dispute about walls and towers?

One can hear the hammering and the scraping of trowels and bricks when windows are converted into vents in a prison. If one listens, one can hear how time is slipping by, slipping by, month after month. I can hear how the walls are falling, blocks of limestone and tufa are falling with a thud into the green or dry grass of the moats.

But I who can look upon it after a time interval of seventeen years, don't see the struggle over the walls any longer. It is unimportant. I see the struggle over me.

I helped our governor and was on his side. He wanted to stop them from razing the walls, he wanted to preserve the towers. Now the walls have been torn down and only one out of twenty towers is still standing. That one he is still protecting, without hope. Without hope?

345

His own power is going down with the walls. With the towers and the walls, beauty disappeared. With me, power is declining. With me disappears also that which some women regard as joy and beauty. Falling towers often evoke hatred. And the hatred is not always directed toward the one who is tearing down the tower but toward the tower itself. It gives rise to hatred—not because it falls and disappears but because it doesn't remain standing, enticing: since one doesn't own a tower rising high above the plain and the woods, since one cannot dominate the tower, one must hate it.

The women's dreams about the towers. The men's envious dreams about other men's powerful, dangerous towers.

*

Madeleine was under arrest and imprisoned for two days in the house of Pierre Milouin, who had followed her like a waiting dog for many years, until he began to follow her as a drunken soldier follows a whore: in those days he used to shout "whore" after her in the street.

She was imprisoned in his house for two days. But *bailli* Cerisay and the brothers Calvet got her out.

The demons of the Ursuline Sisters accused her of witchcraft. They have turned their hatred toward her. The demons are longing for her. The demons are claiming that they are bedding her.

The Ursuline Sisters, the possessed ones, are demonstrating at public séances what happens when the demons are lying with Madeleine. Bontemps said:

"For two days she has been with M. Milouin, that distinguished man. For two days and two nights—are you listening?—for all of forty-eight hours. Milouin who has always been hot for women! For forty-eight hours. She probably got what she needed. Now that no one else can give it to her. Of what she has a need for. Then he got tired of her and let her go. But for forty-eight hours! Milouin looks

346

completely worn out now, do you hear! You're not answering! Here's your food."

*

I am seeking the motives, now that the walls have disappeared and only one tower remains standing in the city that I called mine.

At one time I wished to become the father confessor of the Ursuline Sisters.

I have confessed it for Madeleine.

At one time it had something to do with the Tranchant girl. I was indifferent.

I have confessed it for Madeleine.

At one time I took revenge on the apothecary Golet and on Jacques de Chasseignes and several others and had them convicted for libel and false accusations. I took great pleasure in that.

I have confessed it for Madeleine.

At one time I was a victor and rode into the city with a twig of laurel in my hand and I felt a great deal of satisfaction.

At one time I was attacked by Milouin, who was in love with Madeleine, and by Jacques de Chasseignes, who also wanted Madeleine. I recall that I felt much satisfaction at being so handsome and stately a man that they hated me unto death.

I have confessed it for Madeleine, but she answered that she already knew all about it.

*

June

Of course, I know much about the motives: they, my enemies, want to be *right*.

They will never be right (and in the final analysis it is a matter of the right to live) unless I am proven wrong. It doesn't matter in which way I am proven wrong. Or?

347

But if I am proven "wrong," they will be "right" as long as they have the power to live.

If Minet (in whose house I am now imprisoned) is proven wrong, then the Ursuline Sisters are proven wrong. If Minet and the nuns (and the monks!) are proven wrong, then Tranchant and the "Razing Party" and Laubardemont will be proven wrong. If Laubardemont is proven wrong, the Cardinal is proven wrong, and if the Cardinal is proven wrong, then the King and France are proven wrong.

If France is proven wrong, then the whole world is proven wrong. And if the whole world is proven wrong, then God is proven wrong—since he has created it and filled it with content. And if God is proven wrong, the demons are right. And if the demons are right, the way they are speaking through the mouths of Sister Jeanne and the other possessed women, then I—yes, then I am proven wrong.

I can still smile at this kind of logic, it is childish. But it is dangerous since it is so easily available, so easy to acquire. It hurts when they try it on me. Then I scream.

I try to train myself not to scream before that which is and that which is to come. Or I think: When it comes, that which is the worst, that which they are preparing, then I have already screamed. Then it makes no sense to scream. Then I will have seen through the possibilities of the scream to make it *better*—to make it *less* painful to me: those possibilities do not exist any more. Then I can refrain from screaming. That is my logic and that too is childish. And it causes me pain.

*

Bontemps noticed that I cut my finger when I borrowed his knife and tried to cut the hard and dry bread. The knife slipped. I cut myself between my thumb and forefinger. It didn't hurt. I put my lips to the cut and

348

licked it. I then forgot all about it when I was chewing the bread.

Two days later the demon Asmodeus claimed through the mouth of Sister Jeanne that I had signed a pact between him and me with my own blood.

When the physicians came back to examine me, they discovered the cut.

I forgot about the knife and said that I had scratched myself with a needle. An accident, no, a little mishap. They found no needle but a lie, my lie. Afterward I remembered the knife and changed my story. They found that I had lied and had made evasive answers.

But that is not a new kind of logic: it is my own logic. If my logic (which is theirs) is deficient, then God will cease to exist for me. Then I will be all alone and that I will surely not be able to bear.

*

When they had examined me closely, prepared and got me ready, I learned how they had even prepared themselves.

They showed me a document from the learned Sorbonne, acknowledging that the demons were indubitably playing their game in this city that I called mine.

They based their confirmation of facts on the following: that many of the possessed women had been lifted by an invisible hand three feet into the air above the heads of the exorcists and the spectators and had remained suspended there for several minutes. Everyone knows that this is a fabrication. Or, is it? *Jointly* (it is claimed) the spectators witnessed such a miracle. But *separately* (it is claimed in the rumors reaching me) they saw nothing but prone, kicking, screaming women.

If I could have seen the documents before they were handed over to the learned gentlemen, I could have pointed out that this floating in the air has never occurred here. (But I would have done so with a feeling of doubt in my heart.) However, they didn't show me the documents, the false protocols. Consequently, the men from the Sorbonne could base their views on sworn facts. In the presence of such weighty facts I myself would have certified that demons no doubt existed in this context.

Those who are to judge me can put their conscience at rest: they don't see *me* any longer, they hardly see the case and the circumstances, they only see the testimonies. This is the kind of logic with which we operate. It is my own, there is none other for me either.

Then they discuss whether the Devil is lying or speaking the truth when the men of the Church, the exorcists of the Church who have been appointed by the bishop of Poitiers, force him to speak through the mouths of the possessed. This is one theory: that the Devil is lying—that's how cunning he is! That might be my salvation: I could be saved through the lies of the Devil. Another theory has it that the power of the Church is so great that the Devil, fearing *it,* speaks the truth when he says that I am the prince of the demons in this locality.

To have doubts as to the power of the Church is blasphemy. This has been eloquently explained by learned men. I have pointed out that doubt is always to be encountered on the path of the Christian and that the saints were often filled with doubt. They have claimed that such a remark is blasphemy.

I am locked in here. I submit to the power of the Church but I want to know what is the real view of the Church. And that I will not know as long as the Holy Father in Rome keeps silent.

If I don't submit, then I lose God. At times a thought (perhaps not blasphemous?) has crossed my mind: Whether one can serve God *without* submitting to Him in everything? One may argue with Christ. Only with him, but not with the saints. He is a human being in his divinity.

350

The saints are former human beings. They are locked into their sainthood and there is no discussing with them: their time is spent clinging to the firm and blind faith which they have had and which carried them forth to the saintly sphere; without it they are lost even in their later holiness. One can argue with Christ the Son. Facts may be tested and new facts included, the moods of the human heart and the demands of the body may be contemplated. One cannot argue with God the Father. One cannot argue with Laubardemont. One cannot carry on a discussion with the Cardinal in which he is forced to change (for the sake of the welfare of the country) what he regards as useful facts. Thus, the demons speak the truth. If I don't submit and acknowledge it—then I further confirm that they speak the truth.

*

The Demons

One day they took me to the convent across the street and we—I and the possessed ones—were made to join a procession from their house to the church which I used to regard as mine more than the other churches here: Sainte-Croix.

We are all accomplices, I thought while walking in the procession behind the exorcists, Bishop Roche-Pozay, my colleagues, Laubardemont, and all the judges.

I was surrounded by city guards and on one side I had old Bontemps and on the other the notary, Nozay. There were many people about. I saw faces that I recognized, people whom I had promised to bury and children I had baptized. Many faces were filled with shame. Some people were smiling at me. Some were shouting how thin and wretched I looked and then I straightened up and walked very erect (which was taxing). I looked for a face that I knew would not be there. Several faces indicated triumph.

351

My own face also showed triumph at one time, I thought. Now the turn has come to these faces. After the triumph is gone one's face turns lifeless unless one dies at the moment of triumph. It is the last reflection of the day. All faces that show triumph will sooner or later turn lifeless.

I looked for a face with tenderness in it: not fear, not triumph, but tenderness. When we arrived in the square, it is only a few hundred paces away, I saw a face in a window in the house of the former royal procurator Louis Tranchant. It was his daughter Philippe who was standing there although she and her husband, the present procurator, live in a house with a fine view on the other side of the square. She was standing there in order to have a look at me. Her face expressed no hatred, no sorrow: it was an empty face. I felt some sort of gratitude for that.

In another window facing the square, on the second floor of Daniel Drouin's house, no one was standing. I felt a deep sense of gratitude for that.

*

They asked me to exorcise the demons. The bishop of Poitiers, whom Christ would declare my enemy but whom the Church and perhaps God call my brother and superior, wanted conclusive proof that the demons that he now so firmly believes in, actually exist.

Before I began, I asked the bishop to bless me. He *threw* the blessing at me and his fingers moved as if flicking away an insect, a louse.

I asked to be allowed to exorcise the demons in Greek. The bishop then asked me to submit written questions, delivered beforehand.

There is nothing to answer, nothing to reflect on this. Except perhaps: then there is time to quickly translate the questions for the demons, in case they don't master Greek (despite the Church's statement).

*

The Women

I have never truly seen them before. Their faces have passed by my eyes, I knew the names of some of them, but I haven't *seen* them. Nor can I have felt much desire for them.

First they showed me the signs of the pacts that existed between the women and the demons, that is to say: between the women and me. They were ashes, human hair, nails, small lumps of dried blood, eight orange seeds, a small bundle of straw, and something else, I don't know what. They held it all up before my eyes. I had been placed near the seat of Laubardemont; the exorcists, the possessed Ursuline Sisters, and the officials had all taken their place in the choir. I denied any knowledge of the pacts and the signs. The physicians testified that they must be the work of the Devil. Laubardemont burned everything in a brazier that had been brought in.

*

The Women

I saw one face after another, they were eight in all. All of them gave the impression of being possessed by demons. Sister Jeanne was quite beautiful. Behind her twisted body there was or had been a soft, young face. Now it was stiff and tense. Her forehead and eyes had been beautiful, as had her neck and her very black hair visible underneath her cap.

I don't know why I looked at her as if she were dead. For she was alive, her mouth was alive, her full lips were moist, her eyes moved and various parts of her body twitched convulsively. There was a sort of lopsidedness about her, I don't know just where, perhaps in her back.

One of the women was called Séraphique, a big and strong peasant girl whom they had to quiet time and again. Another one was called Catherine, she lay on her bed with closed eyes as if she were asleep. Sister Claire—middle-aged—kept staring at me stubbornly, persistently: just staring. Her hands were folded but her lips didn't move. I don't know whether she reproached me for something or whether she was merely studying me. There was no bond of antipathy or sympathy between us, although I have heard whispers about her strange passion for me and her curious behavior and cries. At first I believed that she was looking at something behind me; but when I turned my head to look, there were only the flock of witnesses and beyond them the vault and then the hot street, the sharp yellow light above the square. It was the 23rd of June.

One woman was called Sister Anne. She was quite old and her face seemed so dissolved that her features no longer hung together. She mumbled my name continuously. When her features were still joined—a long time ago—her face might have been beautiful. She kept her palms together—not the way a saint does when depicted in prayer but cupped as when a child hides a small insect and is about to show it soon, to surprise someone with it.

There were three other women, I didn't hear their names. I don't believe that I had seen them before. Seventeen or eighteen of the women in the convent are now supposed to be possessed.

They had taken me here so that I could demonstrate my ability to exorcise the demons. I was given the manual with the rules for exorcism and they put a stola over my shoulders. They sang *Veni Creator Spiritus*. The voices sounded so remote, yes, I thought my own voice came from a distance. Then I stood up and asked the bishop from whom I was to cast out demons. He said: "You are to exorcise these women." Then I replied, "Monseigneur, I am forced to believe in possession by demons since the Church believes that it exists, although I don't believe that a sorcerer, a *magus,* can make a person possessed by demons unless that person himself wills it."

Then they screamed at me. I don't want to suggest that

354

they already howled (as they did later) but they screamed. A tumult arose among the exorcists. They cried heresy. I barely heard more than the sound of their voices, their words slipped past me and I recall that I thought: Now I have reached the stage when the words slip past me, when I find them to be meaningless. What moved and frightened me—and I must admit: enticed me and somehow flattered me—were the sounds from the throats of the women. I felt a kind of power when I heard them.

*

The Women

They *howled* when I turned to face them. I had not known that the language of the demons was so coarse.

I started with the one whose name was Catherine, the one with the rigid, sleeping, or dead face. I awakened the demons in her. She turned her pale, narrow face toward me. She had a narrow, white glance, I thought. I have never seen eyes like that before. They didn't look at me, they wrapped themselves around me. I must admit here that I felt a sort of desire—not masculine and not what I believe is feminine—but some kind of desire to touch when I saw her eyes. They didn't look at me: they touched me. When she began screaming, then the one who is called Séraphique also began screaming and had to be calmed. While she was lying there gasping, the prioress, Sister Jeanne, and Sister Claire, who is a relative of the Cardinal, began screaming. They sprang to their feet howling at me. I tried to call to their demons in Greek to get answers to my questions, but the demons didn't hear me. Sister Jeanne, who is also called Mother Jeanne, but who gives no impression of being either spiritual sister or spiritual mother, but rather of beauty warped and of physical and spiritual distortion, screamed at me with the frothing from her mouth spattering my face: "Oh, how you are shrewd!

355

You know very well that one of the conditions of the pact between you and us is that we are not to answer you in Greek!"

The bishop gave me no assistance. Through his silence he admitted that the Church has no power over the demons. I myself do not dare admit anything like that or pursue such a line of thought.

The women howled at me. They tore off their caps and uncovered their hair, this black, grizzled, or blonde, whirling, sweaty women's hair. When I saw their hair, I again felt temptation. They tore their clothing. We all thought: that it was the demons who with the help of the possessed hands tore the clothing off the women's bodies. They tore their clothing. The naked, distended, or flabby breasts were turned toward me and I remember thinking: Now I can see these women's true faces. They revealed their legs and thighs, they twisted themselves in curious postures testifying to fierce desire, insane passion. They touched their breasts and abdomens as if wanting to lift up their breasts and intimate parts to me. I felt horror and repugnance but also a kind of satisfaction in my horror and disgust: a kind of desire.

Time and again I tried to shout to the women: "I am innocent!" They didn't hear me, and I felt in my heart and in my body that I was not innocent. I even thought that the demons who were raging in these women's bodies, were demons that I had brought there and let loose. But I shouted: "Miserable creatures!" I shouted to all the spectators: "There you see devils and demons let loose! There you see devils raging against one another!" I tried to remain calm, but I felt desire, I felt temptation. I shouted: "There you see demons who are tearing themselves away from themselves!"

Then the women rushed at me. They came toward me as a wave of hatred and terrible passion: a wave wanting to embrace and caress and whip and carry and drown. They wanted to scratch me, paw me, bite, kick, and embrace me:

they wanted to kill me. All this they wanted and did not want. There was a willpower in them that was not their own. Since then I have thought that the willpower was mine.

If they hadn't held back the women and had taken me away, then the women and I would have mingled as executioners and victims intermingle. Then I would have lost myself. I felt a desire to kill and to love, and I felt a great hatred in my heart. And a sort of remorse that I hadn't touched these women before, while I could. Now I was calm. I knew that I had to appear calm even if I was lost. They took me away. When I was led out, I heard the screaming behind me. The women cursed me and supplicated me. They shouted: "Do you remember, prince of demons, that you came to me at night, do you recall that you gave me pleasure, that you penetrated me, that you lay down with me, that you begat a devil's brood with me, that you lashed me with flowers and that you caressed me with your claws!"

I was wet with perspiration, it clung to my face and my shoulders and I froze. But I walked out calmly, my movements were restrained and dignified. Someone said when I walked past: "He is as calm, dignified and restrained as only an innocent man of pure heart can be!" Someone else said very loudly: "That's the way only a hardened sorcerer and a prince of devils can act!" A third person shouted to me: "I believe you are innocent, monsieur pastor!" And others shouted: "You can see that he is innocent! You can see it in his noble, beautiful, suffering, and handsome face!" But farthest inside the choir, some of the women screamed: "Do you recall, O do you recall, prince of demons! You came to me at night and lay with me!"

I couldn't remember what had not happened and was not true. But within me there was nevertheless something that did remember.

*

357

When the guards took me back to this place, I was walking between Bontemps and notary Nozay, holding my head high. I looked neither right nor left. When we walked up the stairs to my prison garret, I was thinking: Now I won't manage another step. But I did, and the next one and the next one after that.

"He has a good physique," said a soldier who was walking behind me, sweating and breathing heavily in the heat. "Such a fine physique even though he is a priest," he said. "He's as vigorous as an officer."

In the doorway, Bontemps said to me:

"There you saw what you have let loose! There you saw what you've done. There you got to look at your work!"

*

I am trying to look into myself and learn the Truth. But I find only truths, facts, and a desire which is alive or a desire which is not alive; the memory of a desire which has been forgotten but is awakening.

It is soon August. Friends are working on my behalf and are trying to have me set free.

The physical examinations are continuing and they are at times painful. I am screaming now to be able to keep silent later. I imagine that nothing more painful than this *now* can happen to me in the days to come. That is why I scream when they search for demon marks on my body. Lannoury makes use of tubes and long needles. I have learned that people gather down in the street in order to hear me scream. I know now that it is for them that I scream. This is my message which they convey to others.

Laubardemont himself appears once in a while and wants me to sign a confession that he has formulated. I reply that I have nothing to confess, that my sins have been disclosed to my father confessor, Bacher, who has been allowed to visit me once. Then Laubardemont curses and looks as if he wanted to hit me in the face. His bald pate is shiny from sweat and fear.

He was away from the city for some weeks and then his supporters were very worried fearing that he had given up on the entire matter. But I, who looked into his eyes at Angers, where he visited me, know that he will never give up. He cannot. He and I cannot both exist on the earth any more. Even if there were no exterior, tangible reason to obliterate me, he would still do it. One day this thought came to me: It is he who is afraid. I am the rock on which he builds. If the rock gets up and walks away, his house will fall. If his weight is sufficient to press the rock down into the earth, then his house will be standing on a firm foundation.

I harbor such pictures and metaphors in my heart and in my head.

*

Madeleine, my beloved, you are so far away! You are in danger, they want to defile you by defiling me. I am trying to protect you by being calm and dignified. I have said to Bontemps (so that he can pass it on): "I forgive you, Bontemps, I forgive everyone. I am going to forgive you no matter what you do."

He hasn't done me any special harm. He gossips and refuses to give me a bed instead of the straw I am lying in and he spits perhaps in my soup, but I still don't feel any anger when I see him. He seems to be weighed down by my words, however, and he looks at me with hatred in his eyes.

"Your forgiveness is worth nothing," he says. "I am an honest man and don't need your forgiveness. I can manage without it, I'm sure."

His eyes are full of hatred when he is saying it.

*

Laubardemont is afraid.

His power has grown tremendously but he doesn't quite rely on it. He feels that it is no longer a question of our city

359

walls: what has not been razed, will be razed whether I exist or not. I am no obstacle. He also feels that the demons are strangers to me. I don't know if he believes in them. But I know that he must try to force himself to believe in them. He also knows that the demons will continue whether he believes in them or not—whether they exist or not! Demons beget demons. The screams of the women are signals and avenues for new screams.

We are dignified in our behavior toward each other; yes, he is as dignified as he can possibly be and he is an able government official. Our relationship is pure and simple. In a way he is more open toward me than toward others; vis-à-vis others he must always look for proofs and motivations against me, but before me he doesn't need to do that any more. He says: "Confess that you are a prince of the demons." I reply: "You know that I am innocent." He is silent and looks at me, then he lowers his glance. Before others he rages, commands, threatens; then he shouts, tears papers to pieces, and has people thrown out. He had my mother thrown out when she came with a petition, he had Madeleine arrested and kept in prison for two days, he had my brother in Paris arrested. To me he merely says calmly: "You know what awaits you. We'll no doubt be able to squeeze a confession out of you. It will be cheaper for you if you confess now."

I reply: "I have nothing to confess to you."

Such is our quiet game.

I don't even know if he hates me.

If he were a peasant, he would be digging in the soil by day and by night and everyone would say: "An industrious, an able and conscientious peasant; he doesn't give himself even a moment of rest."

*

But I am looking into myself. It is now July. I am lying here enveloped by the heat, which is rising and coming closer. The guards are sweating and cursing down below,

360

Bontemps breathes heavily and smells of perspiration when he comes up with the soup. Exorcisms are taking place in all our churches. There was a letup for about a week and the demons were listless, but then they called Pierre Barrot back from Chinon and then again the situation improved, with things being speeded up again.

Something very strange has happened. The prioress, Sister Jeanne, and Sister Claire have retracted their accusations against me and have instead charged themselves with self-contradictions and lies and sinful desires. Sister Anne—the soon-to-be old woman—has attempted to hang herself in her cell.

All this serves to confuse the quiet game.

I am looking into myself. Once I was as open as I could be: last autumn and before Madeleine. I was in dread that my desire for her would be gone, my lust forever exhausted. It returned after I had opened myself to her. Now I cannot look any more deeply into myself. There is a content in my life, in my dreams, in my desires, in my longing to go away, and in my wish to behave in a dignified manner which I can no longer reach, grasp, or explain. I say: The walls are of no importance to me, the city is now of no importance. What will happen to me is unimportant. And yet, I am not apathetic. I am awake, answer questions, and I believe I formulate the answers well.

*

I am seeking a principle and I assume that I have found it.

Today the old lady Bontemps came up with my food. She put the dish on the stool and said:

"Here it is, you swine."

She expected me to answer her. When I didn't answer, she said again (in a shaky voice):

"Didn't the swine hear me? Here's your food, I said!"

I turned on my back in the moldy straw and looked up at her, I believe in a friendly manner. She was standing in the door opening with her back to the door and the big key in her hand. She said, louder:

"You swine, you whoremonger! You devil!"

"I forgive you," I said then.

Her bloated face was distorted. She held up the key and took a step forward as if she intended to hit me. But she checked herself and lowered her hand. I didn't catch her eye any more and cannot say that I kept her under control with my eye—the way they say that I dominate women by looking at them. Her brownish-yellow eyes were bloodshot as if from wine and long waking hours. The face loosened up from the grimace, there was weeping in it. She turned around abruptly and walked toward the door opening.

"You rotten swine!" she sobbed. "You rotten swine!"

After slamming the door shut she stood outside crying, I believe. I got up and walked over to the door and heard her mumble something. I remained standing there until she had reached the bottom of the stairs. I felt joy, triumph. I felt that I still have great power. I felt more certain than ever that I had found the principle and the means.

*

The day is near. I have looked into all my unsympathetic sides (the ones I have been able to find) and gone over all my errors and what I call sin and what they call sin. I don't need to scream any more: my scream is now going along its own paths without the help of my throat. I have (practiced) a smile: the smile of forgiveness. I imagine that they will not smash my face to pieces; for it must be shown to all the people. I don't think they will crush my hands and my arms. For everything else I have already screamed and the scream has reached those witnesses who will also see my forgiving face.

Among my unsympathetic sides was above all my arrogance. I still possess arrogance but it is hidden. Then it was my lust for power. I still have it, I know that, but it is hidden. Then it was the girl Philippe Tranchant. She is still there but everything has already been atoned for, I tell myself and think of it as a truth. She is going to suffer. I feel a sort of (theoretical) pity for her, a compassion grounded in a principle.

They will not be able to fill the emptiness after me with triumph: they must for years on end fill it with pain and powerlessness. I believe that even Laubardemont will be filling it with some sort of pain and powerlessness.

At times I look upon him as a fellow player, yes, as an accomplice.

*

All the others except Madeleine I have excluded from my world. My mother also; but my dignity up until the end will give her a pleasure which will be growing, always growing. My sister and brothers are going to be proud of me and so will all my friends: they will reproach themselves for not having done more for me, for not having used force or trickery to free me or help me escape. They will suffer a few pangs of conscience—or many—but above all they will be proud of me. That is the gift that I leave with them. But they have been excluded from my world.

These remain: Laubardemont, Madeleine, and God.

Laubardemont is my tool, my means to attain to my dignity: that of the fighting martyr. Without him I might just be a fugitive.

Madeleine is my wife and the meaning of my life and my death. All the tenderness I possess is turned toward her.

God is my firm principle, He is a means for me, a support. I can calmly say to myself: I am convinced of His existence as a law of nature. I know that I cannot prove this law of nature, for that I lack the necessary mathematical knowledge. Before I was sorry at times that I hadn't studied mathematics seriously and deeply. I am now saying: God exists and is with me. He is an act of will. He contributes to my dignity, He is its foundation.

363

I am now the most powerful man in this city which I once called my own and it gives me a pleasure that I cannot deny.

*

One night I said to myself that I was possessed by demons. It didn't frighten me. If God exists (and I do not doubt it), then He has allowed these demons to enter into me in order to help me. He has power over the demons. Only if it can be proved with the help of mathematics that He doesn't exist, then His power will come to an end. I don't have such knowledge of mathematics. It is a lack for which I am not sorry. Before, in weak moments, I might have. Now I don't do it. I can say: I am the prince of the demons—but only with the approval of God. Before that principle alone am I guilty (guilty? willing? forced for the sake of my dignity?) of speaking the truth. I will deny that I by the power of the Devil, as his servant and his representative, have called the demons to the Ursuline convent.

I can say quietly: Demons spring forth from the love of the soul and the body. God has infused with love the bodies and souls of humans. It is His handiwork. This is my principle, my firm support.

Other voices besides those of the principles are of no importance to me.

*

August.

People are gathering in the city. The sentence has not been pronounced yet but everyone knows. There are many visitors and curious people, and the inns and lodging houses are completely filled.

It is a fine season.

It is generally hoped that the weather will be beautiful.

19

Daniel Drouin's Protocol (5)

§ 11. (Completed and put aside in 1637)

It is over now, a long time ago.

I am sitting writing in this beautiful summer of this year of grace 1637 out at my country place. The children are playing, Charlotte and the wetnurse (we have got a wet-nurse now) are occupied with them. The maid makes the meals and is very good at it. The bees are buzzing and my vineyard, which I see here in front of me, seems to be shaping up well.

We had a girl at the end of April 1634. Then came a boy in May 1635 and last year too we were granted a child, a boy. They are all living. It is good to have girls a well as boys. My family is once again getting quite large.

My desire to write down my thoughts is not as strong as before, and the notes I put down now are primarily concerned with the children, the food we eat, the wine, and some flowers which I consider noteworthy. When I am in town I live a quiet private life. At most once a week, perhaps twice, I walk over to my old favorite inn, "The Hen," to have a glass of absinthe with my friends Petiot and Dolet and my cousin, the coach-builder Mathurin Thiboust. At times I meet the brother masons Antoine and Charlot, but only seldom, they are now working in our neighboring city, Chinon, and in Richelieu, the Cardinal's city.

During the summer months, I have gone through my protocol and my diaries. My hands feel strangely weary as I touch the rustling pages, so often read and corrected. At times I think: Will they be of any value? Cicero says that it is important and necessary for a senator to know the state's constitution, and I can cite him as my authority when I claim that it is necessary for a government official to see and note down what is happening in his city: it may perhaps be of value in the future.

It is to the future that I look.

I am approaching the end of the protocol which I thought would grow as long as I could hold a pen, think thoughts, see and observe. Or: actually my old protocol has been concluded. The last notes were made in August and September of 1634. Since then I haven't written much but have mostly leafed through my papers. What I now write down about my wine, important family occasions, the progress made by our children, etc., is a completely different matter, solely for personal use.

About the other matter I can say: I know that life goes on and is probably just as interesting as before. For I have seen how it goes on. But my pen is not as willing to make notes.

Once in a while I go for an evening walk in our city, up to my grandfather's old house on the castle hill and look at it before the sun goes down. Then I most often continue on to the square tower which is still standing. I put my hand on the wall. It seems to me that it is sweating fear and that it will continue to do so as long as the tower stands, perhaps for a hundred, perhaps for two hundred, three hundred, or a thousand years.

The thought makes me feel depressed.

*

Here are the last pages of my old diary:

April 16, 1634

Today it is Sunday and I really ought to be out at my country place checking on Michel and what he is doing with the wine, but instead I am sitting at home leafing through my papers. Charlotte—my wife—is now quite heavy. But she is so accustomed to giving birth that she is taking it with much composure.

I ask myself: When should one stop begetting children? I don't mean to say that the desire ceases, that I haven't noticed yet, but the responsibility is considerable, though. I am thinking here about the distribution of the little property one leaves behind whenever death comes.

Last night I stayed a while at my cousin Mathurin's. Corisande, his wife for whom I have always had a certain weakness, said something about "Charlotte's never-ending confinements." It is my opinion that my wife is not driven as hard as many others. She is satisfied with her lot—from what I can understand—and cries only very rarely. And the loss we suffered during the plague needs to be remedied. At any rate, I have not figured on having more than two or perhaps three more children.

However, our conversation gave rise to a little ill feeling. Mathurin didn't take out his best white wine, which he usually does when I visit him, but instead a more recent one. Later, Mathurin and I went together to the "The Hen." Petiot and Dolet were there. We talked, of course, about the events in our city.

Urbain Gr. has now come back from Angers. They have put him in canon Minet's house at Rue Pasquin; verger Bontemps and his wife are guarding the prisoner. It is said that they are conducting certain experiments with U. G. People have heard him scream. Physicians examine him and search for signs of demons on his body.

People are shocked and indignant but I am careful not to show my feelings publicly. The demons are once again wreaking havoc in the Ursuline convent. The number of exorcists has been increased by two. Pasquinades dedicated to M. de Laubardemont are being posted on the Ste-Croix gate. I consider it imprudent, since I know the full import of M. de Laubardemont's power of attorney. It is unpleasant to live so close to the church at this time; there is similarly a certain risk for me to have Madeleine de Brone living in my house. But I have remained firm and have not intimated anything to any one except Charlotte.

Charlotte cries whenever we talk about Mad. de B.

The exorcists are now preaching assiduously in all our churches and are saying that it is a deadly sin not to believe in the Ursulines' demons. Their thesis is that through their exorcisms the Devil is always forced to speak the truth.

*

April 25

Yesterday my wife gave birth to a girl. We are very happy, that is, it may be more useful to have boys, they are evidently not so sensitive to demons, etc. But everything lies in the hand of the Almighty.

Had a scene with the maid. She has begun to be sloppy when it comes to her cooking.

April 27

Today I heard from Charl. Calvet that they once again had conducted a big medical examination yesterday. Doctor Lannoury is treating U. G. very roughly. He is supposed to have discovered marks of demons in his anus and on his testicles (in duabus circa anum et in duobus testiculus). It sounds very serious. A few physicians who had been called in from outside have disclaimed any responsibility. They are of the opinion that the medical examinations "are pure humbug" (the words are not mine) and they "don't want to have anything to do with such things."

April 30

The demon Asmodeus has confessed that a written agreement has been made between Lucifer and Urb. Gr. The prioress of the Ursuline convent, Sister Jeanne, has got hold of the document which (Ch. Calvet told me with a smile which was a little on the bold side) "was kept in Lucifer's own workroom and had been signed with U. G.'s own blood; and I believe that Lannoury helped Lucifer get hold of that signature," (Ch. Calvet said it; I am only quoting him).

May 5

My newborn daughter was christened today; with a determination unusual for her, Charlotte, my wife, insisted that the girl be named Madeleine. So she was. It is provocative perhaps—but in the end there are so many with the name of Madeleine! It was Madeleine-Louise and I suppose that for the time being we will call the child Louise. Canon Maurat (who is a friend of U. G.'s) officiated at the baptism; as usual it took place in the Church of Ste-Croix. Godmother: Mme De Lagarde, the wife of the head of our Salt Depot. Afterward a glass of wine in our house.

May 15

U. G.'s brother, my professional colleague René G., has been arrested in Paris, where he had appealed to the Court of the Parlement.

May 21

Had planned to ride out to my country place and stay

there through Sunday but the events going on here make me stay in the city.

Yesterday, the demon Asmodeus wrote a letter to the prioress of the Ursuline convent, Sister Jeanne, promising to leave her body together with the demons Gresil and Aman with—I believe—Leviathan and Behemoth. They would leave signs and marks to show in which places they had gotten out of the prioress's body. During the demons' departure the hands of the prioress were to be tied in order to prevent her from doing herself harm.

The exorcism had been set at six o'clock last evening in the Church of Ste-Croix here on our square. I had decided to be present but there was such a throng that I gave it up. Instead I went over to "The Hen" after my evening meal and heard the news quite late from Dolet who had been in the church. He claimed (and they are not my words!) that M. de Laubardemont broke the promise of the prioress's hands being tied and (Dolet said) "many saw clearly how she pinched herself and that her nails were bloody and that she also used a small knife."

I will not take any stand as to D.'s statement.

May 23

The physician and teacher from Saumur, the Scot Marc Duncan, who was very much interested in the demons' activities here, has now been refused admittance to our city. He has expressed strong doubts as to the existence of the demons. Some persons in Saumur are supposed to be his protectors. Such was also the case with the physician Claude Quillet from Chinon. He was in danger of being arrested but is supposed to have fled to Italy.

May 24

A search has been carried out here in my house! That is to say, not in *my* dwelling but in the apartment that I—

perhaps rather imprudently—have rented out to Mad. de Brone.

I had been given a hint about it by Ch. Calvet and through my wife I had Mad. de B. warned—but Mad. de B., who by the way has had many opportunities to leave and go away, didn't pay any attention to the warning. She remained here! They turned everything upside down in her apartment. Her personal enemies, the apothecary Golet and Milouin, were along to search for Urb. G.'s books on black magic!

I stayed away from my house and visited my cousin Mathurin Thiboust. Every one felt depressed. Mathurin's wife, Corisande, uttered a few sharp words to the effect that I ought to have stayed home on such an occasion. I answered her that as a government official I had to think of my reputation and demonstrate my neutral attitude. She threw in my face something like "your reputation is not so great in any case." Mathurin acted as a conciliator. I think that Corisande's behavior is far from praiseworthy. She knows me and she *knows where I stand!* I walked over to "The Hen" and had a small absinthe and afterward I strolled slowly home, filled with all kinds of thoughts.

My wife told me—with tears in her eyes—that Mad. de Brone had been arrested. Extremely unpleasant!

May 27

Mad. de Brone was imprisoned for forty-eight hours in Milouin's place—"a private, pleasant prison," said Petiot in his coarse manner. That was a tactless remark to make. I criticized him for this and then he immediately regretted his words. That shows what a reproach made at the right time and place can accomplish!

Our *bailli,* M. de Cerisay, and also Louis and Charles Calvet, were apparently the ones who persuaded M. de Laubardemont to let Mad. de B. go free. They were very upset because of her arrest. I myself was also extremely upset but didn't show it so openly since I am a man of self-restraint.

May 28

We all feel a certain pressure. Heavy fines, even imprisonment, are now imposed on those who write and distribute scurrilous songs and such about M. de Laubardemont, the Ursuline Sisters, and the demons.

May 30

Our very highly esteemed *bailli,* M. de Cerisay, and his wife are now accused of witchcraft!

Later

The accusations have been retracted, that is, buried in silence. They didn't dare!

One ought to leave the city for a while. But it may not look so good inasmuch as so many are staying. And actually they cannot accuse *me* of anything. Although—one never knows when demons are involved! My behavior is calm and well balanced.

June 24

Yesterday they had U. Gr. confront the possessed women. It took place in our Church of Sainte-Croix. The bishop was there! I did want to go but refrained from doing so. They led U. G. in a procession from the prison via the Ursuline convent to the church. My wife Charlotte maintains that she heard Mad. de Br. cry, it was very distinctly heard downstairs where we live.

I was at "The Hen" in the evening and was told that the possessed ones were so furious that they wanted to tear U. G. apart. Séraphique A. is supposed to have been among the worst. When they had led U. G. out, the prioress and Sister Claire collapsed from exhaustion on the floor of the church.

July 10

They have now appointed the judges! Most of them depend on the good-will of M. de Laubardemont. One of them—Jacques de Nyau—was at one time accused of robbing a church but got out of it. Several government officials in our area who were asked to serve—declined! Among them were our *bailli* M. de Cerisay and both Louis and Charles Calvet! They refused to become members of the court even though they were pressed hard and received all kinds of threats. Charles Calvet is indeed my colleague! I too might have been called! But fortunately they didn't think of me or they may have recalled certain words that I—taking a great risk—have uttered!

*

July 27

Today I learned that the court has begun its sittings in the Carmelite cloister near the Bartray Church.

July 29

Since it is Saturday, I am going to the country where my family is now staying. I may stay there a few days. A protest meeting by officials and the burghers is being planned.

Aug. 4

Returned from the country yesterday.

The officials and burghers in our city have staged a protest meeting. Naturally, I could not attend since I was in the country. Our *bailli* and the brothers Calvet called together all our officials and formulated a letter, addressed to H. M. the King. In it is pointed out what shame and ignominy this so-called "trial" draws down upon our city. "The trial" (in which the accused has not yet been allowed to appear and defend himself!) is a—parody! (The words are Dolet's and not mine!) Cerisay left for Paris last Sunday in order to look up the king either there or at Saint-Germain in order to speak with our governor who is staying with the Royal Court.

A new prohibition, instituted by M. de Laubardemont: Neither officials nor others in this city are allowed to make critical remarks about the trial or make disparaging remarks about the judges.

U. G. and his mother and his lawyer are supposed to have sent several letters to M. de L., but no attention has been paid to them.

Aug. 14

The trial will begin tomorrow and U. G. will for the first time face his judges. It will take place in our city hall, where I have my office. My wife came back from the country last night. She didn't want to stay out there now, she says. Last night she informed me that she was pregnant once again.

— — —

Saturday, Aug. 19, 1634

I feel as if I have become many years older. And that it isn't the same man who is holding the pen. I am sitting here in my house, at night, and the smoke from a pyre is still penetrating into where I sit.

I, Daniel Drouin, am now forty-two years old and this I have experienced:

On the 15th, 16th, and 17th of this month of August they interrogated him and I was present as long as I was able and until all of us who were forced to be witnesses were chased out.

On the 18th of August of 1634, this year of grace and of

suffering, they tortured him in both the customary and the extraordinary manner with the Spanish Boot.

After the torture, they gave him another beating.

But his mouth did not open to utter anything but weak wailing and lamentation and steadfast but mild explanations that he was innocent of the witchcraft they had accused him of. He forgave them all.

In the evening, before darkness set in, he was burned here in our Square of Sainte-Croix with his back to the church and with his face turned toward the windows in the house of Louis Tranchant.

I am not able to write any more.

*

Aug. 25–30

I want to leave the city, my own city, where the smoke is still so heavy that it seems to suffocate us all. We don't see it any more and don't notice the smell but it still feels that way.

The pen is resting in my hand and is drying up but I keep dipping it again and again. I know that I won't escape from this until I have written down what I saw and heard so that posterity will know the truth.

My family is in the country. I stay home in the evening and write. I have not seen my friends since late in the evening of the 18th of August. I attend to my work, that is to say, I walk to my office and sit there with unimportant papers in front of me. It is the same way with my colleagues. It is as if life has come to a halt in our city and will stand still forever.

*

They interrogated him for three days trying to make him confess that he was a prince of the demons who had bewitched and let his obedient servants in the world of the demons possess the sisters of the Ursuline convent located here.

375

He denied that it was so but pointed out that he like every one else had been very sinful. "I have loved women," he said.

M. de Laubardemont was very dissatisfied, even furious. He is supposed to have tried to bribe Mad. de Brone who inexplicably has stayed in the city and is mostly sitting alone in her dwelling, staring at the square which has been blackened by the smoke. M. de L. is supposed to have asked her to admit that she was bewitched by U. G. and has promised her total exemption from punishment as well as economic compensation. She is supposed to have refused with great firmness. But the threat is still hanging over her.

— — —

*

On Friday, August 18, the judges gathered in the Carmelite cloister by the Bartray Church. U. G. was not present but they nevertheless delivered the judgment on him. He was declared to have practiced black magic, ungodliness, and blasphemy as well as having caused the possession of the Ursuline Sisters.

He was sentenced, with bare head, divested of all ecclesiastical insignia, in a long shirt and with a rope around his neck in front of the main portal of the Church of Saint-Pierre and in front of the Ursuline convent and on his knees, to ask H.M. the King and Justice for forgiveness and after that to be led to the Square of Sainte-Croix, make another public apology in front of our church, be led to the pyre, be tied firmly to the stake in the center of the pyre, and then be burned alive together with his pacts with the Devil and the pamphlet about the celibacy of the clergy. All his property is to be confiscated and appropriated by the Crown.

That same morning, M. de L. sent for the surgeon Fourneau and had him visit U. G.'s prison, where the physician Lannoury was already present. When Fourneau arrived, he heard U. G. shout to Lannoury: "Cruel executioner!" Lannoury then withdrew and F. was told to shave U. G.'s head and all the places on his body where there was any hair growing. When surgeon F. began, M. de Laub. himself arrived and gave the order for F. also to remove U. G.'s eyebrows and nails. U. G. stated that he was prepared to suffer any pain but Fourneau refused to follow his orders despite M. de L.'s threats. He only shaved U. G.'s body.

It was nine o'clock in the morning. They dressed U. G. in a long linen shirt and other old rags and tied his hands tightly together. He wasn't given shoes on his feet but a pair of worn slippers. Thereupon he was driven in M. de L.'s own coach to our city hall. When the exorcists Barrot, Minet, and Lacet had rid the room of demons through various kinds of exorcisms, the final proceedings could commence. The courtroom was filled to the rafters with spectators and witnesses. I stood in one of the doorways.

I didn't manage to listen very long but I did manage to see. In the first row sat Madame de Laubardemont and other distinguished ladies who were relatives of the judges; some of them had traveled far in order to be here. They were staring at U. G. I don't know whether it was fear or something else in their eyes. When he fell on his knees in front of the judges it was so quiet in the room that one could hear people swallow their saliva. What he said was: "Gentlemen, I can only bear witness before God the Father, the Son, and the Holy Spirit, and the Holy Virgin, who is my only legal counsel here, that I have never been a sorcerer and have never committed any sacrilege or approved of or practiced any other sorcery than that of Holy Writ, which I have preached. Christ is my Saviour and I pray to Him that I may be worthy of the blood of His Passion." He appealed to the judges to be spared the suffering of the most extreme torture since he feared that they "might instill despair in me." Many were profoundly moved and his words made a great impression on the women. When M. de Laubardemont became aware of this, he gave an order to clear the room and remove spectators and witnesses.

It was a very warm day.

*

What happened from then on, I partly saw and partly heard about. M. de Laubardemont appealed, threatened, and appealed again and so did the judges. They *begged* U. G. to make a confession, but they received none. They handed him a piece of paper that he was to sign, but he didn't sign it.

It is now being said that the prioress in the Ursuline convent, Sister Jeanne, the one who was so sorely possessed, and Sister Claire, who was also greatly possessed, once again retracted their assertions, declared that U. G. was innocent, and accused themselves of lying and distorting the truth.

"I don't know whether he was extremely unhappy, but I believe that the possessed women were," Ch. Calvet told me afterward. "Those women were more defenseless than he could ever be," Calvet said on the same occasion. I have been pondering his words.

*

— — —

They delivered him up to the torturers. It was the Spanish Boot, both the ordinary and the extraordinary way. They tied both his legs between two planks and drove in ever larger wedges between the planks. M. Grange-Aubin, who was present, has told me all the details, but I can't make myself write about it here. The ones who worked most zealously were not our executioner, Duchesne, and his helpers, but instead the exorcists Barrot, Minet, and Lacet and Trainasse. They wanted to insert bigger and bigger wedges and they grabbed the mallet themselves and used it when they thought that the executioner's helpers were too soft-hearted and irresolute.

I don't want to write any more about it.

*

He didn't scream very much. I have discussed some of this with my esteemed colleague Charles Calvet, who said: "It may have been that he during the torture couldn't find any other words for the pain than that it was *very painful,* that it was *very very painful,* and that the words that he muttered to himself and which were on his lips, although they were not said aloud but were only slowly uttered like moans, were these words that covered everything and were expressive in every syllable: *'It-is-very-painful.'* That is the way I believe it felt to him," said Ch. Calvet.

*

He admitted nothing. He wanted to make confession to Father Maurat, who had been merciful toward him during his time in prison, but M. de L. refused to give his permission.

*

Barrot, Minet, and Lacet stood over him, shouting: "Speak! Speak!"

Grange-Aubin told me how he had heard U. G.'s legs cracking. U. G. fainted, but they revived him.

*

At two o'clock in the afternoon his legs were crushed so that the marrow was running out. They carried him to a room one flight up. M. de Laubardemont appealed to him once more and handed him the piece of paper, but U. G. did not sign it.

It is said that they thereupon gave him a whipping.

*

At four o'clock they dressed him in a shirt impregnated with sulfur, placed a rope around his neck, put him on a cart which was pulled by six mules and brought him to the Square of Saint-Pierre.

All our church bells were pealing.

M. de Laubardemont and the judges marched behind. They were protected by city guards. The people were shouting. I have never seen such a great commotion in our city. They say that thirty thousand curious people had come from all of Poitou and Vienne and Touraine and from other districts. I have no actual numbers and there will never be any available. On a day like that no one counted the number of visitors.

Many people prayed for him. Before the procession started, notary Nozay (whom I will never again exchange greetings with if it can be avoided) read the sentence once again. Once again I heard U. G.'s voice. It was calm and clear but sounded tired. "I am innocent," he said.

In front of the Saint-Pierre Church, M. de Laubardemont ordered that U. G. be lifted from the cart and placed on his knees before the church portal. He fell forward, say those who were standing there waiting and looking, he had no knees to support him. Nozay again read the sentence. Some people maintain that they saw pigeons circling around U. G.'s head. They saw a monk hit him over the head with a stick. Others say that it was Barrot or Minet who hit him.

They put him back on the cart again and brought him to the Ursuline convent. The same thing happened outside the chapel. But when the court notary, Nozay (whom I will probably never again exchange greetings with) urged him to ask the Ursuline Sisters for forgiveness, U. G. replied: "I have never done them any wrong, but I ask God to forgive them."

*

I didn't witness these scenes. I walked home through the

380

crowds and entered my house, and we locked all the doors and bolted the gates. But some people had managed to get up on our roof with ladders, and all the other roofs around the square were filled with spectators. M. de Laubardemont had had stands built for the more distinguished of the spectators, but even since early in the day the stands had been filled with people of the lower classes.

We sat there waiting. My wife was crying and I could hardly speak on account of the emotion I felt. We decided to walk up to Madeleine de Brone and so we did. "We have come to be close to you," I told her when after our repeated knocking and pounding on her door she opened and let us in. She replied in what in my opinion was a firm voice: "I thank you, M. and Mme Drouin. You are very good to me." My wife, who is impulsive by nature, embraced her and wept uncontrollably. Demoiselle de Brone soothed her with some whispered words, which I unfortunately couldn't make out (later I asked my wife about them but she gives evasive answers).

*

———

I am now relating for posterity that I was standing in my own house, in Madeleine de Brone's dwelling one flight up, seeing what was happening that late afternoon, on Friday the eighteenth of August in the year of Our Lord 1634. I was alone in the room. Mad. de B. and my wife Charlotte had withdrawn to Demoiselle de B.'s bedroom, from which I heard them whisper and cry.

I didn't stand there because I was curious. I stood there as a witness and I saw the most horrible that has ever taken place in our city.

The pyre had been set up in front of the windows of the former procurator, Louis Tranchant. In the window could be seen men and women of the Poussaut-Tranchant-Herseur-Minet families and families who were related to them. There were also the stocky, abnormally broadshoul-

381

dered Madame de Laubardemont and other distinguished persons. Also, the new procurator, M. Poussaut, the apothecary Golet, and Messieurs Milouin and de Chasseignes were there. But although I looked close, I couldn't see the procurator's wife, Philippe, née Tranchant. When I leaned out through the open window—it was as mentioned above a very warm day—and observed very closely Poussauts' house, which is located right across the square from mine, I saw that the shutters were closed.

The square was packed with people, as were the stands. People shouted to me from the street asking for permission to come up so that they could see better and get a wider view, but remembering that this was Mad. de Brone's dwelling I merely shook my head and withdrew a bit into the room.

All the roofs were full of people. They hung on supporting their feet against the gutters or putting their arms around the chimneys. It had never occurred to me that people were so afflicted with unhealthy, even loathsome curiosity and craving to witness outrageous acts and scenes.

But neither our *bailli*, M. de Cerisay, nor the brothers Calvet were to be seen—which is the reason I hold them in even higher esteem than before.

———

It is difficult for me to tell about what happened next.

First came the city guards, who had received reinforcements from Chinon, pushing people aside, and then came the procession itself. I heard spectators groan from the heat and the jostling, they shouted and cursed, the mules made much noise. Urb. G. was lifted down from the cart and they tried to place him on his knees in front of the portal of the Sainte-Croix Church while the notary, Nozay, once more read the sentence out loud. (I have decided henceforth—if possible—to avoid speaking to or greeting Nozay!)

Thereupon, the executioner of our city, Duchesne, car-

ried U. G. to the pyre. As is said to be customary, it was
made up of dry wood and straw stacked around a stake.
On the stake hung a sort of saddle or iron chair, and U. G.
was tied firmly to it. I believe that notary Nozay once again
read the sentence but there was such an uproar and confusion that I couldn't hear very much even though I stepped
up closer to the window. I didn't see U. G.'s face. It was, as
mentioned before, turned toward Tranchant's house. But
he is supposed to have uttered a few words and forgiven
every one.

They wanted him to confess that he was a sorcerer but
he continued to refuse. Lacet and Barrot handed him a
crucifix for him to kiss, but the movement of the hand was
so sudden and violent (I could see it) that it was like a blow.
I got the distinct impression that they beat his face with the
crucifix so that he shrank back. Apparently, they wanted
him to shrink back. Some have maintained that "they,"
that is Minet or more probably Barrot or Lancet, had
heated an iron crucifix in a fire inside the church and were
now bringing the hot iron against his lips. His shrinking
back was looked upon as a proof that he denied his
Saviour.

From then on everything happened quickly. Someone,
and I think it was Barrot, or perhaps it was Minet or Lancet, was seized with such a rage at the sight of U. G.'s great
courage and proud steadfastness that he grasped the torch
out of the hand of the executioner and lit the pyre himself.
It is said here that they had promised U. G. that he would
be strangled before the fire was lit—this being customary
in civilized countries—but that they had tied so many
knots in the rope around his neck that it was impossible to
do so. I believe that the executioner didn't even have
enough time to try to do it.

The last I saw of my old friend, at whose side I have
been through all the terrible things that have happened to
him and our unhappy city, was how his body bent forward
in the flames that rose skyward and then how he was en-

veloped by the smoke. I recall that tears ran into my mouth. I must have looked up thus making my chin and lower lip protrude.